Centre for Educational Research and Innovation (CERI)

ORGANISATION FOR ECONOMIC CO-OPERATION AND DEVELOPMENT

Pursuant to article 1 of the Convention signed in Paris on 14th December, 1960, and which came into force on 30th September, 1961, the Organisation for Economic Co-operation and Development (OECD) shall promote policies designed:

- to achieve the highest sustainable economic growth and employment and a rising standard of living in Member countries, while maintaining financial stability, and thus to contribute to the development of the world economy;
- to contribute to sound economic expansion in Member as well as non-member countries in the process of economic development; and
- to contribute to the expansion of world trade on a multilateral, non-discriminatory basis in accordance with international obligations.

The original Member countries of the OECD are Austria, Belgium, Canada, Denmark, France, the Federal Republic of Germany, Greece, Iceland, Ireland, Italy, Luxembourg, the Netherlands, Norway, Portugal, Spain, Sweden, Switzerland, Turkey, the United Kingdom and the United States. The following countries became Members subsequently through accession at the dates indicated hereafter: Japan (28th April, 1964), Finland (28th January, 1969), Australia (7th June, 1971) and New Zealand (29th May, 1973).

The Socialist Federal Republic of Yugoslavia takes part in some of the work of the OECD (agreement of 28th October, 1961).

The Centre for Educational Research and Innovation was created in June 1968 by the Council of the Organisation for Economic Co-operation and Development for an initial period of three years, with the help of grants from the Ford Foundation and the Royal Dutch Shell Group of Companies. Since May 1971, the Council has periodically extended the mandate, which now expires on 31st December 1991.

The main objectives of the Centre are as follows:

- *to promote and support the development of research activities in education and undertake such research activities where appropriate;*
- *to promote and support pilot experiments with a view to introducing and testing innovations in the educational system;*
- *to promote the development of co-operation between Member countries in the field of educational research and innovation.*

The Centre functions within the Organisation for Economic Co-operation and Development in accordance with the decisions of the Council of the Organisation, under the authority of the Secretary-General. It is supervised by a Governing Board composed of one national expert in its field of competence from each of the countries participating in its programme of work.

Publié en français sous le titre :

L'ÉDUCATION
MULTICULTURELLE

From 1982 to 1986 the Centre for Educational Research and Innovation carried out a project on "Education and Cultural and Linguistic Pluralism". The main thrust of the project was to analyse the consequences for education systems of the cultural and linguistic changes brought about by new lifestyles and forms of social organisation.

Under the responsibility of Mr. Norberto Bottani, Principal Administrator, a symposium was organised in January 1985 at OECD Headquarters which was attended by distinguished experts in the field of linguistic and cultural pluralism. The present reader brings together the papers prepared for the symposium.

In a separate publication, Immigrants' Children at School, the results are described of a large study about the schooling of immigrants' children in Europe. A third report on "Educational Policies: Their Interface with Cultural and Linguistic Pluralism: Problems and Perspectives" will summarise the main findings arising from the project.

The views expressed in this report are those of the authors and do not necessarily reflect those of the OECD.

J.R. Gass
Director
Centre for Educational
Research and Innovation

Also available

IMMIGRANTS' CHIDREN AT SCHOOL (May 1987)
(96 87 02 1) ISBN 92-64-12954-5 322 pages £12.00 US$22.00 F120.00 DM44.00

THE FUTURE OF MIGRATION (May 1987)
(81 87 01 1) ISBN 92-64-12949-9 320 pages £10.00 US$20.00 F100.00 DM44.00

EDUCATION AND TRAINING AFTER BASIC SCHOOLING (August 1985)
(91 85 03 1) ISBN 92-64-12742-9 132 pages £8.00 US$16.00 F80.00 DM35.00

EDUCATION IN MODERN SOCIETY (July 1985)
(91 85 02 1) ISBN 92-64-12739-9 108 pages £7.00 US$14.00 F70.00 DM31.00

MIGRANTS' CHILDREN AND EMPLOYMENT. The European Experience (May 1983)
(81 83 02 1) ISBN 92-64-12434-9 64 pages £4.00 US$8.00 F40.00 DM16.00

Prices charged at the OECD Bookshop.

THE OECD CATALOGUE OF PUBLICATIONS and supplements will be sent free of charge on request addressed either to OECD Publications Service, Sales and Distribution Division, 2, rue André-Pascal, 75775 PARIS CEDEX 16, or to the OECD Sales Agent in your country.

CONTENTS

INTRODUCTION:

OBJECTIVE AND METHOD OF A PROJECT OF ENQUIRY

Finding solutions for the educational problems posed by cultural and linguistic minorities presents a challenge for education systems whose political, cultural and social function has been geared to unifying the nation-states that emerged during the 19th century and to strengthening the social cohesion of democratic systems.

Education policies in these countries have always been ambivalent towards cultural and linguistic differences. The fact is that there is a definite incompatibility between the scheme of schooling and the acculturation of ethnic minorities, as witnessed by the hostility that schools in the past showed towards the linguistic and cultural practices of ethnic minorities, leading to veritable crusades against the preservation of regional languages and the survival of what were considered outdated patterns of behaviour and lifestyles. The difficulties that have to be contended with in taking multiculturalism into account in the educational process without descending to the level of folklore are also a sign of the cultural resistance that spreads throughout the field of education whenever it is a matter of dealing with the problems of ethnic minorities.

For more than a decade we have been witnessing the gradual undermining of one of the principal post-war theories of cultural development, that of the increasing homogeneity of Western societies as the result of economic and social progress. Between 1950 and 1975 there was a tendency for the differences within and between countries to diminish, but since then the economic slowdown and the end of urban growth have brought to the fore the diversity that was always latent. As soon as economic progress, with its levelling effect on behaviour patterns, began to lose momentum, diversity -- from being a fast-disappearing relic of the past -- re-emerged as a constituent of the future.

Moreover, any process of consolidation is the outcome of two opposing forces, one pulling in the direction of homogeneity and the other in the direction of heterogeneity. The first of these forces was the more powerful until 1975; as it has grown weaker, it has been superseded by the second, which is still operating today. This phenomenon can be interpreted either as a return to former values during a period of crisis, or as the emergence of new styles of development when growth has been interrupted and the economies of most developed countries have begun to operate more or less in a zero-sum mode.

This has had a fairly appreciable impact on the education policies of most OECD Member countries, as evidenced by the proliferation of bilingual curricula, courses in ancestral and regional languages, courses in native languages and culture, and the like. Despite the increasing number of specific programmes for the education of children from ethnic minorities, the grafting of multicultural education on to the traditional system of education has not been successful: although its importance is recognised, multicultural education does not fit easily into a set of curricula of a monocultural character. The various education systems are not explicitly opposed to attempts to introduce other cultures, but they passively resist any plans to steer education in an intercultural or multicultural direction, being imbued with a vague, inexplicit distrust of any suggestion of a need for a reappraisal of the way the culture developed and transmitted by the school is organised. Despite the attraction of the idealism underlying multicultural education as well as the tempting prospect of adding to the linguistic assets of a society, every system of education has shown considerable reluctance to remodel its curricula and practices along multicultural lines.

This conflict lies at the very root of CERI's project of enquiring into the educational policy responses to the cultural, linguistic and ethnic diversity that prevails in the majority of OECD countries; and the present report represents the Centre's recent endeavours to clarify the various questions underlying these opposing trends, to gain a better understanding of the problem aside from the efforts that have been made to reconcile them and, more importantly, to investigate what is really at issue and the reasons why a situation that previously was perceived quite differently has now become problematic.

It was decided at the outset that, given the emotions and passions aroused by multicultural education, the project should provide the basis of an analysis for the establishment of a theoretical frame of reference for rethinking the problems from an educational standpoint, rather than being tempted to collect piecemeal information on a large number of programmes, with no real hope of ever being able to formulate a model for action or principles for planning education in a multi-ethnic or multicultural society.

Accordingly, the prime objective of the project was not to devise or examine ways of applying a policy already accepted by some, namely multicultural education, but to clarify the problem for which this policy was alleged to be the solution. Irrespective of how it might be designed, did this "solution" fit the problem? And consequently, what exactly was the problem?

The critical moment in our enquiry was a meeting called for 16th to 18th January 1985 in Paris at which a number of specialists working on aspects of cultural and language policy were invited to assess the challenge presented by multi-ethnic societies in terms of education policy and to clarify the fundamental concepts of an epistemological, historical and anthropological character that provide the model for multicultural education. This would entail also their examining the relevance of these concepts, even in relation to cultural issues outside the field of education and the various analogies, models and terminology used to describe the problem.

The original intention for this meeting had been to bring together experts working in different fields and to confront each speaker with a discussant whose task would be to launch the ensuing debate. This procedure was not implemented quite as fully as envisaged which explains not every text in the present record having a critique appended. Nevertheless we invited a distinguished observer to follow the proceedings throughout and eventually to give an overview of the main concepts/interpretations as these were put forward and of the reception with which they were met. This was Mr. Walo Hutmacher, Director of the Sociological Research Service at the Canton of Geneva's Public Education Department, and his commentary ably concludes the report.

The twelve papers in this report are grouped in accordance with the four themes adopted by the conference: the history of multicultural education, cultural identity, the dilemmas of equality of opportunity, and multilingualism.

I. PAST AND PRESENT: OLD PROBLEMS, NEW ISSUES

1. THE SCHOOL AND DIVERSITY: BASIC EDUCATION IN FRANCE BEFORE THE REVOLUTION

by
Jacques REVEL
Directeur d'Etudes,
Ecole des Hautes Etudes en Sciences Sociales, Paris

We have been living for nearly two centuries in societies in which schools and education, albeit in very diverse ways, play a central role in shaping the collective identity and in reproducing it from day to day. The development of the State, the centralisation of government and the growing identification of the nation with a territory are all factors which explain why education has become a key issue in political strategies and a very widely accepted value in our societies. It has not always been so. Or rather, education's methods of management and representation and its social functions have changed profoundly with the birth of contemporary States.

This observation immediately shows the limitations of a historical approach to the problems that we have gathered to discuss here. There is probably never any absolute break in the historical process and it would be easy to demonstrate the long-term continuity of education models (1). However, I should like in the present paper to highlight the special features of traditional society -- roughly preceding the Industrial Revolution -- for two reasons. I believe that it is important not to ask more of historical experience than it can give and not to overwork its lessons. I shall return to this necessary caution in a moment. But, above all, it seems to me that by stressing the specific nature of the old educational systems, we are in a better position to understand the original features of those with which we are familiar now. We tend to take these original features for granted and are too often inclined to think that they represent the only possible picture. A look at history may help to bring a sort of ethnological perspective into our discussions and make us somewhat less dogmatic.

Yet it is out of the question here to trace a general history of educational practice in every type of social and cultural context. Even assuming that we could marshal the facts and had the necessary information -- which is not my case -- such a history would, in my opinion, be meaningless. The history of educational systems is, more than any other, shaped by national frameworks, each and every one of which must be considered. No doubt, broader systems of reference exist such as those devised by the Catholic Church which prevailed at least until the 18th century and sometimes later. No doubt, too, some educational blueprints have travelled well beyond any national frontiers, as was the case for the educational model that the Society of Jesus began to fashion in the middle of the 16th century and was then so extraordinarily successful throughout Europe. Nonetheless, such shared references and glorious models are never sacrosanct. Every individual society receives, adapts and reshapes them according to its own national traditions or circumstances. Indeed, this is amply demonstrated by modern experience: the same blueprints and values are employed very differently from one national group to another, even in societies that seem to be very similar. I have therefore chosen to consider the French example, the one on which I am least ignorant.

This personal reason combines with a far more serious one. Because France, more than any other European country, experienced an exceptionally marked and early centralised process of government building, the problem of an educational policy arose here in more radical and apparently more "modern" terms than anywhere else. Although recent historical literature tends to rehabilitate the role of social demand in educational growth in the centuries preceding mass education and hence to play down the role of deliberate State action, the latter has still been of fundamental importance, from the major statutory orders of the 16th century to the educational debate which played such a central role during the French Revolution (2).

Seen from this angle, the French case appears in many respects to anticipate subsequent trends. We will ensure that this assumption is treated with caution and will not let ourselves be sidetracked by superficial similarities. Another restriction: I shall only discuss one part of the educational system here, that concerned with basic education, which would today be equivalent to what we call primary schooling. Under the "ancien régime", schooling was relatively widespread in French society only for the rudiments, and by no means general at that level. From secondary level, the selection mechanisms which prevailed in a society with a very strict hierarchy excluded anyone who was not in some way or another connected even tenuously, with the mobility (3).

I must finally remind you that the terms of the problem as put at this meeting can hardly be taken as they stand when we are speaking of French society between the 16th and 18th centuries. There was migration, of course, and minorities, sometimes of considerable importance. But they did not have the same significance as in our 20th-century societies and raised very different problems, which elicited a very different response -- or non-response. There have always (or nearly always) been migrant groups and minority cultures, but that does not imply that, at different periods of time, their features have been unchanging.

Migration in preindustrial society is a difficult subject to approach and, when all is said and done, is still a largely unknown factor (4). While the historians have long agreed it with P. Goubert that staying put was the main characteristic of "ancien régime" society, they now recognise the importance of migration, even though it was nothing like as extensive as it has become since. But the word conveniently covers widely differing movements. It includes both micro-movements linked with the complementary nature of town and country life, for example, or with the fluctuations of employment markets, and interregional movements, such as those from the traditionally labour-exporting mountain areas to the agricultural plains and the urbanised areas which were always short of extra manpower. The micro-movements, following their multitude of tiny, usually imperceptible, routes (and which must also include the great mass of matrimonial migration linked with the consanguinity interdicts restated by the Council of Trent), generally raised few problems of cultural transplantation and adjustment, especially as the migrants concerned very often returned finally to their point of departure. The interregional movements, on the other hand, meant a real break in social and cultural ties.

Similarly, a distinction should be made between temporary migration, which was usually seasonal, and permanent migration, which could be prompted by many factors: forced migration of the Protestants after the revocation of the Edict of Nantes, leading to a virtual Reformed Church diaspora; more or less voluntary departure to nearby or distant new territories; lastly, flows for which there is no simple explanation but which, over the very long terms, indicate a kind of region-to-region drift like the one that has been drawing the "French" to the Aquitaine Basin ever since the Middle Ages. Many more distinctions are possible. But the contrast which strikes me as most important, for the issues with which we are concerned, is the one between urban immigration and every other kind of flow. In the towns the influx of newcomers was large and concentrated enough to raise problems of integration and adjustment; elsewhere, migration was less intensive, and schooling, in any case, less widespread.

Urban immigration occurred throughout Western Europe from the late Middle Ages on, and gathered pace in the 18th century: a spectacular movement, it was also composite, not to say contradictory. For instance, there is a world of difference between organised and controlled occupational immigration accompanied by the rapid reconstruction of social structures around a trade -- as, for example, studied by N.Z. Davis in the case of the printers of Lyons in the 16th century (5) -- and the instability of the marginal groups who roamed around the large cities, although it was often easy to slip from the first category into the second (6). Moreover, the fact that this immigration to the cities was constantly fed by more or less distant rural regions cannot justify the tempting conclusion that the new arrivals were necessarily backward compared with their urban host environment.

Even though whole schools of literature once thrived on contrasting the ignorance (or, as from the 18th century, the innocence) of the countryside with the ambiguous enlightenment of urban culture, things were not so simple as all that. Admittedly, Jean-Pierre Poussou did indeed find huge differences in literacy between immigrants and city-dwellers in Bordeaux: respectively 49 and 64 per cent literacy among men (able to sign their name) and 23 and 43 per cent among women. M. Garden arrived at similar conclusions for the traditional trades of Lyons during the same period. But Jean-Claude Perrot observed the opposide differential in Caen during the Enlightenment, and this slight advantage of immigrants tended to increase as the Revolution approached; at the other end of the kingdom, M. Vovelle made a similar observation for a number of large towns in eastern Provence (7). The socio-economic aspect of migration is relevant here, of course: selective migration (of craftsmen, for example) in Provence and to Caen, influx of unskilled manpower to Lyons and Bordeaux. The extreme instance was the hyperspecialised migration from certain Alpine valleys, which regularly provided large contingents of schoolteachers.

We must be still more cautious when considering minorities in traditional society. Indeed, monarchical France's own image of itself had little room for the recognition of legitimate minorities. This was a holistic type of society, regarding itself as a necessary whole, in which any conspicuous individualisation was perceived not only as deviant but, still more, as dissent. On the other hand, groups united by strong ties of solidarity (blood relationships, neighbourhood, trade, shared membership of a guild, a corps, or a political or geographical community, etc.) were readily accepted. The position of these groups was set in a general order and admitted in a broader system of interrelationships. But groups which could find no place in this order were cast out from society and regarded as beyond the pale.

It should be noted, in passing, that this is a persisting pattern in French history: although the Revolution substituted a community of individuals -- political and social subjects -- for the corps and communities of the "ancien régime", and although democratic individualism carried the day over the organic whole concept, the society it established was no readier to accept the existence of collective individuality -- and that is still a characteristic of the France of 1985 (8). This is one of the features which I said earlier make it necessary to trace the history of socio-cultural practices first in the national context.

THE PRINCIPLES BEHIND THE SUPPLY OF EDUCATION

Let us now consider the effects of these general principles on educational practices. Between the 16th and 19th centuries, there was practically never any question of using school education as a means of integrating "minority" groups. There were, in fact, two cases in point. The first consisted of the groups which were totally excluded from educational institutions, including the gipsies (called Egyptians in those days), whose nomadic lifestyle has been obstinately repressed by all western societies. The second, more frequent, case concerned the introduction of parallel educational systems. This applies to the Jewish communities, which had their own schools and, for essentially religious reasons, quickly showed very high rates of literacy, as in Alsace, for example. It was above all the case for the large Protestant minority, whose example deserves rather closer analysis since it is perhaps the most significant.

In the 16th century, at a time when centralised absolute rule had not yet been pushed to the full, the Protestant Reformation (like the Catholic Counter Reformation which responded to it a little later) was able to build up the network of elementary schools needed to meet the demands of the new faith. In 1598, the Edict of Nantes acknowledged this success by authorising the legal existence of Reformed Church schools in a number of places (Article XXXVII); but it must be appreciated that this network was purely and simply juxtaposed to its Catholic counterpart, and there was no desire to run the slightest risk of contamination, even during this period of abated religious strife. By the end of the 1660s, the compromise was in any case challenged and the Edict of Fontainebleau, which in 1685 revoked the 1598 provisions, decreed the closing down of the Protestant schools: "We prohibit the special schools for the education of children of the Reformed Protestant Religion and all other things whatsoever which may indicate any kind of concession to that Religion" (Article VII). This prohibition was, in any event, quite theoretical: recent research has revealed that Reformed Church families often preferred to resist the obligation to send their children to a Catholic school, despite the injunctions of the King's administrators; they chose instead to keep their children away from school and, when they had the means, resorted to the services of a tutor or else pooled resources to pay a private teacher (9).

Quite apart from the more obvious political vicissitudes, I think the most constant feature over the three centuries from the 16th to the 18th was indeed the strict educational separation of the two communities: it was as much demanded by the minority -- even between 1598 and 1685 -- as it was imposed by the majority. And even when, at the end of the 17th century, the monarchy tried to impose a single school on the Protestants, it was not with the intention of assimilating them through education, but in order to put a stop to the insupportable threat to order represented by the existence of an independent -- and hence foreign -- body of education within the kingdom.

In fact, I doubt if anyone looking for situations under the "ancien régime" which at least approximately conjure up present day problems should be searching among the minorities. He should instead consider groups which are not defined according to numerical size in society but by their deviations from a more or less explicit norm, which was roughly that of urban manners and customs. These deviations showed themselves through a number of social "disadvantages" which the school might try to reduce. Such handicaps might be linked with low social status, as in the case of the urban or rural working class. They might be associated with particular linguistic practices and, for example, differentiate between dialect-speakers and French-speakers. They could also be the outcome of inegalitarian sexual casting, where women were traditionally doomed to ignorance or less knowledge.

It might be objected that in most of the cases I have mentioned (not forgetting that the same person often suffered from several handicaps at once), the "minorities" concerned were, in fact, substantial majorities. To tell the truth, I think this observation is no impediment. What makes a minority in a traditional society, such as the "ancien régime" in France is status, not number, and its more or less marked social disqualification, not the claims of the organised group. It is this status and this lower social position which justify a special educational effort on their behalf, in the same way as for that other minority group, children. We shall see presently what kind of treatment they received.

This effort, which was a many-sided one, found its place in a very different socio-political and socio-cultural context from the kind we ourselves know in which the choice of an education policy is not basically -- or in any event solely -- linked to the existence of a centralised government or a policy of planning and standardisation. Even in France in the 16th to 18th centuries the educational effort and supply were connected with a host of individual and collective initiatives. The Church (or rather, as we have seen, the Churches) through their various bodies (often competing), communities from city-dwellers to villagers, and private initiative did as much as, and even more, than the State, which was mainly concerned with providing a legislative framework conducive to the development of the school and with keeping an eye, theoretically, on its proper operation.

In the case of elementary education, we also know that the attitude of the Crown and its representatives was always quite ambiguous in the 17th and 18th centuries. Might the school not siphon off subjects who were essential for economic activity? "Though a knowledge of letters is absolutely necessary to a republic, it is certain that they must not be taught indiscriminately to everyone; just as a body studded all over with eyes would be monstrous, so would a State whose each and every subject was a scholar." (10). The disquiet expressed in Richelieu's Political Testament was variously repeated a hundredfold and finally by the Physiocrats during the Enlightenment itself. The absolute State reserved its solicitude for the elite-forming institutions in preference to small schools.

So what did the teaching of the rudiments of learning aim to do? Schooling first responded to two religious concerns -- to which education always played second fiddle. The school had to dispense the first essential elements of the Christian faith while at the same time providing surveillance and early control over young souls. Throughout the post-medieval period, the Churdh had thus been the strongest bastion of educational activity.

But it would not have succeeded if it had not met favourable factors in the firld. We owe an important change of perspective in this regard to recent students of literacy. The historians of the school, in an evident spirit of apologetics, have for too long put most emphasis on the role of institutions in the development of education. In the French case -- which is the one which ought, in theory, to provide the best illustration of this traditional interpretation -- François Furet and Jacques Ozouf have demonstrated the significance of local conditions for the success of the school (11). A detailed study of literacy growth rates and the identification of forms of rejection or saturation show that the educational effort succeeded where it was wanted, i.e. where acquisition of the knowledge and know-how that the school dispensed could lead to social promotion. It goes without saying that this promotion could vary widely: it could be practical, symbolic or a combination of the two; it could also be identified with higher social status. The historians of literacy have adopted the migration experts' "push-and-pull pattern", but observed that there are few cases where setting up an elementary education network depends on "push" alone, i.e. on deliberate action by institutions (as, for example, in Lutheran Sweden). In 16th to 19th century France, "pull" -- i.e. general social "demand" -- was undoubtedly more influential than the regulations imposed by the authorities.

It was necessary to set right the picture of an educational system which is still too frequently thought of as consistent, systematically planned and organised and which has been regarded as one of the essential factors for the social and cultural standardization of France, both before and after the Revolution. The creation and management of teaching institutions were the aggregate result of usually unco-ordinated initiatives whose effects were cumulative. Can we draw the conclusion that this heterogeneity of the educational fabric made it more adaptable to the different fields in which the school had taken root, and, for example, helped diversify educational practices on behalf of groups that were poorly integrated in "ancien régime" society? This was by no means certain.

All the educational practices referred to a common educational plan which was basically religious. The elementary school had to teach the rudiments of the faith (the Catechism), morals (it had to regulate conduct) and secular knowledge (reading, writing and arithmetic), all three elements being closely untertwined. This intention was thus to provide the child with a complete education, but in doing so it imposed a set of exclusive constraints -- and hence gave little opportunity for the recognition of social and cultural differences. A classical textbook such as L'Escole paroissiale, published in Paris in 1654, exerted a profound influence on all educators in the 17th and early 18th centuries (12). As did La Salle's Conduite des Ecoles Chrétiennes seventy years later (13), the textbook drew on experience in a

Paris parish and made the school a place for the organisation of behaviour and attitudes. Organisation of time: children must always be kept occupied for fear that they might be tempted to become unruly and immoral. Organisation of space: the pupils' placing, and their collective movements, were minutely regulated. Organisation of bodies, posture being exactly defined in order to permit constant control over personal disposition, from prayer to reading and walking about the classroom.

This drilling of school life was matched by an unchanging order of learning from the lowest to the most advanced levels, in a series of steps to measure the child's individual abilities. In this process, where the number of intermediate levels varied from one author to another, there was never any question or adapting teaching content or form to the socio-cultural potentialities of any particular group. From learning the alphabet to fluent reading and arithmetic, the school only recognised individual performance, to be checked against a scale of knowledge that was the same for all. La Salle put this very clearly: "It is of the utmost importance that a pupil be never put into a class for which he is not yet ready, because otherwise he would be in such a state as never to be able to learn anything and in danger of remaining ignorant throughout his life. No account must therefore be taken of age or physical size, nor of the time that a pupil spends in a class when it is being decided whether to move him up to a higher class, but only of his ability" (14). For the school only recognised, evaluated and concerned itself with individual ability.

The same educational model inspired most initiatives in the classical period, wherever they might be taken. To quote an example, which I mention both because of its own importance and because in many respects it mirrors today's realities, there were the urban charity schools which sprouted up in the second half of the 17th century. In town, children raised a special problem which was a social one. Ever since the end of the Middle Ages, city authorities had been disturbed at the rise of juvenile vagrancy which was assuming ominous proportions throughout Western Europe: whether abandoned by their parents, runaways or out on the streets looking for adventure, stray children (who were often the offspring of recent immigrants maladjusted to urban society) formed bands which were in varying degrees a threat to public order. Begging and theft, but also pure vagrancy, undermined the social and political tranquillity of the city. There were several possible responses, beginning with repression, which was unfailingly used. But the school represented a different response and it was very soon realised that it could become the vehicle for a policy of good order. In the middle of the 16th century, a declaration by the Burgomaster of Valenciennes had already stated this clearly:

> "We do inform you and let it be known that established republics and cities were of old, very well prepared and organised so as to entrust and commission good masters to educate children from their earliest age and teach and instruct them in good doctrine, morals and an upright and honest way of life, and to maintain and accustom them in due subjection and respect, 'so that, when coming of age, they be both more tractable and ready to accord their Burgomaster all honour and obedience'" (15).

Clearly, the educational blueprint was inseparable from the political. It found its full expression as from the middle of the 17th century, when it was contemporary with the "great confinement" (of beggars) and can be regarded as one of its dispositions. In Paris and Lyons, the school network was meticulously reorganised to provide a very precise coverage of the city, to whose surveillance it actively contributed.

Still more interesting was the whole series of initiatives, local at first, whose aim was to fix this floating population and to keep it under control in school. In Rouen, Adrien Nyel transferred, significantly, from the General Hospital to the schools charity and was instructed by the municipal authorities in the late 1650s to open "premises which are suitable and capable of containing the poor children of this city and its outlying districts". In the 1660s, Charles Démia undertook a similar operation in Lyons using different methods. With the support of the burghers and the archdiocese, and encouraged by the city notables, he too opened charity schools for the education of poor children "and to take arms against idleness and licentious living". The first opened in 167 and, by his death in 1689, sixteen were firmly established. Finally, the same principles inspired the Christian schools that Jean-Baptiste de La Salle organised from Rheims in the 1680s, which, by the early 18th century, covered two-thirds of the kingdom with a relatively dense network run according to common rules by an Institute of Laymen.

In theory, these free charity schools were exclusively reserved for the poor, and the children or their families had to give the teachers a certificate of poverty. In actual fact, the very success of this formula drew a much more varied population to these schools than had been their founders' aim. While the schools in Lyons mainly attracted working class children (whose fathers were craftsmen or labourers) at the turn of the 18th century, the Frères des Ecoles Chrétiennes recruited much more widely among the lower and middle bourgeoisie, alive to the good reputation of their teaching. Although small in terms of numbers, this tendency towards a sort of social mix in the charity schools raises a doubt. It suggests that the education given there could be taken by all and that it was not therefore accompanied by any special approach for poor children. Indeed, a scrutiny of the curricula used in these institutions shows that they made very few innovations as compared with the general pattern of elementary education.

Much though the great reforming treatises were concerned with detailing every aspect of the management of school time and space, they proved relatively conformist as regards teaching content and methods. The only noticeable novelty was the preference for teaching children to read French instead of Latin, which La Salle and the Port-Royal pedagogues recommended simultaneously. But, apart from the fact that Latin was to remain the major subject for the teaching of reading until the end of the "ancien régime" (and that it was retained in a number of charity schools), the reasons behind the choice of French were very general and in no way concerned with suiting a particular public (17). Otherwise, elementary education was the same for all. Démia did introduce some manual work in his schools, but this was always very marginal compared with learning "the obligation to work hard and faithfully and the means to employ to bring their work to fruition".

The ambiguity of this plan is very evident. It did indeed aim to put children into school and forcibly to contain this unstable and marginal population. But it did so more through discipline (as the army was to do later with the introduction of compulsory military service) than by providing an education suitable for those taken in. The school which adapts to the public it wishes to contain is a school-institution which drills and disciplines rather than a school which transmits knowledge (18).

Many more examples could be given of such inflexible curricula for very different social situations -- such as the way the school considered (or, to be more precise, refused to consider) linguistic diversity in a country where, at least from the 16th century onwards, the proclaimed unity of language had become inseparable from the assertion of nationhood (19). Such constancy and so little readiness to adjust raised a problem. Institutions' inflexibility and their tendency to reproduce themselves might of course be mentioned, but do not provide an entirely satisfactory answer since, as we saw in the case of the charity schools, educational institutions are quite capable of inventing new forms even though teaching content changes but little. It would be more justifiable to refer to the actual function assigned to basic education by traditional society: acquiring knowledge was, we are told, always secondary to the two religious and moral concerns which basically justified the supervision of children. This imbalance tended to increase, in fact, as the school targeted less advantaged groups, all the effort being laid on inculcating Christianity and discipline. thus -- contrary to what was to happen, for example, under the Third Republic -- it is not in the institutions that one should look for the didactic experimenting which the "ancien régime" by no means overlooked. That explains why the many new initiatives and educational forms were paradoxically matched by the relative uniformity of teaching matter.

FACTORS IN THE DEMAND FOR EDUCATION

But we have so far only considered educational supply. We have only observed the school from the viewpoint of the institution and those who promoted and managed it. The prospect changes quite sharply when we finally look at it from the demand side. We are, admittedly, very largely reduced to hypotheses since "ancien régime" documents contain few comments by the users of the school. What did they want from elementary education?

First, I think, that it would give them access to a kind of conformity which was social rather than cultural. The progress of literacy between the 16th and 19th centuries amply demonstrates that this promotion played a decisive part in individual, family and collective hopes of the school. For a constantly growing population, access to the basic rudiments of knowledge did indeed offer a distinctive pattern of social promotion whose strength lay in its conformity with normality. Other signs also confirm the existence of this symbolic demand. From the 17th to the early 19th centuries, the so-called pedlars' literature was responsible for the very wide circulation of cheap books. The fact that this very disparate collection of books included a number of didactic works is constantly mentioned: catechisms, arithmetic textbooks, books on etiquette, etc. The common characteristic of this material was that in most cases it was no good for any real learning: the arithmetic books clumsily imitated the medieval treatises and offered their readers impracticable exercises; the books on etiquette imperturbably suggested a code of behaviour which was in the main unusable in their readers' daily lives (20). But little matter: these books were less made to teach real practices than to confer on those who owned them a sort of potential mastery of arithmetic or good breeding. As we know, in the matter of symbolic property, possession is often nine-tenths of the law -- and access to school probably did not escape this rule.

This prevailing symbolic usage does not in any way mean that nothing practical was necessarily expected of elementary education. For example, the way in which the written word was used in 18th century urban society shows this well (21). And, as we know, mass education only really succeeded because the knowledge stored up by the children found a use in society. This does not necessarily mean that the school dispensed immediately operational knowledge in the form of know-how. In the 17th century, Démia considered that if children were able to read, write and count, they would already "be fit to work in most of the arts and professions: since there is none in which this basic knowledge will not be of great help and provide a channel for advancement to the most important employment". This was a vague objective which suggested a very general destination for a maid-of-all-work education. We find the same definition since the late 19th century with the sacrosanct certificate of primary education, an all-embracing sign of elementary schooling. It gives all the honours to a non-technical concept of education that is one of the predominant features of the French educational tradition. At this point, we can see that the borderline between symbolic and practical usage was uncertain. But the consequence may quite evidently have been a relative indifference to teaching content and a fundamental enhancement of educational form.

I shall conclude, however, with a reservation. We have so far pretended to believe that curricula were received as taught. But we know that this was not the case at all and that cultural objects were reworked or diverted unpredictably in contact with society and the strategies which used them. Where we think in terms of general curricula and undifferentiated teaching material, it is necessary to see what children in a particular social position did with what they were taught. Yet we practically never know how the story goes on from there. When we are lucky enough to have documentary evidence for the sequel, it usually describes the experience of autodidacts who remained outside institutional education and were for that reason the subject of biographies (22). This apart and before the 19th century, we are mainly reduced to hearing the story from the school side and to tentatively reconstructing the expectations of society, losing track of the real issues involved in an education. This shows the obvious limits of our investigation.

NOTES AND REFERENCES

1. Two recent examples: on literacy and the primary school, FURET F. and OZOUF J., Lire et écrire. L'alphabétisation des Français, de Calvin à Jules Ferry, 2 volumes, Paris, 1977; on "secondary" education, COMPERE M.M., Du collège au lycée (1550-1850). Généalogie de l'enseignement secondaire français, Paris, 1985.

2. General background: CHARTIER R., COMPERE M.M., JULIA D., L'éducation en France du 16e au 18e siècle, Paris, 1976; LEBRUN F., QUENIART J., VENARD M., Histoire générale de l'enseignement et de l'éducation en France (edited by L.H. Parias), Volume II, De Gutenberg aux Lumières, Paris, 1981. These two books are the best recent summaries of the history of education in France up to modern times.

3. See COMPERE M.M., Du collège au lycée, op.cit.; and JULIA D. and FRIJHOFF W., Ecole et société dans la France de l'Ancien Régime, Cahiers des Annales, n°35, Paris, 1975.

4. The best systematic approach in a very broad regional framework (since it covers nearly a quarter of the kingdom) is in the thesis by POUSSOU J.P., Bordeaux et le Sud-Ouest au 18e siècle. Croissance économique et attraction urbaine, Paris 1983. Some very useful information is given in the earlier study by NADAL J. and GIRALT E., La population catalane de 1553 à 1717. L'immigration française, Paris, 1960. On migration in rural areas, see the recent book by POITRINEAU A., Remues d'hommes, Paris, 1984.

5. DAVIES N.Z., Society and Culture in Early Modern France, Stanford, 1975, Chapter 1, "Strike and salvation in Lyons".

6. GEREMEK B., Les marginaux parisiens aux 14e et 15e siècles, Warsaw, 1971, French translation published in 1976; Truands et misérables dans l'Europe moderne (1350-1600), Paris, 1980.

7. POUSSOU J.P., contribution to Lire et écrire, op.cit., Volume 2; GARDEN M., Lyon et les Lyonnais au 18e siècle, Paris, 1970; PERROT J.Cl., Croissance d'une ville moderne. Caen au 18e siècle, Paris, 1975; "Y a-t-il eu une révolution culturelle au 18e siècle? A propos de l'éducation populaire en Provence", in Revue d'histoire moderne et contemporaine, 1975, pp. 89-141.

8. I am of course referring here to the study by de TOCQUEVILLE, L'Ancien Régime et la démocratie, 1st edition, 1856, and to two recent books by DUMOND L., Homo Aequalis, Paris, 1977, and Essais sur l'individualisme, Paris, 1984.

9. MANEN H. and JOUTARD Ph., Une foi enracinée: la Pervenche. La résistance exemplaire d'une paroisse protestante ardéchoise (1685-1720), 1972.

10. RICHELIEU, Testament politique, quoted by de DAINVILLE F., "Collèges et fréquentation scolaire au 17e siècle", in Population, 1957, p. 475.

11. FURET F. and OZOUF J., Lire et écrire, op.cit., Volume 1.

12. L'escole paroissiale ou la manière de bien instruire les enfants dans les petites escoles par un prestre d'une paroisse de Paris, Paris, 1654. This anonymous treatise is now agreed to be the work of Jacques de BATENCOUR, priest at Saint-Nicolas du Chardonnet, one of the most active centres of Catholic reform in Paris.

13. Avignon, 1720. See POUTET Y., Le 17e siècle et les origines lassalliennes, Rennes, 1970, 2 volumes. Concerning this text, see also the analysis by FOUCAULT M., Surveiller et punir. Naissance de la prison, Paris, 1975.

14. Conduite des écoles chrétiennes, republished in Cahiers Lassalliens, No. 24, Rome, undated, p. 274.

15. Quoted by CHARTIER R., JULIA D. and COMPERE M.M., L'éducation en France, op.cit., p. 48. The text dates from 1564 (my underlining).

16. On Démia: COMPAYRE G., "Charles Démia et les origines de l'enseignement primaire à Lyon", in Revue d'histoire de Lyon, 1905; on J.B. de la Salle: POUTET Y., Le 17e siècle et les origines lassalliennes, op.cit.

17. Apart from the argument of social usefulness. LA SALLE: "What possible use is reading Latin to people who will never require it at any time in their lives?" (quoted by POUTET, Le 17e siècle et les origines lassalliennes, op.cit., p. 160).

18. At the same time, the education of girls -- and especially poor girls -- suggests similar conclusions, even though their share of special subjects is more notable. Apart from the basic curriculum that they shared with boys (reading, writing and arithmetic), they were taught to spin and to sew and greater emphasis was laid on moral and religious education. Admittedly, these additions reinforced the more traditional features of the curriculum, since women, like the poor, must first be kept permanently occupied.

19. See de CERTEAU M., JULIA D. and REVEL J., Une politique de la langue -- La Révolution française et les patois, Paris, 1975; for the 19th century, WEBER E., Peasants into Frenchmen, Stanford, 1976.

20. I am referring here to the unpublished works of HEBRARD J. on the arithmetic textbooks published by the Bibliothèque bleue and to my own current research on books on etiquette.

21. See ROCHE D., "Les pratique de l'écrit dans les villes françaises du 18e siècle", in Pratiques de la lecture, edited by R. Chartier, Marseilles, 1985.

22. See HEBRARD J., "Comment Jamerey Duval apprit à lire", in Pratiques de la lecture, op.cit., pp. 24-60; I would remind the reader of Il formaggio e i vermi. Il cosmo di un mugnaio del Cinquecento, by GINZBURG C., Turin, 1976, now a classic, which clearly illustrates these unorthodox ways of appropriating legitimate culture outside the normal channels of transmission. Also see DAVIES N.Z., Culture and Society, op.cit., Chapter 7, "Printing and the people".

Commentary by Gérard NOIRIEL

Ecole Normale Supérieure de Paris

Rather than present a formal commentary on Jacques Revel's paper, what I would prefer is to add a further element to the argument he has developed by way of an example that illustrates the magnitude of the changes that have taken place in schools over the last two centuries.

Revel has described the school system of what was essentially a rural society, which had no policy as regards integration (indeed no genuine educational strategy at all) and where the schools, run by the Church rather than the State, still mirrored diversity. What I propose to do is to examine the school system in a more advanced age, namely under the Third Republic (1870-1940), when it came completely under the control of the State. This turned the school into one of the main channels for spreading a uniform ideology, refusing to recognise cultural differences and instilling the values of the French nation and the concept of the superiority of French culture. The example I have to give illustrates the paradoxical effects of this particular school system as regards the integration of the children of immigrants who were enrolled between the two world wars.

It was during this period that the offspring of the vast numbers of Italian, Polish and other immigrants who came to France during the 1920s were exposed to French schools. The steel area of Lorraine, of which I have made a special study (1), was at this period the region with the highest percentage of immigrants in France (and this during an era when, proportionately, France had more foreigners on its soil than did the United States). But, in addition, it was a region that symbolised French nationalism more than any other, by virtue of the fact that it had been indelibly marked by the wars of 1870 and 1914. The combination of these two factors was to have profound social effects as regards immigration.

Yet the primary school was only one of the means whereby this national ideology was imposed. The Lorrainers, traumatised by the war, would gather to mourn their dead in front of the memorial that every commune insisted should be built to their memory. The Fourteenth of July and, still more, the Eleventh of November were commemorated with intense popular fervour. All this helped to sharpen the deep-seated hostility towards foreign workers, even though they constituted the majority of the population in many areas.

With the economic crisis and the unemployment of the 1930s, this hostility developed into aggressive xenophobia. The research we have carried out (particularly the interviews of retired people living in the area) has shown that school was a particularly uncomfortable experience in this respect. Children who were of foreign origin were a target for insults from their French classmates, and their teachers were zealous exponents of patriotic fervour.

For the young second-generation immigrants, this hostility on the part of the French population had a profound traumatic effect and the results of this stigmatisation are still noticeable fifty years on. As was said in 1982 by the mayor of a working-class commune in Lorraine, who is of Italian extraction and was a schoolboy during the 1930s: "I well remember the nightmare of mistakes in spelling or grammar, and on essays the frightening marginal comments like 'Not French' or 'Bad French' which I felt, probably wrongly, were full of innuendo."

This is a good example of an education system that completely disregarded the specific cultural characteristics of the foreign children in its schools. In classes where the numbers were too large, where there might be twenty different nationalities and where only a tiny minority spoke French, no special provision was made and no special educational strategy contemplated. Aside from the teaching profession, nobody considered that the children of migrants posed a real "education problem".

However, despite this complete lack of an "education policy" for the children of immigrants, it could be argued, particularly from the standpoint of the French State, that the process of educating these children has been a "success". Even in the 1930s teachers were talking about the keenness of their Italian and Polish pupils, and their rapid progress in mastering written and spoken French. Their highly successful results in the Certificat d'Etudes Primaires (Certificate of Primary Education) was proof of the effectiveness of this "do-nothing" approach.

For anyone concerned today with the "problem" of educating the children of immigrants, this example from the past gives food for thought. The success of an educational policy or a teaching strategy in respect of a "minority" is not merely a question of adopting a more appropriate technique. It is determined to a far greater extent by general economic and social conditions. In this particular case, the school was a powerful factor in the abandonment by the children of immigrants of their culture of origin; for their generation this stigmatisation was a fundamental psychological incentive which filled them with a fierce determination to integrate within French society by ridding themselves of the slightest trace of any difference. This collective integration was brought about through the working class, its values and its organisations, with the school being the springboard for access to skilled jobs and participation in the political life of the community.

NOTE

1. NOIRIEL G., Longwy, Immigrés et Prolétaires (1880-1980), Presses Universitaires de France, Paris, 1984.

2. MULTICULTURAL EDUCATION POLICIES: A CRITICAL ANALYSIS

by
Etienne VERNE
Consultant to the INSEP, Paris
(Institut supérieur d'éducation permanente)

INTRODUCTION

The education of migrant workers' children is an issue today in many countries, and in fact this public concern extends to the immigrant population as a whole, adults as well as young people, in the labour force and outside, and second and third generation immigrants and new arrivals alike. The specific measures adopted in the industrialised countries for the education of all these migrants have primarily been designed to tackle the economic and social problems which migrants raise for the host countries. They are also a response to the reactions of local social groups concerned at the presence of migrants.

The education measures proposed and the problems raised by the integration of new arrivals do not appear so novel or unusual when viewed from a proper historical standpoint. In our societies migratory movements towards boom areas or new frontiers are not an innovation of the second half of the 20th century. The populations of some countries were until quite recently built up largely by successive waves of migrants. The economic - and indeed cultural - dynamism of these countries with no history other than the immediate past does not seem to have suffered.

So spontaneous or directed immigration is not a new phenomenon. Neither is the integration of newcomers with earlier arrivals or long-established local groups. Yet the social problems that migrants pose for the industrialised countries now seem more acute, and the measures designed for them, especially in education, seem more specific. Above all, local people's sensitivity towards migrants seems to have sharpened. We say "seems to have sharpened" because here again a closer look at history would no doubt reveal this to have been a constant response. Migratory movements are one of history's constants, and one of its motive forces. If reactions have sharpened, two other factors are no doubt at work: the formation of public opinion via the media, and the consequences of public opinion in the political arena.

These observations are not intended to minimise the significance of migratory movements in the historical ebb and flow of populations, still less the importance of the problems that they pose for our societies, but lead into an understanding of them. One must understand that it is not first of all a question of the difficulties that immigrants create within those social groups integrating them, but rather the new kind of sensitivity and reactions that are developed within these groups that accept them or accept them badly. All of these behaviours and attitudes, both individual and collective, that immigrants face today in a diversified and unequal manner, would seem to be new phenomena, had history not already forged the words xenophobia and racism. If one took for example two civil rights, the right to education and the right to vote, one would see that the demand for these rights is less marked by the violence of immigrant groups than by the reactions of refusal of the "nationals". Behaviour patterns and attitudes in the host countries help toward an understanding of the social mechanism by which in a given situation one social group transfers to another responsibility for its problems, difficulties and failures, amounting in some cases to rejection. They also help towards an understanding of the ritual and exorcism by which all social groups purge the guilt and anxiety produced by these mechanisms of defence and rejection (Levi-Strauss, 1973 and 1983).

From that standpoint migrants are not the only parties involved, since they are not the only ones to face this reaction. It is no doubt because they do not raise a specific problem that migrants have customarily been included in a broader group, that of minorities. It could easily be demonstrated that the nature of interactions and the transfer mechanisms that they encounter among the majorities are not different in essence.

Two features are generally accepted as describing minorities: the <u>linguistic</u> dimension and the <u>cultural</u> dimension. The first is far from applying to all minorities. Yet it is through language <u>or</u> culture, or <u>both</u>, that social groups are identified as minorities. A third dimension should be included: language and/or culture, are perceived only in relation to the culture and/or language of majority social groups, so the concept of a minority is bound to be a relative one. By "minorities" therefore we generally mean linguistic and cultural minorities. These, at any event, are the two aspects which the specific education programmes for minorities seem to have singled out.

"Culture" is of course used here in the sense employed by anthropologists, who have defined it in various ways. In the present paper, unless otherwise mentioned, "culture" will always denote the behaviour patterns and attitudes specific to a given social group. Culture thus includes language, but also takes in the group's beliefs, perceptions, way of life, structure of social relations, etc., as well as its cultural and social institutions. Culture is thus very close in this case to the definition proposed by Malinowski (in <u>The Dynamics of Culture Change</u>, 1961) of culture as as instrumental reality, an apparatus allowing the satisfaction of fundamental needs, i.e. organic survival, adjustment to the environment and continuity in the biological sense. Where culture is otherwise defined the word will be suitably qualified. That will be so, for instance, when we speak of sophisticated culture, learned culture, school culture - a set of practices where culture refers not so much to a way of life serving the social dynamic as to a set of objects produced by a particular culture.

The evolution of education policies is significant in this respect. Measures originally conceived for migrants are now being put forward to deal with all minorities, including them in a so-called multicultural scheme of education. Multicultural education seems to flourish on diversity, and hence on the acknowledgement of differences, to the point where the intercultural dynamic becomes the object of an education project covering not just the minorities but all social groups, majorities included. This range of education policy, from education for migrants to education for minorities, from multicultural to intercultural education, is diverse and sufficiently widespread now to merit closer examination.

During the 1960s greater emphasis would no doubt have been placed on another dimension, the economic one, rather than on culture. From the economic standpoint, however, the specific education measures for minorities are no different from those taken for any group with a low socio-economic ranking. As we shall note again further on, the social and educational failure of the programmes based on an economic approach to educational and social success is at least partly the reason for greater awareness of the importance of other factors, first and foremost the culture of the economically disadvantaged groups. It is the case, moreover, that minorities which are not economically disadvantaged may have the same cultural claims. But as a rule there is a considerable overlap between areas of poverty and the groups that occupy them: foreigners, immigrants and ethnic minorities.

Multicultural education is, in broad terms, a response to the problems raised not only by the education of migrants' children, but by the education of all minorities, too. We may accordingly take the concept of "minority" as the starting point for a brief outline of the development of multicultural education. With due allowance for its imprecisions, the concept will also provide the starting point for our critical analysis of multicultural education.

Before proceeding further with this critical examination we may briefly present the education practices that multicultural education covers. We will then outline the framework for our critical analysis of these practices.

The purpose here is not to close up analysis but rather to open it out and allow others to continue in turn elsewhere. The points proposed here for analysis are chiefly intended to help define an area of great complexity, and lead on to the significance of practical decisions, both past and future.

THE DEVELOPMENT OF MULTICULTURAL EDUCATION

Approaching the critical analysis of multicultural education through the concept of minorities and hence through the education response to the economic and social problems that minorities raise, we may first distinguish three phases in its history.

The prehistory (which is not the least significant part) of multicultural education corresponds to the time when minority groups each assumed their own education needs, or also immersed themselves completely in the surrounding culture. The history of multicultural education proper begins with recognition in the public education system of the culture of minorities. In the early phase the chief concern was to teach the official language more effectively to children who heard and spoke another language at home, in order to offset their linguistic handicap. Put briefly, it was as though the compensatory programmes based on enhancing family incomes and greater educational activism came up against a core of resistance in the language spoken by or around the children. So early multicultural education programmes took the form of intensified teaching of the official language, and hence of the language of schooling.

Attention quickly passed from the language spoken by minority groups to their culture, of which the language is only one component, especially since certain minorities are distinguished from the majority not by language but by a set of values, individual and collective behaviour patterns, attitudes, ways of life, relations with the environment, social structures, etc., which make up their culture. A change of direction occurs here: we could well say that this is the point at which multicultural education comes into being, when we move from intensive teaching of the official language to teaching foreign children their mother tongue.

Originally we had intensive teaching of the official language to economically disadvantaged children, and still more intensive teaching for children whose mother tongue is not the language used at school. The purpose of all this was to give greater equality of opportunity at school and hence in life. From intensive teaching of the official language we move, in the second phase, to teaching minority children, and first and foremost migrant children, their own mother tongue at school. Education becomes bilingual, and bicultural too. Bicultural-bilingual education can be justified on educational ground: learning and development in the mother tongue at school as the best education strategy for proper mastery of the official language. Again, leeway in learning at school can be put down to the fact that children have been deprived of their mother tongue. The perspective is still one of integration, or assimilation. Bilingual-bicultural education can also be justified in the name of cultural identity and the right to be different. A second point of change occurs here.

Bilingual education represents the first change, but it keeps within the dominant educational and social order: it is a change that affects little more than the curriculum, and it is still consistent with the dominant ideology: integration and unification via the school, social success via educational success, educational success via mastery of recognised skills and in particular skill in the official language. The second change breaks with this scenario: it seeks to preserve differences, or indeed promote them, in the name of the cultural values particular to each social group. The second change leads on to a third: after assertion and development of cultural identity, laying claim to cultural autonomy either with the aim of establishing a sort of multilingual cultural coexistence or for the deliberate purpose, in some cases, of waging a cultural struggle against the dominant culture.

In the third phase of development the promotion of particular cultural values no longer seems to concern the minorities alone but every social group. All of them, minorities or not, have to become familiar with the culture of others, and with other cultures. Teaching everybody different cultures from their own becomes an integral part of the new curriculum. This, as a rule, is what is proposed under the heading of intercultural education.

This survey is of course an impressionistic one, and the development of multicultural education is not so straightforward as our outline might indicate. Moreover, the sources of its development are far more diversified, and so are the social movements and the movements of ideas that run through it. From that standpoint multicultural education is a good sounding box for a whole range of debates at the heart of the modern world. We shall find their echoes in the critical analysis later on. But it seemed necessary, before that point, to demonstrate what multicultural education may cover.

There was also a need, right from the outset, to indicate how the majority's awareness of minorities had evolved, at least in the sphere of education. In the early phase the question is simply one of integrating minorities in the majority. In the second phase the majority tolerates, or accepts, "private" domestic use of the minorities' own language and culture. In the third phase the majority may acknowledge the values particuliar to minorities and accept the risks of an intercultural dynamic. These levels of development must now be defined against their background before they can be analysed.

CULTURAL DYNAMIC AND SOCIAL CONTROL

In the document that prepared the way for this paper, the CERI Secretariat suggested that multicultural education should be considered "not as a problem to be solved, but as a potential solution...so that the main question that has to be asked is the following: what is the problem? Is this solution, regardless of its configuration, in itself capable of solving the problem?" (In CERI, "Education and Cultural and Linguistic Pluralism, Proposed Plan"). These are the two questions that this paper will endeavour to answer: first considering what is the problem to which multicultural education intends to bring an answer, and second examining the relevance of that answer.

In its most advanced developing phase multicultural education seems like an educational programme that does not only concern different minorities, but all social groups who are either the majority or minority; each group must be concerned with their own culture, but also the interrelationship with other cultures.

In actual fact this justification for multicultural education does not stand up to close examination. The assumption of cultural ecumenism conceals the relations that every minority culture maintains with the dominant culture. Cultures may perhaps all have similar values to share, but they do not have equal opportunities to assert their particular values. Even if all cultures were of equal worth, they would not all have the same opportunities of making this known. A review of minority cultures quickly shows the cultural scene to be composite. But the juxtaposed and interwoven fabric of these cultures cannot really conceal the relations that each one of them maintains with the dominant culture. This latter may be the national one ("French culture", for instance); it may also be a transnational culture, for instance that conveyed by the culture industries, and the standard English used to disseminate their products.

Culture's expression, especially in the case of minorities, cannot be assessed without some reference to culture's power, and hence to a dominant culture. A particular culture will be dominant because of the power that it exerts over other cultures (its chief feature), but it too is composite and dispersed as well, more fully grasped through what is called "mass culture", an industrialised form which follows market patterns, a transnational culture, a culture growing outwards through all these manifold networks, still looking for its own language but already heavy with linguistic signs.

Multicultural education may equally well serve as the vector for a dominant culture under cover of safeguarding other individual ones. Before seeing multicultural education as the triumph of local cultures we need to assess how permeable each of these local cultures is to the dominant one that surrounds them. We therefore propose a different interpretation here, with the following hint of argument:

i) First, multiculturalism is a de facto situation in society to which the school has so far felt bound to remain impermeable;

ii) Next, the dominant culture is not a culture like all the rest, taking its place among the pattern, but one which penetrates all the others and indeed lives off them, restructuring them in its own way. It is this reshaping by the dominant culture that perverts all attempts at cultural authenticity;

iii) The agency for this shaping of society is the education system, once the dominant culture's chief promoter and still effective even if it is now rivalled, and perhaps outdistanced, by others;

iv) Last, the education system may no longer be crucial and almost undisputed but it still plays its role and does so with greater impunity and greater openness to the "second class" cultures and languages since it has triumphed over them.

Multicultural education can thus be seen as a fresh attempt by the State to control the cultural dynamic of society. The formation of nation-states has not halted this dynamic. While the nation-states have by and large achieved control over the economy and education, they appear less capable of dealing with the cultural dynamic displayed by the various social groups in society. Placed in this context multicultural education will not necessarily seem a pointless venture but rather an inappropriate answer.

Like many other projects in this field, multicultural education is an attempt by the State to control the cultural dynamic, and in particular an attempt to control the cultural dynamic when it is a source of intercultural conflicts. But it can in no sense provide a solution to the clash of cultures, without which there would be no social dynamic. To support this interpretation we may now examine the policies focusing on minority education, and in particular education policy relating to migrants. After that we shall analyse cultural policies with regard to minorities, and in particular the language policies which States conduct. In all of these cases we shall see that the cultural aspect is crucial to any understanding of the education policies that are proposed and, at the same time, is quite irreducible by those policies.

MINORITY: A SHAPELESS CONCEPT OR A PSEUDO-CONCEPT

The succession of transformations in the education policies that States apply are no longer any surprise. For decades, in the name of the same principles, the same agencies have tirelessly devised the same scenarios which yield the same effects and lead to other problems. That is the way with educational reform. The targets of this unremitting policy drive may vary, but the standards are the same. Their rationales and their accompanying programmes can be tirelessly repeated, with the only imaginative effort being to locate or handle social groups which had previously eluded diagnosis and treatment. The problems tackled by earlier education policies may not be overcome but already -- and perhaps for that very reason -- the focus shifts to new targets which topical events have drawn to the public's attention.

These successive targets of public attention may -- it matters little -- be the populations of distant regions, prone to reactionary and dissident behaviour when national unity has to be built up; the children of the people, as victims of ignorance, when the mode of industrial production calls for standardized skills; the children of the working class, suffering under individual and collective handicaps, as an affront to equality of opportunity; or else children in the third word, as victims of educational imperialism or the inequalities of the trading system. We are not saying these successive efforts are negligible; we are simply noting how the same kind of interventionist logic crops up again and again when States are called upon, in various ways, to use their educational authority to overcome the problems raised by society. In that logic, it is for the State to resolve education problems, in particular by means of the education system that it controls.

Among the social groups to have thus benefited from public attention recently is an imprecise or at least heterogeneous area, the hope no doubt that focusing on it would finally make an end of particularisms, and hence of differences. This area -- this remaining area -- is what are termed minorities, the residue and the discarded part of societies which are not yet through with generating differences.

"Minorities": a relative concept if ever there was one, since the "quantitative" criterion is not always applied. A disjunctive concept as well, since minorities can be "national" or "foreign", localised or dispersed, immigrant or long-established, new or old, ethnic or political, religious or social, and so on. The factors that identify them may be highly varied, too: language, socio-economic status, sex, housing, region, race or ethnic origin, geographical origin, way of life, religion, and so on. In the industrialised world "country people" are a minority, but so are old people. In France, Protestants form a minority, but they are the majority in the United Kingdom. In Canada, English-speakers are the minority in Quebec but the majority in the other provinces, and there is no hesitation in such cases in talking of a dual minority or majority in describing the situation. Women too are said to be a minority, even where they form the larger part of the population. It may be noted in passing that the idea of a minority is rarely coupled with a majority, though that alone could justify the description.

In the case of multilingual States, such as Switzerland, the concept of minority is still more difficult to use. It could well simply describe groups of immigrants, if the native Rhaeto-Romanic group was not itself a minority (and within that minority group in turn we should need to determine which is the majority language: Romansh, Tyrolean or Friulian). In Belgium the concepts of majority and minority seem to be quite outlawed.

The socio-political determinants seem no clearer than the linguistic ones: a numerical majority does not always mean a dominant social and political position. To add to the confusion, a good many individuals would find difficulty in saying whether they belonged to a minority or not, and in identifying its configuration.

These brief observations should be enough to designate "minority" as a pseudo-concept. It is a pseudo-concept that has its uses, however, for it provides a picture, fashions the imaginary social pattern and provides an introduction to the complexity of the social sphere and the way it comes about. In this sense the pseudo-concept may help us to think through this complexity, and what ties it together. But as a mean of bringing order into the social sphere, qualified by clear-cut criteria, it is quite inoperative. Yet that is the most frequent way in which it is used.

A concept as shapeless as this would attract little political and social attention if it were not accompanied, in certain cases, by more specific determinants -- including one which has triggered off the bulk of specific educational schemes over the last twenty years: socio-economic status.

In one of the preparatory papers the CERI Secretariat proposed the adoption of the four criteria suggested by Thurow (1980) to identify minorities:

i) The probability of the minority's finding employment, relative to the majority group;

ii) The earnings opportunities for those who are employed, relative to the majority;

iii) The number of minority group members breaking through into the high-income jobs in the economy;

iv) The group's economic history.

This definition deals purely in economics. Identifying minorities by these four economic criteria has the advantage of tackling the education problems of minorities as an extension of policies designed to cater for all economically disadvantaged groups. If the problem raised by education for minorities is first and foremost an economic one, the measures required are twofold -- financial, increasing the income of disadvantaged families, and educational, offsetting socio-cultural handicaps. The purpose of all this is to ensure equality of opportunity. Identifying minorities by economic criteria has a further advantage: it means that the conceptual and theoretical framework employed for analysis of social stratification can be used for the social minorities as well; they are simply one example of the social division into classes identified by their position in the production process.

In spite of these advantages the economic definition of social minorities comes up against a number of difficulties:

-- The first is the failure of the social and education policies which have aimed to offset the education deficits of disadvantaged groups through economic and education measures. The lack of success of many programmes of this kind has been explained by the cultural resistance which groups, and cultural minorities especially, develop. Moreover, this cultural resistance may be similar to the resistance to the school's educational influence displayed even by majority social groups when faced by a different dominant culture.

It is as if the social and education policies designed to bridge the gaps between social groups ultimately came up against an unavoidable core of resistance that can hardly be described otherwise than through the generic word "cultural"; with culture denoting here, at least, a set of things learnt individually and socially, well before the formal school process of learning, and also the fact of belonging to a social fabric, to a particular history, whose form and life seem barely affected by schooling;

-- Above all, identifying minorities solely on the basis of their economic status leaves out all the minorities whose position may be comfortable or heterogeneous. Should we disregard the education problems raised by the Jewish communities in Los Angeles, the Indo-Chinese immigrants in Paris, or the Basque community? Economic reasons to not account for the fact that Catholics, a religious majority in France, insist on an education system separate from the public system. Nor do economic reasons account for the presence almost everywhere of alternative, ethnic or religious schools, or simply for the fact that some children attend two schools belonging to quite different systems.

All these factors, and others as well, no doubt, account for the move away from the concept of the minority to that of the minority cultures -- to lay emphasis, undoubtedly, on the cultural aspect. Where the earlier concept of the minority still holds, in spite of its ambiguities, this is due more to political than to economic criteria. In such cases the minorities are seen as human groups which are culturally and economically dominated in a given social context; or, again, are disadvantaged for reasons of culture and language, in particular the ethnic minorities.

We need not trouble here with the range of definitions by which certain social groups have been styled minorities. We may simply note that they have all given rise to specific programmes and that these programmes were felt to be necessary and possible in a period of economic growth where funds could readily be found. They nonetheless proved unsuccessful; in particular, as we mentioned above, in the case of minorities defined not simply by economic factors, like every other disadvantaged group, but by cultural factors as well. It seems likely that this failure has helped, in the education field at least, to draw attention to other determinants that, in a period of economic crisis, have come to assume greater importance: spoken language, national origin, culture. The process has gone so far that these latter features are said to account for the failure of earlier programmes with their heavier emphasis on socio-economic status: giving financial assistance to disadvantaged families cannot alter cultural habits and linguistic behaviour.

We have thus moved gradually from the idea of deficit to the idea of difference. If educational and social problems are tied up with spoken language, culture, ethnic origin and race, measures aimed solely at raising living standards are bound to be inappropriate. Can enhancing the socio-economic status of Bretons in France or Jamaicans in the United Kingdom solve the problems of particularism, nationalism, separatism, irredentism or tribalism?

A SEPARATE MINORITY: THE MIGRANTS

Study of a special minority, migrants, brings us back again to this cultural factor. The case of migrants and the minority groups that they form in the host countries illustrates particularly well the importance of the cultural and linguistic variables. The education system is not alone, moreover, in feeling its impact. Business and the social and medical services also experience difficulties. As a consequence, immigrants are certainly the minority group on which the greatest concern focuses. Unlike national minorities, migrants and hence migratory flows are monitored more closely and in two places: the country of origin and the country of destination.

Like all minorities, immigrants form a very diversified and heterogeneous group; first of all from their nationality of origin, their language, their culture and their socio-economic level. In many cases, one and the same nationality may mask different ethnic origins, representing a diversified pattern that nationality does not reveal. These differences are compounded by others of another order: there are long-standing residents, recent permanent residents, circular immigrants and also immigrants already holding the nationality of the host country, or again immigrants from other parts of the countries: Andalucians in Barcelona, West Indians in Paris, Porto-Ricans in New York, etc. Matters go so far as identifying the traditional occupants of a region as migrants because they have become local minorities (native groups) or because they are identified with new arrivals (Chicanos). All these groups have special features which are further complicated by the legal status of each one in the host country (political refugees).

The main characteristics of immigration today are well known, and need only be recalled briefly here:

-- Immigration into the host countries has stabilised, but the immigrant population there is rising through births and the admission of family members. The decline in migratory flows resulting from the legal obstacles the host countries are gradually introducing is occurring at the same time as more and more members of immigrant workers' families are swelling the school rolls and the workforce. The foreign population is continuing to rise and the second generation phenomenon is developing, the children of immigrants who have to be educated. As a results, immigration is exerting an increasing influence on population figures in the host countries. In the United States, for instance, legal immigration is said to account for 25 to 30 per cent of annual population growth;

-- Political immigration and illegal immigration, still fairly high although estimates vary widely, are on the increase in a number of countries (Kelly, 1982, pp. 37-42; Bustamante, 1981; Abstracts of the Sixth Seminar on Adaptation and Integration of Immigrants focused on undocumented migrants or migrants in an irregular situation. Geneva, 12-15 April 1983. Published by "International Migration", Vol. XXI, N° 2, 1983);

-- There is now international legislation governing the movement of workers within the same economic community, as with the EEC, and also bilateral agreements such as those between France and number of its former possessions or between Portugal and Sweden, etc.;

-- Even in countries with a nil net migratory balance, the number of foreign pupils in the education system is increasing and will continue to do so. And their proportions are increasing still more rapidly than their numbers by the combined effect (as in France) of the falling numbers of young nationals, the continuing admission of members of immigrant families, and higher fertility in foreign than in French families. In coming years a rising tide of foreign enrolments is thus to be expected all along the line of school classes (Bastide, 1982);

-- The concentration of migrants in specific geographical areas (regions, suburbs, districts) raises special problems: allocation of national and local resources, disparities between regions, segregation, etc;

-- Despite discussions and even the implementation of explicit policies promoting the migrant's return, immigrants are increasingly tending to remain permanently in almost all the host countries. In spite of this there is a general failure to assimilate them. Immigration for employment purposes is being converted into settlement through the ties which the children represent. Immigrants do not easily integrate, and few, if any, leave. Yet many policy decisions are still based on the opposite assumption, that based of return;

-- There is continuing debate over the segregation of immigrants: Is it greater today, or not? Do immigrants' children today stand less chance of succeeding at school than in the past? Have they less opportunity of finding a job? In the United States discrimination against Hispanic immigrants is today said to be far greater, though it was apparently virtually non-existent at the start of the century. A. Girard, in the preface to a study on immigrant children in France, notes that "the school career of migrant children follows a similar pattern to that of French children", although he does note that they "progress somewhat less quickly and are less numerate in the longer secondary cycles" (Bastide, 1982, p. 3).

All these factors help to clarify the configuration of the groups of migrants. But alongside them there are others which are less directly noticeable and pose greater problems for the national majority. They have to do with the demographic threat, the language threat, the civic, racial and cultural and in some cases the religion threat. This is the case, for instance, with the demographic growth usually displayed by migrant groups: demographers estimate the time at which the national majority will become a minority, sociologists put forward critical thresholds beyond which equilibria are a risk in a geographical area, and so on. The national majority feels threatened by immigration. What is at stake is far more than the national unity represented by a shared language and a cultural community. The threat -- or what is perceived as such and generates individual and social reactions of rejection, segregation, racism and xenophobia -- extends to the values which a nation is said to hold in common and which appear jeopardised as soon as assimilation or integration seem to be impossible or even merely remote.

When the limits to assimilation have to be seen, others may invoke the merits of pluralism and respect for minorities. Pluralism, all the same, has its limitations too. It is as though the presence of migrants among social groups aware of the unity they have fought to win were making the unity brittle by reintroducing differences. The presence of the foreign body compels society to consider its relations with what is different. That means some destabilisation, of a kind which serves patterns and postures of defence and rejection rather than a positive cultural dynamic. And if pluralism is impossible the alternatives are rejections, encirclement or assimilation. The threat is felt all the more keenly because, in spite of governments' efforts, immigration is apparently not so fully monitored as it is said to be. Some switches and contradictions in policy would seem to bear this out.

Immigration is customarily accounted for by the manpower needs of the industrialised countries. If that factor alone accounted for immigration it would be most difficult to say why legal and illegal immigration persists in countries where few if any jobs are available. Immigration can be explained by the needs of the industrialised countries -- population and manpower -- but it is also due to the needs of those who emigrate: finding paid work, but more fundamentally breaking out of the poverty circle (Galbraith, 1979), reconstituting the family unit, etc.

Everything suggests that migratory movements follow a logic which is not simply economic. Above all, the problems which immigrants face, and those which they create, do not appear to be simply economic ones. As with minorities in general, the case of migrants again brings us back to consideration of cultural, ethnic, linguistic, national, racial and religious factors. Behind the teaching of their own language and culture to minorities -- and that is one of the aims of multicultural education -- there is always the fear that the preservation of the culture and language of others threatens national cohesion, erases the historical roots of peaples, or the historical legitimacy passed down by the fathers of the nation, and the rights acquired in the course of a shared history, and hence opens up a process of conflict between social groups claiming to be racially, ethnically and culturally different. The social imagination of descendants with historical legitimacy on their side is fostered by the fear of being dispossessed of that legitimacy by the new arrivals or the social groups which stand outside that tradition, or at the very least of having to share it through some fresh fraft onto the social body.

The causes of controversy surrounding multicultural education, and in particular the teaching of their own language and culture to migrants, are mainly economic: why should public money be spent in public institutions for minority groups? But there are social reasons as well: should differences be deliberately maintained when the public service ought to be promoting social cohesion? Above all, there are ideological and axiological reasons: why threaten national unity and abandon the development of the nation? At this level, when we are dealing with unity and pluralism, identity and difference, we have to look to political philosophy when it raises the question of the "social bond" (what is it that holds a disparate society together?) and hence the question of social division (cf. for instance Debray, 1981).

It is here that multicultural education is vulnerable to criticism: when the established social bond is weakened. If multicultural education gives rise to conflict it is not on account of its content or its teaching methods. While it is serving integration and assimilation, through transitional programmes for instance, it is fully in line with the aims assigned to the public education service. But when it becomes one of the ways selected by the minorities in order to assert themselves and to emphasize their right to be different, and hence to live in a different way, the "iron law" of democracy is at stake: the rule of the majority. Is there then a threat to the social bond and its arithmetical rule, or is a new form of democracy foreshadowed, in which minorities may live otherwise than under the law of the majority?

The pressure which all minorities exert on the dominant social group brings us back to their cultural dynamic. We must accordingly attempt to define and understant this cultural dynamic if we are to account for the development of multicultural education and assess the relevance of the answers that it supplies.

CULTURAL MINORITIES AND CULTURAL RESISTANCE

In order to understand the development of multicultural education as briefly outlined in the introduction we have to recognise that the early programmes very quickly hit upon an unavoidable fact, what we have so far termed the "cultural fact". Far from glossing over it, the programmes in fact brought it out sharply. From that point onwards it is as if the education system had taken it over to make it the central subject of its teaching. The process of acceptance reaches its culmination when multicultural education is defined in this way:

> "Multicultural education is an interdisciplinary process rather than a single programme or a series of activities. Included in this process are the concepts embraced by cultural pluralism, ethnic and intercultural studies, and inter-group and human relations" (California State Department of Education, State Board of Education Policy on Multicultural Education, adopted 9th March, 1978).

Anthropology has never given any other definition of education, even in those societies which have no formal schooling.

How can the succession of slippages concerning the purpose of multicultural education be accounted for? That is the question that has to be answered, and the answer should help us towards a fuller understanding of both the meaning of multicultural education and what is at stake.

In the case of minorities in general, and migrants in particular, it is as though, after the failure of the major economic and educational programmes that were to change the academic career and social future of the disadvantaged social groups, there had been a return to a more directly educational form of intervention dealing with cultural and linguistic differences. From that standpoint multicultural education, in its various forms, benefited from the failure of the educational programmes based on raising socio-economic status and on the treatment of socio-cultural "deficits". That failure can be accounted for by the inadequacy of the budget allocations for these programmes, and now by the lack of material resources. The failure is understandable, from the confution between "deficit" and "difference" that the education philosophy sustained: it views difference simply as a handicap.

But the failure in terms of resources is perhaps compounded by a theoretical inadequacy: how far can the educational needs of minorities be inferred simply from the socio-economic characteristics which they may share with other groups? How far do linguistic, cultural, ethnic and national characteristics explain the resistance of minority groups to standard schooling? To what extent can the economic criteria and the cultural ones be brought properly together, as in discussion for example of a "sulture of poverty" (Hoggart, 1957) or a "culture of the oppressed" (Freire, 1972)?

The disadvantaged minorities showed particular resistance to the financial, social and education programmes that were supposed to change their educational and social destiny. They perhaps caused them to fail. If that is so we need to understand the reasons. The failure of education for gypsies in Western Europe is a good example of active resistance. The first explanation to be put forward is that the programmes adopted have been unsuitable. Since socio-economic variables are no longer essential, emphasis is to be placed on the cultural variables: ways of life, systèms of thought, the feeling of belonging to a propre social group, shared language, structures of relationship, history, culture, etc. Educational programmes try to integrate all these variables to develop an educational scheme focusing on the particular characteristics of each minority.

The link may well seem tenuous between compensatory education which tackles poverty through primarily financial assistance and "dialogue between cultures" which seeks to tackle the human being itself, racism and war through the promotion of an international cultural community. Yet link there is, and it can be traced, in the education field at least. The failure of the earlier economic programmes has helped to bring out the phenomena of cultural resistances. By extension we have come to be concerned with cultural minorities as a whole, including those whose socio-economic status is not low. That has happened by extension, but also as the result of other factors, outside the school. But although a fair number of multicultural education programmes are still marked by their socio-economic origin, in particular those focusing on the linguistic dimension, the fact remains that what has most frequently led to multicultural education is the hard core of the cultural.

Of course the development of multicultural education is not simply the result of the failure of earlier programmes and a sort of desperate determination among practitioners and theorists to mop up pockets of resistance appearing as a consequence of educational measures or identified as the cause of persistent failures. The failure of earlier programmes is not due simply to theoretical weakness and practical inadequacies. Behind multicultural education, and buttressing it, there are social movements and hence social conflicts which resound through the world of education. But it must also be recognised that multicultural education, as a part of the curriculum, stands today at the end of a logical educational process whose successive stages are not difficult to identify.

There is a formal education logic on the one hand, but a social movement as well: the genesis of the concept of multicultural education and the development of the programmes that illustrate it can be understood only taking into account both the social demand for a specific form of education and the policy response thereto; the demand and the response forming a system indeed! To what demand are policy makers responding when they decide on a new curriculum, especially in the case of a "culture" curriculum (in the same way as we speak of a "mathematics" or "history" programme)? What social demand are policy makers fostering through their intervention? And what power does their response carry for it to maintain such demand in their respect? The education debate is not the only ont to raise these questions about the interactions between civil society and the State. But they need to be considered when we are questioning both the legitimacy and the limits of intervention by public education systems, controlled largely by governments, in the case of the culture of different social groups, their cultural dynamic and hence their future as differentiated groups, their cultural identity and hence inter- and intra-cultural conflicts.

We need, therefore, to understand the reasons that impel governments and their agencies to develop programmes of multicultural education. To understand why governments should initiate or assist these programmes in their own education system, but also to understand why this particular social demand is addressed to public education, that is to say, why social groups hope that their culturel identity and their cultural dynamic, the protection or promotion of their culture, shoulc be a matter for schools. How far are the "cultural" programmes designed to achieve better academic results or better education for minorities compatible with the survival of the minority? How can the cultural and linguistic identity of a minority social group be secured and promoted through formal education, as it currently functions? When we see the role that formal education has played, and the role that is still being assigned to it, in the emergence and consolidation of modern nations, it is really astonishing that the same type of formal education should be expected to serve, and possibly satisfy, the specific cultural needs of minorities. These questions should bring us to consider how far additional government intervention in these areas, through the imposition of new curricula is relevant or legitimate. They should also bring us to consider the novel social practive of looking to the education system for everything: income, social mobility, skills, jobs and now -- ironically, but why not? -- culture. We only need to list the successive demands on formal education systems to grasp the importance of some de-escalation. Unless the education system is supposed to become so bloated that it bursts.

If consideration of the matter were to rest here, we might simply encourage states not to intervene and the social groups not to ask for anything, in particular not to look to schools to satisfy such essential and such intimate needs as those relating to their own culture, or the organisation of the relations which minorities maintain with the dominant culture. But to go no further would overlook another factor: the resistance which certain minority groups put up to cultural domination and the steam-rollering of their identity; passive resistance in some cases, active resistance in others, sometimes backward-looking and sometimes forward-looking, and involving both a refusal of formal education as currently imposed and a quest for alternatives, and the refusal of specific treatments in the school context for their particular cultural, religious and linguistic characteristics. A corollary of struggling for academic recognition of particular cultural features is the refusal, by other cultural communities or indeed within the actual community concerned, of specific cultural treatment. The cultural claims of these communities do not necessarily include the involvement of the school. And in a number of cases, especially with regional features, it would not be very difficult to show that the pressures on the school are stronger where the regional culture and language are already dead or nearly so.

THE CULTURAL DYNAMIC OF MINORITIES

To trace the links between compensatory education and multicultural education is still not to justify the latter. The successive stages in the transition from one to the other do not conceal the fact that two sets of principles are involved: one, of social principles based on the democratic ideal and promoting equality and the other, a social reasoning based on the autonomy of social groups through affirmation of their right to be different: the principle of differentiation versus the principle of equality. The multicultural education curricula now being developed cannot conceal the fact that they are based on either one principle or the other. In actual fact, as these contradictions suggest, there is no single educational principle underlying multicultural education as the response of education to cultural diversity -- not the principle which we have so far been following, of which the characteristic is an obssession with the democratisation of success: ensuring that the greatest number achieve the same success measured by the same academic standards, or at least that all have equal chances of achieving that success. Multicultural education is not merely one of the many stages in the process of democratisation of teaching and educational methods.

Underlying multicultural education there does indeed seem to be emerging a principle which is no longer merely the democratic ideal in its twofold form of democracy through education and democracy in education, but one which no longer seems to fit entirely into the notion of democratic equality as represented by the same treatment for all, the same chances for all and if possible the same results for all, but one which, on the contrary, proceeds by affirming differences, the right to be different and to receive unequal treatment, though this may still be given in the name of the same democratic values. Behing multicultural education are also all the cracks which the democratic states have not been able to fill in and which weaken the great democratic structures managed by them. Behind multicultural education, and therefore going well beyond the problems of education of minorities, is a set of social movements on the institutions managed by the nation-states: the political institutions, the business enterprises, the educational system, the hospital system, the information system, the legal system, the cultural industries, etc.

It is worthwhile recalling which are the sensitive areas where these social movements, which are often interdependent, appear:

-- The "linguistic" fronts, active or dormant, in various states such as Belgium, Canada, France, Spain, Switzerland, the United States, etc., and the constitutional conflicts for maintenance of or access to, the status of a national language;

-- The pressures exerted by the various minorities according to the cultural dynamic they embody, for their recognition, preservation or promotion;

-- The regionalist, native, nationalist movements seeking a language, sometimes lost, autonomous political institutions, or even a state which has not always existed, or more generally cultural rights that have become forgotten or distorted; ethnic consciousness has been increasingly aroused in recent years in minority groups, including those in societies that are as centralised as those of France or Spain, while the phenomenon is not confined to those countries in which it is recurrent, such as Belgium, the Scandinavian countries or Northern Ireland;

-- Ethnic, religious or racial conflicts and the search for a new ethnic expression, a new culture, as a revolt against the cultural melting-pot and the planetary culture;

-- The struggles of the various groups of immigrants seeking economic, social and political citizenship in the countries to which they have migrated, or recognition of their cultural and linguistic distinctions; and

-- More widely still, social movements against war and in support of peace, seeking a transnational community by affirming a common humanity.

All these social movements are to be discerned behind multicultural education, going beyond the problems of getting immigrants to schools and beyond the principles on which they are taught: schools are being asked not so much to absorb differences as to take account of them. Taking into account a language or a culture is usually the double banner under which claims are made by various social groups, whether regional, ethnic, immigrant or native. But these two banners fail to hide a third which is that of the political power of these entities, participation in that power, control over that power or the seeking of autonomous power. Minority groups not only have educational and economic difficulties. They are usually oppressed groups whose modes of resistance have to be taken into account and, in particular, the ways of resisting education which some of them have developed over their history. It is as if the nation-states were today obliged to pay for the consequences of excluding minorities in the past (Arendt, 1951).

The impact of the various social movements on the educational system would not deserve to attract much attention if education systems has not been marked by a long tradition of a single language and culture. No one appears to doubt that schools have indeed accomplished one of their historic missions: to legitimize, produce and reproduce a national culture. And no one doubts that this task has been broadly achieved, even where particular cultural features have been able to stand out despite this cultural levelling. And where the State has protected national differences, cultural diversification is still represented by single-language cultural blocks placed aside one another. In accomplishing this task schools have resorted to the gradual introduction of a school culture of their own which has rapidly become dominant and has thus contributed to cultural homogeneity by imposing itself (Bernstein, 1971; Bourdieu and Passeron, 1970), even if human differences reveal, here and there, residual anomalies within the pattern of the behaviour and attitudes imposed and made universal by the schools (Le Bras and Todd, 1981). Governmental cultural policy in schools has always been to maintain a single culture within frontiers or within linguistic areas fixed by history and the constitution.

To reverse that tradition today would be a piece of historical irony which would require an explanation: why schools are being called upon today to protect, if not actually accentuate, differences which their task was previously to absorb. If this reversal were a proved fact it would also raise doubts as to how far schools can really go in the direction of cultural pluralism without losing their true nature, and without also obscuring the nature of the cultures with which they have become involved. How far can the schools organise the absorption of cultural differences, or their inculcation as is done in multicultural education, otherwise than by melting cultures together? How can the various cultural communities entrust their cultural future to the schools, in a cultural environment that has already become familiar and is in any case dominated by a school culture tradition? Here there is an ambiguity in the call of social groups for culturally diversified education. In what condition is the culture of a community which believes that it can entrust its preservation and promotion to the education system? And if the schools took on this work today, it would still be necessary to ask what institutional principle would be represented by the undertaking of such contradictory political tasks by the same social institutions, even if they were undertaken at different times in history.

Awareness of an ethnic or regional identity, or of a minority status, can be hidden for many decades by the myth of national unity and identity, of ethnic homogeneity, or of mass culture or planetary culture. It can also be hidden by an analysis in terms of social groups or the evocation of proletarian internationalism. Today, ethnic or racial claims, nationalist or regionalist movements, and movements for independence or autonomy, have broken up communities which were merely a façade. The alliances between immigrant workers and regionalist movements in France, for example, or the links between regionalist and feminist movements for a cultural war against the same internal colonialism, are evidence of the same refusal to be assimilated. It is sufficient to record the breakdown in national unity, the failure of the "melting-pot", and to resort to pluralism as a way out, closing the door on any ecumenical cultural ideology.

For all these reasons, a present-day analysis hesitates between two extremes. On the one hand, for instance, there is denunciation of the cultural idealism of the regionalists. In affirming the significance of regional or ethnic identities they are felt to be victims of their imagination but sufficiently convinced of it to give it a semblance of truth (Bourdieu, 1982, pp. 125-148). At the same time there is recognition of the "fragmentation impulse" (Debray, 1981, p. 463) which has gone on unchecked by the cultural amalgamation effected by the schools. If it were possible to choose between these two interpretations it would be easier to define the meaning of multicultural education. This meaning is not to be found in the content of multicultural education curricula but in the significance of the social movements which those curricula are intended to support. In itself, the fact that the social movements concerned are putting pressure on the public education system for it to accept this "teaching imperative" (Malinowski, 1970, p. 79) needed for the development of any culture is already doubly significant: a sign of a weakening in a cultural dynamic which can only be spontaneous and not assisted; and a sign also of danger that the schools may amalgamate scattered and marginal cultural elements for their own benefit. It is to this direction that the proposed interpretation will incline; and to justify this, it will be necessary to consider the direction taken by the social movements developed by the minorities.

THE MEANING OF SOCIAL MOVEMENTS AND MULTICULTURAL EDUCATION

The cultural, political and social movements which call for the identification and recognition of any minority thus raise two questions: What is the meaning of these movements? What is their influence on the educational institutions?

i) First, the significance of such movements: what economic, social, political or religious analysis can be made of movements that are so heterogeneous but are all accompanied by a demand for social and even political recognition and by a claim to an identity that is to be recognised or rediscovered? The question is a capital one because it involves understanding of the cultural dynamic and of social movements. The tools of analysis that might be used for social analysis or cultural anthropology would be quite inadequate to help us understand such refined and diffuse social movements as those developed by the minorities.

The question is still a difficult one if it is simplified to the following: how, and in what respects, could it be possible to modify today the significance of the processes of exclusion, neutralisation or assimilation achieved with minorities by the nation-states? What, in other words, according to the principles of the triumphant nation-state, justifies any different social treatment for minorities? What could lead those states, which yesterday were factors for unification and against differences, to preserve a variety of cultural heritages within the nation, protect and promote them?

These questions immediately evoke as many replies, on lines that are already familiar. Briefly, they are:

-- Those based on the crisis of the state, a crisis which arises from dissidence, but also from the resistance developed by a society of citizens necessarily heterogeneous and resenting control by the state over all its components;

-- More widely, those based on analysis of the crisis of internationalism: amalgamation through a worldwide culture is falling apart in the face of the balkanisation of the world; membership of a class is not proof against membership of a nation; while membership of the nation does not override membership of an ethnic or religious group: in Ulster one is first and foremost Catholic or Protestant, as one is a Basque in Spain... It is as if cultural roots were stronger than identification with a nation-state, at least in every case where a cultural group has not identified its own culture with that of the nation-state;

-- Those based on the return of culture against economics: the economic crisis is strengthening the feeling among various social groups that they have the same cultural roots, and is reminding them of the predominance of culture over economics. Migrations, for instance, sharpen the need to belong to a cultural group;

-- Those based on the persistence, and hence the reemergence, at a time when the weaknesses of the industrial societies have become so clear, of the anthropological bases of all social groupings. The breakdown of a standardizing industrial culture is allowing large remnants of older cultures to remain;

-- Those based on the demand for autonomy and hence refusal of the principle of "common identity" (Castoriadis, 1975, 1978, pp. 303 and following) imbued with the idea of society as a whole and the application of global solutions.

ii) Connected with the question of the signification of the social movements covered by the expression "minorities" is that of the impact of those movements, and hence those minorities, on educational institutions: how far is multicultural education a response to the diversity of cultures, or does it amount to recognition of the culture of minorities? And recognition for what reason? What justifies special teaching for minorities in the school system, particularly teaching off the limits of the general curriculum? Why have the educational systems that have developed over the last two centuries on the basis of uniformity of language and cultural homogenisation in the name of the culture and of the nation not succeeded in wearing down these differences existing within a national culture? Resistance to economic facts: the standards of living, the system of production...? Resistance to political facts: power in the hands of a historical ruling class...? Or, more broadly, resistance to anthropological facts going beyond production systems and social conflict? And why, if the educational system has so far been quite successful in assimilating different social groups, should the same system be less successful today, should it encounter resistance and take this into account, and should it try to deal with it in other ways than by ignoring or repressing it?

Here one can see clearly the two frames of reference that can help us understand the same phenomenon: the appearance in various forms of multicultural education curricula. On the one hand there is, even in multicultural education, the persistence of the long task of assimilation that the educational systems have been pursuing since school attendance became compulsory, to the present time when they are turning on the last few minorities in order to integrate them better. On the other hand there is, even in the same multicultural education, recognition of the facts of cultures and their irreducible nature.

In the second frame of reference the argument might be a simple one: it is under the pressure exerted by the various minorities that schools are becoming open to their cultures. The multicultural education is nothing more than the response which the active cultural minorities are succeeding in obtaining from an educational system which has hitherto ignored them. More broadly, it is the resistance to the imposition of cultural uniformity, the standardisation imposed by a dominant culture, the identification of that culture with the nation, and also its extension to a worldwide culture that is being expressed by the demand for and, obtaining of, a multicultural education. And to take the argument to its conclusion, the schools which were the main instruments of the campaign against cultural non-conformity in the preceding period are now to become the places in which the various cultures, including the minority cultures, are to be recognised and taught.

In addition, the opening of schools to various cultures, and in particular minority cultures, is all the more necessary today as the schools will remain a socially marginal institution if they do not subscribe to the cultural flows that are arising. Schools must return to teaching cultures because cultural diversity has not disappeared, the more so since their teaching is unsuited to the economic needs and the cuiltural values of geterogeneous social or ethnic groups. Schools, which have contributed to cultural desertification by imposing their own culture, must now turn back in order to take into account the pockets of cultural resistance which they encounter as they spread their cultural defoliant on new social groups. To say this is to recognise that the educational system has not achieved the homogeneity which its promoters expected, and has not eliminated linguistic, religious or cultural differences rooted in a region or in an ethnic or racial group. This is incidentally true of other transcultural institutions: the information system, political power, national trade unions, churches, business enterprises, all of which face the same differences and the same resistances. All these institutions have worked to forge national unity going beyond local differences, and all appear to have failed in the same way.

The schools will be even less able to escape from this opening of their doors to diversity as the balance today is swinging toward identification and affirmation of those differences. There is something attractive in the idea of schools as a new refuge for oppressed cultures, a bastion of resistance to the uniformity imposed by industrial-scale production of information and cultural products; of schools which may have lost the leading role in inculcating and spreading the dominant culture, leaving this to the "culture industry", but which are organising resistance by defending both culture in general and the promotion of other cultures against the standardised worldwide industrial version. In a state without a nation the school once more becomes the melting-pot of national unity. In a nation-state the threat is no longer internal but external. The multinational industries, including those of culture, transfrontier flows and the technologies which make these possible, have weakened the nation-state. It is therefore up to the schools to resist the cultural flows imposed from outside by cultural industries and impersonal networks of dissemination, to resist mass standards and standardisation, and to do so by building on the local cultures which have withstood the process of breaking them down which the schools had hitherto pursued.

This argument is an attractive one but it is also problematical: can the educational system cope with this about-turn and adapt itselt to the plans for cultural and even political autonomy put forward by certain minorities -- especially since these claims for autonomy are never unanimous? It is rare to find a social or ethnic group with a clear statement of its wishes concerning multiculturalism. Teaching children their mother tongue is as much disliked as it is demanded by members of the same minority linguistic community (Rodriguez, 1981). Can one and the same school carry on at the same time the work of affiliation to a particular community and that of assimilation to the national community? Can one and the same school obey the principles of common identity and of differentiation? Can it abandon its work of social acculturation in response to the demand expressed by certain social groups to have a different relationship with public institutions? Does the single culture which has so far predominated, the ideal of a single-culture state that is still pursued, allow for cultural diversity?

The idea is an interesting one but it is also optimistic. It does not stand up easily to examination, and we shall therefore undertake to disprove it. Other theories can just as well be put forward at the stage in which we now are evolving a general theory of culture and cultural dynamics.

First we encounter all the objections raised to multicultural education, and in particular those based on the "ethnic dilemma" (Glazer, 1982; Smolicz, 1981): by giving minority groups opportunities equal to those of majority groups, one condemns them to remain minority groups. To state this dilemma is in fact to say a number of things: first, that ethnic differences are a social and vocational handicap which must be concealed, on pain of seeing the fact used by dominant groups to discriminate against minorities. This amounts to saying that ethnic differentiation and socio-economic progress are incompatible, or that equality of opportunity is possible only in a culturally unified society. Above all it amounts to saying that the demand for ethnic recognition is part of a general prospect of cultural or inter-cultural conflicts.

Ethnic claims which are the work of minority groups are still a part of the search for benefits available to the majority: "recognise that I am different from you in order that I may become the same as you". One thinks immediately of the mechanism of mimetic rivalry analysed by Girard (1972, 1978), of the desire common to different social groups for a same object, a desire which has to be based on the premise that there is an enormous difference between the groups withour which they could not be opposed to each other. The more the differences become blurred, the more the rivalry develops, even when the desired object has disappeared or when those concerned are no longer certain what is to be desired. And when they no longer know what they are divided about, there is still rivalry because one may always suspect others of having a desire. "Each antagonist tries at all costs to be different from his adversary. This inverse and symmetrical desire to be different identifies them still further. thus, paradoxically though logically, the efforts they make to distinguish themselves makes the rivals more and more similar. This constant return to identity which haunts antagonists sharpens their rivalry. Men are incapable of recognising that there is no difference which justifies their disputes. The more intense the rivalry becomes, that is to say, the more the differences melt away and the rivals becomes doubles, the more the knowledge of their identity becomes intolerable. And they are in the last resort opposed to each other simply because they do not see that they resemble each other and that nothing separates them" (Dumouchel and Dupuy, 1979, pp. 170-171). Cultural differences, and the affirmation of those differences, could be merely vague ideas destined to disguise what the various social groups have in common, namely their rivalry for the same thing. They all have the same aim, and all come to compete, no longer for that aim which they all desire, but with the desire of the other social groups. Social groups are victims of this mimetic rivalry, at the same time as they are kept alive by it.

This mimetic rivalry between social groups has as a corollary within each individual a desire, and particularly in the psychology of minorities, a double identity, which is a source of conflict, and cannot be properly resolved otherwise than by creating a third loyalty, as can be seen among second-generation immigrants (Moscovici, 1976, 1979). Does cultural pluralism assume, and does multicultural education aim at, a pluralist identity? And if the social institutions are there to protect social groups from violence, how can multicultural education given at school contain violence which breaks out away from school?

On the other side of the ethnic dilemma, the other way of by-passing multicultural education would be to reduce thqe culture of ethnic minorities to a residuum. Does the notion of a "minority ethnic culture" have any meaning? Would it not be better to speak of a sub-culture, so greatly does the culture of minorities resemble a by-product or a remainder? Present-day social customs or individual behaviour, which have no explanation or meaning other than in terms of the culture of the social group, are of little importance compared with the behaviour that is based on the social position of that group. Usually, the culture of integrated minorities is already nothing more than a sub-culture, an integram part of a dominant culture.

To say this is not to remove what relevance there may be from the objections to multicultural education. It has already been pointed out how much the reduction in the status of minority cultures to a sub-culture made it impossible to take account of this. Underlying these questions -- and here we are speaking superficially -- what is at stake is roughly the following: is it or is it not worthwhile to concern oneself with, and therefore develop and finance, multicultural education projects? Should one or should one not call for multicultural education? If the claims to cultural identity are nothing more than a residue of the cultural history of the social groups concerned, it is undoubtedly not worthwhile. But if those claims are backed by a capacity for self-sufficiency and self-organisation on the part of minority social groups, if ethnic expression is what a group is defining by its acts because it wishes to exist as a fact of history, then the questions are relevant and deserve much more attention.

Taking up the case of migrants, it was pointed out earlier that geographical displacement did not always destroy the needs to belong and to have roots (Gokalp, 1977). These are the same needs that lead some to look for their roots, others to retrace the steps of successive migrations, and the majority to maintain links with their original home. The need for a home is trill a feature common to many cultures. It is all the more strongly felt when it is awakened by the distance from the culture to which the group belongs, as is shown by the way in which migrants are rejected by host groups. The need for a cultural location survives a change of that location (de Certeau, 1980, p. 133).

From this point of view it would seem that multicultural education can provide for cultural pluralism. On the other hand it seems less well placed to provide for the dislocation of cultural links and to satisfy the need for a cultural location. Schools can hardly offer more than a substitute location, proposing a culture which for the most part remains superficial. to say this is once more to point to the cultural tension suffered by many social groups caught between their underlying culture, that of the roots, and the culture imposed on them from above, i.e. that produced ans disseminated by cultural institutions, including schools, as the approved academic culture, and by the cultural industries, as the mass culture. Among all these strong influences, multicultural education is likely to cut a poor figure.

CULTURAL POLICY AND LANGUAGE POLICY

As we have seen, ethnic assertion does not appear to escape the "ethnic dilemma" inasmuch as it seems to reveal a desire to become like others. For a minority to assert its cultural identity is hence no more than the incidental outcome of belonging to a broader cultural entity that embraces all social groups, and can only by understood as part of the dynamic of social movements. The latter are always minority movements, and assertion of their identity (and indeed of their proposed character) points up the limits on their autonomy.

It has been demonstrated that an external link is necessary before the question of autonomy can arise (Dupuy, 1982, pp. 162-185), the autonomy of cultures, or of minority social movements, can be posited only in relation to an external agency. Here that agency, which gives meaning, is bound to be the State. the linkage is especially clear since the ethnic or regional issue has never been the minority's preserve, for internal discussion alone; the State has always taken a hand, developing cultural and language policies, whose present-day equivalent is on offer as multicultural education as anything but a continuation, in deceptive guise, of the State's drive to achieve social uniformity. The best proof of this will lie in a review of the policies concerning language teaching, including minority languages.

As an initial approximation we may see multicultural education as the policy response of nation-state to the assertion of a "new pluralism", a "new ethnic awareness", a "new citizenship", and the development of various "isms" -- indigenous, regional, national -- or, more broadly, to the persistence and upsurge of a minority element. Through multicultural education in its own school system the State is responding to a social demand over which it does not wish to cede control, especially not to the minority groups themselves: the introduction of a regional language in schools is a matter for bargaining with the public education machinery and, if that proves successful, permission is granted by the State.

There are plenty of illustrations of the State's varied interventions among minorities: the establishment of national agencies to handle "cultural promotion for immigrants" (France, 1975), bilateral government agreements about immigrants, the numerous recommendations adopted at international conferences, the continued control by some governments of their nationals abroad (by setting up a fully-fledged national education system in foreign countries for instance), social or cultural funds especially for immigrants, and so on. But the best illustration of State interventionism is surely the continued control of their citizens by the countries or emigration. The many recent bilateral agreements between countries of emigration and immigration demonstrate this: a State's power over its citizens no longer seems tied to the territorial principle.

In other cases multicultural education is deliberately incorporated in very traditional projects in particular when the argument of ignorance is deployed. That argument holds that ethnic groups clash and cultural relations set up conflicts because we do not know each other properly and have formed a false picture of other people's culture. The notion that cultural conflicts arise from ignorance of other people's culture goes back a long way. It was in fact one of the notions that shaped the old projects devoted to the construction of national unity. Multicultural education for social harmony has returned to square one here, no doubt overlooking the element of mimetic rivalry, and hence violence, that learning about the culture of others entails (Girard, 1978). Intercultural education generally revives this old project with the aim of making each pupil aware of the value and dignity of the culture of every social group, whatever its language, religion, race or ethnic origin; yet it has never been found to settle the conflicts and violence that may crop up between ethnic or racial groups, or at least to settle them as effectively as the strategies based on cultural indifferentiation. Whence the notes of caution sounded from time to time: it is not prudent to try, as cultural pluralists would have us do, to launch more affirmative action in favour of diversity until we are more certain that that is what is generally desired: today's tolerance towards minority groups should not automatically be construed as a stance favouring pluralism (Edwards, 1981, pp. 50-51). Even those who believe that schools should concern themselves with preserving their pupils mother tongue are most careful to add that they should not foster separatism (Fishman, 1980a).

But it is the State's role in cultural policy and particularly language policy which best illustrates that the States control over culture and language is still overwhelming and that what is happening is at best the incorporation of neglected cultures and minority languages in the formal schooling system. This is by no means a new development, and is quite in line qith the education, language and cultural policies that have been followed to date.

We describe this as incorporating culture in the schooling system because cultures are not simply a collection of historical data or cultural product (books, tools, oral tradition, rituals, celebrations and so on), or just a vocabulary or a language that has been "grammaticised" for school purposes. A surprising number of languages are currently being manufactured all over the world in the cause of "teaching the spoken language" and "teaching the mother tongue", on the pattern of the official languages. That is so even in countries where a standard official language has been imposed and is in general use. When a culture is reduced in the hands of education professionals to an academic programme patterned on the compulsory official programme we are no doubt seeing the "ironic triumph of the dominant cultural forms" (Olneck, Lazerson, 1980).

States have manipulated language in this way precisely because language is one of the signs of social heterogeneity. It has always been subject to social and political control (de Certeau, Julia, Revel, 1975; Illich, 1981). The designation of an official language has almost always been accompanied by restrictions on the use of other languages, i.e. rules and regulations discriminating against the minorities who speak other languages. Social and political struggle over language is thus a normal part of the social order (Macias, 1982). For instance, a language spoken by a minority may be recognised as a language of instruction but not as an official language. In Manitoba, Canada, French is recognised as a language for use in schools but not as the province's official language. In New Brunswick, on the other hand, French, though still a minority tongue, is used both for instruction and as an official language of the province. The situation is further complicated in Canada by the fact that the Federal Government has officially adopted bilingualism for federal institutions and services, but education comes under the provincial governments.

In spite of all the manipulation, a wide diversity of languages are still used in a given country, and linguistic clashes still arise. National and foreign minorities ask (and the request is usually granted) for their own languages to be taught as part of the official programme. Moreover, governments seem to reckon that linguistic diversity will continue. The State can accept linguistic plurality more easily when the imposition and inculcation of the official language has become irreversible, both in attitudes down-grading bilingualism when the mother tongue is itself socially devalued; upgrading bilingualism when it means acquiring a prestigious or noble second language and the accepted ideas or myths of the community (Macias, 1982).

The State can more easily tolerate a degree of diversity when in practice the official language is used by everyone. Some programmes of multicultural education use a minority mother tongue as the language of instruction, for instance, but their daring is justified by reference to the official language: teaching of the mother tongue and instruction in it will allow all the pupils concerned to achieve greater mastery of the second (official) language (Cummins, Krashen et al., 1981).

In the debate over bilingual education and whether it holds back learning of the official language, everyone appears to accept that the important thing is to learn the official language: the chief interest of instruction in the first language is to assist learning of the second language (and, people add, to assist adjustment to the cultural environment) so the State has not relinquished its long-standing aim of incorporating all its citizens in a single linguistic community, via schooling in particular, by devising, legitimating and imposing an official language. Bourdieu (1982) has noted that strategies subverting the objective hierarchy in the fields of language and of culture are quite likely <u>also</u> to be strategies of condescencion reserved for those who are sufficiently secure in their place in the objective hierarchies to be able to disown them without seeming unaware of those hierarchies or incapable of satisfying their demands. That applies first and foremost to the State.

In any case, most multicultural programmes set off not from their national local languages but from the (foreign) language used by minority groups. How far a minority preserves its language does not seem related in the first instance to its use at school. When it is observed, for instance in Australia, that Greeks preserve their language best and Dutch least well, the concepts generally referred to as explanations are "ethnic tenaticy", or else "central values" (Smolicz, 1981, p. 23). Smolicz draws a distinction between cultures centring on language, those for which language is a central value (French, Polish, Greek), and cultures based on the family, religion or other ideals (Jews, Southern Italians, Irish). Other writers note that the permanence of preservation of the language of a given linguistic minority is quite closely linked with the group's size and concentration. That is so with Spanish in the United States and French in Quebec; but it is also the case with extreme minorities which have protected themselves (or been fossilised) in reserves. In all these cases preservation of the language is predictable and is not primarily due to its inclusion in the school programme.

Behind these explanations there looms the issue of the relations between language and culture. For some people language is the most important aspect of a culture since language is the chief vehicle for transferring culture from one generation to the next. For others, the linguistic signs of a culture are of less importance than the cultural, religious and economic ones; language on its own is very rarely a source of disturbance, in particular at school, and cultural differences are more significant (Otheguy, 1982). Both these approaches help us to differentiate two types of multicultural education -- the one focusing on language and hence bilingualism, the other focusing on culture, and hence multiculturalism. An attentive look at these two types of programmes will no doubt show that those focusing on language tend to encourage assimilation, while those focusing on culture tend to foster pluralism.

At the heart of the discussion lies the matter of mother tongue: is the mother tongue learnt at school, can it be taught? The answer seems obvious when we observe what is said and appears to be done at school. It is less obvious when we note that a mother tongue is acquired before schooling starts. Psycholinguistics distinguish between the acquisition of mother tongue and learning a second language, and draw a large number of inferences for education (Krashen, in Cummins et al., 1981, pp. 56-61): the mother tongue is acquired spontaneously, it is not taught (or is taught only secondarily), unlike the process of learning a second language. In fact most of the psycholinguistic approaches, although they display great optimism concerning bilingualism and rate dual linguistic skills highly, cannot conceal that they usually serve assimilation, which remains the norm, rather than pluralism. Few give rise to pluralist programmes (Mackey, 1976; Legaretta, 1977).

The economic and sociological approach to language seems to tell us more than the psycholinguistic approach. Otheguy (1982) comments that the majority of black Americans have not drawn any great benefit from their monolinguism. Hispanic Americans who now speak English only are quite often as poor as when they arrived. Otheguy concludes from this that exclusive use of English among immigrants is a consequence of economic integration rather than the cause (idem, p. 306). The remaining factors are social ideology, to a substantial extent, and educational demography.

It was Ivan Illich (1981) who demonstrated that the mother tongue itself was simply an education product invented long ago by monks to the detriment of the vernacular languages (idem, p. 69). Teaching of the mother tongue marks the first stage in universal instruction, but its development as an education product is in fact the first distortion the move from the vernacular language used to satisfy daily non-market needs to a mother tongue used for the process of education and instruction. The term "mother tongue", writes Illich, from its earliest use, makes language an instrument in the service of an institutional cause. Today, he says, mother tongue means at least two things: the first language that a child learns, and the language which the State has decided should be the citizen's first language. So "mother tongue" may mean the first language fortuitously assimilated, a form of speech generally quite different from that taught by educators and parents who consider they should act as educators. Dependence in respect of the taught mother tongue may be taken as the paradigm of all other dependences typical of human beings in this age of needs defined by products (Illich, 1981, pp. 74-75). This shows how the issue of the school language lies right at the heart of mercantile relations, and is a reminder that monolingualism is the unfailing sign of citizens of those nation-states which have enjoyed compulsory education for several generations (idem, p. 81).

The dominance of the authorised, legitimate language in most countries, and the internalisation of that dominance, has no doubt reached a point of no return, and bilingual education is unlikely to change or even stabilize the situation. In any case, the linguistic debate is no longer between the language spoken by minority groups and the national language; in a number of countries it is now between the national language and international English, for the same mercantile reasons that restricted the use of vernacular languages to essentially domestic purposes.

We have seen the process of including abandoned cultures and derelict languages in school programmes, that is to say imposing the latent programme of education on fields that had for some reason previously escaped it (Gorz, in Dauber, Verne, 1977, pp. 111-118), through teaching the culture and language of minority social groups, and there is no reason to believe that multicultural education will reverse these trends -- rather the contrary. Through multicultural education in its various forms and differing guises, states are continuing the social drive to unify or indifferentiate social groups, marking out the boundaries of minorities' autonomy.

MULTICULTURAL CULTURE

The cultural autonomy of minorities is under threat: indeed, asserting that autonomy is like aspiring to a lost paradise. Minorities are so permeable to other cultures that any education policy which took cultural autonomy as something given or as a target would be based on dogmatic principles alone not on any analysis of social realities. A sounder basis for policy is to acknowledge the multicultural reality into which minority cultures dissolve.

Multiculturalism is a fact, describing the position of social groups in relation to one another across the planet: the dividing lines between various cultures have never been insurmountable. Multiculturalism also describes the situation in a given area: the persistence of unassimilated pockets of different cultures in the context of a given national area, and the establishment (through immigration, contamination or dissemination) of new social groups each with their own culture. The point is soon reached where we cannot clearly draw cultural frontiers, rank cultures or tell where this one begins and that one ends. The very concept of culture has to be reviewed, in fact: the concept draws in signs and seeks to differentiate one conglomerate of signs from another but we must not forget that each culture survives only by striving to mark itself off from the rest. Even on the scale of a city ward or district the differences in neighbours' behaviour can still be accounted for by culture.

Moreover, multiculturalism describes the cultural position not just of social groups but of individuals within their social group. For instance, a set of individuals may belong to a given cultural group identified by national or geographical origin and language but some of these individuals may at the same time belong to another cultural conglomerate incidental to the first. The Berber culture does not preclude some members of that group from belonging to this "immigrant culture"; and that does not preclude some members of that group from belonging to the so-called second- or third-generation culture. We are all cultural hybrids, if not cultural mutants. History, education (including what is termed "culture" at school), travel, meeting people, books, films, our experience (via the media or not) of the culture of other people, all lead on to this hybrid state. Each person's culture is of mixed birth.

Multiculturalism is hence an integral part of the culture of each individual and of every social group. Ours is a life of "plural culture" (de Certeau, 1980). The fact that culture today has a global dimension explains why the intercultural, the pluricultural and the multi-cultural are inevitable factors in our own culture. In the past children at school studied the cultures of others as if they were ethnological, historical and geographical objects. Nowadays various cultures flow through a school and confront one another there (more in the playground, in fact, than in the classroom). Devitalised cultures suddenly take on new life an call for appropriate educational responses. We even go so far as to require minority children to assimilate their own culture through the education processe; we protect cultures, just as we protect rare species or areas of countryside. Education programmes concern themselves, in clumsy or inspired ways, with the particular cultural situation of pupils; and pupils are now showing a continuing interest in these matters outside the classroom. Cultural differences are present, in many schools, before they are brought in by the education process.

Before becoming an education programme, multiculturalism was a fact of history. Down the ages it has described the cultural situation of most human groups, marked as they are by diversity and permeability. These groups have never presented a wholly impermeable barrier to cultural influences from neighbouring peoples or more simply to the missionaries, traders and warriors that every culture has seen fit to send out. By way of illustration, the great movements of flocks and herds, except over uninhabited lands, did not occur without cultural shocks; empires were not formed by the arrangement of cultures side by side in watertight compartments; the great civilisations of the past all left a cultural heritage and if they died the reason was not cultural inadequacy but the hammer blows of other cultures; single travellers, and the great population movements, have always taken their cultural baggage with them, subsequently losing, integrating, inculcating or sharing it in the areas they occupied.

The contemporary era is not exempt from this swirl of cultures. The cultural dynamic may be moderated; the last remaining empty habitable spaces do not exert the same attraction since they belong to states even before they are populated; the great migratory movements seem to have halted, or else are hard to discern over relatively short periods. That does not mean, however, that new demographic pressures may not generate fresh migratory turbulence. The dynamic also seems moderated because the cultural products of the planetary village tend to smother local expressions of culture. Yet it has accelerated too: cultural changes seem to speed up and amplify as the cultural bombardment to which we are subjected increases in intensity and scale. The swirl of culture made possible by industrial technology has heightened awareness in some quarters at least, of the emergence of a worldwide culture that cares nothing for cultural heritage, cultural individuality or the clash of cultures.

Moreover, any cultural individuality seems to be assessed against the yardstick of this worldwide industrial culture, against the yardstick of the culture produced by a single culture industry, so that we find concretions of the "youth culture", type, or "second-generation immigrant culture", etc. Taking a wide field such as "Western culture" or "industrial culture", it would not be hard to conceive of minority cultures as so many artificial by-products of just one dominant culture.

CULTURAL POLICY AND EDUCATION POLICY

Multiculturalism is a fact for social groups and for individuals, but cultural and education policies -- in particular -- make it an affair of State as well. Current circumstances no doubt help this trend. Yet the emergence and development of nation-states has always gone hand in hand with a cultural policy for the peoples who were to grow into a nation. That was so even when nation-building was not the mission originally legitimating the State's developments, and in modern times it is one of the first tasks proclaimed by the State in most new nations, just as it remains a substantial concern in a number of older countries.

A more detailed study of individual states' attitudes towards national culture, viewed in particular through the language policies that they pursue, would no doubt bring out the following trends:

-- New states concerned for their national unity, and hence cultural unity, sublimate local indivuduality in the deliberate promotion of a national identity, to the point of losing their souls by rejecting official use of national mother tongues in favour of a foreign language;

-- States still concerned to preserve the geographical and economic equilibria among their component nations, either through constitutional and legislative checks that uphold and protect the status quo by disallowing any movement, or through the political imposition of one nation's cultural power upon the rest. The more common case here is the status quo accepted freely or not, and sometimes flying in the face of cultural and economic realities. Open linguistic and cultural warfare may also obtain, and the most aggressive linguistic minorities are to be found here;

-- States which have largely managed to establish a national cultural and linguistic community and endeavour to preserve or restore what remains of cultural individuality out of nostalgia but also due to a resurgence of regional activism;

-- Modern states formed by successeive waves of migration, with distinct and antagonistic strata of migrants, where older immigrants today have to cope with newcomers and it is not clear what point has been reached in cultural integration, assimilation or differentiation;

-- Lastly, states where the cultural front no longer involves internal clashes but lies in the protection of a fully-formed national culture now under threat from external influences.

In every case the school is called upon to play a particular role, which differs according to the dominant cultural policy. The school is thus at the service of a cultural policy.

These policies face two main developments at present: the renewal of regional, indigenous or national cultures, and the novel behaviour of immigrant groups. States have already come across these developments, but the setting in which they face them today is very likely different: local ethnic minorities, especially their activist fringes, are more aware of what they have lost as the State has evolved; the immigrants come from countries which have recently achieved independence, from countries where the State has asserted itself, to look for work in a tight job market. The host countries have to inhibit immigration and overcome the social and economic problems that immigrants raise, and at the same time put forward programmes, especially in education, which are designed to take their special characteristics into account.

We have to consider what compels individual states to concern themselves with the pockets of individuality that they have not so far managed to absorb, those that they have helped to establish (by drawing in foreign labour, for instance), and also those that they have allowed to form. States in fact continue to conduct a two-fold cultural policy: at their frontiers, where they meet other cultures, in order to protect themselves against some and to contaminate, or indeed dominate, others; and within their borders to control or absorb cultural individuality -- or to protect and possibly promote it. The background to all this is a situation where it is no longer clear whether the states (and which ones) are in control or whether cultural power has shifted elsewhere, into the multinationals of science and culture or into the hands of the culture industries.

Schools have always had to cope with this complex of cultures, and the development of the education system has generally met with cultural resistance. By imposing its own culture it has gradually managed to wear down the surrounding cultures, vis-à-vis the dominant culture, and exhibits the same standardizing role that grammar has played in respect of language. Through this success, the culture which schools inculcate has gradually become the shared culture that the State needed to become identified with the nation. Standing in a position of weakness in relation to local cultures, schools were bound to be monocultural and secure their position by imposing a monoculturalism and monolingualism before in law and after in practice. The education culture had success imposing itself over all. That culture is characterised by the imposition of a standard national language, and more importantly by the inculcation of knowledge, know-how, patterns of behaviour, attitudes and social customs of a given cultural field, which is that of industrial culture. The exceptions are few and of little significance: it is easy to demonstrate that the study of minority cultures is subordinate to that of the dominant culture, that the teaching of minority cultures applies the same standards utilised for the teaching of the dominant culture, that the cultures of minorities are in fact included in order to integrate them more fully in that same dominant culture, and that teaching of a minority's mother tongue is still proposed in order to help the minority children master the dominant language. One difference is that nowadays schools know somewhat better how to make use of the specific cultural features of individual groups in order to achieve fuller assimilation. And since the culture that schools propagate is largely undisputed, they further have the power to incorporate cultures which have turned soft into the education process.

In these circumstances, the more recent acknowledgement of the special cultural and linguistic features of certain minority groups in society usually falls in with the dominant attitude of facilitating access to the official culture. That acknowledgement came about under pressure from the "minorities" themselves, from regionalist movements, sometimes from states, from employers of foreign manpower, from teachers having to cope with cultural resistance, and so on. It took many different forms: bilingual education, bicultural education, inter-cultural programmes, etc. But schools seem to adapt well to these various types of programmes when they have long managed to impose their own culture, which remains the yardstick of success. It is easer to accept a few departures from the norm when the norm is our own, just as it is easier to speak a local language in public when we have already demonstrated our perfect mastery of the official language. All this leads back to the same conclusion: multicultural education will not breach the monopoly that the official culture and the standard language have established, for it forms an integral part of the monopoly programme. Needless to say, states will be ready to pay the due price for teaching another language and another culture since they feel certain that, through the formal education process, they will keep their radical monopoly of the language and culture that is taught.

CULTURES IN THE FORMAL TEACHING PROCESS

In putting forward, at least in certain cases and through diverse channels, a policy of multicultural education, governments are making use of a configuration to which we have long been accustomed, since it is the peculiar sign of the state's role within the society : any social problem must have an institutional response. The successive tasks that the state has assigned to its education system all tell the same story. To present the fact of multiculturalism at school, for instance by teaching the culture and mother tongue of minority groups to children from the dominant groups or using each person's mother tongue as the language of instruction, or teaching cultures, that is the culture of others (possibly making use of the presence of minorities within the school), is also to run the risk of making cultures academic by incorporating them in the programme, and to put forward a scholastic conception and use of culture. Can culture be taught, apart from the culture which is described as "cultivatec culture", that is the culture recognised and disseminated by the school?

An education system today which deliberately addresses itself to collating, glossing and promoting minority cultures seems most surprising, and a number of frivolous reasons spring to mind -- exhibitionism, diversion, a harmless graft, or providing an alibi? We first need to consider (looking beyond the proclaimed intention) how serious this apparent change of course is.

Once serious factors are seen to be at work several interpretations are possible:

i) We may be dealing with schools seeking to set themselves up on the fringe of dominant cultural circuits and devoted to teaching local culture and minority languages; a few such schools already exist. A type of resistance school, dispensing linguistic and cultural instruction to protect and defend minorities. An approach of this kind is the point at which several cultural currents converge: indigenism, ethnicity, cultural identity and authenticity, anti-hegemonism, regionalism, and so on. It may be based on alternative projects, and in particular the range of ethnic schools to be found in various countries;

ii) Alternatively, the education system may be sufficiently sure of itself and its mission of social integration to handle dominated, unobtrusive cultures with impunity and without neglecting its chief mission (or perhaps as a means of accomplishing that more effectively);

iii) The introduction of multicultural programmes may also be construed as a failure by the school to carry through its assigned task of homogenisation: state schooling has not produced the cultural and social unification that was expected from it. Regional, ethnic, religious and national differences persiset, and so do cultural clashes. Cultural integration is an illusion: schools should acknowledge their failure and work for autonomy claimed by cultures which have withstood assimilation, even if the social groups concerned are far from all sharing the same view of the culturalism and multiculturalism that they desire.

The wide variety of existing multicultural programmes would justify all these interpretations. The very fact that these programmes exist shows that the education system has rediscovered the range of cultures under the one which it devised and imposed. Ultimately we need to ask how the school has come back to culture through the rediscovery of cultures, and why it has made culture one of the compulsory items in any curriculum. Such a transformation could only occur in schools: making culture into an academic programme. It is a strange twist for culture to make its return via the education process! An education system essentially designed to foster the economic system rediscovers a cultural vocation when the economic system is going to a crisis. The comeback of culture, including in schools, represent a revenge of things cultural on things economic, especially when culture is to be industrialised to save the industrial economy. That leads on to the last interpretation for multicultural education, as one response to the economic crisis: the provision of multicultural education being an acknowledgement of the predominance of things cultural over things economic.

Schools are themselves a cultural product. In their present form they are the product of a dominant industrial culture. They have themselves contributed to nourishing the industrial culture, as well as working for their own account on a longer standing task, access to learned culture and the objects of that culture, including learned language.

Though they are the product of a culture, schools are also on the fringe of the cultures which spring up and develop in the flow of daily existence, in particular through all the cultural patterns which develop ourside mercantile relations. That culture cannot be taught; it is learned throughout the course of life; the learning process is not confined to one particular age group; it is learnt everywhere: it is not acquired in one place only but throughout society, and it is indistinguishable from the other threads in daily life.

So what purpose does the multicultural education dispensed at school serve, and what social problem does it help to settle? If the problem is cultural violence, multicultural education in the formal schooling process, open and available to all, is unlikely to be the answer. In that case, it would be hazardous, as mentioned earlier, to make multicultural education into the problem. Yet that is what occurs, we feel, in a familiar trend that appears to describe the relations which the education system maintains with all the major social problems: where it is unable to control them, the school (like any other social institution) is affected, by them; and to get away from this the school proclaims itself to be the solution. But the only solution that the education system can usually offer is to include the problem in the schooling process, for instance by embodying it in a new academic programme.

All the major social problems -- health, demography, education, security, inequalities, and so on -- are tackled in this way. It is the typical response of the all-providing State (Rosanvallon, 1982). Inequality of opportunity in life, for instance, has produced compensatory education in schools. By the same logic, intercultural clashes and cultural inequalities have led to programmes of multicultural education in school. Now, if multicultural education is unable to respond to cultural violence, it must provide an answer to another -- which is bound to lie within the logic of the school curriculum itself, both the declared curriculum and the hidden programme of the education process.

An educational analysis of the multicultural programmes on offer in schools, or at all events, those that operate, should demonstrate this: multicultural education programmes are first and foremost for academic use. They are secondly at the service of States, which are responsible for the plausibility and operation of the societies that they administer. The first category contains all those programmes where emphasis lies on "bilingual bicultural education", whose declared aim is to bring pupils speaking a minority language "to a high level of mastery of the majority language, a satisfactory level of cognitive and educational development, and adequate psychosocial and cultural adjustment" (California State Department of Education, 1981). The second category includes all those programmes which apeak of education for a multicultural society rather than multicultural education, with the aim of ensuring "the development of a culturally diversified but socially cohesive society" (Schools Commission, Australia, 1979).

On the one hand we find social movements and the cultural dynamic of the various social groups that make up society; and on the other we find the State, endeavouring to channel that dynamic for the common good and in the national interest. Between the two lies machinery in which the school holds a key place. Multicultural education as dispensed by and in schools has to be viewed in the context of these two poles, and of that testing area. The education system is there, along with other institutions, to manage the transit of this twofold flow: the movements from a composite society towards a homogenous State, and the flow from the State towards the various social groups that it administers. The strains are first and foremost political ones, although cultural violence does not simply aim at political control of cultural power. Most frequently the cultural power of minorities seeks to make schools acknowledge their modes of cultural expression, first and foremost the teaching of their language and the use of their language as a vehicle of instruction; the political power exercised by the State through its control of the education system leads it to channel this demand for recognition, to acknowledge it and integrate it in the school, in highly varied and usually ambiguous forms.

The educational power exerted by schools, in the context of this twofold demand, leads to the production of special programmes, even in cases where multicultural education is defined as a philosophy that has to imbue all school activities. In actual fact, an examination of these programmes shows that schools are working largely for their own account. Much the same conclusion would be reached from a review of the gap between response to social demand and the policy which States actually conduct.

BIBLIOGRAPHY

ARENDT H.: The Origins of Totalitarianism. 3 vols. Harcourt, New York, 1951.

BASTIDE H.: Les enfants d'immigrés et l'enseignement français. Cahiers de l'INED, 97, PUF, Paris, 1982.

BERNSTEIN B.: "Class, Codes and Control". In Vol. 1: Theoretical Studies towards a Sociology of Learning, Routledge and Kegan Paul, London, 1971.

BETANCES S.: "Cross Cultural Education and Ethnic Conflict in Guam". In NABE Journal, V, 1, 1980, pp. 71-91.

BOURDIEU P.: Ce que parler veut dire. L'économie des échanges linguistiques, Fayard, Paris, 1982.

BOURDIEU P. and PASSERON J.C.: La reproduction, Minuit, Paris, 1970.

BUSTAMANTE A.R. (Ed).: "Mexican Immigrant Workers in the U.S." In Anthology n°2. Chicano Studies Research Center Publications, University of California, Los Angeles, 1981, 180 p.

CASTORIADIS C.: L'institution imaginaire de la société, Seuil, Paris, 1975.

CASTORIADIS C.: Les carrefours du labyrinthe, Seuil, Paris, 1978.

de CERTEAU M.: La culture au pluriel, Bourgeois, Paris, 1980.

de CERTEAU M., JULIA D., REVEL J.: Une politique de la langue, Gallimard, Paris, 1975.

CHURCHILL S.: The Education of Minority Groups. An enquiry into problems and practices of fifteen countries. OECD/CERI, published by Gower Publishing Company Ltd., Aldershot, Hampshire (United Kingdom), 1983.

CUMMINS J., KRASHEN A., et al.: Schooling and Language Minority Students: A Theoretical Framework. California State Department of Education, Office of Bilingual Bicultural Education. Sacramento, California, 1981.

DAUBER H., VERNE E.: L'école à perpétuité, Seuil, Paris, 1977.

DEBRAY R.: Critique de la raison politique, Gallimard, Paris, 1981.

DUMOUCHEL P., DUPUY J.P.: L'enfer des choses. René Girard et la logique de l'économie, Seuil, Paris, 1979.

DUPUY J.P.: Ordres et désordres. Enquête sur un nouveau paradigme, Seuil, Paris, 1982.

EDWARDS J.R.: "Psychological and linguistic aspects of minority education". In Education of Minorities. World Yearbook of Education 1981, Kogan Page, London, 1981.

EPSTEIN N.: Language, Ethnicity, and the Schools: Policy Alternatives for Bilingual-Bicultural Education. Institute for Educational Leadership, Washington D.C., 1977.

FISHMAN J.: "The Social Science Perspective". In Bilingual Education: Current Perspectives, 1980a.

FISHMAN J.: "Minority Language Maintenance and the Ethnic Mother Tongue School". In Modern Language Journal, 64, 1980b, 167-173.

FREIRE P.: Pedagogy of the Oppressed. Herder and Herder, New York, 1972.

GALBRAITH J.K.: The Nature of the Mass Poverty. Harvard University Press, 1979. French translation: Théorie de la pauvreté de masse. Gallimard, Paris, 1980.

GIRARD R.: La violence et le sacré. Grasset, Paris, 1972.

GIRARD R.: Des choses cachées depuis la fondation du monde, Grasset, Paris, 1978.

GLAZER N.: "Affirmative Discrimination: Where is it going"? In International Journal of Comparative Sociology, 20, 1-2, 14-30.

GLAZER N.: "Politics of a Multiethnic Society". In Ethnic Relations in America. The American Assembly. Columbia University, Prentice-Hall, 1982, pp. 128-149.

GLAZER N., MOYNIHAN D.P. (eds.): Ethnicity, Theory and Practice. Harvard University Press, Cambridge, Mass., 1975.

GOKALP A.: "Le paradis perdu de la culture originelle". In Autrement, 11, 1977, pp. 188-194.

HOGGART R.: The Uses of Literacy. Chatto and Windus, 1957.

ILLICH I.: Le travail fantôme. Seuil, Paris, 1981.

ILLICH I.: Le genre vernaculaire. Seuil, Paris, 1983.

KELLY C.B.: "Immigration and the American Future". In Ethnic Relations in America, 1982, pp. 28-65.

LE BRAS H., TODD E.: L'invention de la France. Librairie générale française, Paris, 1981.

LEGARRETA D.: Language Choice in the Bilingual Classroom. TESOL Quarterly, 11, 1977, 9-16.

LEVI-STRAUSS C.: "Race et histoire". In Anthropologie structurale II. Plon, Paris, 1973, ch. XVIII.

LEVI-STRAUSS C.: "Race et culture". In Le regard éloigné, Plon, Paris, 1983, pp. 21-48.

MACIAS R.F.: "Opinions of Chicano Community Parents on Bilingual Preschool Education". In VERDOODT, A., KJOLSETH, R.: Language in Sociology. Institut de linguistique, Louvain, 1976, pp. 135-165.

MACIAS R.F.: U.S. Institutional Language Policies and the Spanish Speaking. A Hospital and Medical Services Case Study, 1982.

MACIAS R.F.: "Language Diversity among United States Hispanics". In SPIELBERG, J. (ed.): Proceedings. Invitational Symposium on Hispanic-American Diversity. Lansing, Michigan Department of Education, 1982, pp. 110-136.

MACKEY W.: "A Typology of Bilingual Education". In Bilingual Schooling in the United States: A source book for Educational Personnel. Ed. Francesco Cordasco. McGraw Hill, New York, 1976, pp. 72-90.

MALINOWSKI B.: Les dynamiques de l'évolution culturelle. Recherche sur les relations raciales en Afrique, 1961. Trad. fr.: Payot, Paris, 1970.

MOSCOVICI S.: Social Influence and Social Change. Academic Press, London, 1976. Trad. fr.: Psychologie des minorités actives. PUF, Paris, 1979.

OLNECK M.R., LAZERSON M.: "Education". In Harvard Encyclopedia of American Ethnic Groups. Harvard University Press, Cambridge (Mass.), 1980, pp. 303-319.

OTHEGUY R.: "Thinking about Bilingual Education: A Critical Appraisal". In Harvard Educational Review, 1982, 52, 3, pp. 301-314.

RODRIGUEZ R.: Hunger of Memory: The Education of Richard Rodriguez. Godine, Boston, 1981.

ROSANVALLON P.: La crise de l'Etat-Providence. Seuil, Paris, 1982.

ROTHBERG I.C.: "Some Legal and Research Considerations in Establishing Federal Policy in Bilingual Education". In Harvard Educational Review, 1982, 52, 3, pp. 149-165.

SMOLICZ J.S.: "Culture, ethnicity and education: Multiculturalism in a plural society". In Education of Minorities. World Yearbook of Education 1981. Kogan Page, London, 1981.

THUROW L.: The Zero Sum Society. Basic Books, New York, 1980.

TIERNEY J. (ed.): Race, Migration and Schooling. Holt, London, 1982.

WEINBERG M.: A Chance to Learn. The History of Race and Education in the United States. Cambridge University Press, Cambridge, 1977, 471 p.

3. POLICY DEVELOPMENT FOR EDUCATION IN MULTICULTURAL SOCIETIES : TRENDS AND PROCESSES IN THE OECD COUNTRIES

by
Stacy CHURCHILL
Ontario Institute for Studies in Education, Toronto

INTRODUCTION

This paper is a review of the policy-making processes that have been used in western industrialised societies to adapt their educational systems to the needs of different cultural, ethnic and linguistic groups during the past two decades. In short, it is about how education has become "multicultural"; only part of it deals, however, with so-called "multicultural education".

Two phenomena should be distinguished:

i) The process by which educational systems adapt to accommodate diverse languages and cultures reflected in the make-up of each country's population;

ii) The multicultural education movement, a social phenomenon of the last two decades or so, which promotes a certain set of methods -- particularly school curriculum change -- as a solution to the general problem of accommodating linguistic and cultural diversity.

The first of these is the more general, as it emphasizes the general objective of accommodating diversity; the second emphasizes a certain means to this more general end.

Both these phenomena are currently dynamic realities that affect policy making in almost all the OECD countries, both at the level of central educational authorities (national, state, provincial) and in local decision-making that reaches down into the school and affects the everyday reactions of teachers to classroom and school situations. The possibility for a cross-national review of these processes is opened up by a remarkable degree of similarity of problems that is often hidden by more obvious differences of national culture and methods of organising public education. The educational systems of the OECD countries share many common elements, particularly regarding the functional assumptions underlying the goals of education for citizens of industrialized societies. Other authors have pointed out, more cogently than we are able, to what extent modern industrial countries share similar concerns and problems in education (Husén, 1982). One shared assumption is that the role of schooling is to support one or two dominant national views of culture and the primacy of one, sometimes two, languages. Only Switzerland (because of its recognition of four languages within the framework of the canton system) and the Yugoslavian federation constitute legally sanctioned exceptions; the rapid evolution of Spanish law and practice is now tending in the same direction (1). Still, in the period since World War II and, more particularly, since the late 1950s, this monolithic agreement about the role of the school as the main tool for imposing dominant languages and cultures has begun to be eroded on a broad scale.

A great "thaw" has occurred, at least in terms of political rhetoric about schooling and tolerance of cultural diversity. The purpose of this paper is to point out major trends and processes which have been at work. One main source for generalisations on the policy-making process has been the Centre for Educational Research and Innovation (CERI)'s project of enquiry into "The Finance, Organisation and Governance of Education for Special Populations".

The first stage of this enquiry was the completion of surveys of current practice by 15 countries -- not published, but still held for consultation in the OECD by those who are professionally interested. These are here acknowledged, when appropriate, simply as "(FOG national survey)". The main conclusions of the enquiry as they relate to linguistic and cultural minorities were summarised by the present author (pp. 233-292) in the final CERI report "The Education of Minority Groups" published in 1983. These sources are now complemented by national case study reports submitted as part of the ongoing CERI project on Education for Linguistic and Cultural Pluralism, as well as by the author's continuing exchanges with educational officials in a number of countries.

This paper deals with a limited number of issues:

i) The social context of decision-making about the education of linguistic and cultural minorities;

ii) The main stages of development of educational policies for minorities in the past two decades;

iii) The relationship between the policies developed and the role assigned to the culture of minorities in the context of majority educational system.

When we talk about the "aims" or "objectives" of policies, no attempt will be made to go beyond the obvious and directly perceived implications of policy in order to determine the ultimate outcomes that might be pursued. To talk about ultimate outcomes or objectives of policy-making is to engage in theory-building that is best left to general treatises on sociology and political economy.

THE SOCIAL CONTEXT OF DECISION-MAKING ABOUT THE EDUCATION OF LINGUISTIC AND CULTURAL MINORITIES

The policy process and the role of majority opinion

The participants in the process of making educational policy vary widely from country to country in accordance with political and constitutional arrangements. As a result of the development of mass education systems, certain overriding tendencies have made themselves felt in most OECD countries. The most important is a tendency towards a certain type of bureaucratisation, i.e. the development of technical and managerial apparatuses staffed by persons with high levels of expertise and specialisation. This general tendency of modern society has had as its corollary the partitioning of decision-making into different spheres -- those issues dealt with by "professionals" (on the basis of their presumed expertise) and those that are the concern of "politicians" and the "general public". It has been the author's experience to see very great degrees of similarity in attitudes about the appropriate boundaries between the professional and non-professional decision-making spheres, even in political and social systems with very different arrangements for running schools. To take an example, the approaches used to educate the severely handicapped have long been left to the "experts", and political interventions to change what the "experts" do are rarely tried without recourse to extensive consultation of other "experts". The size and problems of managing mass educational systems have resulted in very distinctive national configurations of policy makers who, despite their differences, often adopt similar stances on what are the appropriate responses to similar problems.

One of the most obvious factors in decision-making about education of linguistic and cultural minorities in all countries is that the most important decisions are generally outside the boundaries that are left to professional opinion and expertise. Or, to be more exact, any proposed change to the _status quo_ automatically engenders political and other reactions from those outside the narrow confines of the educational administration apparatus. Decisions about what language to use and when to use it, about the way the curriculum deals with the national culture(s) in relationship to those of other regions and countries, about grouping pupils on the basis on language or ethnicity -- all are topics on which opinions are held not only by politicians but by everyday citizens. For the better part of a century (at least), most countries have based the organisation of their state and institutions on the idea that language -- an officially sanctioned language or limited number of languages -- is a crucial part not only of national identity but of social cohesion that must be promoted and defended at all costs. Policy-making that threatens to recognise an alternative language, culture or ethnically-based world view is an explosive matter that arouses heated opinion even among those who are generally passive on most public issues. Such opinion makes itself felt in all national educational systems, regardless of their degree of centralisation or decentralisation. Even in a system so legally pluralistic as the Yugoslav Federation, the central role given to language and ethnicity as a principle of organisation for the entire fabric of social institutions, confirms the supra-ordinate place accorded to these issues.

The importance of public opinion for decision-making on language and ethnicity in educational systems is a crucial point in explaining how the policy process operates. Simply put, we can distinguish different aspects of this:

i) At any point in time, there is a dominant, socially acceptable viewpoint on the role of language and ethnicity. Even where social strife exists, it is usually possible to identify the dominant viewpoint. In our western industrial societies, we can usually refer to this as the "majority" viewpoint, even though the majority in question is only the majority in control in a given place at a given time and may not be the total national majority (e.g. the French majority in Quebec, the Walloon and Flemish majorities in their respective parts of Belgium, etc.);

ii) The response of the educational system to problems presented by the education of linguistic and cultural minorities is always confined within the bounds of what is tolerable for dominant (majority opinion); stepping beyond these bounds usually results in strong political interventions that can override what educational policy makers have done. The response may go outside the legal system and result in violent opposition to changes such as has happened in the U.S. in response to desegregation of schooling. Dominant public opinion is an external constraint, a brake or a straitjacket, on decision-making;

iii) The dichotomy between external public opinion and internal "professional" opinion is rarely clear in matters related to language and ethnicity. The professionals employed within educational systems tend to be drawn from the national (regional) majority and they tend to share the same opinions as the majority. In fact, in some cases, where legitimating a minority group's language or cultural pretensions would threaten the status of the professionals, their attitudes may be even less responsive than those of some sectors of outside opinion.

The crux of the policy-making problem for multicultural societies is that the final power for decision-making on minority needs and rights is taken within the constraints of dominant public opinion under circumstances where the majority, rather than the minority, is usually in control.

The truly fascinating problem we must come to grips with results from the evolution of the last two decades. In most OECD countries, despite the weight of majority opinion and the strength of past tradition, major changes have occurred in the ways educational systems provide for the needs of minorities. What processes and forces resulted in this breakthrough? Why should the educational establishments and the majority opinion of countries respond to demands from groups that are numerically small and, often, politically weak? A full answer would involve, of course, an analysis of the full range of forces at work in society as a whole. We shall confine ourselves to much more limited explanations based on the operational characteristics of educational systems against the broader backdrop of social changes, which are taken as a given. Before looking at these systems in detail, we should attempt to specify the main elements of context: a) Who are the minorities involved? b) What are the main social trends affecting minority status?

Types of linguistic and cultural groups concerned

For the purposes of our discussion, it may be best to talk about a limited number of groups whose characteristics are easily recalled by the general reader:

i) "Traditional" linguistic and dialectical minorities of Western Europe having long-established territorial bases;

ii) Resident foreign workers (mainly in Western Europe) whose status is assumed to be non-permanent and not to lead to naturalisation;

iii) Immigrants who have acquired, or are in the process of acquiring, national citizenship in their countries of current residence;

iv) Descendants of persons whose nationality was changed as a result of territorial conquest (French-speaking Canadians, Hispanic Americans in the U.S., now augmented by recent arrivals);

v) Indigenous peoples characterised by ancient folkways, usually in the process of disappearing (Native American Indians, Sami/Lapps, Torre Strait Islanders, Maori, Pacific Islanders, Aboriginal peoples of Australia, etc.).

Many analyses treat the education of these groups as separate issues of concern, and for many purposes this separation is appropriate. But when we sketch the evolution of policy for a longer period, it is obvious that the processes of dealing with all the groups then are historically intermingled.

It is extremely difficult to arrive at any global estimates of the numbers of people who might fit into these categories. "Belonging" to a minority often involves considerable ambiguity, both in the psychology of those concerned and in the implications of such status for being recognised by society at large. An idea of the phenomenon can be garnered from a recent report to the Parliamentary Assembly of the Council of Europe on the educational and cultural problems posed by the linguistic and dialectic minorities of Western Europe (Council of Europe, 1981). The rapporteur described some 51 identifiable minorities in an alphabetical list running from the Aaland Islanders and Albanians to speakers of Veneto and the Walloons. The groups range in size from more than 5 million (Catalan, Occitan) to only a few thousand or even a few hundred. These are, of course, members of what we have called traditional linguistic and dialectical minorities of Western Europe [i) above].

Statistics on resident foreign workers are notoriously difficult to track down, even though the criteria for identification are, in principle, quite clear. A working party on migration, organised by the OECD, recently estimated at some 4.5 million the number of foreigners under the age of 25 living in eight European Member countries, which account for the bulk of resident foreign workers on the continent (the U.K. was excluded from the data). These figures did not include either the many newcomers (or their children) who had acquired the nationality of the country of residence nor the children of resident foreign workers who had remained behind in the country of emigration, estimated at almost 2 million in 1977 (OECD, 1983).

Even more serious problems of identification occur when the persons concerned hold the nationality of the country of residence and are perceived to speak its dominant language. In common parlance, third generation descendants of persons from the West Indies residing in the U.K. and holding full citizenship are referred to as "immigrants". Their problems are often dealt with primarily in racial terms without consideration for the implications of differences in home dialect and culture. Many Native American Indians who have lost knowledge of their ancestral languages pose similar problems of identification as separate minorities. The majority of Basques do not speak the Basque language, but they remain one of the most highly mobilized and clearly identified minorities in Europe.

No one is certain where minority status begins or ends in modern pluralistic societies. For this reason, most authorities rarely will cite a precise figure to estimate numbers of affected persons. There are simply no reliable cross-national bases for comparison and aggregation. Difficulties of identifying and counting minority group members are a peripheral phenomenon in the context of our discussion. The number of persons involved in a given situation is often a determinant of the type of recognition given and of the educational solutions proposed for related problems, but on a cross-national basis it is clear that the threshold value for attention in policy is dependent upon the willingness of the majority to listen to minority needs, rather than a result of absolute numbers. Thus it was possible for the Franco regime to ignore the demands of several million Catalans for more than a generation, whereas relatively small minorities in other countries were sometimes dealt with favourably. One may justifiably ask what forces bring about recognition of educational needs for one minority rather than another.

The example of the Franco regime serves to underscore the types of forces with which this analysis does not deal. The end of the Franco era and the revolution in Portugal are pieces of background data, and their main consequence was to increase the degree of similarity found in the institutional arrangements of western industrial nations (which these two countries have subsequently made great strides in becoming). Our analysis of educational policy-making concerns the type of evolution that is characteristic of western industrial democracies, and it was only possible because of the basic similarities of democratic structures operating in most of the countries concerned.

Major trends of social policy development affecting minorities

Any list of social trends and processes is perforce limited and must be preceded by a statement that it is obviously arbitrary. For our purposes, we shall single out a few major social trends that have significantly affected the processes we analyse:

i) Externally-imposed protection of minorities has ceased to be a major force dictating policy

The current period differs radically from that following World War I, when the peace treaties in Europe imposed a series of restrictions on the rights of the signatory powers, intended in part to protect the rights of linguistic and cultural minorities. Little of this was left in the wake of World War II.

ii) The fight of minorities against overt discrimination has been replaced in most cases by a quest for recognition (2)

Two main changes are involved here, concerning the objectives pursued by minorities and who decides the membership of minorities. In some countries, such as the United States until the mid-1950s, the majority members of society decided that certain persons were members of minority groups on the basis of certain criteria (loose racial criteria in the U.S., religion in many countries, etc.) and then excluded these persons from the right to participate in educational (and other) opportunities available to the majority. Resistance to such policies is resistance against overt discrimination. This may be contrasted to a situation such as prevails in some Western European countries with respect to resident foreign workers. Children of such workers are generally obliged to study in the school of the majority, as if they were members of the majority. Thus the majority has decided, so to speak, to include these people in the services offered to the majority; this is formally the exact opposite of overt discrimination. The consequences of such non-discriminatory practices may be disastrous for the education of the minority children concerned, but the practices do not involve exclusion from majority facilities. The minority groups affected may decide to organise themselves and demand their "rights" as a group to have a different treatment; the persons affected decide they are members of the minority(ies) and seek special treatment. We may call this a fight for recognition. Thus, even if the educational and social effects of non-recognition may sometimes be similar to those of overt discrimination, in terms of policy-making and its underlying assumptions, the two are worlds apart. And -- we should note -- in almost all OECD countries today, minorities are pursuing primarily the quest for recognition, not for elimination of formal, overt discrimination of the type that was prevalent in the period between the wars. Interestingly, the success of American Blacks in overcoming many of the overt forms of forced discrimination has led to a counter-movement to reinforce ethnic identity and seek recognition of ethnic and cultural differences in the educational system.

iii) Recognising and helping minorities has become a legitimate policy goal of the state

An earlier CERI study of educational finance at the primary level found a broad tendency of governments to pursue educational equity by making special arrangements for different groups on the basis of recognition of special needs (Noah and Sherman, 1979). This is part of a broader tendency of industrial democracies to adopt measures of social equity to level differences between groups -- part of the tendencies usually identified with the so-called Welfare State. The general acceptance of such social equity goals provided a fertile ground for the development of minority demands, and many minorities have successfully presented their cases for special treatment on the basis of general equity considerations. A typical line of argument (from among a multitude actually found in political activities of minorities) might be that members of a given minority are excluded from well-paid jobs because they lack educational qualifications; this has resulted in relative poverty which, in turn, lowers the ability of families to help their children benefit from schooling and creates a "cycle of poverty"; breaking this cycle requires action to improve housing, incomes and educational facilities that recognise the minority language and incomes and culture, thus reducing the alienation of the children and permitting them to attain higher levels of achievement. Using a line or argument such as this enables the minority to obtain recognition of special status on grounds that are understood to apply to all members of society -- social equity; this reduces the opposition that might otherwise manifest itself to giving special recognition to a group identified on grounds of language, race or ethnicities. Rarely can one "sell" multiculturalism for the sake of multiculturalism.

iv) Economic changes have created new minority problems but have facilitated also the resolution of some problems

Different rates of economic growth between different regions (e.g. Northern Europe and Mediterranean Europe) or different parts of a country (e.g. Catalonia vs. Castile, New York vs. Porto Rico) have often resulted in massive population displacements and the creation of new minority problems. In Western Europe the creation of economic communities has been a particularly potent force in stimulating manpower flows, conceived of originally as being of temporary duration. The now enduring status of resident foreign workers in most of the recipient countries of the European Economic Community and the Scandinavian countries has resulted in very well-known problems, including the unresolved issue of how best to deal with the education of children unlikely to return to their parents' homeland. On the other hand, it is not often pointed out the extent to which the economic developments have also helped put in place the mechanisms for recognising and coping with the problems:

-- The economic integration of Western Europe has been accompanied by the creation of a variety of consultative channels and other mechanisms (e.g. EEC, Council of Europe) that have provided a means for recognising problems and designing coordinated responses to their solution. On the other hand, it is difficult to discuss the current situation without lamenting the slowness of the reaction to the educational issues affecting the children of these workers; but on the other hand, it is equally difficult not to notice the leadership role played by the international organisations in bringing to a head discussions that otherwise might not yet have taken place if the individual countries had been left to their own internal evolution. In fact, the permanency of the rights granted to workers in the EEC countries, who can settle indefinitely anywhere in the EEC countries and freely exercise their trade, provided a model that helped authorities (and the public) to conceptualise the issue of resident foreign workers.

-- A concomitant of the economic developments mentioned has been massive growth in real national incomes. Not only does this provide the recipient states with more resources to create appropriate services for minorities, it also has aided in maintaining the climate of help for minorities. The major growth in programmes serving minorities in the OECD countries during the past two decades owes much to the underlying pattern of long-term economic development. The widespread economic downturn of the recent past demonstrates, of course, the fragility of public good will in the face of adversity. But current economic problems should be interpreted as a political crisis rather than as a total crisis of resources; the total wealth of the countries now suffering from unemployment is immensely superior to what was available, on a per capita basis, only a generation ago. This serves in part to explain why the signs of xenophobia present today in most countries remain at a level which is, by historical standards, quite low, even if profoundly disturbing.

v) <u>The world of policy making on education has been opened up to powerful external forces, including judicial intervention and enforcement of treaty commitments</u>

If one opens a textbook on comparative education from about twenty years ago, the descriptions of educational systems and their operations give very much the impression of educational establishements operating as closed systems. Public schooling is described in terms that indicate the role of a fixed set of participants: parents, children, teachers, administrators, superintendents/ministers, elected representatives charged with matters related to education. That image of an establishment serving "its" public can hardly be compared to the reality of today. The Anglo-Saxon countries, particularly the U.S., have developed a whole new route to policy-making that involves litigation before courts (usually on the basis of individual rights) followed by decisions that essentially override normal political decision-making processes. Although the legal traditions of continental Western Europe and Scandinavia leave little room for such legal recourse on an individual basis (though some limited cases may eventually be taken to international bodies in spite of the multitude of obstacles erected by the governments concerned), the arena of education in these countries has been invaded by different forces, emanating from the international sector.

The international economic cooperation referred to above not only brought new clienteles to the schools, it created new stakeholders, vitally concerned that social problems should be solved: the long-term future prosperity of many Western European countries depends upon the ability to attract and hold quality manpower in areas that have lost their demographic vitality to the point that many have been almost unable to replace their populations by natural growth for several decades (masked briefly by the post-war baby boom). The result of a variety of pressures for immediate solutions has been to create, among other things, a network of bilateral treaties by which emigration countries provide various forms of practical assistance to receiving countries, such as furnishing trained teachers from among their own nationals to provide instruction in the home language of children. Decision-making on the future of the children involved is no longer entirely in the hands of the so-called educational establishments: in many cases, economic ministries have a major hand in pushing for solutions, and the solutions often involve negotiated settlements arrived at through diplomatic channels.

This is altogether a revolution in procedure, as compared to the usual methods for dealing with educational problems as late as the early 1960s. Furthermore, agencies such as the EEC and the Parliamentary Assembly of the Council of Europe provide centres for focusing policy discussion, carried on between persons often recruited from outside educational circles. One is faced with a dynamic situation which escapes the traditional moulds and hastens evolutionary processes. Educational policy makers in the 1980s are, in most regards, outflanked and in a defensive position. The resulting impossibility of controlling policy events has often facilitated changes favouring minorities that would otherwise have been impossible through normal channels.

vi) Linguistic and cultural minorities have learned to mobilise and fight political battles before public opinion

No observer of political happenings since the early 1960s can escape noticing the increasing degree of skill and sophistication shown by linguistic and cultural minorities in mobilising their political strength, such as it is. Although public opinion is often focused by the media on a limited number of trouble spots, several serious studies have documented how widespread is the phenomenon of minority political mobilisation in Western Europe (Allardt, 1979). Some minority groups have been held back by lack of status and, particularly for foreign workers in some continental countries, by fear of reprisals from police and other authorities resulting in loss of work permits and expulsion. When such mobilisation occurs, its strength can come as a shock to educational authorities accustomed to more controlled, orderly methods of interaction, in which they have traditionally held the upper hand. One need only cite the example of the enormous impact made on public opinion in Sweden in 1983-84 by a parent-supported strike of Finnish students in one school; it is the author's impression, from studying the press and from discussions with various persons involved, that the happenings went far beyond the normal range of expectations held either by policy makers or Swedish public opinion. On the other hand, Sweden might also be cited as a foremost example of enlightened policies that have facilitated defence of minority interests by granting the right to vote in local elections to foreign workers meeting certain residence criteria. The effectiveness of political mobilisation is directly related, in the long run, to mobilising power and this, in turn, depends to a considerable extent upon the status of the affected minorities. We will not dwell on status here; as already indicated, our contribution to the CERI report on minority groups (1983) presents an overview of the different levels of status as they relate to the ability to affect the formal political processes. But even nominally powerless foreign groups may sometimes make their influence felt indirectly by attracting the attention of their home governments, who can intervene to help them in their country of residence (a pattern that has emerged with increasing frequency in Western Europe in the last decade).

In the end, however, the power equation of majority-minority relationships is weighted so that the extension of minority rights and the development of better educational provision for the minorities is dependent upon the good will and tolerance of the larger number. This situation dictates a form of dispute settlement that results in marginal, rather than spectacular, gains for minorities; major improvements in services for the minorities come largely through the accumulation of marginal gains over a longer period of time, each building on the other. (For a taxonomy of the stages in development of minority demands in response to varying levels of service, see Churchill in CERI, 1983).

THE STAGES OF DEVELOPMENT OF POLICIES FOR THE EDUCATION OF LINGUISTIC AND CULTURAL MINORITIES

The long-term trends just outlined make it possible to understand the type of policy process that appears to prevail in most of the OECD countries in defining educational services to be offered to minorities:

i) Minorities suffer from various educational problems which are recognised, initially, by educators, who apply existing solutions to them -- e.g. by providing remedial instruction of the type given to the retarded or by streaming minority students into programmes intended for the less gifted. Changes in arrangements to deal with differing languages and cultures are not undertaken by professional educators except in a very marginal manner, within the regular, day-to-day operations of schools and educational structures;

ii) Minority educational needs are translated into some form of tangible pressure that necessitates a "political" intervention to change the constraints under which educators operate. The response can come either from higher echelons of educational administration (e.g. senior levels of ministries) or from outside the educational system proper. In some cases, where status permits, the minorities themselves can play a role by political mobilisation;

iii) The limits on the response of the educational system appear to come primarily from the need to respect what the dominant view of public opinion considers tolerable at any point in time. Direct appeals to majority opinion on the grounds that a minority wishes to have a recognised special status are, in most cases, bound to fall on deaf ears. The changes required to improve services are "packaged", so to speak, in terms of goals that are more generally recognised as useful to majority society. The most successful stratagem of the last two decades has been to present minority needs as part of a generally accepted goal of improving social equity; economic disadvantage is perceived to derive from educational disadvantage, and the remedies to the educational problems of minorities are said to require some changes that, otherwise, would not be contemplated, such as developing school curricula that are different from those used for the majority population;

iv) Once a given set of changes is decided upon and put into place by authorities, the persistence of educational and social problems of minorities creates additional pressures that, if the climate of opinion is right, result in an additional round of improvements and changes to services;

v) The implicit "bargaining" between minority needs or demands and the limits imposed by majority opinion is being increasingly overriden by factors outside the usual framework of educational policy-making. In most of the countries of Anglo-Saxon legal tradition, the courts are playing a greater role; in the countries of continental tradition, international economic agreements have set in motion social changes that increasingly invite intervention in educational decisions by those involved in economic policy-making and by means of multilateral and bilateral international agreements;

vi) Changes imposed by forces outside the usual framework of educational policy-making require long periods to become assimilated into the educational system. Court rulings tend to concern individual cases and leave margins of discretion for applying them to others. Even when they are of broader application, putting into motion the necessary changes to comply with them can take years or decades. Similarly, in Western European countries, despite various engagements by the concerned governments, provision for minority needs is extremely scattered and touches only a minute fraction of the intended beneficiaries. In the case of both judicially imposed and negotiated obligations, the obstacles to implementation are ordinarily presented in terms of "practical difficulties" such as the small numbers of individuals affected, etc. Upon analysis, these practical difficulties can usually be traced to a failure of the policy makers to design the mechanisms that will permit the services to be delivered: thus, educational establishments and local educational authorities may be urged to provide a given type of service but the financial and human resources made available may be so limited that, under normal circumstances, it is absolutely certain that the institutions or local authorities will not be able to provide the services adequately to those who are supposed to receive them. This deliberate "under-design" or "under-planning" is probably partly attributable to a spirit of resistance by those involved in policy-making and implementation; but the resistance itself may be attributable less to a desire to deny minority needs than to the lack of vigour in accepting changes imposed on administrative and institutional structures from outside.

From the above we can see that responses to minority are likely to be highly idiosyncratic and to vary widely within a given educational jurisdiction. Members of a given minority may receive one level of service in one city and a much lower level in another only a few kilometres away; or, because of different degrees of political influence and power, one group may receive excellent services, while another is almost totally neglected. Old minorities with persistent problems, such as gypsies, may be overlooked in the rush to fulfill international agreements covering other groups. In all situations, despite the formal goals of policy makers, age-old attitudes involving racism and cultural stereotypes can slow up changes; this has affected two groups in particular -- persons of darker skin colouring and indigenous peoples, such as Native American Indians, Aboriginal peoples in Australia, Sami (Lapps) and others.

The earlier CERI study of Finance, Organisation and Governance reveals what appears to be a useful model for analysing policy goals of educational provisions made for minority groups. The crucial ingredient in this analysis appears to be the political sensitivity of three related issues: the role of minority language, the role of minority culture and the degree of separateness allowed the minorities in terms of educational facilities. Because such issues are so politically explosive, dominant majority opinion at any one time appears to dictate what response will be made by authorities to educational needs of minorities. This opinion can be summarised in general terms by looking at what is an acceptable definition of the "problem" faced by minorities in education. When the problem has been defined in terms acceptable to dominant majority opinion, then the solutions to the problem appear to flow in logical sequence from it.

Figure 1 (already presented in the CERI report) shows a model presented in six stages along with a variant labelled "1-4(B)". The first column presents a short name for the particular stage of problem definition; the second outlines the major assumptions made by educational policy about the causes of the minorities' educational problems; the third shows typical policy responses; and the fourth shows the expectations that are held out by policy with regard to the use of the language of the minority. The table uses the usual jargon of linguists to refer to languages: L1 stands for mother tongue or first language of individual minority group members, L2 is the second language they have to learn, the dominant language of the country or region where they reside. Thus, for Turkish children living in West Berlin, L1 would be Turkish and L2 would be German. The model is more fully described in the Appendix.

THE ROLE ASSIGNED TO MINORITY LANGUAGES AND CULTURES

Multicultural education as a stage of policy development

The model presented above is not intended to be deterministic. It simply provides an easy means of describing what has happened in policy-making with no pretension to predicting future developments. For the reader, the model may raise more questions than it answers. In the full report on the project, we have outlined how each of these stages of problems definition translates into provision for education; it was an unanticipated discovery to find how consistent the implementation policies are, once the problem definition is arrived at as a starting point. At this point we should attempt only to analyse rapidly the aims of policies in terms of the role assigned to the culture of minorities in education.

A good place to begin might be Stage 3 of problem definition. This stage includes almost everything that is subsumed under the names of "multicultural education", "intercultural education" and so forth. The author has discovered that this classification has been something of a shock when it was presented to persons who promote multicultural education in the belief that it is the main solution to be pursued to minority problems. The shock appears greatest not among minority group members but among those majority group members who are well-intentioned and believe that multicultural education is the means of coping definitely with minority problems. (There is a less potent, though more vociferous reaction, from theoreticians intent on proving the importance or value of one type of "multi-/inter-/cross-cultural" education compared to all the others; being grouped into a single category with rival approaches conflicts with their belief in the ultimate good of their particular brand of the product).

For those persons involved in trying to respond to minority needs in an open, fair-minded manner, a serious psychological effort is required to set aside many of their own deeply-held values concerning the importance of having one language and one culture embedded in an educational system; once they have made this effort and accepted multicultural education as a solution to current problems, they feel somehow deceived to discover that putting it into practice may not end all problems and will not eliminate further demands from minorities for additional recognition.

Figure 1

MAJOR MODELS OF PROBLEM DEFINITION AND POLICY RESPONSES

Model	Assumptions about problem causes	Typical policy responses	Language outcomes
Stage 1: Learning deficit	Language deficit in majority language (L2) due to use of mother tongue (L1). Problem similar to retardation or learning handicap common in special education.	Supplementary teaching of L2. Special grouping for initial instruction, rapid transition to instruction in L2.	L1 expected to be replaced by L2, rapid transition to L2 for school.
Stage 2: Socially-linked learning deficit	Language deficit as in Stage 1, instructional problem definition is the same. Causes linked to family status: broad range of problems anticipated, linked to social status, both at school and after leaving.	Teaching programmes similar to Stage 1 model. Special measures to assist adjustment to majority society: "orientation" for immigrants, vocational counselling, youth programmes, etc.	Same as Stage 1.
Stage 3: Learning deficit from cultural/social differences.	Language deficit recognised as for Stages 1 and 2. Instructional problem definition the same, but greater weight is given to affective consequences of culture differences (e.g. concern for students' self-concept). Partial responsibility placed on society/schools for not accepting or responding to the minority culture.	Language component of teaching the same as Stages 1 and 2. "Multicultural" teaching programmes: teaching about minority culture for all students, sensitisation programmes for teachers, programmes of community contact. Revision of textbooks to eliminate racial, ethnic slurs and stereotyping.	Same as Stages 1, 2 for education and long-term; short-term in-family use of L1 expected, say for one or two generations.

Figure 1 (cont.)

Model	Assumptions about problem causes	Typical policy responses	Language outcomes
Stage 4: Learning deficit from mother tongue deprivation.	Language deficit as for Stages 1,2,3 but a major causal factor is assumed to be (premature) loss of L1 inhibiting learning of L2 for cognitive and affective reasons. Social problems recognised as for Stage 2.	Language component the same as for L2 teaching as in Stages 1-3.	Same as Stage 3, except transition to L2 in school expected to take longer in most cases.
		Support provided for home language by study of L1 as a subject, sometimes also as a medium of instruction.	
	Cultural differences recognised as for Stage 3 but usually less emphasis placed on need for cultural acceptance by majority school programmes.	Sometimes may include "multicultural" component for majority as in Stage 3.	
Variant stages 1-4(B): Migratory alienation	Problem definition superimposed on the definition in Stages 1,2,3 or 4 regarding problems of contact with or integration into majority schools and culture.	Teaching of majority culture language same as for corresponding stage (1-4 above).	Dependent upon residence: return to home language or, if remaining in new country, same as for appropriate stage of country policy (1-4 above).
	Children are assumed to lose contact with culture of origin as result of foreign residence and require help to prepare for return to culture of origin.	Additional instruction in L1 as a subject, often with country's geography and history taught through L1 as medium of instruction. Additional instruction often outside regular school day.	

Figure 1 (cont.)

Model	Assumptions about problem causes	Typical policy responses	Language outcomes
Stage 5: Language maintenance for private use	Minority language of group threatened with disappearance if not supported, due to smaller numbers of minority. Minority disadvantaged in education by weaker social position of language and culture, due to smaller numbers. Minority has long-term rights to survival. Minority expected to enter majority society outside school.	Minority language used as medium of instruction, usually exclusively in earlier years. Majority language a required subject of study, at least from late elementary years (10-12) onward. Transition to majority language usually required for higher levels of educational system.	L1 maintained as domestic, private language of group. Outside home, minority uses L2 at work or in business life. Long-term group assimilation if demography unfavourable.
Stage 6: Language equality	Languages of minority and majority assumed to have equal rights in society. Language of smaller group may require special support to ensure broad social use; education viewed as only one field of language policy application.	Minority language granted status of official language. Separate educational institutions by language, usually under administration by relevant language group. Support measures extend beyond educational system to all phases of official business, sometimes private sector as well.	Indefinite, prolonged use of L1 by minority in home and in considerable part of work or business life. Long-term coexistence of majority and minority groups.

Source: Churchill in CERI, 1983, pp. 246-247.

The most evident component of many models of multicultural education is the emphasis placed on changing the curriculum of school subjects in order to give recognition to different cultural viewpoints: the intent is to begin showing members of the majority that alternatives to a single national/regional outlook on issues do exist. As noted in Figure 1, these approaches rarely include the use of the language of the minorities themselves in proposals for changing curricula. Such language issues may be separately raised -- e.g. through the internationally-inspired mechanisms that promote teaching of "home language" in Western Europe -- but the emphasis on culture in these proposals involves primarily a sensitization to cultural viewpoints aimed at attitudinal shifts. Viewed from the standpoint of those concerned with language issues (which includes many minority group members), the culture being proposed is peculiar: it is as if minority culture could exist without a language vehicle for its transmission. No proponent of such educational solutions suggests, of course, that there should be something called "language-free culture" for a minority, but the policy emphasis and the language of political discourse places language development of minorities in a peripheral area of minor importance.

Types of cultural adaptation

If we take the whole range of minority educational programmes represented in the OECD countries and analyse them to see the rationales for treating the cultures of the minorities in them, we come up with the following major groupings, each with its implicit or explicit rationale:

i) Grouping pupils of same or similar culture: Pupil grouping practices at the level of classroom teaching reflect a number of criteria, of which pupil culture is often one. In many situations, the definition of "culture" may be equated with language background, or language difficulties, but in others the criteria are specifically oriented towards grouping children with the intention of providing them with a compatible environment, particularly for initial transition into a new schooling situtiion;

ii) Eliminating negative elements in the curriculum: Partly through the impetus of the human rights movement and partly through related multiculturalism concerns, many juridictions have undertaken the revision of textbooks and teaching materials with a view to eliminating negative stereotyping of different cultural and ethnic groups. Until recently, for example, the religions of many groups (other than the dominant groups in the relevant country) were presented in strongly pejorative terms (e.g. in English by use of terms such as "superstition" or "worship of..." rather than "religion" or more neutral descriptive terms). More than any others, indigenous peoples have been adversely affected by negative views which so deeply permeate Western cultures that total elimination of the stereotyping is impossible, e.g. because it is an integral part of the literary tradition of various countries;

iii) Sensitising educational staff to minority cultural characteristics and needs: Training seminars and other forms of training for teachers and educational staff dealing with minority group members are a very common feature in most areas where such minorities live in significant numbers. Some components of training programmes are intended to provide information on the life, customs and expectations of minority group members; others are more oriented towards specific pedagogical problems such as how to deal with linguistic differences in the context of teaching. A few jurisdictions have made such training a regular component of pre-service education of all teachers (e.g. Sweden);

iv) Providing culturally-relevant information to groups other than the minorities: A major component of multiculturalism programmes is the development of the knowledge base of persons not belonging to the minorities. Such programmes are reported both as in-school activities directed at children and as community outreach activities involving the populace at large. The programmes pursue multiple purposes: increased direct contacts between majority and minority, elimination of misinformation, and development of positive attitudes towards cultural differences;

v) Providing staff of the same culture: Provision of staff from the same culture as pupils is done consistently when the curriculum involves teaching in the language of the minority. This practice is often extended to other groups where it is felt the children are insecure or unable to cope with the demands of adaptation to the classroom environment, particularly if their home environment is considered primitive or non-modern. In these cases, qualified teaching personnel may not be available, and there is extensive use of teaching aides and so-called paraprofessionals in several countries;

vi) Introduction of culture-related subjects into teaching programmes or changing the content of such programmes: Certain relatively minor changes to the content of school subjects is often a by-product of multiculturalism policies and the elimination of negative stereotyping. Some programme changes go beyond this "cosmetic" approach and introduce totally new topics, either as special subjects or syllabuses or as sub-components of existing courses of study. The areas most affected are social studies, history and literature. The implications of the changes depend upon the clientele to which they are directed. A programme of "Indian/Black/Hispanic/Asian/ Mediterranean Studies" directed at members of an affected minority is a recognition of the right or need of the minority to learn about its own history and customs; a programme addressed to the majority in the same country, particularly if it is made obligatory, suggests that the minority culture has a long-term, general relevance for all citizens. The encouragement of knowledge of the Maori language and culture in New Zealand as part of the national heritage is an example of the latter approach. A variant of the former approach is found in a number of jurisdictions, where the teaching of "culturally-relevant" topics such as social studies, history and geography, may occur in the minority language;

vii) Recognition of the minority language: The role of the minority language in schooling is dealt with extensively in Figure 1 and the Appendix. At this point one may emphasize that, by most definitions, language is an integral part of culture, but that many multicultural programmes are intended to give a place of prominence in schooling to all elements of a minority culture, _except_ its most prominent symbol, language. Most programmes of education for indigenous peoples across the countries studied, despite a number of experimental and limited attempts, do not accord any role to the indigenous language other than as an oral means of facilitating communication with very small children. Recognition of minority languages does occur for other groups in two main forms: recognition as a language of instruction for members of the minority and recognition as a topic of instruction for members of the majority. Making a minority language an elective subject for members of the majority, particularly if the minority language is not a "prestige" language, is a considerable symbolic step (as in the case cited for Maori); making it obligatory as a subject of study is usually reserved for cases of recognition of long-established minorities in a Stage 6 situation. (Note, however, the Canadian exception: the development of Francophone education has occurred in parallel with the elimination of French as an obligatory subject of study in secondary schools and universities.)

The above list, while non-exhaustive, comprises most of the forms of adaptation of educational treatments to the minority culture reported for the countries studied. The overt rationale in each case is relatively clear. Cutting across the different forms are important assumptions about the objectives of cultural adaptation of education and about the nature of minority cultures. The _objectives_ are linked to the definition of the problem to be overcome.

Problem	**Objective**
1. Minority has difficulty in adapting to majority culture	1. Facilitate transition of minority
2. Minority suffers from discrimination and from negative attitudes of majority and majority culture	2. Eliminate visible instances of negative stereotyping and discriminatory-type actions
3. Minority suffers from non-equal status and lack of positive valuation of its culture	3. Provide positive recognition of minority culture by majority society at large

From the minority viewpoint, the first problem definition can be equated with a negative view of their culture and is based on the expectation that they are to adjust to the majority culture. The second definition is neutral or potentially neutral: the emphasis is on the elimination of overt injustice. In practice, the programmes for elimination of stereotyping are sometimes presented as means of helping the minority adjust to the majority culture and, obviously, the objectives are complementary. The third problem definition is positive, in that it places a positive value on the minority culture and seeks to find means of expressing this in formal ways. So-called multicultural programmes often include all three elements with different degrees of emphasis.

How policies define culture

The definition of culture present in most programmes is rarely made explicit. It can be derived from an examination of the emphases of programmes. At the most negative, it implies that the children are not accustomed to "modern" situations or to an environment requiring discipline and regularity. The emphasis of programmes resulting from this problem definition is on helping children to overcome the handicap of their culture and to learn the new culture and its demands. The definition is close to programmes that are labelled "compensatory" and is part of the rationale of approaches i) to v) above. The programmes involved, it should be noted, are not necessarily conceived as being directed at the population concerned on the basis of linguistic or cultural differences. United States Compensatory Education programmes funded under Title I, for example, are intended to compensate for environmental inadequacies that have led children to perform inadequately, and the legislation refers to the "special education needs of the children of low income families", a category that coincides in many cases with linguistic and cultural minorities; the Bureau of Indian Affairs is a major recipient of funds from this source (U.S. Country Survey for FOG project). In a certain sense, one may speak in many countries of a "culture of poverty" that, because it is often correlated with linguistic and ethnic cultural differences, contributes to the view of minority bilingualism or culture as a handicap.

A second operational definition of culture involves considering the home culture as a topic of interest or curiosity because it involves customs different from those of the majority. This definition verges on the folkloric and is not necessarily flattering for those concerned, but it lacks explicitly negative elements. It is often expressed in the warmest terms of human sympathy and understanding. The definition can be used as a means of arousing the sympathy and interest of children and adults belonging to the majority. The emphasis is on human relations and attitudinal change within existing structures. Forms of programme listed above as ii), iii), and iv) are closely related to this rationale. Treating the home culture mainly as a topic of interest is, to a large extent, neutral in value. Other operational definitions are, from the viewpoint of the minority, much more positive. One involves recognising the culture as an enduring need for minority group members, i.e. as a part of their existence that cannot be removed or neglected without causing a form of prejudicial deprivation. The consequences of such thinking, in most modern social systems, are to recognise enduring need as a fundamental right. The most common recognition of this right is the provision of culture-related instruction either as part of the optional curriculum for minority group members or as an out-of-school activity. Obviously, recognition within the school programmes involves a higher level of official commitment in both symbolic and real terms. For various reasons, official recognition of the language of the minority as part of the commitment of the school has been rare until recently, even for established minorities.

The most positive, and most rare, operational definition involves a major shift in public attitudes for its accomplishment. The minority culture is considered an enduring concern for the majority. Modern educational systems were created to provide citizens with the broad minimum of knowledge considered necessary for them to understand their environment and to adapt to it. The implication of recognising a minority culture as an enduring concern, not only for its own members, but for society at large, is that the compulsory educational system has a responsibility to impart a knowledge of its basic elements to members of the majority. This can involve serious changes to the content of programmes of study for the majority, mainly in culture-related subjects. The introduction of obligatory instruction in the minority language is, of course, the most constraining on the majority and is found only in a few cases of established minorities or multicultural states (Belgium, Finland, Switzerland, Yugoslavia and parts of Canada).

The relationship between the major forms of educational treatment that recognise the minority culture, the related objectives, and operational definitions of the minority culture are shown in summary in Figure 2. Some of the major forms of educational response have been separated into two components, depending upon whether the responses affect only the minority or both the minority and the majority. One group of persons belonging to the majority is consistently affected by almost any measure affecting the minority: the teachers and other personnel of the educational system. Form i) or educational response, pupil grouping, is common to many other of the responses; it is entered in the list only in its simple form, i.e. for the limited case of a transitional measure or when it is enduring and corresponds to streaming of difficult or anomalous students.

The juxtaposition of different elements in Figure 2 highlights one very interesting reciprocal relationship between definitions of culture and the extent of recognition received. There is a strong tradition in education, according to which a topic of study acquires a special status if it becomes a matter of formal study and examination ("discipline" is the term sometimes used in English). The operational definitions of "handicap" and "topic of interest" for minority cultures have a connotation that culture is a matter of personal behaviour, such as food, dress, and personal manners of socialising. The operational definitions that imply recognition as a subject of study are psychologically on a different plane and require conceptualising the minority culture as something of general intellectual interest outside the confines of personal behaviour. Conferring status as a subject of study is a major symbolic act both for the minority and the majority.

A review of policies followed in different jurisdictions in the light of the above remarks calls for two generalisations:

i) There is an increasing tendency across different jurisdictions to develop educational responses that emphasize at least a "neutral" valuation of the minority culture, that is encouragement of its being viewed as a topic of general interest and discouragement of negative acts or attitudes toward minorities. This tendency is usually complementary to measures to facilitate adaptation of minority group children to the majority culture and helps attenuate the negative connotations of culture shift.

ii) Even though the tendency towards neutral or positive cultural valuations extends to all groups, the overall impression of treatments accorded to indigenous peoples is that they are still mainly based on a negative concept of their culture, have as a

Figure 2

OPERATIONAL DEFINITIONS OF MINORITY CULTURE AND RELATIONSHIP TO EDUCATIONAL RESPONSES

			Objectives: emphasis			Groups affected		
Operational definition of minority culture	Valuation (Minority viewpoint)	Provision type	Adaptation of minority to majority culture	Eliminate negative factors	Positive recognition	Minority group concerned	Education staff (majority group)	Majority population
Deprived environment	Negative	i	x			x	x	
		v – a	x			x	x	
		Gen.Comp.	x			x	x	
Topic of interest	Neutral	ii	x	x			x	
		iii – a	x	x			x	
		iv	x	x	x	x	x	x
Enduring need for minority	Positive	iii – b	x	x	x		x	
		v – b	x		x	x	(Indirect)	
		vi – a			x	x	x	(Optional)
		vii –a	x		x	x	x	
		vii – b			x	x		
Enduring concern for majority	Positive	vi – b		x	x	x	x	x
		vii – c		x	x	x	x	x

Provision types:

i	Pupil grouping (only), see text	v – b	Minority staff, own programmes or language
ii	Eliminating negative curriculum components	vi – a	Minority subjects in curriculum for minority
iii – a	Staff sensitization	vi – b	Minority subjects in curriculum for majority
iii – b	Obligatory teacher training (usually pre-service)	vii – a	Minority language teaching for transition
iv	Information for majority about minority	vii – b	Minority language teaching for maintenance
v – a	Minority staff, initial transition (compensatory)	vii – c	Minority language teaching for majority

Gen. Comp.: General compensatory measures common to special education for those with learning disabilities.

major component the objective of compensating for the home environment, and fail to include home language (including non-standard forms of the majority language) as a significant basis for intellectual development.

The areas of taboo

The discussion of culture here has lacked one key element: passion. It is as if culture were neutral, even though all experience shows us that it is hotly debated. The reason for this is that key elements of a politically sensitive nature are carefully dealt with by educators and educational authorities in a way intended to limit their destructive potential for social harmony. The main issues are race, religion, sex, and "primitive" behaviour. We should explore them briefly, because they reveal the limits of the extent to which educational provisions can be responsive to minority demands. On each of these issues, our public educational systems will generally tolerate very limited accommodation to minority requests and/or life styles.

i) Race: Positive action to deliberately favour members of a racial minority as a means of overcoming disadvantage -- so-called "positive action" -- has been strongly resisted in all jurisdictions. It took the enormous U.S. civil rights movement to make a dent in the psychological, legal and institutional obstacles to positive action programmes based on race. Almost nowhere is there any admission that members of a race, as such, should be permitted on racial grounds to pursue life styles and patterns that are deviant from the dominant norm. The basic problem for policy-making is that most of the rationales for racially-based programmes favouring minorities run into direct contradiction with legal and moral norms embedded in current institutions. Minorities may argue that perpetuating legally neutral institutions that do not recognise races can result in discrimination on racial grounds simply because human behaviour overrides the legal neutrality; but arguing in favour of a "positive" racial discrimination policy, albeit one intended to further the well-being of those affected, arouses deep-set fears that the precedent could be used in other circumstances to the detriment of racial groups. And, at the same time, any form of positive action in favour of a minority is perceived to be part of a zero-sum game: any win for the minority is perceived as a loss for some members of the majority. The U.S. civil rights movement managed to convince large numbers of influential persons at one point that necessity dictated radical solutions, the outcome of which would not be a zero-sum game but a general social improvement. This is a rare exception that proves the general rule: race is not a criterion that is easily used to define special educational provision.

ii) Religion: There are few, if any, examples in the OECD countries, of accommodation to the religion of minorities in the educational systems in a way that upsets existing arrangements. Most countries seem to believe they have defused religious-based conflict by whatever arrangements are now in place. The secular nature of industrial societies has affected profoundly most minority groups, whose goals are articulated mainly in terms of access to material well-being together with some recognition of their identity and status. Religion becomes an issue primarily when existing curricula or textbooks present other religions in pejorative terms. The main remedy has generally been to eliminate severe stereotyping of the traditionally conflicting religions (Protestant-Catholic in most OECD countries,

Catholic-Orthodox-Islamic for Yugoslavia, Protestant-Orthodox for Finland). Population movements of the past twenty years have brought a new awareness of how culturally biased is most traditional writing about Islam; more recently, particularly in the United States, there has developed an awareness of the need to change presentations of traditional Asiatic religious and ethical systems. The elimination of stereotypes and negative remarks can generally be agreed to; what remains out of bounds for policy is to create special courses and curricula that promote the religious viewpoint of a minority.

iii) Sex: It is symptomatic that most discussions of the issue refer to the way women and girls are treated. Most OECD countries (but by no means all) have moved towards adopting many of the central themes of the feminist movement, including the gradual removal of role stereotyping from textbooks and the slow -- some would say painfully slow -- opening up of educational opportunities to women. Despite resistance, there is a growing movement towards greater recognition of women's rights and women's issues. This runs directly counter to accommodating the culture of some minority groups in the educational system. Comparatively little is written about this, though much is said about it. Particularly in Western Europe, Islamic culture is equated with certain ways of controlling the behaviour of women, and there is an absolute, unequivocal rejection of the rights of families of Islamic origin to dictate what will be the conduct of young women -- together with a resignation in the face of the impossibility of changing current patterns of control overnight. Unfortunately, popular discussion of the issues tends to reinforce negative religious and racial stereotypes: rarely does any educational policy document point out that some of the most condemned practices assumed to exist in Islamic families are still prevalent in many Christian areas around the Mediterranean today and were the rule in most peasant societies of Central Europe until a few generations ago. The near absence of strong official commentary on the similarity between behaviour now reputedly found mainly in Islamic persons originating in remote rural areas (e.g. in North Africa and Turkey), and that which has prevailed in many Christian societies at least until the recent past, has allowed the festering of what is a deep-set cultural issue and the reinforcement of anti-Islamic racist attitudes.

iv) Primitive behaviour patterns: Certain groups suffer particularly from the rejection by prevailing dominant society of their traditional life styles. These are primarily the indigenous peoples, whose needs are perhaps the least well dealt with among those studied in the CERI's FOG project. The issue is simple to describe: many of the assumptions of all school systems in the industrial world are predicated on the disappearance of so-called "primitive" life styles. Hunter-gatherer societies, even when sedentary, are difficult to reconcile with an educational system predicated on the development of abstract cognitive skills using mainly written information sources to produce citizens able to function in a highly differentiated economic system. Many of the indigenous peoples have absorbed the basic motivations and attitudes of the dominant societies around them to the point of harbouring contempt for their own culture and cultural origins. Yet, at the level of the individual child, formal education in many current school systems provides a definition of culture that is more than a slight modification to their own. The message is: "Cease to have your identity and assume a new one, cast off your primitive ways, reject your parents, reject your past, be a different, new person". This negative definition of so-called primitive culture has the most profound psychological and practical consequences. No modern educational system has found even a moderately tolerable set of solutions for the problem, which is the definition of a minority group's whole way of life as a negative value. It is a rejection that goes deeper than racism.

Trends that may be short-term

Our discussion has focused on long-term structural aspects of the response made to divergent languages and cultures within national educational systems. To go beyond such generalisations and deal with specific recent events is to risk mistaking a coincidence for a trend. Despite this risk, it may be worth itemizing a few happenings that may be the beginning of long-term trends.

i) Majority opinion in Western European countries has become increasingly aware of two dimensions of the problems faced by minorities, both in education and in society generally:

-- That the phenomenon of minority problems is deep and cannot be made to go away by use of simple, low-cost measures;

-- That currently applied educational measures are inadequate and generally failing.

ii) Majority opinion throughout most OECD countries is becoming more sensitized to cultural differences and more aware that most societies are culturally and linguistically diverse. This amorphous awareness is an underlying source of unease -- not usually discussed or translated into political issues -- because it directly contradicts many of the assumptions on which societal arrangements are based.

The contradiction appears strongest between two traditional sets of values: on the one hand, particularly since 1945, there has been a growing consciousness of a link between the operation of democratic institutions and respect for individual rights, even if these result in behaviour that is different from that of the majority: it has taken Western societies nearly half a century to internalize the lessons of the holocaust. On the other hand, the political discourse in most countries continues to reinforce the traditional concept that the operation of nation-states requires the maintenance of an officially approved set of cultural arrangements involving only one, or at most a very few, languages, along with very limited cultural diversity.

iii) The support of Western-European governments and majority public opinion for so-called home language instruction of resident foreign workers' children, appears currently rather fragile. The postulate that home language instruction is intended to prepare them for a return to the parents' native land has been the main pretext for making these arrangements. The growing awareness that current policies are not solving problems, together with growing evidence that the return to a foreign homeland is no longer possible, is leading to demands for re-evaluation of these policies. In most countries, there appears to be little broad support for the rationale that corresponds to what we have called a Stage 4 problem definition -- that learning and developing the mother tongue is a step necessary for healthy development of the personality and of the cognition necessary for the minority children to learn the dominant language of the country of residence and to benefit from education given in that language. At the same time, there is increasing awareness that bilateral arrangements for home language teaching result in serious contradictions -- contradictions between the styles of teaching of foreign teachers from the homeland of the foreign workers and those in the country of residence, but, more importantly, contradictions between the formal pretext for education -- return to the homeland -- and the true state of affairs. In turn, this raises serious issues about the nature of a curriculum based on the national language and curriculum of the foreign home country for various groups whose true home language is not the same as the official language of the country of origin (e.g. Kurdish-speaking Turkish nationals, Catalans of Spanish nationality, Sardinians of Italian nationality, etc.). There is every evidence that, in most Western European countries, public understanding of the problem is roughly at a Stage 2 level and that the erosion of confidence in home language teaching will result either in a complete reversion to Stage 2 policy options (i.e. abolition of home language instruction either by direct action or by starving the programmes of adequate human and financial resources), or, in the best of cases, by a shift to a Stage 3 policy definition. The Stage 3 option is strongly encouraged by the movement in favour of "intercultural education" (Council of Europe) or "multi-ethnic education" (U.K. Schools Council).

Recent policy changes in Sweden mark a small reduction in the home language support of the recent past, but Swedish policy remains generally so much more supportive of home languages that it cannot (at least at this time) be interpreted as signalling a long-term trend.

iv) The multi-/inter-/cross-cultural education movement in several Western European countries appears to be gaining momentum as an option for policy makers in search of a way to reduce pressures for more fundamental changes in political and social arrangements. The main factor favouring this development is the current climate of budget stringency in most countries, which rules out important initiatives to improve social conditions or to change governmental arrangements. The relatively strong regionalist pressures of the 1970s have only eventuated in major changes in political arrangements in Spain and Switzerland (Jura). The decentralisation policies of the current French government were not intended as a final solution but as one step in a direction where further progress has been slow. The system of local government in the United Kingdom makes it extremely difficult for central government initiatives to target large-scale special help and assistance for linguistically and/or ethnically identified groups without violating the spirit of local priority definition; this means that local English-speaking majorities control service levels for ethnic and cultural minorities. Further examples abound in different countries.

In this situation, making changes in school programmes in order to sensitize the majority population to cultural differences, offers the hope of improving inter-group relations without large-scale expenditures of public funds and without a backlash from majority opinion -- particularly if the issue of language can be kept separate from the changes. The greatest degree of political movement towards major changes -- the outcome of which remains impossible to predict -- appears to exist in Italy; but the Italian political system has a demonstrated capacity for defusing major regional and cultural differences over long periods of time, and it would be hazardous to predict a clear-cut political solution in the near term to deal with regionalist sentiment. On the other hand, because of the largely political and regionalist form of such pressures, the use of a limited multicultural option not involving changes in the language of instruction appears somewhat marginal and may not prove attractive as a policy option to deal with the situation.

v) In North America the recent political victories of conservative forces in national elections have resulted in two, diametrically opposed, sets of implications for cultural diversity: in Canada, the recent Progressive Conservative sweep to power was based on obtaining very significant electoral support from French-language voters. Failure to consolidate this, i.e. failure to promote existing bilingual arrangements, would constitute a menace to the new political base of the current government, which also is seeking to spread its support among non-English, non-French groups. In the United States, the political tendencies most strongly visible in conservative political discourse tend to emphasize traditional themes centring on nationalist feeling and a return to the values of a generation or more ago, i.e. to values that emphasized cultural and linguistic unity. Obviously, the decentralised U.S. system of state and local government, combined with the large numbers of votes wielded by minorities, provides many opportunities for policies that contradict this apparent wave of opinion visible at the national level.

vi) Economic forces in the Pacific perimeter are promoting cultural adaptation in very dissimilar ways. Generally speaking the economic boom of the last few decades has resulted in strong trade and exchange currents that have put regional countries much more closely in contact with each other than in the past and have created strong economic interests that should favour cultural openness. But the great national differences between the OECD Member countries of the region mean that these forces are acting quite differently. New Zealand has a long tradition of relative openness towards the Maori minority's culture, though it has faced well-known difficulties in reaching a social accommodation between a Europeanised society and an indigenous life style; such changes as have occurred appear to be largely intended to improve the nature of this accommodation. Australia, by contrast, has become much more sensitized to the possibilities offered by the multi-/inter-cultural education movement as a means of reconciling the great cultural differences that have resulted from migratory currents. Policies specifically incorporating such multi-/inter-cultural outlooks have been adopted in various Australian educational jurisdictions. The monolithic cultural and linguistic homogeneity of the bulk of the Japanese population poses quite different challenges; multicultural approaches to education involve what might be described as an attempt to look outside the country and to seek international contacts. By and large the international economic forces acting in favour of openness remain, despite their apparent size, somewhat marginal, and developments in each of the three countries appear likely to be dictated in the foreseeable future by current internal forces, i.e. with little prospect of fundamental change. The only unpredictable factor may be the implications of the rapid economic growth in the Republic of South Korea for relations with Japan (which has, in its work force, significant numbers of persons of Korean origin); the Japanese have a long tradition of regionally-oriented policy thinking that leaves open the door for cultural exchanges and initiatives related to cultural relations, the nature of which is, of course, impossible to foresee.

vii) Within Europe, the so-called "sending" countries for migratory flows, taken as a group, are currently all involved in various forms of intervention in favour of their own nationals in the so-called "receiving" countries. The promotion of these interests is now popular, but it is quite uncertain how long the system of bilateral and multilateral arrangements with receiving countries will survive the growing recognition of the low likelihood that those living abroad will return. The prospect for a gradual retreat from this outside involvement appears very strong as national education systems in receiving countries develop their own indigenous solutions.

Predictable consequences of recent trends

In combination with the long-term tendencies outlined in earlier parts of this paper, the short-term tendencies sketched here suggest that:

i) Current programmes of home language instruction for resident foreign workers in Western Europe are likely to decline unless a new rationale is found for them and supported by the minorities involved, i.e. a rationale based on the need to support development of the mother tongue of children as a means of ensuring their academic success in schooling using a second language;

ii) The multi-/inter-/cross-cultural education movement affecting most OECD countries is likely to persist because it has low financial and political costs compared to alternatives. In countries where the policies concern relatively new minorities (resident foreign workers and immigrants in Western Europe) this is likely to be in a form that de-emphasizes support of the home language in publicly-funded formal education. Conversely in countries of old immigration (Australia, Canada, New Zealand and the U.S.) the political force of the immigrant constituencies is likely to continue to provide a basis of support for the development of home language instruction in connection with multicultural education initiatives. (This will continue to be reinforced in the U.S. through the application of existing jurisprudence affecting those who cannot benefit from education in English.);

iii) The regionalist tendencies of old territorially-based linguistic and cultural minorities, while apparently eclipsed in most jurisdictions by economic and political events of more pressing current concern, will remain a major force for the foreseeable future, as the implications of multiculturalism, even in the more watered-down forms proposed in some jurisdictions, become apparent to larger sectors of the dominant majority populations.

This, of course, is all speculation.

CONCLUSIONS

Across the OECD countries there is a growing willingness to adapt educational systems to take into account differing cultures. Because many underlying assumptions about the goals of schooling and the means of delivering it are the same in the industrialised countries, the processes of policy definition bear some remarkable resemblances that transcend national cultural differences. We have identified a number of trends of policy development, some of which promote adapting educational provision to minority needs, others of which raise obstacles. These trends serve as the backdrop for explaining the main stages in the development of policies for education of linguistic and cultural minorities. The model of stages of policy development, while not pretending to have a predictive value for events that may occur in the future, does describe in relatively succinct terms the main elements that have characterised policies in the past two decades. In turn our analysis has linked these stages to very clearly defined differences in the meaning attached to the culture of minorities in educational policies. The so-called "multiculturalism" approach (which includes a variety of similarly named approaches) is approximately at the transition point in valuation of minority culture and language, the point where policies cease to treat the culture as a net disadvantage and begin to deal with it as, at least, neutral.

Strong positive valuations of culture are only found in the higher stages of the model of policy development. Despite this flexibility, most systems have remained inflexible in their treatment of certain issues that are excluded, more or less by definition, from the range of acceptable cultural alternatives for formal schooling -- positive discrimination based on racial criteria, modifications to the *status quo* in recognition of religious differences within schooling, acceptance of culture patterns that permit the family extensive control over the behaviour of girls and women, and accommodation to so-called "primitive" life styles of indigenous peoples. These out-of-bounds areas confirm the role of what we have called dominant public opinion in defining the boundaries of acceptable flexibility in cultural matters.

Within these boundaries, through constant pressure and the help of a variety of circumstances, almost all minority groups in the OECD countries are showing signs of some progress, and most educational systems are beginning to adapt towards cultural pluralism. This pluralism is integrative and seeks to reach an accommodation with minorities that, for a given state of power relationships, permits the social harmony necessary to promote social and economic development within the western, liberal model. The educational policy-making process outlined is reformist rather than revolutionary. It fits well within a general definition of policy-making advanced by Torsten Husen in a publication some years ago concerning social influences on educational attainment: "Policy can be defined as an institutionalised manifestation in planning and decision-making of ideologically embedded, vested interests" (Husen, 1975, p. 159).

NOTES

1. In all cases, the legal framework may suggest a greater degree of equality between languages and social groups than is actually the case in school practice and society at large. Thus, Yugoslavia, Switzerland and Spain each have a traditional dominant linguistic-ethnic group (respectively Serbian, Germanic and Castillian speakers). Our remarks at this point refer to the frameworks of policy and law rather than to social forces.

2. Our analysis here owes much to the synthesis done by Allardt (1979).

BIBLIOGRAPHY

ALLARDT E.: "Implications of the Ethnic Revival in Modern, Industrialized Society: A Comparative Study of the Linguistic Minorities in Western Europe". Commentationes Scientiarum Socialum, 12, Societas Scientiarum Fennica, Helsinki, 1979.

CERI: The Education of Minority Groups. An Enquiry into problems and practices in fifteen countries. Gower Publishing, Aldershot (U.K.) 1983.

CHURCHILL S.: "The Education of Linguistic and Cultural Minorities in the OECD Countries". OECD Doc., Paris 1983.

COUNCIL OF EUROPE: "Assemblée Parlementaire, Rapport sur les problèmes d'éducation et de culture posés par les langues minoritaires et les dialectes en Europe". In Conseil de l'Europe, Strasbourg, Doc. 4745, 2 juin 1981.

HUSEN T.: The School in Question, Oxford University Press, Oxford, 1982.

HUSEN T.: Social Influences on Educational Attainment, CERI/OECD, Paris, 1975.

LEIBOWITZ A.H.: The Bilingual Education Act: A Legislative Analysis, National Clearinghouse for Bilingual Education, Rosslyn (Va.), 1980.

NOAH H.J. and SHERMAN J.D.: Educational Financing and Policy Goals for Primary Schools. General Report, CERI/OECD, Paris, 1979.

OECD: Migrants' Children and Employment. The European Experience, OECD, Paris, 1983.

Appendix

STAGES OF POLICY DEVELOPMENT REGARDING THE EDUCATION OF LINGUISTIC AND CULTURAL MINORITIES IN THE OECD COUNTRIES

Explanatory Observations on the Models in Figure 1

As previously, parentheses and local citations refer to one of the 19 national surveys/studies contributed to the CERI project enquiring into the financing, organisation and governance of education for special populations -- FOG -- listed in CERI, 1983, pp. 363-364.

If one excludes the countries with relatively old, established minority situations whose major contours were defined at least fifty or more years ago (Belgium, Finland, Switzerland), the models in Figure 1 represent what appear often to be sequential historical stages of policy development. Although no "new" or non-established minority appears to have progressed beyond the Stage 4 model, some established minorities (such as the Franco-Manitobans in Canada), have moved from Stage 1 or 2 to Stage 5.

The lowest stage (not shown in the Figure) consists simply of ignoring the existence of special educational problems of minorities. Most national educational systems have gone through this stage at some point in the past. The history of literacy policy in some countries studied, particularly with respect to dialects very divergent from the majority standard language, illustrates this tendency well. The development of special education for the handicapped in most of the systems under examination has eliminated most situations where severe disadvantage goes unrecognised at the level of the individual minority student, even if treatment methods may be misadapted.

Since all of the countries in the CERI study have specific policies for dealing with at least a portion of their minorities, all have at least some policies operating at the level of the Stage 1 or 2 models. The initial recognition of the problem in most cases has defined the problem in terms of the learning deficit model of Stage 1, with educational provision characteristic of traditional approaches to special education. By various measures, certain groups of students are observed to suffer from scholastic deficiencies: they have poor grades, make progress through the system more slowly than others, may have special discipline problems, and drop out of school in greater numbers and at earlier ages than the national norms. The Stage 2 model of socially-linked learning deficit, sometimes but not always arrived at concurrently with Stage 1, is recognition of the broader social problems associated with deficient school performance: the students' poor performance in school may derive from the unfavourable socio-economic situation of their parents and may lead them to fall into the same situation, characterised by a lower likelihood of making a smooth transition to the adult work world and greater proneness to serious social problems in later life, linked to low socio-economic status and poor educational achievement.

These two stages appear to be universal to OECD countries with the possible exception of two: Finland, where the Swedish-speaking minority was originally perceived by the majority as having a position of higher prestige and social attainment, and Switzerland, where the relationship between the language groups in modern times was coloured by the fact that each of the three major languages (French, German, Italian) was spoken in nearby, culturally prestigious countries, a factor tending to attenuate the superior/inferior status relationships often found in multilingual settings. By contrast it is evident in data from Canada (FOG national study -- Canada) that the same initial (learning deficit) conceptualisation was applied to minority Francophones, whose scholastic achievement was below that of their English-speaking counterparts.

The Stage 1 problem definition, expressed in terms of a deficit model of special education corresponds to the adoption of pedagogic measures aimed at narrowing the achievement gap. Where minority students are enrolled in the majority-language system (true of most countries except those with long-established minorities), the problem has historically been seen as a language deficit, i.e. the students have an inadequate grasp of the majority language. The French and German national studies detail a variety of special measures aimed at upgrading knowledge of the second language; educational authorities in England also appear to stress development of English skills for "immigrant" students. The intent is primarily to bring the students' knowledge of the classroom language up to a level where they can benefit from instruction; this is accompanied by measures of cultural familiarisation in some cases, as indicated in the Danish regulations: "The purpose of Danish language teaching is for pupils to acquire proficiency in the Danish language, and to familiarise them with conditions prevailing in Denmark" (FOG survey for Denmark). The United States Title VII legislation for bilingual/bicultural education makes language deficiency the criterion of admission to such programmes (FOG national survey). The United States programmes also include measures that illustrate the type of action that is characteristic of the Stage 2 model, such as programmes to facilitate job training and placement on the labour market for members of minorities. The Swedish survey reports the largest range of such measures, including summer programmes for immigrants and short vocational programmes for all interested young people.

Even though at this stage the primary problem identified is the students' lack of knowledge of the second (majority) language, several countries have introduced instruction in the children's mother tongue for reasons not directly related to the assumptions of the model. The most common case, illustrated by France and Germany, involves the use of language teachers from the home countries of the students (or of their parents) to teach the language as a subject and, at least in Bavaria, to use it as a medium of instruction for other school subjects; this reflects the "external" impetus referred to earlier, the objective being to facilitate eventual return to the parents' home country. The case study for England and Wales cites a report from research in the early 1970s, in which "the authors discovered that although no official policy had been declared, the first limited steps were being taken to provide tuition" in the mother tongue.

Until relatively recently, many educators felt that continued use of the mother tongue by students might interfere with the acquisition of the second language. Paradoxically, the contradiction between the first and second language support measures may not exist, according to mounting research evidence. Nevertheless, the common-sense belief in the contradiction between the support of the mother tongue and the assumption of the Stage 1 and 2 models, has more influence on public opinion than do research findings.

The Stage 3 problem conceptualisation has become rapidly more popular under the name of "multicultural education" or "multiculturalism". It assumes that minorities suffer from learning deficits at least in part because of the failure of the majority society -- particularly its educational system -- to recognise, accept and view positively the culture of the minority. In other words, a portion of the blame is shifted to the educational system, and, in neutral terms, one may refer to a "mismatch" between the programmes and institutions, on the one hand, and the minority needs, on the other. It is interesting that the recognition of the culture of children may be endorsed officially without provoking, however, the acceptance of the premise that the language of that culture requires support. Thus, in England the Community Relations Commission carried out various programmes to support multiculturalism between 1968 and 1976; however, as the case study observes, the Commission showed "little or no concern for the maintenance of the mother tongues of ethnic minorities, and the West Indian dialects are seen only as causing difficulty in learning, a viewpoint which has been challenged by many sociolinguistic scholars". The essence of the model is the recognition of a right to be different and be respected for it, not necessarily to use a different language. The multiculturalism concept appears to be gaining ground in a number of Western European countries, usually with at least limited recognition of the utility of mother tongue instruction.

The Stage 4 problem definition assumes that a major cause of learning deficits among linguistic minorities may be traced to linguistic deprivation, i.e. failure to develop the mother tongue of children. As mentioned above, research evidence appears to be lending support to this thesis, which is integral to educational programme definitions in a number of countries. The United States legislation, for example, defines bilingual education as a programme designed for children with limited English language skills in which there is "instruction ... in English and, to the extent necessary to allow a child to achieve competence in the English language, the native language of the children of limited English proficiency" (cited by Leibowitz, 1980, p. 27). Countries such as Sweden have adopted far-reaching programmes of home language support, where the goal of transition to the majority tongue is complemented, in terms of the policy statements, by more long-term objectives. A Bill passed by the Riksdag in 1975 set down guidelines for immigrant and minority group policy with the triple aims of equality, freedom of choice, and partnership. The freedom of choice aim means that the "members of linguistic minorities must be able to choose the extent to which they will assume Swedish cultural identity and the extent to which they will retain their cultural and linguistic identity" (national survey -- Sweden). Such an objective implies possibilities of long-term language maintenance, this exceeding the minimum requirements, so to speak, for Stage 4. The Stage 4 model is still based largely on the concept of linguistic deficit but is enlarged to accept the need for support of the minority language at least as a transitional measure.

An examination of policies in countries having established minorities permits the identification of at least two additional stages. <u>Stage 5</u> reflects the type of thinking explicitly written into the Swedish legislation just discussed. It recognises minority groups as being permanently weaker members of society, because of smaller numbers, but recognises their right to maintain and develop their own languages and cultures in private life. This means that the minority languages are expected to be maintained for use mainly in the family, religion, and private social activities. Support for this role comes mainly from the use of the minority language as a medium of instruction in the educational system, particularly in the initial years of instruction. Most minority language students are expected to pursue studies in the majority language, if they go on to higher levels of education beyond some point (variable by jurisdiction). The case studies of Manitoba, New Brunswick and Ontario illustrate situations where, over the years, the age of transition to studying through the medium of the majority language has been gradually shifted upwards. The most rudimentary form of this involves initial literacy instruction in the first years of elementary school using the mother tongue, sometimes combined immediately with use of, and instruction in, the majority language (Churchill, in CERI, 1983). Such programmes are found today in education for indigenous peoples such as the Lapps/Sami and Maori; it is also the case of the Danish minority in Schleswig-Holstein (albeit in private schools) or the Francophones of the Valley of Aosta, in Italy. Cases such as the latter are almost indistinguishable, in terms of teaching practices, from some identified with Stage 4; the main difference is the assumption made about the long-term role of the minority group in the country involved.

<u>Stage 6</u> is the granting of full official language status to the minority language for the purposes of use in public institutions. Where numbers and social dynamism permit, the minority language may also take its place in the broader economic life of the country, a situation only reached in the very old bilingual or multilingual states (Belgium, Finland, Switzerland). The widely publicised constitutional changes in Spain are obviously intended to move towards a situation like this in areas such as Catalonia. The Canadian case study illustrates some of the potential complications and/or flexibility of moving through these last two stages in a federal system: the policy of official bilingualism adopted by the Federal Government applies only to Federal institutions and services, thereby leaving out entirely the field of education, which is under provincial control. Of the three provinces studies, all have given to the French language the status of language of instruction, but only New Brunswick has also adopted it as an official language of the province for all government business.

Figure 1 illustrates these major stages or models of problem definition identified across the CERI project studies, together with the typical policy response associated with each. In order to accommodate all cases, an additional variant on models 1-4, labelled <u>"Model 1-4(b)"</u>, is included: it is the result of superimposing on these models the concept of preparing the students to leave their "host" country. It implies that the school system will provide foreign students with a minimum of instruction in their native language (mainly teaching the language as a school subject) along with some cultural and other information about their parents' country of origin. As the case study of England and Wales illustrates, this model may be superimposed even in situations where there is generally little willingness on other grounds to recognise minority languages for instructional purposes. The impetus in the United Kingdom appears to have come from an official commitment to abide by the Council of Europe Directive of 25 July 1977 that member countries apply a 1976 resolution of the Council; the resolution laid down obligations to provide "more opportunities as appropriate for teaching these (migrant) children their mother tongue and culture, if possible in school and in collaboration with the country of origin" (study for England and Wales, p. 37). It should be obvious, however, that the institution of such measures creates a situation that easily leads to the Stage 4 model, in which home language deprivation is viewed as a major source of educational problems.

The differences between the various stages of the process of problem identification are not always clear-cut. Some of the United States bilingual programmes are of sufficient scope that, even though the official motivation for creating them, as expressed in legislation, corresponds to a Stage 2 or Stage 4 outlook, they are viewed by the recipients in the context of Stage 5, i.e. as tending toward long-term maintenance of group language and culture. A fundamental shift in outlook regarding the minority language separates Stages 5 and 6 from all the earlier ones; Stages 1 to 4 are primarily aimed at treating a handicap. Stages 5 and 6 seek to cultivate a difference which is viewed as a positive asset for the individual and (particularly in Stage 6) for the society as a whole.

II. CULTURAL IDENTITIES

4. ETHNICITY, MIGRATIONS AND MINORITIES

by
François H.M. RAVEAU
Directeur d'études
at the Ecole des Hautes Etudes en Sciences Sociales, Paris

TENTATIVE DEFINITION

If we agree with Durkheim that social facts are concrete facts, then, to deal with them, we need concepts that are operative. When the social scientist is confronted by reality, he is obliged to abandon the comfortable realm of speculation to apply some of his theories arrived at through observation -- not always with fortunate results. The checkered experience of the social sciences over the past twenty years in dealing with the unquestionably concrete problems of violence, deviance, marginalisation and petty crime are, according to Denis Szabo, clear evidence of this (Szabo, 1984). The magnificent structures created by Foucault or J.P. Aron have served only to add to the trials and errors of the different approaches to crime tried out by the grass-roots criminologists, the workers out in the field responsible on a day-to-day basis for devising and applying measures to protect society.

Szabo writes: "The ferment of change in the penal area did not come from the grass roots. It was not police officers, nor prison warders, nor judges, magistrates or criminal lawyers who took the lead in this revolution in ideas, these daring programmes of reform. It was the intellectuals -- academics full of new ideas...". Later on the author notes that the involvement in the various social policy programmes of people from the human and social sciences was becoming increasingly greater, quoting Auguste Comte that "the social science specialists, postulating that by changing the environment, man himself would be changed, were undertaking a Promethean revolution so as to know in order to be able to predict, and predict in order to be able to act" (in Szabo, 1984). But the resistance of existing structures to innovation in social matters and the crisis of confidence in science as a remedy for social problems were fuelled to a great extent by the objective inadequacy of the results (a patently ludicrous cost-benefit ratio) and above all by the failure of the concepts used in the various strategies. It is with this failure of ideas that we shall be concerning ourselves here.

Is it not likely that a similar disillusionment will follow the introduction of education policies?

We are not advocating a pragmatic activism that mixes description and demonstration, action and thought, but we want to examine whether the concepts that are everyday references in our thinking and the vocabulary that we are accustomed to use in our discussions are properly suited to solve (or help to solve) the problems posed by our present-day society. It is by no means easy to abandon a context of reflection where the word rather than the thing itself becomes the object of attention, where the theory incorporates and transposes as a matter of course the dominant ideologies, and ventures into situations where contradictions cannot be glossed over.

In the area of "multicultural education policies" where we are confronted with groups with different systems of references, such as the children of immigrant families and other minorities, are we not likely once again to end up with a stalemate? Are there good grounds for hoping that concepts such as Culture (cultural, ethnic, minority, etc.) and Migration can be of practical assistance in decision making? It is a matter of assessing the differences so as to adjust to these. The measurement of these differences implies solid benchmarks and reliable yardsticks that make comparison possible. Can we go from the Magrebi in France to the Turk in Germany and to the Pakistani in Great Britain without the risk of confusion if our yardsticks are either dissimilar or incomplete? (Bovenkerk, Kilborne, Raveau and Smith, 1979) (1).

Let us pause for a moment to consider the references made either implicitly or explicitly to the cultural differences within host societies and minority groups (immigrant or other). Since most writers also refer to acculturation, it should follow that it is clear what is meant by the original term which would seem no longer to have any meaning except when coupled with an adjective.

More than twenty years ago one of the first of these writers, E. Schils, complained of the shifts in meaning quoting as examples: "high culture, refined culture, elaborate culture, serious culture, vulgar culture, mediocre culture, middle culture, low culture, brutal culture, base culture, coarse culture" (Schils, 1961). He pointed out the extent to which value judgements underlay the use of the term. Round about the same time, J.M. Yunger attempted in this avalanche of terms to fix a few of the definitions by assigning to "sub-culture" and "counter-culture", key definitions that could be used as a reference. By the late 1960s, the futility of these efforts had been demonstrated in the United States and in Europe.

In France, there was a similar proliferation of meanings. Dumazedier and Rippert (1966) gave a number of examples of the increasing variety of associations: "working-class culture, sport culture, middle culture, academic culture, industrial culture, urban culture, mass culture, altruistic culture, mercantile culture, high culture and, of course, general culture". Bourdieu and Passeron (1964) adopt as keywords "learned culture" and "culture of the cultivated class" when it is a question of positioning the heirs to these along their social trajectory.

The dispersion of meanings was even more marked in the United States and Kroeber and Kluckhohn (1978) felt the need to compile an inventory. This jungle of definitions, where there was considerable overlapping, was reduced by them to six major categories: descriptive, historical, normative, psychological, genetic and structural. One also finds this plethora of meanings in the different schools of psycho-anthropology where culture, the action of cultivating the individual, becomes the state of the cultivated individual, the element determining the group personality and cultural identities. By extension it also becomes creative activities, behaviour matrix (Kardiner, 1969) and expression of intellectual and/or emotional life (here we are including religion and language). In the various expressions of social life that it adopts, it takes on a value, becomes imbued with ideologies and in the end assumes the same drawbacks that, in Tylor's view, ruled out use of the concept of civilisation because it had become tainted with normativeness and value judgements on the meaning of history. Bénéton (1975) adds yet another key aspect to the complexity of this "polysemous nebula" by very appropriately drawing attention to the phenomenon of borrowing (very frequent in social science as evidenced by the word "structure" and its passage from biology to linguistics and then to anthropology). The German word Kultur has affected the meaning of the English term and both have contaminated the French term. Thus it is not surprising to find Braudel (1986) stating that "a culture is a civilisation that has not yet reached its maturity, its optimum, nor ensured its growth". There is still a desire for comprehensiveness, which frequently will exist alongside judgements such as those of "maturity" and "optimum". There is also still a concern for a rank order which both hinders and bears out the temptation of the word "culture" which we would like to be neutral. Chaunu (1984) seeks to reconcile a long memory and a short history by suggesting that civilisation is "the superimposing of several cultural layers" and that its role is to "separate the cultures".

Here there are a number of essential points: the need for a comprehsive approach which is able to incorporate all the synchronic and diachronic aspects that characterise a given society and a dynamic view of the perpetual destructuring/restructuring resulting from the interaction with different environments.

This brings us back again to this interface, the point where acculturation occurs, giving rise to "the problems of the intermingling of civilisations and their works" (Bastide, 1960) and "the dialectic which then takes place needs to be kept free of any philosophical postulation in order to remain purely empirical. It presents us with a two-way flow from the superstructures to the infrastructures (and vice-versa) which produces a whole series of chain reactions, either of the values which change even to the ecological level or of the structures which are altered, thereby disrupting the set of values, standards and symbols".

When we examine the vast subject of acculturation, as summarised by Dupront (1965), we cannot fail to note the absence of any consensus as regards the initial terminologies which explains why the final conclusions are doubtful and even contradictory, that is if we can still regard them as being comparable.

The weakening of the concept of culture as the result of its being split between many different meanings is similar to the weakening of the concept of civilisation more than a century ago. There is, however, one thing that still can be learnt from this, namely the extraordinary polymorphism of the way society, within its own confines, expresses itself and, over time, makes it essential to understand the whole before attempting to explain one of its components. Although to some extent a truism, this needs repeating if we are to avoid the sin of pride of which the social sciences are accused by van den Berghe (1978). He would deny them the right to use the term "science" to describe their activities, "if by the word science we mean a logically coherent body of generalisations concerning causal relationships between observable, measurable and predictable phenomena...". "How (he asks) do sociologists get away with claiming an expertise they do not possess? Why is their bluff not called? The latter question is easy to answer: scarcely anybody does any better..." (2).

Although we are reluctant to employ the term "culture" and use it as a reference, the infinitely varied social entity to which it refers nonetheless exists. It was thus to be expected that a number of new words would be coined to replace the use of adjectives coupled with the word "culture" -- the term that emerged was "ethnicity".

It is not our intention here to trace its history -- it is still too early since the term made its first very timid appearance in 1953 in Riesman's The Lonely Crowd (Riesman, 1964). Coined in an English-speaking context, it was given a mixed reception by the disciplines within the human sciences. An extremely good analysis of this has been made by Glazer and Moynihan (1975) who raise the question: "Does (ethnicity) mean anything new or is it simply a new way of saying something old?" We shall not be summarising here the answers given by the authors, which have been quoted and discussed in a wide variety of contexts during the ten years that have elapsed since their book was published. We shall confine ourselves to the remark that, to some extent, it is a new way of describing older concepts that the term "civilisations" covered. The totality of the elements that make it up can be found in the past and the present. It is also a way of giving a new lease of life to the subjectivity/objectivity dualism -- ethnicity can be attributed by one group to another: it is thus identified; it can also be claimed by a group: thus it identifies itself. This is what governs the debate on cultural identities to which rather brief reference was made earlier. But it is also a way of taking into account the conflictual positions that will set majority and minority groups against one another. The "ethnic boundaries" (Barth, 1970), which both delimit the containers and define the contents, become the subject for research because they are more easily objectified by the conflicts engendered by these divisions.

Lastly it is a point of convergence and a required area for research for human sciences disciplines and, in particular, sociology, psychology and anthropology; its use extends into the areas of economics, political science and education sciences.

We were thus prompted to propose the definition: the awareness -- felt or recognised -- of belonging to a group related to an historical or mythical past that can be projected into a possible or utopian common destiny. It is expressed in terms of seven indicators of participation or recognition: biogenetic, territorial, linguistic, economic, religious, cultural and political (Raveau, Galap, Lirus and Lecoutre, 1977).

MINORITY GROUPS: INDICATORS OF PARTICIPATION OR RECOGNITION

We postulate therefore that a holistic approach is essential: the seven indicators identified must be present. Their absence is considered as an act of oppression through a banning of their appearance and their elimination becomes a source of conflict aimed at restoring their rightful expression. Although we do not share the excessive optimism of Gordon (in Glazer and Moynihan, 1975), who sees in ethnicity a general theory of the relationships between ethnic groups, we would mention the fact that an analysis of the socio-ethnological literature of recent years shows that close attention has been paid to this dynamic (Morin, 1980).

As de Vos (1972) has pointed out, there are cases where certain of these indicators are given extra emphasis and others ignored -- or suppressed. This may be the result of the researcher's specialisation or even the existential situation of the group which in a process of self-weighting assigns greater or lesser importance to the one or other factor, depending on the tactical requirements of the moment.

Lastly, we would emphasize the instrumental aspect of the concept. By carrying out a careful diagnosis of the groups studied and evaluating each of the factors involved (which bind the individuals together as a unit), we believe that it is possible to construct a profile of ethnicity. The value of this will be to permit point by point comparisons and, subsequently, as objective an evaluation as possible of differences in terms of distance (which may be of some use in formulating an education policy).

Coupled with the diachronic aspect that introduces and imposes history on culturalist thinking is the monitoring of the group's aspirations.

In some cases, diagrams can be useful and, in order to illustrate the importance of the time factor, we have borrowed from de Saussure (1969) the idea of the cylinder (Fig. 1). The minority that exists incorporates at a synchronic level the seven indicators expressing its ethnicity (we shall be referring here only to the concept of ethnicity enunciated by the group being studied, but this is equally true for the ethnicity attributed by the observer. The difference between the two evaluations provides an initial measurement of distance.)

At the diachronic level, the need for a common past applies to each and/or all of the indicators involved. This past may be an historical one, e.g. the black minority in the United States (or the population of the West Indies) originated from Africa (territory) and has acquired, through the slave trade, a group memory, the consequences of which will affect the other indicators. Slavery, as a reference, becomes a source of cohesion. The same applies to groups that have been victims of various forms of oppression genocides (Armenians, Jews, etc.).

It can also be that this past is a mythical one. A cultural hero may have been the founder of the community: being the descendants of Abraham or Moses becomes a definition of the Jewish people. The need to relate to a common ancestry is such that when history or myth are lacking (or grow dim) this leads to the creation by such groups of legendary characters (or situations). An exemplary attitude (sacrifice, learning, wisdom) provides posterity with a reason for its existence. The figure of Paoli in Corsica is a good example of this.

Another binding force is the sharing of aspirations. A group inspired by the past may be characterised by its future. In which case, some indicators may acquire greater importance. Typical of a "religious" minority will be the vision of a paradise or a place to be attained: "Next year in

Figure 1

DIAGRAM REPRESENTING THE COMPONENTS INVOLVED IN THE DEFINITION OF MINORITIES

Starting from the central synchronic component representing the present situation, the lower section contains the past and the upper section the aspirations.

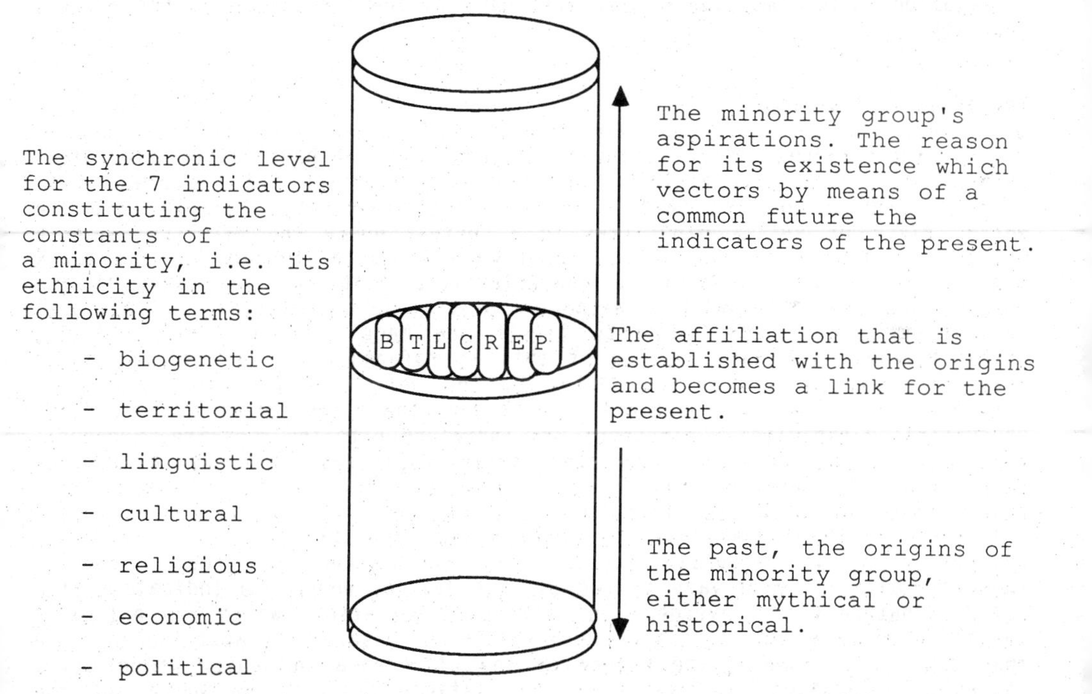

Jerusalem" was for a long time a "utopian" vision of the Jews of the Diaspora. It was achieved several decades ago. A return to Africa, for a long time, rallied the black minority in the United States around Garvey. The messianic vision so well described by Lanternari (1960) acts in this case as a factor promoting cohesion. Other indicators may also be involved in these aspirations: the vision of a classless society for many years underlay the actions of a proletarian minority and social success in economic terms (together with the processes of solidarity that this implies) has been a feature of Indian communities in Africa, Lebanese communities in the Caribbean and Chinese communities in the United States. Achieving political influence and an economic future is a driving aspiration of the Irish in Ulster.

To state that the past must be used as a foundation for the future is a platitude when it is a question of understanding the functioning of a community. However, to deprive a minority of its aspirations, to divert it from the achievement of its desires or attack its roots is to commit a form of ethnocide like that perpetrated deliberately or otherwise by many education policies... a collective memory is often obtained by displacement of another less dominant one.

Let us look now at the significance of the seven indicators adopted in the synchrony. Although always present, they are apparent to a greater or lesser degree depending on the historical situations in which the minority moves. Some will act as a stimulus in the awareness of "the era of togetherness", which is also a parameter of ethnicity: they can be weighted in relation to the importance they will have in the expression of the group's identity.

The biogenic indicator

This concerns primarily the traditional area of physical or biological anthropology. The most visible signs of the difference are the phenotypes, such as skin colour and certain morphological features. Examples are the white, black or yellow minorities in a context where the majority is of a different colour (e.g. the white minority in Rhodesia/Zimbabwe or the black minority in France). It is a characteristic that can be stated by the observer and attributed with or without a pejorative connotation. It can also be seized upon by the minority itself and made into an emblem of its distinctiveness. A good example of this is reference to the colour black: initially used in the United States by the white society as a stigma of exclusion, the term was subsequently adopted by the black community itself and energetically exploited. Blackness was therefore extolled (Cesaire, Senghor): "Black is beautiful" and even particular qualities such as a natural disposition for emotion, music, etc., were ascribed to it. It is at this point that we need to introduce the concept of distance that will differentiate the biophysical features of two population groups. This means objectivising the perceptibility of the difference. A group's opacity (non-transparence) will vary in very slight degrees where the indicators of a corporal nature will converge. In half-caste societies, which are extremely sensitive to this body language, we noted in the case of the West Indians more than ten terms denoting the nature of the difference and which amount to a series of gradations in measuring the distance between the white and the black, e.g. type of hair, facial morphology: nose, lips, eyes, skin texture and shades of colour, etc. (Raveau, Galap, Lirus and Lecoutre, 1977).

Returning to the question of establishing a profile of ethnicity, it has to be realised that this is a double profile, i.e. the one claimed by the minority group "being studied" and the one assigned by the dominant group "undertaking the study". The differences observed between the opinions on either side will provide an indication of the extent of the misconception. The disparagements from one side will often find an echo in the reactions from the other (agressivity, passivity). There are a vast number of ramifications to this assessing of other people. Preconceptions about tall people, short people, brunettes, blondes are legion. The behavioural connotations, frequently related in terms of preference or rejection, physiognomy or characterology are applied in a conscious or unconscious manner -- remember the comment of Sartre about Franco: "His ugly Latin mug" which, coming from a committed philosopher, is evidence of the prevalence of this type of assessment of other people.

The territorial indicator

This is the geographical reference to a place shared by members of the group. We have seen that this can be historicised as an origin (the children of Zion) or as an aspiration (the return home of immigrant minorities in Europe). It can also take the form of a "native heath", where the person's real roots lie and which, through the influence of the imagination and experience (odour, flavour, colour), assumes special significance. Ethnology has taught us, as a result of the work of Lorenz (1970) and Ardrey (1966) the fundamental significance that mammals and primates in particular attach to their living space. Goffman (1972) situates the rituals of social interaction within measured spaces. A threat to these provokes anxiety; an invasion, aggressiveness; an abandonment, nostalgia; a return, security.

And lastly, in this context, the concept of boundaries or limits takes on its full significance (Barth, 1970). The ghetto, with its aspects of protection (gregariousness for the purpose of defence) and vulnerability (the hypervisibility of the community becoming a provocation for the surrounding environment), becomes the symbol underpinning the assembled minority. We know that its dispersion is often the prelude to its disappearance. This may happen spontaneously through assimilation (disappearance of the Asian district in Cuba) (Helly, 1979). In some instances well-intentioned city planners or impatient politicians insist on breaking up concentrations of members of a minority. The main result in most cases is merely to shift the problem rather than solve it, as would seem to have been the case with the policy of geographic desegregation in the United States.

The linguistic indicator

Here we are dealing with a dimension that is more difficult to evaluate. Physical or territorial visibility lends itself to a certain degree of objectivity as regards its measurement; however, it is far more difficult to quantify the possibility or impossibility of intercomprehension with the dominant milieu, the acceptance of a dialogue conveyed through a common medium or the desire for a specificity that prevents individual susceptibility being decoded by others.

The language barrier is obvious in the case of a first generation immigrant community; it becomes far less evident when the minority is a long-established one (and in some instances even longer-established than the dominant invader, as is the case in Great Britain for a Welshman vis-à-vis an Englishman, or in France for a Breton vis-à-vis a Frenchman). The accent that reveals a person's origin is concealed by those who want to "pass" but stressed in a provocative manner by those who often have no other way of emphasizing the fact that they are different.

What is also worth noting is the process of contamination of this indicator by the remainder, e.g. the invention of "black English" by the black minority to show its desire to distance itself from the dominant language as well. The invention of different forms of slang by economic minorities is evidence of this same desire to be incomprehensible for others.

A person may also identify himself as a member of a group by means of a special form of communication, the non-verbal language known as body language. Secret societies are in a way minorities and they make frequent use of this.

Lastly, it is interesting to note the way minorities revive languages that have fallen into disuse in order to demonstrate that they have achieved their ethnicity. Hebrew, the national language of Israel, is perhaps a more appropriate example than Gaelic in Ireland. A "regional" language or dialect is an even more striking example: the Breton minority is reviving its language as are the Provençaux, the Alsatians, the Basques and the Catalans. This effort of "revivalist" recreation underlines the need for a specific and original form of communication which, if it no longer exists, is reinvented and, if it never did exist, is invented. The Creoles are an unusual case in this respect: the black minorities of the Caribbean are rehabilitating this embryonic language and making it a vehicle of communication; in order to teach it, they have written it down and are providing it with a syntax and a grammar. Its creation is becoming a symbol. Each minority endeavours to individualise its form of expression, either by maintaining an original language, or by using their own dialect forms of the language they share with the majority or, failing that, creating a new language.

The reactions of the dominant group to these strange and therefore foreign modes of expression are often hostile and this attitude is clearly expressed in instructions to "speak white" or "speak like everybody else". Bilingualism is not easily tolerated, even in Canada -- it causes a division (which in some cases is the obvious intention).

The cultural indicator

This remains ambiguous. It can in everyday language serve as a reference confirming a difference. We shall be using it here in its most restrictive and "neutral" sense (Bénéton, 1975). We shall be including, among other things, specific ways of enforcing authority inside and outside the family, the way male and female roles operate, sexual behaviour patterns, types of upbringing and education, relationships with the environment (cuisine, dress, housing, leisure activities), the principles governing relationships between individuals (manners and etiquette), etc. All of the behaviour patterns originate from a need to adapt to a given environment, end up by appearing as conditioning factors separate from the context that has produced them and become more symbolic than instrumental.

Here again, it must be remembered that these indices are connoted by all the other indicators: when we refer to black culture, is it the phenotype that is of prime importance or the mode of dress? An attempt has to be made to separate these and this is possible through a study of the community where the biophysical indicator has little or no incidence. Intolerance is generated by conflict between different customs. It is not the foreigner's noise or cooking smells that disturb his neighbours but the fact that his noise or his cooking smells are different, and therefore noticeable. Research that we carried out on Haïtians in France (Bastide, Raveau and Morin, 1974) showed that both communities were equally indisposed when they could smell the odours created by the other, whereas they did not notice, or no longer noticed their own cooking smells. Douyon in Canada has highlighted the conflicts created by different ways of bringing up young children. Families in the Haïtian community, who slap their children when they misbehave, are regarded as "child beaters" by their Canadian neighbours (who use other means of discipline) and reported by them to the authorities. This type of conflict does not arise in a ghetto but only when there is a mixture of races living together (an example of the territorial factor having an influence).

A minority, in addition to the modes of existence that it inherits from the past, creates and invents daily particular ways of dealing with the conditions of life that the majority imposes on it (or offers it). There is a culture of poverty which, whenever it becomes intolerable, is used to justify the dominant classes' large-scale isolation of this minority, in hospices during the 19th century and in today's shanty towns that have become ghettos.

The religious indicator

The religious indicator is often combined with the cultural indicator. However, in this context, it seems to us necessary to keep it separate: the Jewish minority in Europe or in the United States, the Islamic minority in Europe or in the East and the Christian minority in the Middle East illustrate how important such collective demonstrations of a particular faith can be for the purpose of identifying groups. It is also the indicator that is most deeply imbued with temporality. It is often an explanation of origins and a promise of future redemption. It may become a means of compensation and increase in importance when oppression prevents the operation of other indicators. The example of Ireland or Poland demonstrates how powerful this form of expression can be as a rallying point. The hope of a messiah cherished by oppressed peoples is, in Lanternari's view, a universal form of defence. Here again, in addition to the element of heritage there is also an element of borrowing or creation. Did not the black Muslims in the United States choose this form of religious expression in order to differentiate themselves from the Christianity of the white majority? The black churches in the United States had already transformed and adapted Protestantism for this minority but they needed to go further, differentiate themselves to a greater extent in order to feel more at ease in an even more distinctive community. This dynamic is quoted as an explanatory factor in the theory which maintains that Christianity owes much of its success during its early stages to the slave or destitute minorities of the Roman Empire (Bastide, 1935). Has not the creation of what we now call sects represented attempts to win support on the part of individuals wishing to band together in order to express their distinctiveness more effectively? Their success is understandable when the other ethnicity indicators are at work and their failure demonstrates that the operation of a single indicator is not sufficient to bind individuals together permanently in order to structure a minority.

We have, of course, so far avoided defining too precisely the content of the word "religious"; however, if we adopt the connotation of faith and the right to hope, and the expression of a shared affection unsullied by an overly oppressive rationality, it is not difficult to find this religiosity running through many minority groups and even without any church structure or the existence of appointed clergy.

The economic indicator

A distinctive feature of a community will often be its form of economic activity, the types of commercial dealings it has with its environment, its wealth or its poverty. An object of ostracism when the essential activity is frowned on by the majority (e.g. the Jewish minority: usury in a Christian society), it will be an object of envy if it involves a particular expertise. Minorities can be analysed in terms of economic infrastructure; their subsequent financial success and social success are effective means of defence against forms of oppression directed against the minority's other forms of expression -- the most obvious example being that of the Jews in the West. However, the price to be paid for this is an increase in the visibility of the group within its environment and an increase in the forms of oppression. In some cases, wealth can be the starting point for the creation of an affluent minority and (like poverty too) it can give rise to a spatial segregation (residential area), a particular form of religious expression (the "fashionable" churches) and particular cultural rituals (marriages of money, etc.).

It may seem paradoxical but, while as Lewis (1972) says, poverty creates its own culture, every established minority has an economic specificity. This may be determinant or sequential to a greater or lesser degree but it is always present and closely linked to the other indicators. For example, trade is a specific activity of the Chinese in the Indian Ocean, the Indians in Eastern Africa and the Lebanese in the Caribbean area and it demonstrates that the survival of the minority depends on the exercise of a particular economic activity. The question of cause and effect is not our prime concern here: whether this economic activity engenders, structures and justifies the existence of the minority or whether it is merely a necessary adjunct to its survival is, strictly speaking, of secondary importance. The main fact is that this activity exists and must be taken into account when analysing the "metabolism" of a minority.

The political indicator

Here we shall be using this term in its primary sense meaning the organisation and administration of a community and the ways in which power is acquired. We have seen in the case of the "religion" indicator that there was a certain see-saw movement with the political dimension (present-day Poland being an example). This channel of expression is inevitably involved in the problems posed by a minority group's resistance to oppression. The political indicator is constantly involved in the tactics of defence and the strategies for achieving progress. Léonard (1961-64) has shown how the Protestant minority in France has systematically been amongst the opposition, with the dominant authority being Catholic. This goes some way to explaining the existence of an alliance between this form of expression of Christianity and atheistic movements. Since this form of expression was the one most visible to those in power, it was the one most frequently outlawed. There are many overt and covert bans that are imposed, for example, on the Indian minorities in the United States and foreign minorities in Europe.

It is worth noting that the political aspect can sometimes take on a messianic character: the promise of a classless society without discrimination is very much akin to the promise of a land without evil that captured the imagination of the Guarani minority in Brazil (Bastide, 1960a). The dualism oppression/resistance that characterises the struggle of various minorities to assert their rights can be analysed in terms of social classes, as is amply illustrated by the recent history of the Equal Rights Amendment in the United States.

WHAT, THEN, CONSTITUTES A MINORITY?

Coloured minority (biophysical indicator), local or regional minority (territorial indicator), linguistic minority, cultural minority, religious minority, economic minority and political minority -- seven descriptions headed by one of the seven indicators that we have discussed all too briefly. Behind each one of them, however, will always be found the other six, although their presence will be more or less apparent depending on the particular case in point. The unwillingness of the English-speaking majority in Canada to accept the French language in Quebec led to a conflict where all of these indicators were involved. The fact that the solution was political did not prevent all of the other forms of expression playing a part, with each assuming in turn what appeared to be the major role. The Catholic Church, which during the two centuries of oppression had been the lynch-pin of this minority's resistance, found itself stripped of its role which was taken over by the political parties and the cultural institutions.

During the course of this analysis explaining the indicators and illustrating their functions we have placed the emphasis mainly on the ethnic aspect of minorities. The reasons for our choice of references are obvious. The social sciences have emphasized extreme concepts, degrees of maximum strangeness, where the gaps are widest as is the case in the cultural or racial areas (to which here we have applied the term "biogenetic"). In the remarkable book by Gould and Kolb (1964) we find, for example, a definition of a minority as "a social group which, within a larger cultural and social system, claims or is accorded special status in terms of a complex of ethnic traits which it exhibits or is believed to exhibit". The meaning sometimes needs to be broadened to include within the relationship between dominant and dominated other social groups that do not necessarily have this ethnic connotation.

The concept of minority is still somewhat vague. The concern of those international organisations that have endeavoured to define it has been one of protection -- a noble but somewhat restrictive aim: anxiousness not to offend pluriethnic nations or to create problems by making a study of them is largely responsible for the timid attempts that have been made (Azcarate, 1945; Bagley, 1950). Is a legalistic approach a productive one for describing an entity that seems to us to have more to do with the socio-cultural and the psychological?

What are the preconditions for acceding to the status of a minority?

First of all, to be sufficiently numerous to have the ability to reproduce a number of linguistic, cultural or ethnic traits. There is considerable vagueness as to Figure 2 which it is no longer possible to retain the ability "to reproduce". It is somewhat like the problem that exercises geographers, i.e. how big does a piece of land entirely surrounded by water have to be for it to be regarded as a continent and not an island. Can the related psycho-sociological concept of insularity be applied equally to Australia, Great Britain, Guernsey, Borneo and Sark? Have the 150 Hurons in Quebec the same claim to the status of a minority as the 30 million blacks in the United States or the 50 000 Catalans in France?

The second requirement is not to be "dominant", but here again the concept is vague: is this a question of demographic, economic, political, cultural and religious domination or all of these at once? This power relationship is essential as a means of highlighting the differences but do all differences engender minority situations?

A minority cannot exist without there being a majority. To define oneself as a member of a minority means a wish to see oneself as different from a larger entity. It is a psycho-sociological reactivity to the oppressive character of a neighbouring unit.

In addition, an important question is whether there are fixed and immutable minorities or simply successive transitions to minority phases in accordance with the aims of actions or reactions and their strategies.

We have therefore proposed ways of defining a minority on the basis of what seem to us to be the constituant elements. The danger would be to assume that this fragmented analysis conveys the entire living essence of a community. Other factors more commonly taken into account, such as the cohesiveness of the group and its patterns of leadership, must not be overlooked.

However, we do not think that a classification of the various types of minority can be based on generalities such as "foreign minority" or "Jewish minority". It is rather by attempting to weight the seven indicators referred to earlier within a context of temporality and by establishing a specific profile that we would be able to reach an understanding both from within such communities through the values they attribute to themselves and from outside through an analysis of the opinion of the dominant society. In this way the distances can be measured and an assessment made. Migrations produce minorities and Sowell (1981) in his study of ethnic groups in the United States was able to demonstrate the extent to which their evolution was influenced by the circumstances governing their appearance. How long they had been established is one of the factors that needs to be taken into consideration but it is not a determinant in forecasting success or failure in economic terms, for example. The scale that was established by ranking

Figure 2

EXAMPLE OF TWO PROFILES OF ETHNICITY ESTABLISHED BY THE WEST INDIANS IN FRANCE (A) BY THE FRENCH ON THE WEST INDIANS IN FRANCE (B)

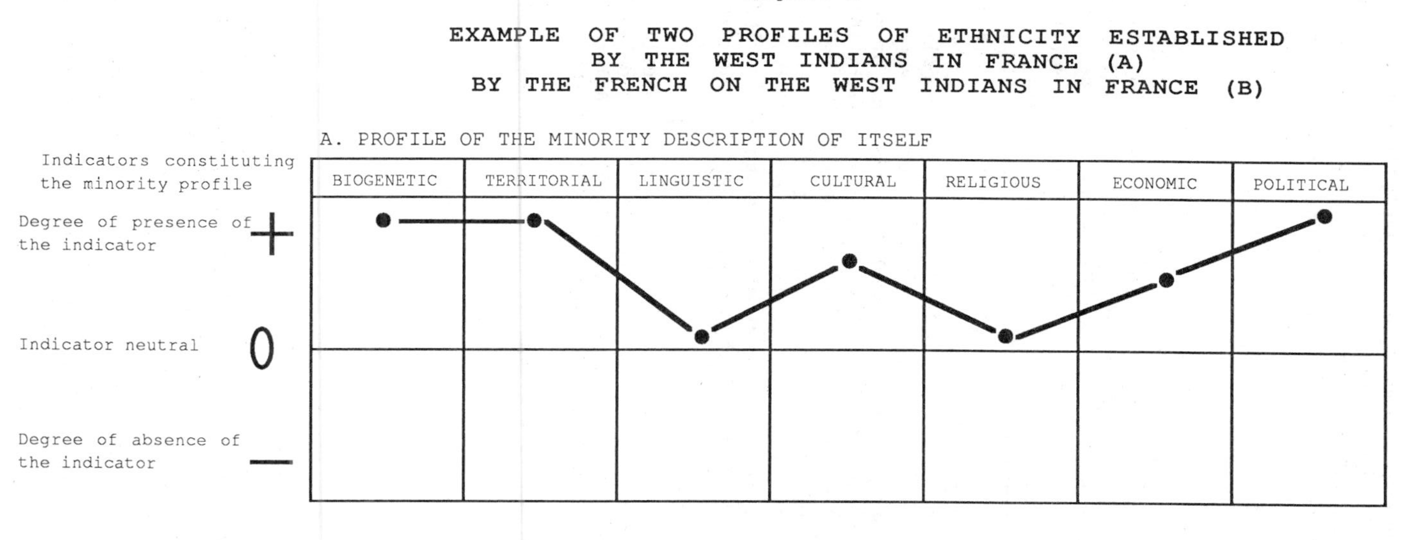

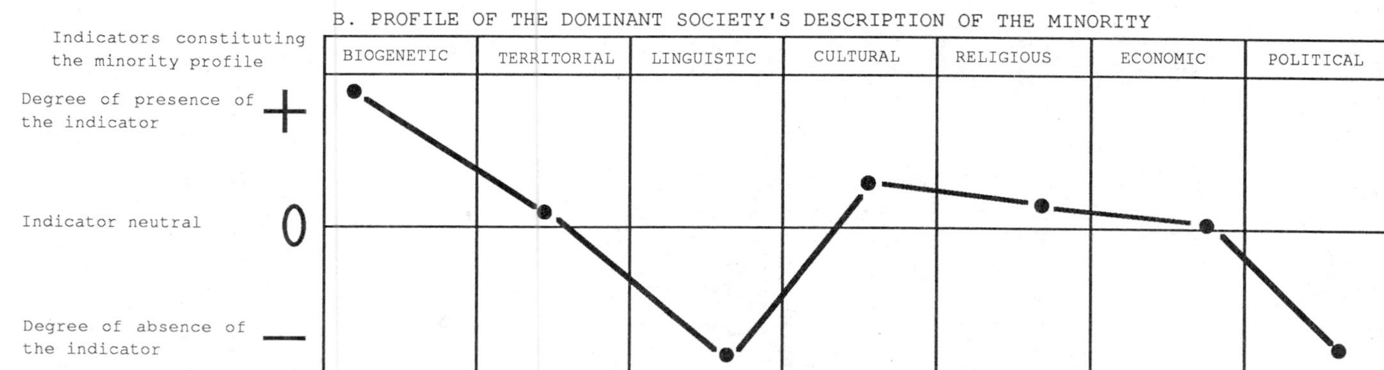

A MISMATCH BETWEEN THE TWO PROFILES INDICATES A SOURCE OF FRUSTRATION.

average family incomes clearly shows that the most recent arrivals are not the poorest at the stage of the second and third generations. In this case the economic indicator is expressing the other indicators of references. "The educational panacea is indetermined by the history of groups like the Jews, the Chinese and the Japanese who first rose by their labor and their business and only later on could afford to send their children to college" (Sowell, 1981).

The reasons that motivate the departure of migrants need to be taken into account when comparing the vast flow of economic migrants with that of political migrants. Here again these factors, although important, are still not determinant. Referring to the children of immigrants (for the most part Polish, Italian and Spanish) Sauvy (1953) wrote, "were it not for the occupational segregation, assimilation would be virtually total". Noiriel (1984) pointed out that "in France one out of every three inhabitants is a first, second or third generation immigrant" and that "in the 1920s this country had the highest immigration rate in the world", but admitted that at present there was a marked atmosphere of intolerance. The new immigrants of "Maghrebi", "African" or "West Indian" ethnic origin, by their profiles, objectivise new distances that create new problems. Bouneb (1985), in what is an outstanding work, demonstrates the determining role of the phenotype of the young French-Muslim in the success or otherwise of his process of adaptation: the more he resembles a Frenchman and is therefore less noticeable, the better his integration. We wrote as one of the conclusions to a piece of research on West Indians in France that "depending on whether you are white or black (and to what degree), you will be considered as a somebody or a nobody". Thus there are degrees of intolerance within the host society, despite the fact that it is itself not homogeneous.

Unlike the United States where Sowell could study the adjustment process of the nine largest minority groups without analysing the Anglo-Saxon majority, it would not seem possible in Europe to overlook the indigenous population: it is as important to establish the ethnic profile of the host society as it is that of the immigrant minorities. Having thus defined both protagonists, it is then possible to initiate dialogues and education policies.

NOTES

1. National or international comparability requires extreme care in insuring that the areas of research are clearly defined and the methods and techniques clearly specified. But the most difficult aspect of all is the theoretical basis underlying the problem and it is this that is the most important in this context.)

2. He also says, "Like the rain maker, all the sociologist has to do is convince enough people that his sustenance is a relatively small price to pay for the virtual certainty that he cannot do any harm and the hope that he might do some good...").

BIBLIOGRAPHY

ARDREY R., Le territoire, Paris, Stock, 1966.

AZCARATE J., League of nation and national minorities. Washington, UNO, 1945.

BAGLEY J.J., General principles and problems in the international protection of minorities genese, Washington, UNO, 1950.

BARTH F., Ethnic Groups and Boundaries. The Social Organisation of Culture Difference, London, G. Allen and Unwin, 1970.

BASTIDE R., Eléments de sociologie religieuse, A. Colin, Paris, 1935.

BASTIDE R., Les religions africaines au Brésil, PUF, Paris, 1960a.

BASTIDE R., "Problèmes de l'entrecroisement des civilisations et de leurs oeuvres", in GURWITCH G., Traité de sociologie, PUF, Paris, 1960b.

BASTIDE R., RAVEAU F., MORIN F., Les Haïtiens en France, Mouton, Paris, La Haye, 1974, 232 pp.

BENETON P., Histoire de mots: culture et civilisations, Presses de la Fondation nationale des Sciences politiques, Paris, 1975.

BOUNEB K., "Adaptation des Français musulmans", Thèse de 3ème cycle, 1985.

BOVENKERK F., KILBORNE B., RAVEAU F., SMITH D., "Comparative aspects of research on discrimination against non-white citizens in Great Britain, France and the Netherlands", in Problems in international comparative research in the social sciences, Pergamon Press, Oxford; UNESCO, 1979 -- Chap. 7, pp. 105-122.

BOURDIEU P., PASSERON J.C., Les héritiers, Paris, Editions de Minuit, 1964.

BRAUDEL F., Civilisation matérielle et capitalisme, Vol. 1, 2 and 3, Flammarion, Paris, 1986.

CHAUNU P., L'historien dans tous ses états, Perrin, Paris, 1984.

DE VOS G., "Social stratification and ethnic pluralism: an overview from the perspective of psychological anthropology", in Race, 1972, pp. 435-460.

DOUYON E., Information communicated privately.

DUMAZEDIER J., RIPPERT A., Loisir et culture, Le Seuil, Paris, 1966.

DUPRONT A., "De l'acculturation", in Grands thèmes. XIIème Congrès international de Sciences historiques, Horn, Vienna, 1965.

GLAZER N., MOYNIHAN D.P.: Ethnicity, Theory and Experience, Harvard University Press, Cambridge (Mass.), 1975.

GOFFMAN E., Interaction ritual. Essays on face-to-face behaviour, Penguin Books, London, 1972.

GORDON M., "Toward a general theory of racial and ethnic group relations", in GLAZER N., MOYNIHAN D.P., pp. 84-110.

GOULD J., KOLB W., A Dictionary of the Social Sciences, The Free Press, New York; Unesco, 1964.

HELLY D., Idéologie et ethnicité, Presses de l'Université de Montréal, 1979.

KARDINER A., L'individu dans sa société. Essai d'anthropologie psychanalytique, Gallimard, Paris, 1969.

KROEBER A.L., KLUCKHOHN C., Culture: a critical review of concepts and definitions, Kraus Reprint Co., Milwood (N.Y.), 1978.

LANTERNARI, Les religions des peuples opprimés, Maspéro, Paris, 1960.

LEONARD E.G., 1961-1964: Histoire générale du protestantisme français, PUF, Paris.

LEWIS O., Les enfants de Sanchez. Autobiographie d'une famille mexicaine, Paris, Gallimard, 1972.

LORENZ K., Essais sur le comportement animal et humain. Les leçons de l'évolution de la théorie du comportement, Paris, Le Seuil, 1970.

MORIN F., "Identité ethnique et ethnicité. Analyse critique des travaux anglo-saxons", in TAP P. (Ed.), Identité collective et champs sociaux. Production et affirmation de l'identité, Privat, Toulouse, 1980, pp. 55-58.

MORIN F., "Présentation de Minorités, revendication d'identité ethnique et mouvements nationalistes", in Pluriel, 1982/83, Nos. 32/33, pp. 3-11.

NOIRIEL G.,"Histoire de la migration en France. Note sur un enjeu", in Actes de la Recherche en Sciences sociales, 1984, N° 54, pp. 72-76.

RAVEAU F., GALAP J., LIRUS J., LECOUTRE J.P., "Phénotype et adaptation", in Ethnologie française, 1977, N° 7, pp. 255-276.

RIESMAN D., La foule solitaire. Anatomie de la société moderne (translated from the US work The Lonely Crowd), Arthaud, Paris, 1964.

SAUSSURE F. de, Cours de linguistique générale, Payot, Paris, 1969.

SAUVY A., in GIRARD A., STOETZEL J.: Français et immigrés, PUF, Paris, 1953, P. XVI., INED, Cahier n° 19.

SCHILS E., JACOB N. (Ed.), Culture for the millions, D. Van Nostrand, Princeton, 1961.

SOWELL T., Ethnic America. A history, Basic Books, New York, 1981.

SZABO D., "Révolution permanente et éternel renouvellement: la criminologie en situation" in Continuité et rupture dans les sciences sociales au Québec, Presses universitaires de Montréal, 1984.

TAPINOS G., L'économie des migrations internationales, A. Colin, Paris, 1974.

THOMAS W.I., ZANIECKI F., The Polish peasant in Europe and America, Free Press, New York, 1918-1920.

UNESCO, The cultural integration of immigrants, Paris, 1958.

VAN DEN BERGHE P.L., Man in Society, Elsevier, New York, 1978.

Commentary by Françoise MORIN

University of Toulouse (France)

I quite agree with Mr. Raveau that words get flogged to death and that considerable confusion reigns in the vocabulary of social sciences. However, I would have preferred him to take as an example of this conceptual vagueness the term "identity", which is much more of a problem today than the word "culture". Because it is used in all disciplines, the concept of "identity" has acquired so many meanings that it is now of little practical use. Yet it is one of the key concepts in the current problem of minorities.

Mr. Raveau himself contributes to this lack of conceptual precision, since according to him the term "ethnicity" is only a "new word coined to replace the use of adjectives coupled with the word 'culture'". And a few lines further on he tells us that it is also "a new way of describing older concepts that the term 'civilisations' covered". If that were the case, then the words "culture", "civilisation" and "ethnicity" would be synonyms. But although the history of the first two terms (1) does show that since the time of their formation during the enlightenment they have often been given the same meaning and sometimes used interchangeably, they can by no means be said to have the same meaning as the third term, "ethnicity". The latter is a recent concept, first used in the United States in the 1950s and widely employed over the past fifteen years to define the dynamic and often circumstantial processes connected with claims to ethnic identity. So I do not agree with Mr. Raveau that "there has been a failure of concepts", since those concepts do not have the function he attributes to them, i.e. that of "solving the problems posed by our present-day society". Concepts are tools, and they have to be constantly sharpened and brought up to date (even if this involves "deconstructing" them, as Africanists are doing now with the concept of the "ethnic group") (2) in order to work out an operational problematic approach -- an approach unfortunately lacking in Mr. Raveau's paper.

On the other hand, I should like to stress that ambiguity may arise when specialists, while referring to the same basic scientific literature and therefore to its concepts, often understand them differently because they themselves belong to different societies and speak different languages. To illustrate this, I should like to quote the example of an international conference (3) on the same theme as this one in Paris (i.e. minorities and migrants), held in Berlin in 1982 and attended by both European and American specialists. During the discussions on the very first day we realised that considerable linguistic confusion reigned. The Americans talked about "ethnic and racial groups" and could not understand why the French talked about "national minorities and migrant workers". Behind this linguistic problem lay the differences in national histories and ideologies. It is difficult to use the word "race" in French because it is a negative term associated with racialism; while the word ethnie is used to describe societies in remote parts of the world, not people living in France. Not only does this word have too exotic a flavour, but recent French history (and in particular the use made of the ethnic ideologies of regionalist movements by the Nazi occupiers during the war) means that it is still taboo.

To add to the conceptual confusion there were our differing images of the nation and thus of national and ethnic identities. The United States recognises that it is "a nation of immigrants" and an "ethnic mosaic"; hence the notion of "hyphenated identity", which enables American Jews, Black Americans, Italian Americans etc. to claim this double identity and to campaign for recognition of their rights in the national context. France, on the other hand, the "Republic One and Indivisible", rejects plurality and mistrusts diversity. Because a claim to be a French Breton, a French Jew or a French Arab is inconceivable in the national context, some minority groups, particularly territorial minorities, have in recent years been calling for more than just a say in their own affairs and claiming the right to manage those affairs independently or even as a self-governing nation. So it is understandable that when American and French researchers meet to discuss ethnicity they should find themselves talking at cross-purposes. The former understand the word in terms of claims to equal rights to education or employment, but in the context of American law and the United States constitution. The latter are referring to movements which often challenge and defy the State and its laws and constitution (e.g. French as the sole national language), not to mention those (like the Basque, Catalan and Occitan movements) that reject the French frontiers.

So confusion may arise between researchers belonging to different cultures and national contexts, even if they use the same scientific vocabulary, since they understand it according to their own national situations. So I believe that at an international conference like this one, each researcher should make clear the national context from which he comes and to which he is referring. As Europeans we may share more or less the same historical fabric, but we still have different concepts of the State. For example, there is nothing resembling French Jacobinism in Great Britain or in Spain, and this has to be taken into account in comparing education policies or studying cultural policies with regard to ethnic minorities.

My second comment on Mr. Raveau's paper concerns his manifest concern with scientism. After mentioning the founders of positivism, Durkheim and Comte, he sets out to evaluate ethnicity, which, according to him, "is expressed in terms of indicators of participation -- or recognition -- which are biogenetic, territorial, linguistic, economic, religious, cultural and political". He believes that these seven indicators will enable him to construct a profile of ethnicity, the value of which will be "to permit point-by-point comparisons and, subsequently, as objective an evaluation as possible of differences in terms of distance". Speaking of these indicators, he emphasises that "physical or territorial visibility lends itself to a certain degree of objectivity as regards its measurement", whereas "the cultural indicator remains ambiguous", and is more difficult to quantify. What is the purpose of these measurements? Mr. Raveau says that the weighting of these seven indicators and the establishment of a profile of ethnicity allows a typology of minorities to be defined and measurements made of the distances between the profile drawn from the "inside" by the community itself and that drawn from the "outside" by the dominant society.

What would be the use of this typology and this measurement of distances? To draw up a scale or hierarchy of the minorities? To show that there are strong and weak ethnicities? That some minorities have ethnicities which are a handicap because they are "too visible" and thus difficult to integrate? Mr. Raveau does not answer these questions but at the end of his paper he proposes that the ethnic profile of the host country should also be established. The comparison of these two profiles (minority and host society) should make it "possible to initiate dialogues and education policies".

I do not think that dialogue can be based on profiles, nor that education policies can be constructed by comparing these profiles; for the latter say nothing about the relative strengths of the dominant society and the minorities, and in no case allow their interactional dynamic to be grasped, nor an analysis made of the crisis factors that lead to the emergence of the ethnicity in question. Indeed, to talk about emergence is to adopt a dynamic approach to ethnicity, i.e. the one which many English-speaking authors (4) call "situational". This approach goes beyond measurement of the content of ethnicity, and focuses on studying the situations in which the ethnic groups interact. These situations engender the ethnic frontiers governing the identities which a group adopts or which are imposed on it by others. This dynamic approach helps to explain why ethnicity may flourish or decline according to the fluctuations of historical, economic, social and political circumstances in which the ethnic groups find themselves.

Although Mr. Raveau never precisely defines his approach, it does not appear to be the one just described. He mentions the diachronic aspect of ethnicity (whence cylinder diagram illustrating the time factor), but he does not show why a minority group is induced to refer to a historical or mythological past, nor does he analyse the mechanisms that lead it to construct a project for a common future. His quantitative approach (which here takes the form of measurements, construction of profiles and typologies, etc.) reminds me of the objectivist approach to ethnicity developed by some authors (5), who start from the principle that every ethnic group is a cultural unit characterised by a certain number of objective traits (Mr. Raveau's seven indicators). This attributive and categorial approach to the ethnic group obscures any dynamic interaction with others (in this case with the dominant society) and makes for a rigid conception of ethnicity. This is true of Mr. Raveau's cylindrical model, when he says that "the synchronic level for the seven indicators constituting the constants of a minority" represents its ethnicity. On two occasions in his paper, he emphasises that "the seven indicators must always be present". Even if one of them predominates over the others, as in the case of coloured minorities or territorial minorities, "the other six will always be present, more or less apparent".

Depending on whether the objectivist or the situational view of ethnicity is adopted, we can understand why one or other indicator is present or absent. Take the Occitan case, for instance. If the objective signs of Occitanity are listed, they turn out to be "minor" matters. The language is now no more than a _patois_ spoken by a few peasants, the territory never existed and the culture is gradually disappearing. So the indicators are weak, not to say non-existent. But if Occitan ethnicity is seen in the light of its interactional relationship with a dominant society, i.e. that of the centralised State which has imposed the French language and French culture and manages the economic and socio-political area from Paris, refusing to acknowledge its specific history, it is easier to understand how the _langue d'oc_ became a _patois_, Occitania's history a blank page and the "country" a meridional region with all the negative ethnic connotations that this entails. Ethnicity then turns into political awareness of this power relationship, and this leads the Occitans to try to recover the stolen identity of which they have been robbed, learn their language anew, improvise a history and fabricate a country often more mythical than real.

So the important thing is not to wonder whether we are concerned with 1, 2 or 7 indicators of Occitan ethnicity, but to analyse this process of improvisation which has used "hibernated" residues to transform a culture from something disdained into an emblem. But in order to understand the dynamics of this minority enterprise, it is essential, above all, to study the dominant societies and the history of their linguistic, cultural and economic policies; and in looking at regional cultures and ethnic minorities, to ask why some States, like Mexico, are today adopting a policy of ethnicity management, or why other countries, like France, have no multiculturalist policy.

Indeed, in the context of this meeting on "educational policies and minority social groups", analysis of the dominant society cannot be disregarded. So long as France does not acknowledge itself to be a multi-ethnic society composed not only of migrant communities but also of territorial (Breton, Basque, Occitan, etc.) and non-territorial communities (Jews, Armenians, Gypsies, North African repatriates, etc.), would-be multicultural education policies will continue to relegate the latest arrivals.

On the other hand, if it is officially acknowledged that France is a multicultural country, then from primary school on children can learn how the various communities in France live and move and have their being. Then the "difference" of each latest migrant group, that difference which today raises so many problems, would be merely one distinguishing feature among others.

NOTES AND REFERENCES

1. BENETON Ph.: _Histoire de mots : culture et civilisation_, Paris, Presses de la Fondation nationale des sciences politiques, 1975.

2. AMSELLE J.L., ELIKIA M'Bokolo (Eds): _Au coeur de l'ethnie : ethnie, tribalisme et Etat en Afrique_, Paris, Edition de la Découverte, 1985.

3. FRIED C. (Ed.) _Minorities: Community and Identity_, Berlin, Springer-Verlag, Dahlem Konferenzen, 1983.

4. This approach to ethnicity is adopted, in particular, by BARTH F., _Ethnic Groups and Boundaries_, Boston, Little Brown Co., 1969; COHEN A., _Urban Ethnicity_, New York, Harper and Row, 1974; BENNET J. (Ed.), _The New Ethnicity: Perspectives in Ethnology_,

Saint Paul, Minn., West Publishing Co., 1975; and EPSTEIN A.L., Ethos and Identity, three studies in ethnicity, London, Tavistock, 1978.

5. The same concept is found in: NAROLL R., "On ethnic unit classification", Current Anthropology, Vol. 5, N° 4, 1964, pp. 283-312. ISAAC H., "Basic Group Identity: The idols of the tribe", in GLAZER N. and MOYNIHAN D. (Eds.), Ethnicity: theory and experience, Cambridge, Harvard University Press, 1975, pp. 29-52.

5. FROM "IMMIGRANTS" TO "MINORITIES"

by
Abdelmalek SAYAD
Centre de Sociologie Européenne,
Ecole des Hautes Etudes en Sciences Sociales, Paris

Although immigration has long featured in French population history, and in the demographic and social history of labour, its contemporary terminology is relatively recent. Even more recent (and still very tentative) is today's shift from the expressions immigration and migrant (as in "migrant workers", "migrant populations", "migrant families", "migrant colonies", "communities", etc.) to the expression minorities, as in "ethnic minorities", "cultural minorities", "economic minorities", -- doubtless by contrast with minorities that can be described as "historic" -- "foreign minorities" (or of foreign extraction), minorities with no territorial base -- here again doubtless by contrast with "national" minorities or minorities for which a territory of origin can be assigned -- "allogeneous" minorities as opposed to those who could be described as "indigenous", and so on. The term "minority" used instead of "migrant" group, community or colony is highly popular and socially acceptable nowadays because it is so very ambiguous, i.e. it can mean several things at once which the user generally declines to specify.

Before we accept "minority", or the way it is nowadays used purely for convenience, the term should logically be scrutinised in regard to the various meanings attached to it and the various uses to which it can be put. "Minority" should not be confined to mere recording of a given situation, or worse, to the social categorisation it entails. In this it behaves no differently from a whole range of other terms (including "marginality" and "marginalisation") one of whose most objective effects is to bring about as naïvely and naturally as can be (at the same time as putting a name to something in the usual way) what amounts to a form of social classification.

To restore its dynamic meaning of a process of identification, self-identification, self-definition or self-assertion, we must look back to the original mechanisms producing the minority condition, rather than merely describe or just take note of it. "Minority" logically contrasts with "majority", as "dominated" contrasts with "dominant". But if the expression is not to be an absolute, an abstraction, or an attribute detached from the conditions in which it is effectively applied, it would be better to specify on each occasion in what respect a minority position is being referred to. To be in a "minority" absolutely (i.e. in all relationships and all fields of existence) would ultimately mean no longer to exist or no longer to exist independently -- to depend for one's existence on others. It would also involve receiving and accepting (with no alternative) the designation "minority" as given and imposed by others -- to be defined by others (hereto-definition instead of self-definition) as being in a "minority". Conversely, to define oneself willingly as being in a "minority" (always in respect of some specific relationship, according to some criterion for identification and distinction, as an emblem or standard to rally around), is to affirm one's existence as such, proclaim one's independence and guard against any identification with the others. It is to choose the criterion by which one regards oneself as in a "minority". Those two ways of being in a "minority" are clearly poles apart, contradictory in all points. The populations they concern are different. So are the historical backgrounds leading up to the formation of the two kinds of "minority" position, the relationships with respect to those positions and the ways of conforming to them, i.e. of behaving (the ways of assuming the "minority" condition and the ways of behaving in that condition).

What is the significance of the lexical shift from "immigrant groups" to "minorities"? Does it really correspond to any actual change observable in the internal structure of the immigrant population, or in the situation of that population within French society? If so, the reasons must lie in parallel trends in the morphology of the populations concerned (demographic, socio-occupational, cultural or behavioural structures). Further, since they are very closely bound up with them, they must lie also in the system of relationships that the populations maintain with the society of immigration and, correlatively, with the society of emigration (systems of attitudes towards one or other society, systems in inverse relationship with one another).

An opposite yet complementary approach would be to look less at internal change within the immigrant population and more at the society actually producing the language and the lexical changes in it. In other words, is the vocabulary changing more because of changes in society than of changes in immigration? The different ways in which society designates what it is not and has no wish to be, and that which is not it (i.e. what is foreign) and does not wish to be it, are only the reflection of the various ways in which society can perceive and represent itself. The shift from "immigrant" to "minority", i.e. from one name to another for the same social reality, is less the consequence of any necessary evolution in the immigration process, or in the population concerned by that process than to some extent an outcome or better, a sign of genuine change in the relationship of the immigration society to itself.

Algerian immigration into France is particularly significant in this context. It is significant in more than one way, as will become clear, since Algerian immigrants are among those who, for various reasons, cannot easily be described as "minorities" without far-reaching implications. So, a broad picture may be helpful of how they historically formed an authentic "Algerian community in (or better 'of') France", thus showing under what conditions they can be called an ethnic, linguistic or cultural "minority" (or "national" for lack of the expression "regional" since "immigrant minorities" have no "territory" of their own within France) and the various implications of calling that particular community a minority.

The significance of this shift cannot be fully appreciated without a twofold investigation to shed light on the two sets of social conditions which seem to determine in this particular case how the word "minority" is used. One objectively entitles the Algerian "immigrant" population in France to be designated a "minority" on account of a number of properties it possesses in itself. Some of those properties are attributable to immigration (to compile a history of immigration is to compile the history and the sociological analysis of the acquisition of the new properties), whether the designation is actual or only possible. In other words, we need to look at the set of conditions presiding over the formation in France of a relatively autonomous "Algerian" population (or of Algerian origin), that is to say the conditions endowing it, or allowing it to endow itself with intrinsic characteristics acting as criteria for identification or self-integration (criteria of authenticity, self-expression, self-definition or distinction, etc). Identification may be by ethnic or international origin ("international" being only the modern version or the modern formulation of "ethnic" in political, national and even nationalistic language. Identification may be by community in language, religion, or culture. Beyond and inherent in all these forms of community is identification by community in the same special condition, the condition communally shared by all immigrants, made up of a greater of lesser exclusion and more or less intensely felt stigmatisation.

The other criteria justify calling that population of "immigrants" a "minority", unless the same combination of conditions (the conditions from which the new vocabulary stems and the uses made of it, those uses being socially determined) is being allowed to project upon an object constituted for the purpose of classification formulated in another field and another context, for other uses and purposes. An enquiry along these lines involves both looking back at how the new vocabulary originated and at the social categories on which it is based. It also involves explaining the conditions under and limitations within which it can be applied to a social continuum for which it was not originally designed, and at the implications of so applying it. What must French society be or become, what changes must it undergo, to be prepared to describe as a "minority" (therefore, within French society) what was previously only a group of "immigrants" (and therefore, outside French society).

ALGERIAN IMMIGRATION: HISTORY OF ITS CONVERSION INTO FAMILY IMMIGRATION

This might look like no more than a difference about words, a lexical or semantic quibble about "immigrants", "migrant population", "immigrant community", "minority", etc. In fact it masks the real issue which is, of course, family immigration. The history of Algerian immigration into France illustrates the transformation very well.

Nowadays "immigration" means the kind of population movement experienced since the first half of the 19th century, closely associated with or directly dictated by employment needs. But employment immigration (i.e. exclusively of workers and therefore nearly always of adult males) always tends to become "population immigration" (i.e. of whole families, not just workers). The two forms of immigration do differ in kind, not just in degree as some suppose, treating family immigration as just another "increase", worsening or ultimate excess in immigration of single males. Labour immigration, insofar as it is exclusively of workers, is a phenomenon mainly or wholly confined to the world of employment (the world of factory, mine or building site, of abstract economics). But like it, accept it or not, family immigration impinges upon the world of the city (the world of the polis and therefore of what is political; the world of street, housing, school, law court, civil and marital status, and of culture, the world of demography as opposed to that of economics). In the employment world the migrant is only a worker (an operative, or unit of labour) but with family immigration he becomes much more: a progenitor, moving beyond the world of production into the world of reproduction. Nowadays, to say anything useful about immigration, about the changes it has undergone and wrought or, more specifically, about the most suitable terms in which to discuss it, methodological principle and even epistemology itself require us to look first at the meaning and actual function of family immigration, then at the social conditions initiating change, as the ultimate source of contemporary discussion of immigration and its various components, especially the cultural aspects.

Only with hindsight, having watched the immigration process from inception through to culmination can one analyse it confidently in terms of strictly labour emigration and immigration, unequal levels of development and, more broadly, unequal relative strengths of the countries concerned, with the emigration countries as dominated, underdeveloped, "third world", and the immigration countries as dominant and developed. Algerian migration to France provides an excellent illustration as having been the first ever migration into the developed world from what we nowadays call the "third" or "developing world". However, while unequal relative strengths are undoubtedly the necessary condition for the process itself to occur, if not continue, can that necessary condition be regarded as sufficient? Everything suggests that it is in the nature of the migration process to break free of the rules that generate it. That is the lesson to be drawn from family immigration and its developments.

We must now consider what the substitution of the term "minority" for "community" or for the more ordinary "immigrant population" represents and what conditions that substitution requires. The term "minority" is itself new in certain respects (e.g. when applied to new instances, to certain immigrant "populations" and "communities" to which it had not yet previously been applied). We shall try to assess what it introduces that is new, what it changes with respect to the older denominations and what it assumes to have actually changed in what it designates. But first it may be helpful to look briefly at the history of Algerian immigration into France, a history which begins strictly speaking with family immigration, the history of "the Algerian community settled in France (not merely migrant there)".

The beginnings of family immigration and the social conditions giving rise to it

The first signs of family immigration appeared before the second world war, i.e. more than four decades ago. But another way of putting this, depending on whether the development is thought precocious or late, is to say that the first signs appeared only on the eve of the second world war, or nearly four decades after the first workers had begun to migrate. However, the movement did not really get under way on any scale until the 1950s.

Since an identical cause produces an identical effect (i.e. the many disruptive, social, economic, cultural and sometimes political factors seen as generating emigration, at first just of males) or more precisely since an identical cause operating more powerfully produces an identical effect to a greater extent, family emigration can be regarded as the culmination of a process beginning with labour emigration. This was because all the internal causes conducive to emigration, already long present, came to a head in the aftermath of the second world war around the year 1950. On top of the now endemic impoverishment on the land came an increasing proletarianisation of the rural classes, greater poverty and in some cases extreme psychological, economic and social distress (disease and famine, several years of scarcity) especially affecting the rural population, partly as a result of the economic blockade of North Africa from 1942, partly of the succession of drought years during the same period. As the usually high population growth became intolerable, there was conclusive and increasingly marked disruption of the social structure and of the moral values of rural society in general, partly under the influence of emigration itself.

The communal tradition was found in its most complete form in Kabylia, Algeria's leading region in terms of volume and tradition of emigration to France. It involved land held in common (the basis of the group and the only form of economic capital common to the group), and pooling of resources and accommodation. All these provided the background for complete group integration (a single source of authority inside and outside the home, identical material and symbolic interests, an undivided sense of honour) and seemed a key condition for migration, especially migration over long distances (France) and for long periods (several consecutive months or even a whole year), a kind of "long stay" emigration. The migrant could be confident that "his" family (wife and children) as just one component of the extended family, could rely on the common ownership system and, more generally, on all the men left behind, a community of males of which the migrant was only one component, just as his (conjugal) family was only one component of the combined unit of undivided families. His wife and children could expect not only subsistence (joint ownership), but also protection, assistance and psychological security (the well known Arabic concept of "haram" or "hurma", with honour and authority being indivisible).

But emigration gradually spread to new regions and new social groups, even the relative "land-owning aristocracy" and lastly, the "marabout families". The latter were a kind of "clerical aristocracy" living on their knowledge and religious power and they, like the land owning aristocrats, refused to demean themselves by accepting cash, paid work from others or for others (still less in an infidel country or for infidels, an attitude especially characteristic of the marabout tradition). As emigration bacame commoner, involving all the men in any given family, and a permanent feature with longer stays abroad, it undermined the earlier common ownership system which had made it possible.

Emigration was originally intended to shore up the social cohesion which had helped to produce it, by helping to restore the economic basis. But it could not last without becoming a serious threat to the integrity and survival of the group. Every extra migrant was another fissure in the community, another attack on the sense of belonging and of fraternity which held the group together. As a process of learning to individualise (the migrant taking an individual approach to his own body, to work, to spending time and money, to place etc.) emigration was ultimately bound to undermine the foundations of the earlier solidarity, the sense of brotherhood (extended to the whole group) and then, the whole of the earlier social order, i.e. the earlier modes of production and of social relations. Discovering and becoming familiar with the most basic concepts (the concepts of return and of profitability) in the logic of productivity, experience of the relationship between amount of work supplied and remuneration received, experience that worktime can be calculated, all these generated and to some extent taught the migrant a calculating approach. This, when applied to the living and working conditions and to the social relationships of the traditional rural world, undermined everything on which the earlier social order was based: the sense of brotherhood underlying family joint ownership and more broadly, all social relations patterned on brotherhood.

So it happened that the common ownership system which at first (i.e. so long as it was inherently natural or experienced as a natural state of affairs) had permitted emigration as something subordinate to itself, then underwent a complete change in nature and attitude, committing itself wholly to serving emigration. A new form of common ownership appeared almost deliberately (no longer natural but "cultivated"), solely to meet the requirements of emigration, to which it would henceforth be subordinate. Common ownership at least in part (sharing roof and board, now that the productive value of land hardly made that worth sharing any longer), was reintroduced for the time that the emigrant would be absent. But this was outside its original context, and most important of all, outside its objective basis, i.e. the common ownership of the total heritage including that bequeathed by ancestors, that partly acquired by local work and partly by the work of the emigrant. The proportion accounted for by the emigrants' contributions, however, increased continuously, ultimately becoming preponderant or even exclusive of any other. The common ownership system was reintroduced sometimes as a pure obligation towards the migrant by relatives remaining behind, but giving them no claim on him in exchange, and sometimes as merely help provided for the migrant's family during his absence, for which he often paid in money.

Accepting the unacceptable: the effect of war on family immigration

The result of the trend was that from May 1952 to August 1953, taking just that short period as an example, an average of 100 families migrated across the Mediterranean to France each month. In October 1954, on the eve of the war of independence, some 6 000 families were residing in France with about 15 000 children. For the reasons mentioned above, family migration did not always start from those areas or social classes which had pioneered migration, but in the migration of single males. Then the latent propensity for family emigration became critical, open almost everywhere, partly as the result of the final upheavals of the war of independence which ended with the resettlement of the rural population.

This was another form of migration although it only involved small distances. The resettlement involved displacement by altitude rather than by distance, a movement of mountain and plateau dwellers down to the plain. The disruption engendered emigration. Although all the underlying conditions appeared to be satisfied for family emigration to follow the workers' emigration, it did nevertheless require the excuse of war, as a case of force majeure -- imposed violence attracting, in return, ways of behaving that were themselves breaches of custom (the custom of peacetime). It required a "needs must" situation to bring people openly to admit and do what they would not normally be prepared to admit to themselves or to one another, or to do: if migration was inevitable, towards resettlement centres or elsewhere (exodus to the town) then one might as well emigrate quite safely to France where the head of the family, husband and father, was already installed. For the family to emigrate to France, which group custom would frown upon in ordinary times, would now be preferred so far as possible to the new situation brought about by war (permanent insecurity for those staying on in their traditional abode, or regrouping in special centres).

Once the first step had been taken justified by war and emergency, family emigration to France became commonplace, with the continuation and intensification of a process which had needed war to come to full and open fruition. The war thus gave countenance to what had previously been experienced and regarded as shameful or scandalous. It was certainly this which gave rise to the saying that the war had acted as a kind of "accelerator of history". Between 1962 and 1967 27 000 Algerian women emigrated to France.

Before Algeria stopped emigration to France in September 1973, and before that decision was confirmed in July 1974 when the French authorities suspended all new worker immigration into France, family regrouping had been on a relatively small scale (only 183 families in 1969 and 1 685 in 1972). That process, the only form of migration tolerated by France and Algeria, gradually increased thereafter:

Arrivals in France

Year	Families	Persons
1974	2 317	5 663
----	-----	-----
1979	2 892	6 619
1980	3 447	7 902
1981	3 142	7 166
1982	4 097	9 064

With 710 000 persons in 1975, and 795 920 in the 1982 census, the increase of 86 000 poorly conceals the demographic vitality of the Algerian immigrant population and all the resulting changes: 130 000 births (births probably reported in the census as being of Algerian nationality); 96 700 persons reported arriving in France after 1975, and also the net excess of departures (including deaths) over entries which can be estimated at over 100 000. Accordingly, the Algerian immigrant population in France must have grown by the order of over 1.5 per cent per year.

Algerian immigration, one of the oldest waves of immigration into France, has been remarkable for its consistency and continuity over time. It has been a long process, beginning in the first decade of this century and extending to the present day with practically no interruption, except perhaps for a few years during the Second World War, some other periods of economic crisis when entry of immigrant workers in general and of workers from the colonies was more rigorously controlled, and for political crises as during 1957-1960 when, owing to the Algerian war, travel by Algerians in either direction was closely controlled.

At the individual level, a feature has been the permanence of migrant stays abroad. The Algerian migrant worker, even when planning to migrate alone, thereby faithfully complying with the strict definition of migration as "labour migration" exclusively, and thinking of himself as exclusively a "labour migrant" and so refusing to bring over wife or children, arrived in France relatively young and, at least for the post-1945 generation of immigrants did not leave the French labour market until nearing retirement age. Still today, the Algerian immigrant population displays very marked stability as regards residence and, more broadly, settlement in France: in 1982, of the 796 000 Algerians recorded, 378 000 were reported occupying the same accommodation as in 1975; 71 per cent were in the same commune and 81.4 per cent were in the same département.

A "settled", no longer "immigrant" population

Another indication of the increasingly pronounced family character of Algerian immigration is the extreme youth of the population or its very high proportion of young people: the 380 400 aged under 25 account for 47.7 per cent of all Algerians residing in France as against 45.5 per cent in 1975. This compares with 36.2 per cent for the French population and 40.6 per cent for the foreign population in France. The under-15s (254 920: 130 080 boys, 124 840 girls) alone represent nearly one-third of the total (32.0 per cent) -- and of course the great majority of the under-25s were reported in 1982 as having been born in France.

Side by side with this large and fast-growing proportion of young people, the older Algerian immigrant age groups, especially those deciding to live in France without their families, are tending to decrease both in relative terms, especially because no new workers are being allowed in, and also in absolute terms as that generation ages. Those returning to Algeria after retirement, early or otherwise, those declared permanently unfit to work (the immigrant group most exposed to industrial accidents and sickness), comparatively early exhaustion, and mortality are all found among that group of immigrants, whether or not they are replaced by other migrants.

This means that the number of births attributable to Algerian families is constantly rising: according to nationality of mother, such births were 16 810 (legitimate and illegitimate) in 1975 and 20 617 in 1981; according to nationality of father, the number of (legitimate only) births was 18 032 in 1975 (of which 2 257 to French mothers) and 20 910 in 1981 (to 2 560 French mothers). Algerian women have high fertility rates even after emigration: although declining from 5.5 children per woman in 1975 to 4.4 in 1982, the average number of children is higher than for other foreign women (3.4 children per woman in 1975, 3.2 in 1982). The Algerian population is accordingly among those with the highest proportions of large families: 3.99 persons per household (including unmarried males and those living alone) as against the national average of 2.7 and of 3.34 for the foreign population. Marriages in France also give a good idea of the internal cohesion of the Algerian immigrant community, and also of how it is becoming increasingly rooted in France: in 1977, 2 598 Algerian males married and in 1982, 3 337; in 1977, 1 704 Algerian females married and in 1982, 2 899.

For completeness, there is another group we should doubtless add to the population usually referred to as the "Algerian immigrant population" which, in fact, is on the way to becoming a "community of Algerian origin" as attested by the growing number of persons acquiring French nationality and especially, the fact that any child born to an Algerian family in France automatically has it. This other population group of Algerian origin, (improperly referred to as "Harkis and their children") resulted from the exodus to France at the end of the Algerian war and thus in different historical circumstances from the immigration to France of Algerian workers and families, the so-called "Muslim French of Algeria" (who should now doubtless be referred to as "French muslims"). They numbered some 180 000 in 1963 and are today thought to amount to 400 000, two-thirds of whom are French-born under 30s; this population is also increasing rapidly, with a birth rate of the order of 30 to 35 per 1000, in striking contrast with that of 1.8 per cent for the French population.

In reality there are, then, 1.2 million Algerians and French nationals of Algerian origin constituting one "community" or "minority" (or the same "communities" or "minorities") within France as a whole. In spite of everything which might separate one from the other (Algerian nationality as a distinction between those with and without, conditions of origin, territorial and socio-economic differences, different political administrative treatment, etc.) they participate in one sociological and cultural reality and are therefore "perceived" identically (as "Algerians", Maghrebins", "Arabs" without other distinction) by French society.

As the years have gone by, social, economic, cultural and political change have affected not only the Algerian immigrant population in France but also Algerian society in general and, more especially, the peasants and the Algerian rural world as a whole. The latter are still substantial suppliers of migrants. Changes in Algeria itself are reflected to some extent in the migrant community in France. In the last analysis, the earlier pattern of Algerian males migrating mainly for work has now developed into a form which had best be referred to frankly as immigration for settlement: 350 000 Algerians of whom 220 000 were in the labour force in 1962, and now 796 000 of whom 318 700 are in the labour force. Without any deliberate policy in this respect, and it is doubtful how far there ever could have been one, this started as a form of immigration which everyone concerned including those involved thought of merely as labour immigration (adult males, bachelors or living alone in France only for reasons of employment and therefore _temporarily_) which has inevitably ended by changing into an immigration of whole families, for settlement. Whether the shift was wanted or not it ultimately imposed itself upon all concerned, thereby confirming what is almost a law in this field: no labour immigration can fail, if it lasts long enough, to turn into settlement immigration and conversely, any immigration reputed to be for settlement (and having been from the outset) must in fact have begun as labour immigration.

HOW THE WORD "MINORITY" IS USED

Yet, however important these changes within the immigrant population may be, do they warrant using the term "minorities"? The word, as it is currently employed, certainly was not specially invented to describe immigrants; if it had been, they would be a kind of "internal" minority completely integrated into the French situation. Indeed, the current usage of the term is evidence of the struggle for "autonomy" waged by communities who see themselves as "minorities", much as elsewhere the term "culture", and especially "popular culture", was used with different shades of meaning to symbolise a struggle that went beyond a mere quarrel over words (the "dispassionate" crusade for "culture"). "Popular" culture was a new kind of culture which had to assert itself vis-à-vis academic, learned, "class" culture and its devotees who, therefore, had every incentive to impose the definition of what was _their_ culture. The concept of "minority", in fact, nearly always implies "cultural minority" or, for bolder spirits, "ethnic minority".

All other things being equal (as if they could be), one gets the idea that the only possible criteria for separateness, that is to say, self-identity, are derived from a few distinctive traits of speech or behaviour (so-called "cultural" differences), or from ethnic considerations. Acting as a constituent and perpetuating principle, the latter consolidate and explain the other, "cultural" differences. Like various other words that confer identity, status, social rank and, simultaneously (merely, some would say) indicate, the term "minority" is not a neutral word: it serves both as a cause and a weapon.

When applied to immigrant communities, especially to the groups that inspire the most intense resistance (racism, discrimination, prejudice of all kinds), the word "minority" is merely an extension of prevailing usage found, for instance, in "the Breton minority", "the Occitanian minority", to take only some examples of minorities who refer to themselves this way more often than they are so referred to. The feelings of resistance use "incomplete" or "non-assimilation" -- or, still worse, "non-assimilability" a refusal to let oneself be assimilated, a kind of bad grace tantamount to hostility -- as their pretext. Nobody is as "non-assimilable" as someone who does not want to be assimilated, even when that person has actively "assimilated" the language, culture and _mores_ of French society, and not been merely passively "assimilated" in the manner of a body that is directly "metabolisable" by the enzyme activity of a unified and unifying French society. One is not casting doubt on the sincerity or honesty of this extension of the "minority" label, or seeing in it some form of intentional manipulation, when one says that often its only _objective_ function (i.e., not perceived by those who employ it) is to shore up a position by recruiting other "minorities" with quite different origins and characteristics, in order to act as reinforcements. In the context of struggle, it is as though the number of actual or potential "minorities" were a trump card -- the more we are, the stronger we shall be and the greater will be our victory. "Minorities multiply and unite, even if you have to invent your minority status or have it invented for you"!

A very careful critical analysis should, however, precede any lumping together of all "minorities" of whatever origin, history and present condition, such as is practised by militants in the heat of action. What constitutes an immigrant "minority", self-styled or otherwise? Looked at objectively, all of the characteristics which go to define such a "minority" -- or which the "minority" claims as its own -- are "handicaps" and function willy-nilly as _stigmas_. This will continue to be the case for as long as the play of forces between immigration and emigration countries (to which immigrants are always returned, even when they take out the nationality of the host country) works against immigrants. It is, indeed, almost a law of nature (of social physics) that stigmatisation breeds revolt against the stigma. The revolt begins by public appropriation of the stigma raised to the status of emblem -- "I am an Arab", "I am a Muslim", etc. -- and normally ends with institutionalisation of the group founded on the stigma (the "minority").

It is quite obvious that this purely negative process of forming, of being formed into a "minority" -- of forming because of being formed -- has nothing in common, especially in France, with those other "minorities" that possess (in their own eyes and in the eyes of the dominators) an infinitely greater degree of autonomy and legitimacy. The two kinds of "minority" are separated by the vast distance between the dominators, even when dominated ("dominated dominators"), and that of the absolutely and wholly dominated ("dominated dominated").

Commentary by E. TEMIME

President of GRECO 13, Marseille (France)
(Groupement de recherches coordonnées sur les migrations internationales)

Mr. Sayad's thesis about the shift from the expression "migrants" to "minority" is definitely sound. But one reservation which he clearly expressed in his paper does seem to need stressing: he is concerned with a particular instance of migration, that of Algerian migration into France and, as was emphasized during the long discussion of the subject at the recent GRECO Migrations French-Algerian Seminar in Grenoble (1), while this is a typical example it is also an inconvenient one for those setting out, as we are, to look beyond individual cases in an attempt to reach general conclusions from combined experience.

French-Algerian relations, even at the minority formation stage, were largely determined by the colonial heritage. The laws governing the relationships between the communities and the question of nationality must surely be seen as direct consequences of that heritage. A study of inter-cultural relationships cannot possibly overlook the distinctions made between nationals of "French stock" and "French nationals of Algerian origin". The colonial heritage confers both a conflictual character and intermingled feelings of belonging to two communities that are not always easy to unravel.

And even these terms can no longer convey the real, profound complexity of the question; the "pieds-noirs", too, are "French nationals of Algerian origin", and of many other different origins as well. And then the rather dubious expression "French muslim" was invented (2) to denote one particular minority -- as if in the lay Republic of France it were possible to define any minority by reference to a purely religious criterion.

So my purpose here is to try to see how far the example Mr. Sayad has selected and defined may enable us not only to analyse a given situation, but also to "go further". Can we define and classify so-called minority groups by reference to a single group, i.e. establish a typology of minorities without too many illusions, acknowledging that such a classification is bound to be arbitrary, simply as a guide to joint reflection on membership of a minority and the consequences this may have at the level of the transmission or acquisition of traditions and knowledge?

So we will reconsider the <u>definition</u> of minority itself, though at some risk of offering an unduly simplified picture. Arguably, then, belonging to a minority necessarily implies a <u>feeling of belonging</u> to some group, i.e. an <u>explicit reference</u> to some community "other" than the majority community in the country of residence. A child may say "I'm Algerian" even though he may not be according to law (by this we mean the law of his country of domicile, i.e. France). This implies that the reference is geographical, whether the speaker is designating himself by that word or being so designated by others. And this can apply whether or not the speaker was born in the reference country. A man may say "I am Irish" even though he has British nationality, with forbears in England for several generations.

Here we touch on something which when taken to extremes may be against all logic. One instance of this is reference to the Jewish community which, as we shall see later, does not apply merely to Judaism but very definitely to the "people of Israel", a constant reference to Jerusalem (for centuries, while Palestine did not exist as a state, Jewish or non-Jewish). Here the feeling of belonging relates to myth (3), and yet is strong enough to be kept up and persist, even in totally isolated communities. In the end it does not much matter what the Ethiopian Jews were originally, or that in their case the myth of "returning" borders on the ludicrous. To some extent this merely makes it all the more remarkable, as a particularly striking example of a reality that is much more common than we will usually admit. For instance, Algerian _pied-noir_ families of Spanish, Italian or other origin were said to have "returned" to France, though many of them had never even visited it. At all events, no one has ever thought of disputing the sincerity of their attachment to France, nor even their membership of the French community.

So to define oneself as a minority does imply membership of a community based on origin, however remote or even legendary, and on history, on the past, recalled all the more emphatically as it blurs or vanishes. Membership of this community must be proclaimed all the more often and forecefully if there is some doubt of it and above all if that community is threatened. It is no accident that regional movements grew up and minorities asserted themselves with the development of centralising and authoritarian states at the end of the 19th century. It became important to remind the dominant and, in its own way, imperialist nation of the heritage that had gone down in history.

For the establishment of minorities also depends on the _transmission_ and _reproduction_ of a _past_ (actual or mythical). The individual immigrant as an individual may be ignored or relegated. He is merely a foreign element of one kind or another, different from the world surrounding him, not necessarily disturbing because he is an "outside" element, his presence being, by definition, temporary. A group of immigrant workers, "colonial" soldiers called up and placed alongside one another does not in itself constitute a minority community. A minority in that sense can only develop when it creates or installs a "family environment", passing on to others the traditions and values which are its own and those of the country of origin or country of reference, whichever expression may be preferred.

This brings us right back to Mr. Sayad's definition: the immigrant group can become a minority group only when migration has become "family migration" and the group's special characteristics can be handed on through the family unit, although as soon as we try to generalise we find that here, too, there are reservations. Some migrations had that family character from the outset, and the groups they formed at once constituted minorities, even though their permanent settlement has naturally modified their essential traits. In the relatively recent past this has applied to Armenian migration, into France as well as into the United States and more recently still, to migrations from south-east Asia. Family cohesion and the handing on of values are facilitated by the very form of the migration (which here often took place for political reasons). The point should be made, though we shall come back to this, that language is not necessarily the most constant or most easily transmissible characteristic. The migrants may be keen to safeguard it and thus have access to a twofold culture, as the first Armenian migrants were; but by the third generation, knowledge of the language of origin has fallen off appreciably.

Can minorities of this type be placed in the same category as communities with a strong family character implanted somewhat artificially and haphazardly in times of crisis or conflict? In France we may point to the families of "Harkis" resettled after the end of the Algerian war in the 1960s. By the second generation they are, in the end, tending to merge with the other migrants of Algerian origin, whose migration has itself changed into family migration, and to lose the specific features inherent in the conditions under which they arrived; and there are other less well known and even more surprising instances, such as that of the Montfuron Albanians (4) who arrived in France after the Second World War with their wives and children. These are definitely minorities, but because of their origin, isolation and exceptional or deliberately marginalised character their presence can be ignored and regarded as no more than a temporary phenomenon, since each small community seems bound to merge naturally into the French context and thus disappear as such, since it is not clearly enough "visible". Then neither the government nor what is usually called "public opinion" take any more notice of them, or even realise that they constitute minorities.

So, for a minority really to exist, it is not enough merely to speak of belonging (real or mythical) and transmission of values. That belonging and those values must be proclaimed and defended. They have to be asserted within the minority group or determined <u>from the standpoint of others</u> -- which is what my point about visibility means. Every minority doubtless asserts its identity itself by keeping itself to itself, maintaining its "purity" only by refusing to have anything to do with anyone else. There lies the fundamental difference between immigrant and minority. The status of the immigrant is essentially provisional or temporary; he is only "passing through" and possesses, so to speak, no transmissible characteristics; he is "defined" by his place in the economic system and only becomes visible or disturbing when he forgets that place. The existence of a minority, on the other hand, depends on the constant and continuing assertion by a group of its membership of a particular community; and the traits of that minority are meaningful only if transmitted from one generation to the next, any element exterior to the group being regarded as "alien" by definition.

The fact that the existence of the minority depends on the transmission through the family of its specific traits may even mean that a "mixed marriage" is seen as a betrayal of the group; this applies to any group claiming or feeling itself to be a minority. Marrying a Corsican does not make you Corsican; for the family and community you are still a foreigner. You may be admitted to the community, but only in certain cases and on certain clearly defined terms. For a non-Armenian woman to enter an Armenian family which has maintained its traditions means marrying the "family in-law" and acquiescing in becoming part of a minority; otherwise she will never be accepted as a member of the family.

Naturally these statements are too categorical and may overstate the case in many ways. But the point is worth stressing. The development of mixed marriages in the older Jewish communities of western Europe was surely a sign of total assimilation, the last gesture of breaking with the community whose religion and rituals had been maintained more through family loyalty than deep conviction. A mixed marriage can in this case be a conscious, deliberate gesture. In this sense "breakaway" and "betrayal" are different words for the same thing.

But the fact of belonging or refusing to belong to a minority is only partly deliberate. Being an immigrant, as we have seen, is in itself a transient condition. Belonging to a minority means something quite different. This is all the more difficult to explain and delimit in that it depends on "other people's perception". The few French people who chose Algerian nationality after 1962 have great difficulty in making people forget that they were of French origin. The son of an Algerian immigrant, though he may be French by law, is considered as an Algerian in principle (so long as he has not renounced Algerian nationality).

One point must be made here in connection with "other people's perception". It can have two aspects. Even a lone individual (without reference here to the definition of minority) may be regarded as a foreigner because of his language or his behaviour, or merely because he does not belong to the village. It may not even matter that he is a member of some other group or community; what does matter here is that he is "not like everybody else".

This inevitably takes us back to the point that the concept of minority does imply membership of a community, an old idea that again relates to the concept of marriage. "Looking at the family" of the future spouse means recognising his origins, identifying the group to which an individual is attached. To some extent, it also means transferring him to another "camp". It also involves asking him to define himself by reference to the family group, by reference to his origins. And in some cases that is or can be felt to be an aggression, or at all events a form of rejection.

This shows how very tricky it is to draw up a typology of minorities; at best, only certain distinctions can be established on the basis of diversity in situation or behaviour between:

-- Those who are members of what is already a long-established migrant group and may really be in search of an identity which has been somewhat blurred through time and, often, through deliberate forgetfulness. This applies to a good proportion of the population of Italian origin resident in France for several generations and generally, fully assimilated; here it is difficult to speak of a double culture or even to use the term minority. The reference here is much more French than Italian;

-- In contrast, the much "stronger" minorities who have retained their own personality and cohesiveness better, some continuing to speak their language of origin, though this is infrequent by the third generation. It is more usual for cultural habits and traditions in the broader sense to be maintained. The Armenian community in France provides an excellent example of a "lasting minority". However, one would still need to ascertain the weight of events on minority behaviour, which is perhaps due to the fact that solidarity has been not only maintained but nourished from abroad, this continuing solidarity and common reactions being cemented by a common reference to the past. In this case the expression "double culture" does have a meaning, corresponding to something real and alive, with no need to relearn or seek out a "lost identity". The feeling of belonging to a minority community is strong enough to be maintained and passed on from one generation to another;

-- A third case is of a group that "constitutes itself" into a minority, trying to discover or rediscover its roots, to maintain links which it may feel are being threatened by a wholly natural "assimilative" trend. An example is the "pied-noir" Jewish community, French nationals for more than a century and naturally French-speaking. Though their religion is a link, it is not enough durably to maintain the cohesion of the group, or the reality of its community; hence the return to a language that has become once more a living language, the maintenance or creation of "Jewish schools". This may be a spontaneous phenomenon, it may be artificial in certain respects; that need not concern us here.

Whatever the value of this typology, and we do not claim too much for it, it has the advantage of emphasizing a number of points. In the first place it enables us to stress the differences in situation and in the weight of history in the formation of minorities and the expression of solidarity. How could the very special relations between France and Algeria not have deeply marked the community of Algerian origin? Colonialism, which has never really been forgotten, created strains and rejections, whereas cultural differences are doubtless largely attenuated by the inheritance of living together over a long period, even though that period was conflictual from beginning to end. National reference today is all the stronger because the traces of those conflicts could not possibly disappear in the space of a few years but remain alive even for a generation which did not directly live through them.

But once we have become aware of the special features of Algerian migration, and of the circumstances in which the Algerian minority in France was constituted, we can still recognise it as a typical minority. France has no Algerian schools; there is no real "double culture" for children born in France and considered as French. The maintenance and sometimes the strengthening of minority status is due as much to awareness of the differences as to the assertion of those differences, and sometimes to the attendant of "segregation" -- much more, in any case, than to the handing on of traditions, or a religion that is often reduced to ritual and the observance of certain customs and feast-days, or a language that is largely forgotten.

From this standpoint the school does no more than take account of the fact of minority status. If it helps to emphasize that fact, it does not do so through the diversity of the education it offers, but insofar as it is the reflection of a community and of rejections which it sometimes helps to highlight. Its role might perhaps be to play down these rejections or get them into proportion.

NOTES

1. Proceedings of this seminar have been published by Publisud in April-May 1985. The seminar was largely dominated by the discussion on how far Algerian migration was or was not typical.

2. A term which is all the more interesting in that it was not coined as a spontaneous or popular expression but is actual official administrative language.

3. More attention should be paid to the question of how long the "return" myth has been propagated, and how, and what it actually means.

4. This community is an example of the case, doubtless more common than we realise, of a group of individuals "transported" to a foreign country as a result of the "vicissitudes" of war; the group settled in Lubéron on land largely abandoned by the indigenous population. By the second generation it had become largely French-integrated, in spite of the prevailing conditions, which were largely favourable to endogamy and the maintenance of family structures.

6. TECHNOLOGICAL DOMINATION AND CULTURAL DYNAMISM

by
Paul-Henry CHOMBART DE LAUWE
Directeur d'études
Ecole des Hautes Etudes en Sciences Sociales, Paris

Technological domination and cultural dynamism! This somewhat ambitious title should leave the reader in no doubt as to the author's intentions. Research experience gained in France and in various other countries by an international team of colleagues (1) has prompted me to give some thought to the dominant position enjoyed by those in possession of the latest technology and, therewith, a feeling of superiority which prevents them from appreciating the contribution that others can make. Such an attitude is not unconnected with the discrepancy between rhetoric and reality that is now constantly being noted in international meetings. We would all like to avoid such discrepancies but are rarely capable of doing so, and I cannot be sure of having entirely succeeded in this paper.

The general remarks made and points raised for theoretical consideration are based on factual experience, though the link between them is not always easy to demonstrate.

The aim here is to analyse, on the one hand, how domination operates and, on the other, how the dominated groups can achieve self-expression. It follows then that respect for cultural pluralism and recognition of cultural dynamism as a factor in social and technical progress is of fundamental importance. But is this creative, evolutionary role played by cultures not part and parcel of a certain concept of democracy and of education? And in this field do we not all too often suffer from delusions? The study of minorities and immigrant groups provides an opportunity to challenge conventional thinking.

While the aim of education in a democracy is to enable every individual to be a free agent relating harmoniously with others, always within the framework of a society's institutions, the processes of domination are a major obstacle to those wishing to achieve this. Good intentions thus come to nothing.

In an attempt to overcome this obstacle and to make a contribution to current discussions on these questions, I propose to consider the topic under five headings: 1) The relationship between technological domination, civilisation and culture; 2) The processes of technological domination; 3) Cultural dynamism and development; 4) A different education? A different concept of life? (Comments on self-management and self-training); 5) Dominated group pedagogy and dominant group pedagogy.

TECHNOLOGICAL DOMINATION, CIVILISATION AND CULTURE

Domination may be political, economic or cultural. As the year 2000 draws nearer, it is becoming increasingly technological. For thousands of years, whenever one group of human beings has possessed more advanced technology than its neighbours it has tended to dominate them -- a phenomenon that has been intensified, first by urbanisation and then industrialisation. Today, everyone is aware that with nuclear energy, satellites and data processing, the opposition of dominant blocks operates at global level. With the change in scale, does the nature of the process also change? The computerisation of societies would indicate that it does, to the extent that technology affects not only the human race as a whole but also the intimate details of our everyday lives.

From the viewpoint of the diversity of cultures, the question may be expressed in the following terms: industrial civilisation has a standardizing influence on the way we live in that it imposes the same technology on all societies. Those with the most advanced technologies have power over those who are less advanced. Whether intentionally or not they impose, with their technologies, patterns of work organisation and political, educational and cultural institutions.

To make this clearer, I should like to come back to the concepts of civilisation and culture that I have discussed at greater length in several published works (2). A civilisation is made up of a group of countries and societies which are distinguished by a limited number of salient features common to them all and which set them apart from others. These features may relate to art or religion for example -- like the Muslim or Chinese civilisations --, an imposed political and social organisation -- like the Roman civilisation --, or ways of organising work or economic resources or of using land, as in olden times the Neolithic or Paleolithic civilisations or the civilisation of the hoe (iron age). The industrial civilisation falls into this last category.

The new technologies made possible by scientific progress and which lead to the setting up of ever bigger and better workshops, factories and enterprises, impose on the world an industrial organisation, centralisation and concentration, and a new balance (or imbalance) between town and country that together tend to standardize work practices, urban development, the economy and bureaucratic administration. Whatever might be the differences or even contrasts between the USSR and the United States, both blocks belong to the same industrial civilisation. The same motorised pumps and irrigation techniques are used by peasants in India and in Africa. The same television technology is used to bring news to the whole planet.

Depending however on the regions and countries involved, some differences persist while others appear. Civilisation meets with support or resistance in different cultures depending on the attitude of their representatives. But the very concept of culture requires further explanation. Not wishing to revive the numerous discussions which have taken place on this topic, I shall mention two main approaches only. The first, based on Anglo-Saxon anthropology, is that a culture consists of all the behaviour patterns, social structures and ways of thinking of a society. Variations on this theme have been listed in surveys and number between 180 and 250 depending on the author (3). According to this approach, culture relates more to society, and civilisation to humanity. According to the other approach, which is that of French-speaking authors and in particular the "Annales" school, culture is defined in terms of various European traditions of individual development, education (Bildung), the 18th century definition of a gentleman ("honnête homme") and the idea of individual and collective progress (4).

By underlining the dynamic aspect of culture -- "creative culture" and "active culture" -- I have taken a different approach from those mentioned above (5). It entails not simply identifying the numerous traditional cultures within industrial civilisation, but stressing the innovative capacities of cultures in course of change. Every culture, in every country, and in every social group can, thanks to its cultural heritage which is constantly being renewed as a result of contact with other cultures and transfers of industrial technology and know-how, contributes something original to the construction of a new world. Culture asserts itself as a movement that starts from within groups and which leads them to define their own identities and to formulate intentions.

When we speak of multicultural societies, of minorities and immigrants, we can measure the enrichment and potential for innovation offered in all areas of life in society. At international level, industrial civilisation will come to a dead-end if it fails to respect the diversity of cultures which guarantees constant renewal, dialogue and freedom of expression and is therefore the prerequisite for a truly democratic concept of community life. If it were to use technology to impose a sort of universal culture, it would perhaps continue to invent increasingly efficient tools, but this technical progress could lead to social decline and, at world level, result in a scientifically organised bureaucracy, functioning like some infernal machine.

Nevertheless, the concept of universal values, interpreted in different ways by different cultures, remains a deeply desired ideal. Human rights declarations are a reflection of this and the current insistence on people's rights is also aimed at ensuring that this active diversity is maintained while respecting the principles of the equality and freedom of individuals and groups.

Let there be no misunderstanding. It is not a question here of condemning technological progress. On the contrary, technology has no doubt not yet progressed far enough to meet the aspirations of individuals and groups. At its present stage of development it brings undeniable material benefits but, by creating unbearable inequalities between countries and between social groups within individual countries, it reinforces the ways in which domination operates. Thus the question is often asked nowadays whether it is possible to change the way those in power view the world and also decision-making procedures, in other words, whether a new world order is possible. But the discrepancy between words and deeds is so appalling that no real solution can be envisaged.

In these circumstances, is the faith placed in new concepts of education justified? To what extent would such education ensure respect for the diversity of cultures and self-expression for individuals and peoples? In what way could it help stop the processes of domination in world industrial civilisation by liberating cultural forces that would channel technological progress, limit its harmful effects and extend its benefits to all men as a fundamental right, that is to say by fighting against inequalities. Is it by means of education that progress will be made? Education itself is bound up with the processes of technological, economic and cultural change. Education is a product of society. To what extent then can it help direct change and break with the processes of domination?

THE PROCESSES OF TECHNOLOGICAL DOMINATION

The term "domination" is taken here to mean the abuse of power, where power is the ability of a social unit (an individual, group, or society) to compel others to do as it wants (6). Conventional theory has it that domination is exercised through fear or dissuasion, the promise of benefits or reward, and through persuasion. This last method has grown out of all proportion since the advent of different media forms which help financial groups as well as governments to impose decisions taken by powerful minority groups.

Domination as between countries or social groups may be political, military, economic or cultural and is often a mixture of all of these. Scientific and technical domination operate at an increasingly early stage and are becoming a precondition for the exercise of the other forms of domination.

Military superiority depends on the possession of technologically ever more sophisticated weaponry. Faster planes, more accurate missiles, and tanks that are the least vulnerable and have the greatest fire-power give their user a decisive advantage over a less well-prepared adversary. Obtaining them involves either paying a very high price to countries better able to produce them, and on whom the buyer becomes to some extent dependent, or having the means to manufacture them oneself. In this latter case, superiority can only be obtained by giving top priority to scientific research which will allow the development of new technologies. It is often claimed that such research for military purposes advances research in other fields. But how, at the end of the second millenium, can we still count on the manufacture of death-dealing weapons to help scientific progress? The indispensable role claimed here for military research is only an excuse used to conceal the desire to dominate that is in us all.

The economic rationale is also equivocation. I have had the opportunity, with an international group, of studying technology transfers for UNESCO. It is obvious that neither the less advanced countries, the developing countries nor even the most industrialised countries can do without such transfers. But importing a "turn-key" factory obliges workers in the recipient country to adopt new production methods, new working relations, a new work schedule and a new way of life. It also means putting the values of efficiency and output first, accepting modernisation as conceived elsewhere and being dependent culturally as well as technologically and economically. It means giving up original forms of creativity which might open up new paths in industrial production itself. Does this standardization of technologies make it inevitable that cultures whose diversity makes for the exchange of ideas, fruitful communication, the assertion of identity and the guarantee of freedom will be stifled?

Technological and economic domination lead to cultural domination. To the extent that scientific and technological superiority are accepted, dominant countries' models are adopted by, sought after and integrated in importing countries. Television programmes, like factories, are also sold "ready to view", and advertising, which has an obvious commercial purpose, also exerts disguised pressure on value-judgements and preferences and has a similar effect. Little by little, that which once seemed essential is rejected and the practices and ways of thinking of the most dominant countries are adopted in an uncontrolled fashion.

In such a context, political domination takes various forms. It is striking how technological progress has in no way eliminated totalitarian régimes, whether they be vestiges of nazism or fascism, an aberration of socialism or a resurgence of religious fanaticism, or whether they take more discrete form and use -- within a framework that appears to be that of a democracy and in limited areas of social activity -- methods which at times are modelled on the worst examples of crimes against freedom. The fact that torture still exists today and that new technologies are helping to perfect the methods used gives food for thought about the relationship between social progress and technological progress.

Let me repeat that it is not a question of putting science and technology on trial. The well-known "perverse effects" must not be allowed to conceal the progress that the development of science has enabled mankind to achieve. The fact that torture still exists must not make us forget about the immense successes in medicine. It is not science that is being called in question but the use thereof. It is surprising that centuries have passed and we are still repeating the warning "science sans conscience" so often without taking heed of it.

The question then arises how a process of domination in which science and technology play a specific role begins and develops. The process operates on the basis of the complementary attitudes of those dominating and those being dominated. On the side of the former, the temptation to use scientific and technological superiority is all the greater inasmuch as it enables them to beat trade competitors and extend their political influence, while at the same time ensuring their national defence. As for the dominated, the loss of initiative, freedom and creation that goes together with over-rapid changes imposed from abroad is made acceptable by the material benefits that modernisation brings.

The way in which land is developed provides a striking illustration of the two sides of this process. The heavy industry model is an obvious temptation for poorer countries or regions and it meets a need: solicited by advertising and subjected to various forms of pressure by the dominant countries, less "developed" countries adopt this model and accept the transfers of technology required to create industrial complexes. But this at the same time accentuates the urban-rural, agricultural-industrial imbalance. Built-up areas spread at break-neck speed due to uncontrollable migratory movements, and in such circumstances construction and the way space is used can no longer reflect the wishes of the local population. New arrivals try to survive in makeshift dwellings or are "rehoused" in buildings of the same design as those to be found in Paris, New York, Caracas or Dakar. On the outskirts of large cities in developing countries, urban life is no longer the collective expression of a group of human beings making their own mark on the earth.

In the mix of populations and cultures, immigrants sometimes try to form separate communities in a desperate attempt to retain their identity. In the industrialised countries, long-established "suburbs" more or less keep their personality but the new "large complexes" built in the fifties, in France for example, obliged residents to live in buildings of a standard design in which community life quickly suffered. Then, first in the United Kingdom and later in France, an attempt was made to solve the problems by constructing "new towns", but the participation of the future inhabitants at the planning stage encountered numerous difficulties. The types of dwelling proposed became the regulation ones and corresponded to the way technical experts and architects thought space should be used. They sometimes succeeded in constructing aesthetically satisfying projects but not enough was done, despite all the studies, to discover the habits of the future inhabitants, their expectations, ways of thinking and perceiving themselves and the setting in which they wished to live.

When these inhabitants belong to different ethnic groups, each with its own culture, the problem becomes more and more complex. Recent research will perhaps make it possible to overcome the differences between planners, experts, politicians, government and those who live in these estates, but this means rethinking the whole approach to decision-making in urban planning and the conception of the use of space, which in turn implies a different perception of society. In this context, the possibilities opened up by computerisation, particularly for industrial decentralisation, will no doubt play a decisive role in the future, for better or, perhaps, for worse. In this respect, science and technology still do not go far enough. Is it possible to ensure that they are applied in the interests of consumers instead of submitting resignedly to whatever developments occur?

To escape from technological domination -- in urban planning as in other fields -- and to obtain maximum benefit from scientific discoveries, efforts must be made to see how various forms of manipulation, intentional or otherwise, help to create an attitude of submission and acceptance amongst members of a culture in the process of losing its roots. The way in which the physical environment is developed, determining what people see every day, how they do things and how they relate to each other, corresponds to a certain ideology of those in positions of power and may not be in harmony with the cultural aspirations of those living in that environment. If, at the same time, similar cultural models are imposed in another way by advertising and the mass media, the room for self-expression left to different cultures becomes more and more restricted. There is a danger that the new "communication" technologies may turn into tools of oppression.

Political propaganda in countries where freedom of the press has become a mockery is, naturally, an intolerable form of oppression, but at least it has the merit of being obvious. In democratic countries, the concentration of a large section of the press in the hands of a single individual or group makes it easier to impose an ideology. A television serial viewed by an audience of hundreds of millions in a very large number of countries over several years, and purveying a system of values and a conception of life peculiar to the dominant classes in a given country, has a significant impact on those who follow it avidly. If to this are added the effects of commercial advertising which encourages the adoption of the consumer habits of these same dominant classes, concern is heightened as to the ability of various cultures to express themselves.

CULTURAL DYNAMISM AND DEVELOPMENT

Inequalities are accentuated as a result of the accumulation of scientific knowledge and, in the most industrialised countries, the increasing rate of such accumulation. When compared to this dominant civilisation, and the material progress it brings, the traditional cultures attached to different ways of thinking appear as an obstacle to modernisation. And so indeed they are when they try to preserve their identity by refusing new technologies, threatened as they are by the domineering attitude of the dominant countries. On the other hand, as mentioned above, cultures can incorporate external contributions as a source of enrichment if culture is perceived in a dynamic sense.

Is it possible for dominant countries and groups to change their attitude, and thus for the recipient countries and groups to change theirs too? The economic and political obstacles are such that there appears to be little hope of this, as is confirmed by the discrepancies between words and deeds. However, no valid solution is possible without such a change. Moreover, the success achieved by multi-ethnic societies should give food for thought. Economic progress in the United States, the most striking example of an immigration country, has not suffered. Switzerland, with its three different languages, provides another type of example. France itself was constituted by different ethnic groups, has been influenced by numerous invaders and has long welcomed refugees and immigrants who have played their part as workers and in economic development and have helped enrich French culture.

Technology transfers could operate on the basis of exchange rather than domination (7) if those in possession of new technologies made the effort to appreciate the contribution that recipient cultures can make. This would have the twofold effect of preserving cultural identity while, secondly, a two-way process would benefit technological development and scientific research inasmuch as the meeting of cultures would cause received technical and research wisdom to be challenged and would encourage the recipients to become creators of new technology themselves.

Such a change in approach cannot be effected in all fields overnight. But numerous examples are already helping to pave the way, and it would be interesting to compare different experiences in this respect. I should like, for my part, to consider one case only, relating to the development of agricultural land. It concerns immigrant workers who returned to their country, Mali, after working for several years in France. Before leaving, they followed a training course on methods of irrigation and also learned about various other techniques. Their objective was to set up new co-operatives which a research worker from our group has already had the opportunity to speak about on several occasions. The problem that arises now is how to rebuild a village which is to be flooded as a result of the construction of a dam. How should the new village be constructed? The traditional design is no longer suited to the new conditions of work. On the other hand, the validity of construction designs and plans imported from Europe is highly debatable since the shape of the houses and the plan of the village make it impossible for the balance of family structures and social relationships in various areas to be maintained. Some other solution must therefore be found. The traditional style should not be preserved at all costs, nor should external models be adopted without question: the villagers must go ahead and create something new together. Research workers in several fields are now studying this problem along with the villagers whose preferences will at all times be taken into account. It is an experimental site that is involved here but the lessons to be learnt from this example can, through comparison with others, help considerably in finding new solutions on a larger scale.

Between the existing cultural heritage and new technologies accompanied by new cultural models, culture can clearly be seen here as a movement forward in the sense in which I referred to "active culture" and "creative culture". In this sense, there can be no real development if the residents of a country or members of a group are not given the opportunity to express themselves and take charge of their own progress via modernisation of a type adapted to their aspirations.

What agents may intervene here in the confrontation between outside experts and the inhabitants of a region, town or village? What kind of resistance, counter-culture or creative movements will be effective? Where may dynamic forces come into being? How can efforts that are dispersed pave the way for more important changes and the real take-over by those concerned of the control of their own development? What role can education play, not only in schools but also in the context of the adult self-training which will be discussed below?

On the outskirts of towns, the problem arises in a stark and worrying fashion. By definition, the arrival of immigrants from different regions or countries produces a mix of cultures which has the unfortunate result that the inhabitants of these urban areas lose the stability of their traditional way of life without finding any clearly defined alternative paths. But in the resulting social disintegration, it can also happen that new forms of expression emerge amongst particularly under-privileged populations. Respecting different ethnic groups and cultures, and taking account of the various ways in which they may find expression can give food for thought to those in charge of development, technical experts, administrators, architects and urban planners. Could not the meeting of cultures be the opportunity for real renewal ? But here again, such a transformation is possible only if there is a change in attitude at all levels, amongst the dominating groups and amongst those who are dominated without being able to find a behaviour model that corresponds to the new identity they are in the process of creating for themselves.

With respect to identity, there is one error that must be avoided. When an identity is imposed from the outside on minority or immigrant groups, they quite rightly react against it. Tacking a false identity on to others in this way can even be akin to a racist attitude. However, every group has a need to assert its identity. In which case it is preferable to talk about a process of identification from within in the sense of something that is expressed and created. But the identity expressed takes on a different aspect according to whether the group concerned is a "minority" or is made up of temporary immigrant workers. In the first case, ethnic groups who have long been integrated into the society of a country, or other groups of more or less long-established immigrants who have opted for permanent integration see themselves as citizens of the country in question and think of themselves as being considered minorities, or better still representatives of a particular culture within the general culture of that country. In the second case, temporary immigrants who choose to return to their country after working for a while in France are entitled to the same benefits as French workers but continue to define their identity in terms of their country of origin. These two cases therefore pose different problems with respect to education.

A DIFFERENT EDUCATION? A DIFFERENT CONCEPT OF LIFE? THREE NECESSARY IDEALS

To come now to the role played by education. If we want to succeed in finding new methods of decision-making to build a genuine democracy, we come up against three ideals of education which serve a useful purpose as long as they are recognised as being ideals. They are self-management ("auto-gestion"), self-training ("auto-formation"), and self-analysis ("auto-recherche").

One hundred percent self-management can be considered as a dream of the future, but the trend towards self-management is real and can be beneficial if it obliges its supporters to prepare a proper defence of their quest for a new form of society. Then the question of self-training arises. Progress in finding new approaches entails preparation but, once again, external cultural models accompanying the technical ones mentioned above prevent the representatives of a group or country from really creating new structures which would give them the chance of achieving all-round development.

Here again, it is helpful to compare examples. In the north-east of Brazil, a sociologist from our group conducted a survey on the demand for education. She noted that what parents wanted was in almost all cases training, the only possible escape route from very poor living conditions. There can then be no question of contesting the model proposed in the framework of the educational institutions of the most industrialised countries. The imported educational model is integrated in the context mentioned above, i.e. a whole series of types of pressure exerted with regard to the development of the environment, and the organisation of work and daily life.

Returning to the situation of minority groups and immigrant workers in the industrialised countries, we find aspirations of the same type, but always with certain differences between, on the one hand, long-established cultural and linguistic minorities and naturalised immigrants and, on the other, temporary immigrants. Both groups are anxious to receive an education that will enable them to overcome their material and social difficulties. They are entitled to send their children to the same schools. But the former want to be taught in a way that allows them to keep their cultural identity and to learn regional languages, the languages of their countries of origin. The latter require rapid instruction in the language of the host country and, at the same time, want their children to be able to continue to use their mother tongue.

In such circumstances is it possible to talk about self-training? Can local inhabitants educate themselves using imported techniques and at the same time try to find their own forms of expression? Are permanent immigrants wishing to become integrated into the host country able to come together and discover for themselves how to assert their new identity while still remaining attached to their national culture? Relations between the state school system and the self-training of minority groups in fact raise the question of instruction in good citizenship and in local customs and culture and, over and above the relations between the State and society in general, in concrete situations for specific categories of citizens. It is not possible here to deal with all these problems, but it is useful to bear in mind that they underlie the present discussion.

As for self-training, it remains utopian in the sense that it is never all-embracing. For a movement to be initiated entirely from within, a catalyst is needed to set it off, and this is difficult to contrive. Not wishing to go into all the methods that have been used by the various adult education movements, by organisers or local culture associations (8), I should like merely to ask the question: is it possible to envisage self-training without self-analysis, i.e. without attempting to understand the situation in which a social group or society finds itself? Such an effort at understanding is, however, like self-training itself, dependent on external intervention.

Who, then, can intervene in this way? At village level, would it be a research worker from a town? At factory workshop level, would it be an expert in labour questions? The question here again, in another form, is that of dominant groups. Intervention? Yes, but by whom and how? No residents' association, training group, theatrical company, trade union or sports group ever comes into being quite spontaneously. It is to be hoped however that, increasingly, it is those concerned who will themselves go in search of external assistance and who will choose which type they want. This comes back to the meeting between different cultures, between individuals from different backgrounds, and between the technologies of the industrial civilisation exported by trained people and experts of all kinds and local cultures.

Self-training and self-analysis experiments

Of the self-management experiments whose successes and failures are well known, shantytowns or urban areas in Latin America provide one of the most instructive examples from the present standpoint. Some were the result of political revolution or breakaway movements, coups and sometimes armed struggle. Others, like that of the Tépito quarter in Mexico city, which I have already described elsewhere, vigorously asserted their identity and succeeded for several years in running a system of self-management for development, consumer questions, welfare measures and culture. Even if such achievements do not last, they do demonstrate the ways in which progress can be made and reveal the pitfalls. Other popular movements in the outskirts of Mexico city have been studied by O. Nunez (9). In Peru, womens' groups have set up self-managed canteens for the people which are playing an increasingly important social and political role.

In Venezuela, an architect from our international group has for some ten years been monitoring "ranchos" districts which are experimental development areas where it is possible to follow building and organisational operations carried out by the people themselves (10). The need for self-training can be seen from the relations between the technical experts and local inhabitants. On the one hand, the inhabitants have to learn how to work in collaboration with the architects and, on the other, the architects have to consider what they can learn from the inhabitants. The same thing happens in Africa, where a young architect in a suburb of Abidjan worked together with young locals who had organised themselves into groups and assumed responsibility for the construction of sanitary installations.

Immigrant workers who had first gathered together in Paris have gradually taken over responsibility for the organisation of their own affairs by calling in experts whom they have chosen themselves. Once again, in such cases of collaboration self-training works both ways, each side learning from the other in the framework of a joint project. It is not enough to ensure that local inhabitants participate in projects planned by engineers or architects, the experts must also participate in the inhabitants' projects.

This self-training of those involved in planning and carrying out projects needs to be compared with the literacy and community development programmes that are taking shape in many areas (11). It is possible only if those involved realise their situation and needs, and for this to happen some outside assistance is generally necessary. It also requires self-analysis by those concerned, based on this understanding, and the formulation of a project relating initially to a limited number of needs and extended subsequently to cover a series of technical, economic, social and cultural fields. Self-training is effected as part of this very analysis, whence the advantage of assistance from people trained in the humanities, on condition both that they are good listeners and that those carrying out the project can work with them as equals.

In the case of immigrant workers in a host country who have a return project, it is easier to form self-training and self-analysis groups, possibly with the help of trained research workers either from the same country of origin or from the host country who will be accepted by those concerned in proportion to their degree of understanding. The types of technical training required are chosen in accordance with the projects formulated in the groups. Thus, an introductory course on irrigation techniques in France, corresponding to the needs expressed in the return project of workers from Mali, made it possible subsequently to set up irrigation schemes and the corresponding co-operatives in Africa.

In the case of regional, ethnic, cultural or occupational groups wishing to retain their identity and culture, or immigrants who have definitively opted for integration in the host country, it is more difficult to form self-training groups since projects are usually less well defined. But it is possible to take the analysis further. I have often mentioned the group of workers who, for fifteen years now, have been undertaking research on the work and experience of workers in the factory and at home, assisted by researchers whose help they requested. This is an example of a continuous exchange of ideas between manual workers and intellectuals in which each side learns from the other. The workers have supervised the writing of several publications which have made an appreciable contribution to research into the living conditions of the working classes, while at the same time developing methods of self-training (12).

DOMINATED GROUP PEDAGOGY AND DOMINANT GROUP PEDAGOGY

In the self-analysis and self-training used in adult education, theoretical and practical knowledge must complement each other. An expert trained in an educational institution could very well help to stimulate self-expression among movements originating within a dominated group. But this trained expert, whatever his level, can only be effective if he himself has already succeeded in changing his attitude, his system of values as mentioned above. It is at university and "Grande Ecole" level that change is most urgently needed. The industrial civilisation has generated top-level experts in all fields, but has not yet proved capable of making them understand that their science and technology can be instruments of death as well as of progress. The confidence they have acquired as a result of the success of western rationalism prevents them from appreciating the richness of other cultures. They run the risk of failure with regard to technology and science itself unless they learn to listen to those for whose benefit they are supposedly working.

There is no question here of making a value judgement. Most experts from towns who work in rural areas, or those trained in the most developed countries to work in the so-called "developing" countries, love their work and give their all to whatever project they undertake, often in very difficult conditions. It is not they who are being called in question, but the system of which they are part. If it is agreed that no real development is possible unless based on a movement from within and unless those concerned have the chance to express themselves and be creative, and if we consider that there can be no real meeting of cultures unless we get away from the idea of a world in which superiority is always on the same side, then sweeping changes in education must be envisaged at all levels.

Research workers and technical experts, unwitting agents of technological domination, can be made aware of the manipulation which causes them to misjudge the capabilities of those with whom they work in the field. They need to be trained for their new tasks in universities and "grandes ecoles". At the same time, social workers, organisers and teachers in the various adult education groups also need training for their tasks and need to meet with the experts on the one hand, and those directly concerned on the other. Certain problems can be solved by setting up interdisciplinary teams, but the initial question always recurs, i.e. the trend towards self-management based on the training in their own environment of those directly concerned. Self-support and self-management cannot be envisaged without self-training and self-analysis.

The humanities could play an important role in this respect. But research workers in these disciplines also need to consider their own training and ways of thinking. Strenuous efforts have been made to promote understanding between cultures, but the fact is that a new departure is nevertheless needed now. In all social _milieu_, analysis must begin from within. Those directly concerned are themselves increasingly taking on the role of research workers. This does not mean to say that professional research workers have a smaller role to play, only a different one. It is no longer a question of research _on_ a culture, but of being with those involved and discovering _with_ them the potential for creation and progress. Between the politicians, technical experts, economists and administrators on the one hand, and those directly concerned, the inhabitants of a region and the citizens of a country on the other, they can act as instruments for promoting understanding and economic and social progress.

Here also, there is an increasing need for new methods and for research workers in the humanities to change their approach. If they were to work in collaboration with education experts in all fields, the results might be encouraging. Such co-operation is still in its infancy. Numerous international bodies are working in this sphere; to name but one for the moment, the World Council of Comparative Education Societies organised a major conference in January 1984 at which subjects of concern included confrontation between cultures, respect for minority groups and the need to avoid any element of domination in relations inside educational institutions. Several committees studied problems concerning international trade and interdependence, and also relations between the sexes, regions and minorities, and ethnic, social and cultural groups.

These concerns are shared by the international group mentioned above -- Transformations sociales et dynamique culturelle (social change and cultural dynamism) -- which is made up of research workers from some 15 countries who are trained in the humanities (13). At present we are trying to identify with greater precision how domination and manipulation occur in different fields, and how to get round them. The question which could now be put is how the change in educational establishments themselves is to be brought about. On what points do education experts envisage working in collaboration with research workers trained in the humanities?

Training and work

The efforts being made in various countries to develop a closer relationship between educational institutions and industry need to be based on analysis of the societies, regions and groups involved. Technological modernisation should be accompanied by modernisation of teaching methods. Readier access to technical skills is a must, since, by breaking down the barriers between those who lead the way and those who follow, it can help counter the technological domination we have been criticising.

Further, research workers have demonstrated, in surveys on youth unemployment, the extent to which poorly conceived training in schools (or the lack thereof) compounds the difficulties encountered in working life. There is in the industrialised countries, and also increasingly in the developing countries, a growing need to alternate periods of schooling with periods of work in industry. The student who is exposed to working life early on, before going back to complete his school or university training, and the worker who receives instruction not only in technical matters but also in economics, the humanities and literature will overcome the lack of understanding which is paralysing social progress at the present time. Recent French legislation on workers' rights (the Auroux Acts) will facilitate this approach.

Given the economic situation of the least industrialised countries, such measures are for the most part still utopian, but experiments are needed to prepare the future.

Minds can meet on some points. There are experts and decision-makers from the most industrialised countries -- as yet not many, unfortunately -- who have understood the need for a change in attitudes. It is interesting to note that their approach with regard to the inhabitants of recipient countries is usually influenced by their experiences in community instructional schemes. Then there are some decision-makers from the "developing" countries, also few in number, who manage to overcome the burden of conventional and unsuitable models, the temptation to take the easy way out by copying their counterparts from the industrialised countries along with their faults, and the temptation to use the knowledge they have obtained for their own benefit and that of their families and friends. To what extent will these two groups be listened to and will they be able to organise themselves so as to bring about institutional change?

These different questions are relevant when considering minority groups and immigrant workers. These latter appear to be underprivileged both at work and in their private lives. Again, the solutions vary depending on whether they wish to be integrated in the host country or to return to their country of origin. In both cases, instruction in writing and language is needed and this can be given in schools and through special courses. In both cases, there is a demand for technical and scientific training courses, but there can be discrepancies in the level of ability in the host country language and in the nature of the technical courses. Workers who wish to return to their own country need to make use of their stay to acquire the technical knowledge that will help them in their return projects, while those wishing to stay want to be given the means to make careers in the industrial firms in which they work. In both cases, careful thought, an understanding of the situations and self-training are necessary preconditions if workers are to avoid being directed, in spite of themselves, along paths which correspond more to the interests of their employers than to their own aspirations.

If progress is to be made in this direction, it is therefore necessary to study reforms both in education and in the organisation of work. An active role is played by the many associations set up to co-ordinate the two, but the scale of the changes required is such that governments must also be involved. Dealings between the government, experts and workers draw attention to the difficulty of communication due to differences in education. A person's level of ability and his technical and scientific knowledge, although very important, should not cause him to feel superior in his dealings with other people.

A political question

While, in this respect, the pedagogy of dominated groups -- in which self-training plays an essential role -- is indispensable, it should not be forgotten that, as mentioned above, dominant group pedagogy is no less so. But since no one is going to oblige the dominant groups to acquire this necessary training in human relations and to change their ways of looking at things and systems of values, it is up to them to take the decisions themselves since it is they who have the power.

While self-training and self-analysis need an outside stimulus to act as an initial catalyst, such a stimulus cannot in this instance, and at this level, come from above. It will come from below to the extent that senior management understand that they have much to learn from the other social classes and other cultures. It will not be possible for such changes to be worked by countries acting alone, but rather by constant contact between countries. International organisations therefore have a fundamental role to play here, but one that must be linked to developments in each country.

How can feelings at grassroots level exert pressure on the dominant groups and so stimulate self-training and changes in attitude? There are four main possibilities: political parties, trade unions, NGOs, and international organisations. Changing the system of education in universities, state schools and the top training centres is a political matter, falling within the jurisdiction of the legislature. But politicians themselves require a stimulus from outside their parties. Of the work of the many national and international associations in this field, the educational projects conceived by SOMO in the Netherlands would seem to provide a very cogent example. The research carried out by this body, financed partly by the trade unions, is undertaken at the request of the workers. Studying decision-making systems in multinational companies is important as a means of countering measures taken without any consideration of the human factor. Other examples could be mentioned in Canada, Sweden and various other countries (14).

The idea that education is necessary for development is gradually gaining ground and if it becomes as widely accepted as may be hoped, a change in attitude towards minorities, immigrants and those on the fringes of society becomes possible. In all countries, those in power must change their ways of looking at things and their systems of values. This is true not just in the most industrialised countries, for the dominant groups in developing countries are also concerned. On a wider scale, if it is understood that all men are one with respect to hunger in the world, the fight against racism and respect for other cultures, then it may be possible to bridge the gap between rhetoric and reality and to speak effectively of a new world order.

NOTES AND REFERENCES

1. Transformations sociales et Dynamique culturelle -- international co-operative research by representatives from fifteen countries constituting a network of individuals or teams carrying out comparative research. Four collective volumes have already been published. The present address of the Secretariat is the Centre d'Ethnologie Sociale, at Montrouge, France.

2. In particular La Culture et le Pouvoir (2nd edition), Paris, Harmattan 1982, see pp. 90-94 and 118-121. La fin des villes, Paris, Calmann-Lévy, 1982, Chapter II: "Domination et culture". "Crise Economique et Cultures Novatrices" in Le Monde Diplomatique, March 1984.

3. One of the best-known works is that by KROEBER A. and KLUCKHOHN C., Culture, a critical review of concepts and definitions, Vintage Books, Random House, New York, 1963.

4. See the still relevant book by FEBVRE L., MAUSS M. et al., Civilisation, le mot et l'idée, Renaissance du livre, Paris, 1930.

5. See La fin des villes, mythe ou réalité, op. cit. Chapter II.

6. CHAUVIGNE Ch. and BRIZAIS R. See also, for example, the recent book by GALBRAITH, The Anatomy of Power, Houghton Miffin, Boston, 1983.

7. See the collective work "Domination or Sharing?", UNESCO, Paris, 1982 and La fin des villes, op. cit.

8. See the collective work La Banlieue aujourd'hui, L'Harmattan, Paris, 1982.

9. BOLIVAR T. in La Banlieue aujourd'hui, op. cit. and "A la périphérie de Caracas. Les barrios de ranchos" in: Culture-action des groupes dominés (a collective work still to be published).

10. See for example: BELLONCLE G. et al. Alphabétisation et gestion des groupements villageois, Club du Sahel, Karthala, 1982.

11. A group of workers, Nous travailleurs licenciés, Paris, Ed. Christian Bourgeois, 10/18, 1974; and also Le Mur du mépris, Paris, Ed. Stock, 1978.

12. FREIRE P., 1970, The Pedagogy of the Oppressed, Herder, New York. It is important also to talk about dominant group pedagogy.

13. See Culture-Action des Groupes dominés (Civilisation uniformisante et pluralisme des cultures). Limited edition. Edition being prepared. Work cited under (1) above by the international research group.

14. See in particular PRADERVAND P., "Penser globalement, agir localement", Economie et Humanisme, n° 268, Nov-Dec. 1982, pp. 19-31.

Commentary by Chris MULLARD

University of London and University of Amsterdam

The main themes of Chombart de Lauwe's paper arise from a provocative and highly original engagement with what might be termed "the process of domination and the possibilities of the expression of the dominated". A central concern of the argument rests on a plea for the respect for the "pluralism of cultures" and essentially the dynamics of culture as a coercive factor in social and educational progress. Indeed the skilfully constructed argument reaches its apex in a call for another education, another conception of the world: an interrelated demand which itself is based upon three depictions of essential practice -- self-education (l'auto-formation), self-research (l'auto-recherche), and self-management (l'auto-gestion).

Clearly an argument as complex and visionary as this could lend itself to a number of scorching critiques if it were not for the fact that it is basically located within an alternative paradigm and hence conception of an ideal world in which the relations of domination are so to speak exchanged for the relations of equality. The sensitivity of approach which refreshingly recalls to mind the "underdog" research tradition pioneered by Alwin Gouldner and others in the 1960s and the political empathy which strikes a similar cord and concern with the liberation of oppressed peoples then distinguishes this contribution to the seminar as one which seriously attempts to relate to the aspirations of ethnic minority groups in Europeanised societies and those majority groups still contained and oppressed within the neo-colonial structures and institutions of domination. Whilst such an orientation protects Chombart de Lauwe's paper from any crass or ideological critique focused around the classic rail-road metaphor, it does not, however, exonerate it from a critical appreciation culled from an account of the inconsistencies and contradictions embedded in the argument -- inconsistencies and contradictions which could provide a basis for a set of policies and practices designed to bring about the very opposite of what is advocated by the author.

For instance, the first stage of the argument, which makes the connection between education and technology, is patently obvious on one level within a given interpretation of history. There can be little dispute that technology, as an agent of domination, tends to act against the dynamic of cultural diversity and in so doing constitutes a force towards uniformity that leads to a regressive social tendency. The point that is being made here is, of course, that in addition to bringing material benefits technology also accelerates inequalities between different countries and between different groups within different countries. But the problem with such a premise is that whilst it might appear to convey a certain truth, its actual meaning cannot just be gleaned from the assertion of the "fact" but instead relies upon a rather particular understanding of the deep economic, social, and general historical processes of capital accumulation and regeneration necessary for the making and remaking of Europeanised, "First World", and mainly White forms of political, economic, and cultural hegemony.

This problem of historical context and hence the precision of conceptual formulation reasserts itself far more dangerously in two further parts of the early argument, which attempts to set the equation between Western technology and Third World oppression.

Firstly and in relation to the process of technical domination two dynamics are in a sense identified: the material and cultural. Whilst the material dynamic, based upon a notion of technological determinism, suggests that the dominated nations exchange what amounts to their liberty and power for material advantages, the cultural dynamic appears to provide a justification for this apparent happening or state of affairs. That is to say the material advantages of technology per se and of the acquisition of technological capital (which in the Third World sense is actually a commodity) are articulated within the framework of a dominant cultural discourse through the various kinds of media. The identification of these two processes is all well and good, but the questions which arise from these descriptions are: i) How are these two dynamics really connected within the overall process of technical domination? ii) What in a far clearer way than presented is the role of ideology in this process? iii) Where is the Western state and how does it function to maintain technical domination and the maintenance and development of (White) Western power and capital?

Although some of these questions are hinted at, without analysis, in the second part of the early argument, their virtual contextual absence leads the author to an interesting, though highly problematic, conclusion, which can be expressed as follows:

i) The acceleration of technology and scientific knowledge accentuates social inequalities;

ii) Traditional or dominated cultures are viewed by secularised dominant cultures as obstacles to progress;

iii) Traditional or dominated cultures view technology as agents of oppression;

iv) Therefore traditional or dominated cultures reject technology.

Now the problem of not having a thoroughly worked out historical context for this kind of analysis has become quite clear. For on the one hand the reader or audience is left with a firm impression of ambiguity. Yet on the other there exists the possibilities of a tremendous imaginative and creative leap that could be made if only... So to put the dilemma succinctly, the conclusion has brought us to the point where it is necessary to ask: Is there detectable in this process as suggested in the title of the paper the working out of the dialectic? Or have we only arrived at a kind of socio-political stalemate, where the dominant attempt to provide technology to the dominated countries, which in turn reject it?

If the former, then there should have been evidence in the earlier analysis not only of a historical appreciation of the capital accumulation and regeneration process, but there should have also been an argument that addressed itself, or at least incorporated, ideas on the role of the (inter)national capitalist state, class, gender, race and ethnic power, ideology, and particularly the role of racism and ethnicism in the modern (inter)national social formations and, finally, for the purposes of the point being made, an account of the global context of East-West as well as North-South relations and the competitive contest between the two dominant world ideologies, Socialism and Capitalism, as played out in the Third World.

As these concerns were hardly addressed then it has to be assumed that the author retreated from the full implications of his earlier position to a intellectual and implicitly ideological vantage point, which favoured an explanation in terms of a stalemate situation -- the creation of a somewhat, in my view, artificial vacuum across which it would appear that an imaginative leap could be made to the way forward. In fact, this is what substantively happens throughout the remainder of the paper, relying upon a set of non-historical and basically cultural and moral arguments to rally support, research effort, and policy considerations for, yes, an imaginative, but also a rather dangerous way forward if the proposals suggested continue to remain decontextualised, dismembered from any restructural theory of social change and largely stripped of their fundamental political and economic as well as their cultural, racial, and ethnic implications for the restructuring of Europeanised and mainly White Western societies.

Both the problems and real dangers for the perpetuation of the racial and ethnicised forms of economic and cultural hegemonies can be seen in the argument that proposes that the way out of the stalemate situation and the "egalitarian" way forward is to be found in a movement from "relations of domination" to "relations of exchange". In practical terms this means that the possessors of technology, the dominant nations, should attempt to learn what benefits their technology could bring to the receiving or dominated nations on the terms of the receiving of dominated nations. Although a textual illustration of this new orientation is given in the example of the construction of a Mali village _with_ the people, it is nevertheless only an orientation.

For not only does it echo an earlier post-Bretton Woods Conference era of development/underdevelopment theory and practice, which sounded through the "aid and development", "partnership", and "transfer of technology and democratic institutions" years of the 1960s to possibly the even less benign North-South dialogue with its doctrine of mutuality in the 1980s; but, without a clear conception of what is actually being exchanged, it can be seen as yet another though more sophisticated form of techological domination. As closeness in concept, thought, and practice to the language of mutuality economics of the Brandt Report is in itself a reminder that all exchanges are undertaken within and bounded by the interests of the dominant rather than those of the dominated.

What then is being said here is that technology is non-exchangeable until it is converted from its status as a commodity for Third World, dominated societies, to its status as the capital _of_ these societies. For this to happen the philanthropic partnership or mutuality schemes, however dressed, have to be abandoned, and not renegotiated in an exchange, for an actual non-conditional repayment of the historical debt owed to the dominated by the dominant societies -- the debt that has arisen as a result of centuries of slavery, pillage, colonialism, imperialism, appropriation of resources, exploitation, and all those other forms of aggression, power, and dominance which have decisively shaped the history and wealth of Europeanised and predominantly White societies.

Without a recognition of these historical happenings and their theoretical and analytical importance in the field under discussion, then any way forward that depends upon an empathetic plea to more from "relations of domination" to "relations of exchange" can be interpreted in any way a dominant nation so wishes to interpret it and consequently help to legitimate even further rather than delegitimate and deconstruct the existing relations of power and domination.

Given this and what I referred to at the beginning as the inconsistencies and contradictions inherent in the analysis, the concluding section of Chombart de Lauwe's paper perhaps speaks for itself. Because whilst few, if any, can fail to agree with the three ideas discussed -- self-education, self-research, and self-management -- the question which should hover over all of our heads and the question which is continuously begged in the paper has little to do with idealism or the futuristic myth. Instead it is a question about how is it possible for the dominated to control, let alone undergo, the processes of self-education, self-research, and self-management when the context is designed, the resources including technology are owned, and the various international policing agencies and bodies, witness the recent politics at UNESCO, are either controlled directly or through the representatives of dominant Europeanised societies.

Thus, whilst a conclusion which calls for the role of experts to change, where the exploited should become the experts and researchers, where the actors themselves become part of the process of change and not just the "detached" researchers of topics, appears eminently sensible and extremely attractive on an emotional level, it will not, in my opinion, do anything that is more than superficial and cosmetic to alter the structural as well as the cultural relations of inequality. Similarly, the challenge to educational institutions in the West to begin to initiate themselves in an understanding of the processes of domination and manipulation with the view to collaborating with social science researchers in beginning the necessary processes which will lead to another, intrinsically more humanitarian and egalitarian conception of the world is equally sensible and attractive -- but again remains almost meaningless (other than in control terms), unless the "another conception of the world" grows out of a historical and structural rather than merely a moral and cultural appreciation and explanation of the existing and dominant conception of the world.

So, finally, despite the flaws in Professor Chombart de Lauwe's fascinating paper, it should be stated boldly that his paper is not only one of several pathways that will lead to the junction where the way forward, along with other ways, can be at least viewed but, if the commitment to change as conveyed in it, is relocated within a more explicit historical context, then the way forward rather than sideways can be both viewed and taken.

III. EDUCATIONAL DILEMMAS

7. THE MANAGEMENT OF ETHNIC RESOURCES: SCHOOLING FOR DIVERSITY

by
Michel de CERTEAU
Directeur d'études
Ecole des Hautes Etudes en Sciences Sociales, Paris

INTRODUCTION

The abundance of statistical and sociological research into cultural and linguistic diversity (minorities, special local characteristics, immigration, etc.) and the educational policies used to "manage" it (1) is such as to justify questioning the very formulation of the problem which gives rise to the research or which its outcome suggests. This is the aim of the discussion that follows. I shall not therefore deal directly with conflicts between minority groups and national educational institutions, nor with the mass of factors underlying the demands of these groups and revealing the shortcomings of the institutions. By "formulation of the problem" I mean the way in which the problem is treated in relation to the crude facts, the way it is presented, and the ideological frame within which solutions are sought. It is a question of identifying the social code which shapes our way of thinking and of whether the facts themselves suggest -- or necessitate -- a change in the framework used as a reference for remedial action.

That the problem of minorities would lead us to question the way it is treated -- or the underlying formulation of the issues -- was inevitable since what is being challenged is the ways in which the education system faces the confrontation with another or other socio-cultural entities. With immigrants or minority groups, other customs pervade the dominant order. An "otherness" clamours for recognition. Unless we are going to accept "solutions" imposed by the relative strengths of the parties, is it acceptable that one party should treat the others according to his own standards and take credit for being neutral and objective? The more complex conventions within which we live accept that the clash of different cultures within a particular system cannot but threaten the assumptions on which the dominant culture is based. Hence the sharpness of the reactions.

Reconsideration of what is at stake in the way in which the problem is formulated seems just as necessary from the historical angle. It has been pointed out many times, for example in connection with migration to richer, more open or more liberal countries, that there is nothing new about migration. What is new is the world in which it is taking place. There is a different set of political, economic and cultural circumstances which changes the significance in all sorts of aspects of political struggle, economic exchange and collective consciousness. As a "fact", it is no longer the same. Continuity is largely illusory, even though it may be found in the statistics of migration. We must therefore consider how this migration operates at present and how to formulate the issue so as to understand what is happening.

Over the last 15 years or so, the progress or revival of ethnic consciousness, has become apparent world-wide and heralds important changes (2). The increase in "ethnic revival movements" has even surprised scientific observers, who were formerly inclined to regard racial, ethnic or religious expression as a relic of the past, but now have to take it seriously, as demonstrated by much recent research since J. Bennett's hotly debated thesis (3) or by the launching of specialist journals such as Ethnicity in 1974 (4). An important body of work is in hand which has enabled "ethnic reality" (which has been taken for granted and therefore left on one side and ignored in the current state of knowledge) to be elevated to an object of scientific investigation. This revival concerns itself closely with studies of the "nation" and "nationalisms", phenomena which, despite the trend that still exists in France, cannot be dissociated from problems of minorities and migration (5) -- which it so happens are largely outside our terms of reference.

An approach to inter-ethnic situations that have become permanent (albeit long assumed to be temporary) calls, therefore, for reconsideration of our standpoint (6). Yet clearly, by its very nature, such an approach excludes the possibility of some neutral or objective analysis to overcome the ambiguity or opposition between heterogeneous groups. At what level can we master or come to terms with these differences? Any authority which examines these differences (even a scientific authority) belongs to a particular system with its own assumptions, rules and logic, and its success, influence and underlying strength end by giving it universal validity.

To begin with -- and this is one of the most important aspects of the question -- it is vital to counter the "realpolitik" which has already fomented so much historical change; "might" is not necessarily "right" and the specificity ("otherness") of the least powerful community has no less right to be recognised than the most powerful. That common interests may exist between migrants or minority groups and citizens of the host country or members of the dominant group, that (with a little cunning) forms of jurisdiction acceptable to all parties can be worked out, that international agreements already provide for redress and changes in the prevailing situation: are all these factors that help to safeguard this fundamental right. But they do not give it a sound basis. If this right is accepted, it follows that the definition of the problem is still liable to fall foul of the independent authority of each community. In a similar perspective to the search for compatibility between nations, no more can be done than to analyse the terms of new socio-political contracts and, in particular, as a precondition, explain the internal changes within a dominant group brought about by or a necessary consequence of its encounter with other groups.

This is the angle from which I would like to consider, in turn (5): first, a critical examination of the conceptual apparatus used to analyse and manage ethnic plurality (6); and secondly, the identification of some of the new or now decisive forms of "belonging" in contemporary minority group or immigrant experience. It is through the reciprocal impressions that emerge from putting these side by side -- on the one hand the challenges to the framework of knowledge of the dominant culture, on the other those things which relate to the changes induced either by the marginalisation of a community or by its dispersal -- that it becomes possible to make new proposals on schooling. Indeed, the school reproduces a society's norms. After all, don't all our own schools play the same role as initiation rites in traditional societies? The school will therefore only be diversified to the extent that contact between ethnic groups itself acts as a school to teach diversity to society as a whole.

CONCEPTUAL ASSIMILATION

Ideological eclecticism

Categories of very different origins are to be found in research on the educational strategies relating to cultural difference. The concepts used, regarded more or less as self-evident, derive from historical and ideological traditions. In the French system, ideas of the "nation", the "national heritage" or "identity" are part of a centralised political philosophy (of Jacobin origin, but often given a nationalist slant which strongly influences reactions to "foreigners" or "autonomists"), whereas concepts of "equal rights", "social bond" or "social demand" belong to a liberal federal-style terminology. There is an ideological gap between "universalism", which is a cosmological and non-historical concept, and "internationalism", which is a political, socialist or legal concept. The terminology of "disadvantage" (cultural or mental) or "handicap", like that of "resistance" and even "minority", refers to an ideology of progress emanating from 18th-century "Englightenment" and is scholastically or medically represented by the grading of abilities in a supposedly progressive way. Among these emanations of "enlightened" philosophy long dominant in educational thinking, categories based on cultural anthropology stand out, e.g. "identity", "difference" (which has replaced the "theory of disadvantage"), "social imagination", "subculture". Out of the idea that culture is a coherent whole in which individual experience is fixed and symbolised, comes the notion of "the space between" ; it is as if there is a vacuum between belonging to one group or to another, and that a choice has necessarily to be made between the two identities -- like considering a journey across a sea as being the time lost before reaching port.

The vocabulary follows a chaotic path of mixed references. Leaving aside "national ideology" or the opposition between "cultural" and "economic" factors, to which I shall return later, this basic list illustrates the many successive ideologies and different disciplines which clutter analyses of the relationship between an educational system and other cultures. This observation, which could be expounded on at length, is not intended as a judgment. But nor is it due to chance. It is the result of a twofold process: on the one hand, the erosion of intellectual assurance when it comes into contact with other cultural assumptions; on the other, the unsuccessful involving of a variety of new intellectual or scientific references in order to try to contend with the situation. A fluctuating eclecticism emerges, as in more and more places within the educational system the often tragic failure of migrant pupils (or those in different linguistic groups) undermines the certainties of those concerned with education. The ideological framework is not independent of the phenomena studied. It reflects the same metamorphoses. It reflects -- whether by more movement or by greater rigidity -- the shifting of strategies of the social institution on which it depends which is usually the school itself. The character of the analysis depends on the ideology of those who undertake it.

Some of the concepts in current usage deserve special attention. First of all, "special local characteristics", which is only significant in relation to its assumed opposite, i.e. the "universal" standard which is supposed to be recognised by all. But are widely circulated notions, such as those put out by the mass media, to be regarded as universal? This overlooks the singularity of the historical conditions of their creation and, still more, the very different ways in which they are used, in other words the special features of their actual use. Or what about values such as "freedom" or "equality"? One forgets that many groups operate on other principles, such as honour, loyalty, contractual allegiance, etc., and that, depending on the society concerned, freedom or equality may take such diverse, not to say contingent, forms that one may well ask if people are really speaking of the same values.

The concept of "identity", often taken as self-evident, is no less strange. Whatever its uses for legal, administrative or police purposes, it assumes that a group (or individual) coincides with a representable object (a system of beliefs and practices, a place in a hierarchy, a way of speaking, etc.) and that it (or he) thereby becomes an object of knowledge both for itself (or himself) and for others. Taken at face value, this concept could be seen as a definition of alienation, since it takes away from a group (or individual) its (or his) interaction with a multitude of systems and the fact that it (or he) is the subject of its (or his) history within a frame of mutually determining relationships. Identity is what ethnology or psychosociology have made of the group by transforming it into an object of knowledge, by a process which defined legal status before the topic itself (7).

This process of definition goes hand in hand with new situations. Thus a highly individualistic society compensates for the gradual disappearance of its internal symbolic hierarchies by an increased stigmatisation of foreigners. The immigrant, the member of the minority group, the outsider, has to take on the role of providing an image which is in contradiction with a norm the character of which is becoming less and less clear. The identity of the "others" who are either dramatised as dangerously unstable or seen in terms of fixed stereotypes, makes up for the lack of character of the others. The immigrant becomes the antidote to anonymity. But whatever social function identification of "the foreigner" plays, it is under brutal attack by the very contact between ethnic groups: foreigners living among citizens of the dominant society not only reject an identity imposed from outside, but also the very idea of identity since they claim the right to be themselves and to live out their own diversity.

Other cases could be mentioned such as the use made of the concept of "difference". But a few examples will suffice to show the extent to which confrontation touches strategic points in a culture and upsets or transforms the conceptual framework.

Cultural or economic?

Many analyses have stressed the failure of educational action programmes based only on the problems of the social environment and the economic interpretation of status or advancement. They have pointed to the importance of cultural factors: ways of life, forms of social behaviour, feelings of belonging, language, familiarity with one's own history, religion, types of habitat, etc. Indeed, it is impossible to resolve the difficulties of Catholics in Northern Ireland, Jews in Los Angeles, or gipsies and Basques in France by socio-economic measures only. Even though in many cases cultural and economic factors work together -- cultural and linguistic difference combining with low cultural status to explain the extent of educational failure -- we need to leave aside an essentially economic approach to the problem in order to stress its cultural aspects.

The policies of those concerned reveal a havering between the two approaches and prove the difficulty of reconciling them. For example, views on the Chicanos in California were long divided between those who saw them as an agricultural proletariat and others who saw them as the alienated survivors of a great tradition dating back to the Aztecs. Two different sets of policies were born of these two interpretations, the first economic, the other cultural. How can one analytical frame of reference, which stresses class relationships and plays down cultural differences, be related to the other, which invokes symbolic genealogies and anthropological structures (8)? In any case, history often demonstrates an opposition between the two. Thus, a strong desire for assimilation by immigrant workers in the United States has put a brake on class consciousness and channelled union solidarity towards corporatism (9). Similarly, in Quebec, the priority given by the Parti Québécois after 1970 to the defence of the French-speaking community increasingly inhibited working class demands over several years. In other circumstances, the same contrast gives rise to the opposite reaction. For instance, in speaking out against government measures which had the effect (or purpose?) of marginalising the "case" of 12 million foreigners in Western Europe, immigrant organisations asserted in their 1979 charter that solidarity with the working class as a whole was paramount (10).

This tension results from the wide disparity of situations and economic circumstances, but it also marks our technical and scientific difficulty in reconciling the two types of analysis that Western society has gradually separated over the last three centuries for reasons relating to its own structure: the first is historical and concerns the dynamic relationship that this society has with itself, preferring to use socio-economic codes; while the other, which is ethnological and relates to "other" societies, tries to understand the unchanging anthropological features of ethnic communities. Nowadays, the confrontation of cultures within our own "developed" society seems to juxtapose the two types of analysis without bringing them together, as though a structure formed by internal historical development was unable to adjust to a structure bent on knowing and dominating the fixed systems outside it.

The presence of "foreigners" in our midst gradually reverses the ethnological or colonial relationship and allows us to reconsider the assumptions. Are we going to treat their presence as an internal factor of "our" history in using the economic approach or as a "foreign body" using ethnological analysis? The alternative is not a valid one (although frequent). It obliges us to think out anew the Western division of knowledge. The immigrants are in a similar position. As inhabitants of a world defined by our systems of knowledge they have to absorb its values and must often situate their own experience of their own country according to a pattern, which, by opposing economy to culture, or productive operations to symbolic images, transforms their traditions into a past which, while still present, is confined to the realm of the unthinkable. But they can also express these different systems of social relations in specific places (for example, home or café, office, factory and administration), and introduce a different practice into the dominant codes, which has the effect of revealing concealed functions and assumptions. Even though its impact is of course felt in a broader framework, I think that the experience of contact between ethnic groups blurs the clarity of our ethnic distinctions (intellectual and administrative) and that we are only just beginning to consider the changes it entails for our ideas.

Individual and collective rights

In particular, the opposition between a "historical" or socio-economic concept of our own societies (in terms of progress) and an "ethnological" concept of others (in terms of cultural structure) seems to be linked with a more fundamental determinant: since the 18th century, as a result of events and for reasons which we have no room to repeat here, modern Western society has been viewed as a combination of individual units and therefore different from the traditional (medieval, classical or "primitive") societies which were governed by the principle of the priority of the group over its members (11). This concept has gradually grown and taken shape in a liberal economy (defined as competition between individual producers), democracy (with one man one vote for the purposes of collective representation), a mathematical science of society (in which the individual is the unit of calculation, ever since Condorcet and up to the INSEE statistics), a legal formulation of individual rights (taken as equal for all) and so on (12). As far as the school is concerned, the official progressive line is therefore to express social needs in terms of individual rights and duties, and avant-garde battles are fought in terms of the equality of these rights (13). Clearly, increasing application of data-processing to social problems reinforces this way of dealing with groups, via an analysis based on the manipulation of basic units.

The old communal rights which gave family, "house" (14), tribe, client network or "nation" priority over their individual members have been outlawed from orthodox thinking or banished abroad to become the symbol of an outlived and alien system in the form of an "ethnological" approach to "primitive" or "peasant" societies.

This system of social relations has been rejected, not to say banned, to a point where in France the collective expression of "family", "house", etc., has in both theory and practice been as far as possible dropped so far as national institutions and representative bodies are concerned, or abandoned to the conservative opposition and, where total elimination was impossible, treated as "relics of the past", or obstinate and irrational opposition (e.g. by the Basques, Bretons and Corsicans) to the democratic march of progress. Where possible, such expression has been transformed into a set of problems relating to a collection of separate individuals. An enormous effort -- an obscure underground "Hundred Years' War" -- has reduced communal rights either by assimilating them with individual rights or by "ethnologising" them.

In so blunt a summing up of such a complex story -- one which is fundamental for the development of the sciences examining social relations on this new basis -- I only want to underline the difficulty we experience today in finding a place for rights of communities (insofar as they represent more than the product of combinations of individuals) amidst the dominant logic of individual rights. In every case the community is reduced to a number of basic units whose combination and correlation can be analysed by economists or sociologists. It is not surprising that the inadequacy of these calculations increasingly prompts the use of ethnological or anthropological models taken from their function abroad and (painfully) applied to "research" and planning at home.

Migrants or the members of so-called minority groups however reintroduce into an administration (legal, economic or educational) based on individual rights, the rights of communities, which cannot be reduced to the sum of their individual members. By virtue of a language, a body of practices or a common history, a social entity exists over and above the variants presented by its members, and it is on this basis that they demand recognition. Before looking at some of the forms that this situation imposes today on "belonging" in migrant or "minority group" experience, it may be useful to see how the more or less hidden forms of these collective rights reappear in structures which treat society in terms of individual units. While these disguised forms refer to the way in which our history has prompted <u>us</u> to put problems concerning <u>other</u> types of belonging, and while they stem from a policy of assimilation which shapes our way of thinking, they nonetheless provide tools for analysing our own situation and may suggest alternative policies.

Behind the mask

Since we are faced with two opposing paradigms (the priority of the community in one case, the priority of the individual in the other), it is not surprising that social experience seen in terms of the first gives rise to curious interpretations of the second. As examples, I shall only consider some of the paradoxical forms in which community experience appears to us concealed in and by our social terminology, e.g. "cultural", "private", "customary", "non-communication". These "translations" give figurative expression to an alien language.

First of all, a considerable part of what we regard as "cultural" -- or which we have transformed into "cultural" expressions and activities -- corresponds to those areas of social life that the individualistic assumptions of our analytical and management structures have made incomprehensible to us in economic terms. We call "cultural" those configurations or fragments of <u>economies</u> which obey other criteria than our own. The word identifies within a different group (or in our own) what we can now only think of as exotic manifestations, symbolic structures or customary practices not amendable to the law of the market (15). Indeed, studies on those social relations covered by the word "cultural" discover an increasing number of systems of exchange, but systems whose rules depend on the pre-eminence of the group, its honour, continuity and spiritual heritage, the allegiance due to its "leaders" by a clientele, and so on. Likewise, since Schumpeter, we have gradually come to perceive in "economic" rationality itself the "cultural" trends underpinning each system, the historical types of credibility that this implies and the impact of non-trading relations. The dividing line between economy and culture is becoming less clear and more permeable. What we call "symbolical" (property, a method of expression, etc.) is no more symbolical than money or financial accounts. Nor less rational. But it is a different economy and has a different rationale from those which have prevailed for us.

It is also remarkable that psychoanalytical research, now directing towards the examination of the "savage" interior of Western life, the style of ethnological investigation previously used on a "primitive" external world, rediscovers in the subsoil of our societies the very same relational, "family" and collective "economy" that a productivist and individualist order claims to have replaced. In this respect, immigrants restore to us our own subconscious, which we have repressed! In any event, our institutions and conventional wisdom no longer respond to this kind of collective law. But by recognising ethnic economies behind the "cultural" mask, which is the result of their rejection by our history, we have an insight into what is at stake (16).

The description of one type of social relationship in terms of another produces a second paradox: the rights of a community as a whole are translated in terms of private rights and duties. The communal is disguised as the <u>private</u>. Belonging to a social organism (aggregate corporations as English law puts it, or to "families" of all kinds, such as ethnic communities, linguistic groups, etc.) was once considered in terms of contracts governing alliances or wars between groups, and not between individuals. Nowadays, it is only reflected in official regulations in the form of prerogatives or special responsibilities of private persons -- except where it is possible to find a diplomatic solution for these problems of belonging (as preferred by the policy-makers in the case of migrants but excluded for many others, e.g. Gypsies, Basques, Irish Catholics in Northern Ireland). Thus, apart from agreements between States on "foreign nationals" (which short-circuit the relations between groups themselves and the host country), the general tendency is to treat ethnic belonging in terms of individuals in a way which is by turn ethical (liberty of conscience), educational (abilities and backwardness), medical (handicaps, social security rights) etc., and to regard the community as an "association" (with its representatives and powers) based on rules and decisions of individuals. In this way a community reality fragments, so that a system of management based on the individual can deal with discrete units and no longer has to confront a different social logic.

Two cases more sharply illustrate the procedures which make belonging a "private" matter: family lineage and religion. In spite of differences, it is possible to compare them in terms of the relationship evident in France between collective reality and private expression. Social organisation (which is productivist) has been separated from belonging (in the family or religous sense), whereas they were for long closely linked. Having isolated them (as one scientifically isolates a chemical body), the socio-political administration has marginalised the domestic and religious economies, which are now reduced to expressing themselves in this new framework in a disguised form: the ethnic dimension is henceforth a private matter. The private sphere serves as a social metaphor often a symptom, or even the root of a fixation for those aspects of family life or religious institutions which have had to be eliminated from public norms in the name of individual <u>activity</u> (the true aim of the market economy and the administration) (18). Fortunately, the issue is not one of returning to a past which was no less restrictive than the present (and probably more so), but of recognising manifestations of fundamental ethnic economies in a private form, i.e. treating this new social form as a possible community form in disguise. That this private aspect is the expression of an ethnic revival (and a particularly strong one in the case of family lineage or religious affiliation) is amply demonstrated by the latest political events, but must be taken seriously for that very reason, including relations between the school and the private demands of migrant parents.

Another collective manifestation within legal systems based on written constitution is provided by customary law. In ways which have often been debated, forms of behaviour usually accepted as legitimate by a group are or can be law-creating. They may even derogate from formal constitutional law. They refer to a collective right existing within the legislative system based on individual representation. The counterpoint that these customary norms introduce at the margins of our regular habits obviously demand official sanction and this has usually minimised their importance. It nonetheless entails acceptance of a different logic, frequently in the form of conçessions to "relics of the past", in other words, a recognition of diversity within our societies and of principles of social relations other than those prevailing in our country. Customary law, which is still ill-accepted, is the Trojan Horse of alien social systems; it introduces the idea of "otherness" compatible with a changing society. It could be used for organised systems to understand not only the data from the past in the present situation but also the implications of the present for the future.

Lastly, we must mention the form taken by the "foreigner" in the communication context, clearly postulated as far back as the Enlightenment. The massive advance of communication has created roads, schools, administrative rationalisation, telecommunications networks, the media and information technology. The role of communication has been to provoke an unceasing struggle against the prevailing opacity of the situation (local prerogatives, autonomous or extraneous communities, etc.) in order to create an universal transparency allowing immediate contacts between citizens and with central government. In France, it is possible to discern two presuppositions, one anthropological (communication is a good thing and we need more and more of it), the other political -- royal and then republican (the rise of the State ensures the nation's progress). Events have fortunately imposed limits on the development of these presuppositions. Restraints include the collective experience of immigrants or minorities, from Gypsies to the Portuguese of today. In opposition to the goal of transparency and the endless striving for total social legibility, we find here obscure differences equivalent to a kind of high treason against "Communication". But behind this irritating mask, there remain two essential factors to which the inflationary logic of information obliges us to return today: first, communication exists only in relation to non-communication, to barriers generating a collective intimacy and to a whole series of closed doors and "secrets" which create internal areas of exchange; secondly, as the effectiveness of democratic life disappears along with the local authorities (leading citizens, regional groups, etc.) which were for long its historical prop, only the recognition and the vitality of communities (ethnic, linguistic or geographical) can resist the (at worst terrorist) levelling due to the fragmentation of the citizenship by government departments.

From this angle, the pockets of illegible social "otherness" which seemed to infringe the law of transparency have an increasingly essential role beyond that qualitative threshold at which the successes of communication are beginning to undermine it. In our Western countries, opacity has become necessary. It is based on community rights that can offset the impact of the economy, which in the name of individual rights exposes social reality in its entirety to the universal light of the market and the administration.

ASSETS AND LIABILITIES OF BELONGING

Mixing

Those communities whose image is metamorphosed and hidden on the national scene by the effects of assimilation are also, owing to migration or marginalisation, themselves being transformed by their adjustment to new situations, in other words by the effects of adaptation. Many factors are involved in this internal transformation: the distance from their base of reference (a territory, a language, local customs, a genealogy), the compulsory adoption of different administrative codes (police, social security, labour legislation, employment conditions) and the expansion of frameworks of distance or spatial proximity (the media, markets, urban life-styles, transport).

A group's reactions to new settings naturally cannot be dissociated from the effects of the "colonisation" it suffers, but they are not however of the same order. The capacity of "adaptation" of which its members are capable is more than the "assimilation" of a foreign body by the host country (an "anthropophagic" phenomenon), in relation to a dynamic they entail using a range of strategies to use the imposed order for the group's own ends. If they were the same thing, adaptation would be merely a passive reaction within a framework of constraints; once again, the dominant group would be left the role of main actor in the story (the agent of evil if it cannot be the hero). The renewed creativity demonstrated by these tactics also leads us to abandon the assumption (ethnological and mythical) that foreign societies are by their very nature coherent and stable systems, that it is necessary and possible to isolate their "authentic" form (scientifically "pure" substances) and that the actual or tentative changes due to adaptation are therefore symptoms of deterioration or alienation. Any group lives by the compromises it invents and the contradictions it deploys (up to a point where it can no longer support them). Identifying it as a homogeneous stable entity would be to regard it as though it were already dead. Immigrant and minority group experience presents the opposite pattern: adaptation processes pushed to the extreme by a sudden acceleration in the rate of change demonstrate creativity pushed to the limit of its capacity. Because it is faster than in normal times, this "trial" of the mechanisms of mobility reveals possibilities and bottlenecks of a social dynamic.

Although violent, the confrontation of "foreign" groups with the host country is not a collision between two systems. It is not the same as the metaphorical clash between heroes or gods of antiquity. It takes place in what are now composite dominant societies, especially in their urban forms, generating an eclecticism which is the constantly enriched material handled by commercial, industrial or mass-media technology. Nowadaways, orthodoxy is multi-cultural. It plays all the cards. The dominant society deals in diversity itself, using methods which make every possible difference accessible to all, free from the hermetic meaning assigned by a particular community and which thus put the separate ethnic autonomies on the same level, subjecting them to the general code of individualised diffusion. Like that circulated by money, every possible social form must be conveyed far and wide by technology networks whose universal growth camouflages specific historical, economic and ideological postulates. This "hybrid monism" (the doctrine that reality consists of only one substance, such as mind or matter) (19) therefore has its laws. It transforms, "rewrites", homogenises and combines flexible contents in a rigid framework.

Reciprocally, adaptation is more brutally imposed on minority groups. It comprises faster adjustment and a necessary selection of types of belonging. It is necessary to determine the forms adopted for the maintenance and even clarification and strengthening of "otherness" in the context of a general mix. There are certain strategic points. They map out a geography of the difficulties encountered in school (as in many other places) and the measures to deal with them. These points correspond to a strengthening or interiorisation of the specific situation under the stimulus or constraint of adaptation to a different social climate. Operations and fixations which are not in themselves new in the group acquire a quite new importance with the erosion or disappearance of traditional sites. Two in particular of the factors of belonging to which the situation allots a new strategic function should be noted: first, practices, which are traditional and individual forms of action, are now deployed in the network of different factors imposed by a different order; secondly, fragments of a collective memory unconsciously or not, involuntarily or not, constitute the anchor points or "stops" whereby a collective resistance is reflected in individuals. The former might indicate the "assets" of belonging, the latter its "liabilities" if by these two words we mean styles of production and forms of adhesion.

Politicisation

Before examining these two historical processes, they must be situated in the more general context which gives the measure of the contact between ethnic groups: the politicisation of "belonging". What until that point has been taken as a setting and a "given", as a set of fundamental principles, becomes an issue of debate and political choice. The accepted tradition is transformed into history in the making. Disputed by others, it is no longer merely the scene of political strife but its purpose. By "political", I mean the positions of strength which govern the experience of immigrants or minority groups in search of jobs, a recognised role and normal advancement. Many aspects of this struggle (which also takes place in the school, of course) will determine the forms taken by the ethnic reference: it becomes an ideology once its politicisation is neglected. I shall only note some of these issues.

A debate on nationalism

The relations between groups are conflictual relationships. It is therefore impossible to subscribe to the idealistic view that these conflicts can be settled through mutual "understanding" or merely by making technical improvements in teaching methods. In point of fact, technical improvement is a mask for the power that a group exercises over others in laying down the norms for their meeting. The competing interests call for political elucidation and expression which are the very ones that directly or indirectly prohibit the kinds of analysis that emphasise certain otherwise positive aspects of the problem (cultural, psychological or anthropological).

In particular, these conflictual relationships take place in an environment which is basically hostile to them and might be described as one with an "obsession with units of measurement". At the present time the reference to all that is national mobilises this "obsession". It gives an initial form to the politicisation of ethnic questions. It provides ethnocentrism the support of public institutions. It organises the revised and amended historiography which in France "forgets" the Sétif massacres in 1945 or torture during the Algerian war (20) and which, by giving the impression that it tells what actually happened, becomes the instrument of nationalist indoctrination that is so efficient in making present-day society conform to a State ethnic model.

Movements are being born or reborn all over the world which identify the State with the nation. Observable in many countries (from France to Israel) and linked with the rise of nationalism over the last three centuries (a complex phenomenon whose resilience historical analysis has not managed to fathom by the usual methods) (21), they convey its logic: for a nationalist, being different is an act of treason. Nationalist tendencies also reflect the internal contradictions in each country. For instance, while the French Constitution of 1958 refuses to identify citizenship with nationality (22), it is legal custom to favour the national law of the home country as regards migrants' political rights. Moreover, whereas the economic market is gradually reducing the relevance of frontiers (multinational companies, etc.), ethnic attachment to a territory ("being one's own home") is returning in force in the collective conscience. It is as though economic internationalisation provokes (like an antibody?) the development of political nationalism. In this reversal of orders, immigrants are both the artifice (their migratory flows responding to the laws of the market) and the victims (their arrival provokes local chauvinism).

Action and discussion are urgently needed against this ethnic nationalism, starting in the educational system, to counter the "nationalisation" of the State, i.e. the "ethnicisation" of political problems. A good subject for lessons on civic ethics! An internationalist tradition could provide the basis for research on the compatibility of different nations within the same State, even though, as it works in France, this tradition has often been a product to be exported, rather than a rule of internal policy. To the extent that no general public debate has taken place on the "nation", immigrants have to bear the sole responsibility as witnesses to an internationalism that is perfectly compatible with the state; but because the relative strengths are unequal they are reduced to being no more than the nationals of foreign powers.

Historical interactions

Another effect of the conflict is that the social existence of a group is constructed. It is neither reducible to a "nature" defined by biological characteristics, nor to a "system" produced by its ethnological or anthropological image, nor to a past disinterred, selected or invented (to support some thesis or other) by historical research. It is made day by day. It is linked with a "historicity", if by that we mean a group's ability to change by re-using the means at its disposal for other purposes and for new uses. The way in which a group is also the subject of its history and not only the product of constraints affects actual analysis of the facts and suggests some rules as regards methods.

i) This collective creativity could not exist in isolation. It develops in the course of reciprocal historical exchanges. It is organised and mobilised by real situations of intercommunication (23). Hence the special importance of the "interrelational" dynamic effect on an immigrant group of its advance from first to second or third generation. It has often been pointed out, from Lévi-Strauss (24) onwards, that isolation produces inertia, while confrontation is a stimulus. In this context, the necessity for adaptation faced by immigrant or minority groups prompts them to be pioneers in using the means at their disposal, even if finally this new use of a heritage is of more benefit to the host than the home country. This interrelational dialectic often lacks the instruments for analysis and therefore for action. Research should continue (25) and might be based on the arguments of feminist studies which found that male and female roles are determined jointly in various historical situations after believing for a time that a female "identity" could be isolated. These mutual transformations, which cannot be dissociated from positions of strength, constitute the greater or lesser daily mobility and the creative hum of any living group. They relate to that law of history which propounds that contact between communities, as between the two sexes, is the true principle of generation.

ii) The ideological, historical or mythical image that a group has of itself at any given moment in its struggle is constantly changing since it is the cause and effect of adaptation, protest, loss or plans connected with a conflictual situation. Naturally at each stage, it also has the role of expressing an immemorial identity, but in fact the collective narrative is subject to constant revision (in which the "details" are often more important than the general plot) and is affected by its re-employment and the different beliefs that are successively based on it. In spite of its apparent greater stability, this image is no less clever nor less subtle than the cyclical tactics it regulates or legitimises, nor more fixed or more legible. It belongs to history. It is a symbol in the struggle. To "depoliticise" it, changing it into an identifying monument, would be to mistake the way in which this instrument of social historical authenticity works and to alienate its users by depriving them of the room for manoeuvre and adaptation that a space for symbolisation allows them.

Internal crisis

Confrontation between ethnic groups is a trial and a decisive moment (a crisis) for the traditional image. It reveals the latter's internal contradictions, which were "held together" by the relative stability of territory, language and the group itself. All the different elements assembled by symbolisation, permitting mobility within the area of the same tradition, are made compatible by a common "soil". Without it, this mix would be a source of fragmentation. Furthermore, the formerly accepted social hierarchies (the "authorities") lose their legitimacy for members of the group who move about and come into contact with other types of social structure. In these and many other forms, conflict with other groups is not the most important thing. Within the minority community, it entails internal strife regarding ways of adapting or resisting. Different strategies reveal or exacerbate tendencies that an autonomous collective policy was formerly able to regulate. Traditional criteria oppose new choices. Hitherto silent solidarity falls apart.

This internal deterioration surprises many immigrant or minority communities. It demands a completely new effort of selection from the past, contracts for the present and common projects that are still possible for the future. It is of course a fact that personal processes of adaptation often gradually take the drama and even the interest out of such crises. In many cases, successful assimilation makes individuals forget the collective problems of their original immigrant community. This is one solution, but it cannot be the only one and means sidestepping the inter-ethnic problem. In actual fact, it is for various reasons less frequent (e.g. increasing immigration, the second generation's political claim to belong to two societies). In any event, it is still also necessary to analyse the strategies of what we might call diaspora policies (26), which are able to elude the constraint imposed by the alternative of assimilation or a return to the country of origin, and which places collective experience itself in a transitional vacuum of between the two.

Are Algerians and Bretons fighting the same battle?

Finally, we must consider the delicate problem of the relationship which may exist between the social forms assumed in one and the same country by ethnic "otherness" of external origin (e.g. in France, Portuguese or Maghrebins) and ethnic otherness due to the country's domestic history (e.g. Bretons, Basques, Corsicans). In administrative and legal logic, they are separated by a simple distinction: are you French citizens or not? This classification is neither very clear nor automatic. The various communities living in France have obvious ethnic and social differences which from the point of view of their particular economic organisation should not be confused. But from a political standpoint, the problem is different: legal recognition of collective rights also affects these communities and can forge a political solidarity between them. In this respect, citizenship, which is in any case quite liberally granted in France (the Italian or Maghrebin communities living in the country contain some members who are "naturalised" and others who are not) is neither impeded nor privileged by "cultural distance" (Basque society differs more from Ile-de-France customs than Piedmontese society), nor the geographical dislocation assumed to be peculiar to emigration (some Corsican, Basque or Breton immigrants in Paris have been separated from the local origins for one or more generations), nor even the historical fact of having a different past (which is just as much the case in France for the 200 000 Basques as it is for the 900 000 Portuguese). In any case, an immigrant from the former Upper Volta and one from Vietnam are no closer to each other than to a Parisian and the way they are treated in Paris separates them even more: to put the first two in the "foreigner" category masks their difference; at the same time, naturalising them as the only way of giving them access to political rights (beginning with the right to vote) would be granting them political legitimacy at the price of a procedure which generally means obliterating their distinctive character.

Instead of a policy that makes the foreigner a fetish by isolating him or offering him citizenship as the only way out, it might be preferable to have an alliance between communities which together claim recognised rights because they belong to an ethnic group and already play a part in political life. We might then have a slogan such as "Algerians and Bretons shoulder to shoulder", which rejects the "foreign" ghetto for the former and the domination of national ideology for the latter (27). As a logical component of decentralisation or a federal structure, this alliance could procure for each ethnic community the political means for developing its own distinctive character without necessarily being a third alternative imposed on all of its members.

Catalogues of practices

Styles

Migrant experience takes on a wide variety of forms according to the stage of establishment in the host country. Thus, "immigration for work" (adult employment, mainly for men, at places of work) is qualitatively different from "immigration for settlement" (family involvement in civic life). The "first generation", estranged by belonging elsewhere and still bound by a whole network of economic and family ties, differs from the second, which takes advantage of belonging to two communities, like the "Beurs" (second generation immigrants of maghrebin origin in France) (28). The same applies to minority communities according to the levels at which their difference can still be asserted: an economic power, a linguistic unit, a set of customs, local institutions and their own means of expression. Minority social relations vary with the tone they are able to use.

To these disparities are added the internal distortions due to the impact of surrounding society. For example, while collective consciousness is increased for the whole group by family immigration, it is contradicted for its members by the individualistic behaviour and ambitions demanded by participation in the socio-economic structure of the host country. Or else, and this is another paradox, an increase in the cultural demands of French minorities is linked with an economic and political decline, so that these communities increase their demands at a time when they depend more on the resources granted by central government.

It is therefore very difficult to determine common forms and stable types among the variety of directions taken by adaptation or resistance. A definition of situations in terms of socio-economic categories or "households", administrative status, or population or budget country, takes static cross-sections that leave out the very operations (strategies, tactics, conventions) whose effects are being calculated. While statistical analysis can be used to measure trends by means of comparisons and correlations, it does not show their underlying dynamics.

It is possible to include an analysis of the actual procedures used by minority groups to appropriate, change and improve the situations imposed on them. We would then no longer be concerned with their circumstances but with the operations they use to make their history, not out of static states, but from specific action and "styles". The too-rare studies on the different styles of procedure and imprint which are nonetheless also scientific (29) may serve as a model; they should be extended to the styles which, in the busy hubbub of a school, factory or street, also characterise the operations of the members of different communities. One or two comments in this connection will show the "assets" of belonging.

Ways of speaking

A first sign of the importance which must be attached to these forms of action is shown by a group's relationship to its language. According to recent research on the "ethnography of communication" or the "ethnography of speaking" (30), a group is less distinctive for the language it speaks (the dictionary and grammar as defined in linguistics) than for the use made of this language, the way it is employed socially, the forms this takes, conventions, subtleties and the clever turns of phrase which adjust language to a labyrinth of interlocutory situations that add up to an interrelational economy of language. These uses are of course hinged to the characteristic structure of the language, but they constantly generate new lexical or syntactic forms. They add unexpected possibilities to the "treasury" of language. What is more, they adapt extremely well to external linguistic additions which they "treat" (as in painting) in their own "manner" or style. They even outlive the language in which they operated; they may be found outside the "maternal" or local environment in foreign languages whose untapped resources are developed by a proliferation of new "slants" which are often regarded as verbal or grammatical "mistakes" (31). Far from a group being identifiable by its language (in other words, finally, by the system representing it in our linguistics) and far from its autonomy being measured by conformity to the "purity" (decided by whom?) of its language, it is typified by these operations that begin in the realism of a linguistic heritage and are likely to extend elsewhere into other regions.

The spoken word is of course the privileged and most recognisable mode of use. It differs from written usage by the virtuosity with which the uses of the spoken language adjust to a greater number of individual situations. Its "exploits", achieved with a mastery which is slowly being recognised (having long been measured according to its compliance with the laws of written language), are proof of a tactical art of adaptation to constant change. Owing to its mobility, the spoken word combines two characteristics: 1) it clarifies a group's specific style in practical language terms better than the written word; 2) it depends more on the (up- or down-grading) hierarchical differences that govern the relative strength of groups and hence of their practices (this applies to turns of phrase, idiomatic expression, accents, etc.). Being the most sensitive form of verbal communication, the spoken word combines a greater inventiveness, able to give shape to all the musical and semantic resources of a language in different circumstantial exchanges, with greater violence, which may be passive (repressed) or active (domineering), due to the fact that the spoken word is used in social conflict. While written language is more distant from poetic speech and social stigmatisation, the spoken word reveals more and constantly overlaps with a style of creativeness and situations of conflict (32). It associates the art of doing with the struggle for existence, the very definition of a practice.

Specific practices

The group's procedures therefore continue to borrow materials and operate in linguistic settings transformed by the prevailing situation (e.g. by new types of socio-economic exchanges). Similarly, a community's specific ways of inhabiting a space are preserved where the actual living conditions have changed; adjusting to these new conditions, they enable the community to take over the new landscape (33).

A threshold is no doubt crossed where such practices begin to crumble away, gradually yielding to the customs of a new community and to the pressure of a different socio-linguistic environment. It is at least already possible to see from these socio-linguistic analyses some of the consequences of contact between ethnic groups.

i) If the ways of using a space (linguistic, geographical or other) survive the transformation of that space and if they are more characteristic and more lasting than the places they fill for a time, then these practices, as well as their art and combination, must first be granted the right and means to express themselves in ways of living, caring and teaching, in the situations created by migration. From this angle, too, one can recognise within the group the activities by which it creates its history and renews itself, instead of alienating itself, finding its identity in its place of origin and its previous history.

ii) The apparent similarity of linguistic systems has become deceptive -- as in the case of geographical, anthropological and other systems. This similarity is the effect of coherent verifiable procedures developed by Western linguistics. It is produced by a particular set of practices which, outside our mother tongue, are applied to an increasing number of foreign languages. It is the result of specific "forms of action" linked with our history and with criteria that are peculiar to ourselves, just as ethnology applies our own ways to different societies. From this standpoint, linguistics stems from a society's ability (mentioned earlier) to use other languages in the same way as its own. It applies methods that are certainly valid and effective, but wrongly assumed to be universal, which disguise the difference between our own practice of a language and other types of linguistic practice.

There is in fact a real difference between languages according to the ways in which they are spoken. This fact particularly calls in question the kind of teaching which often assumes that, although obeying different rules, language is the same kind of reality in every society. On the contrary, spoken language in, for instance, the Maghreb or in France, Mexico or the United States, is a field organised according to different social practices, consequently it not only differs according to varying norms within similar systems but according to functions that are qualitatively foreign to each other. For one group, language is the spiritual articulation of a fundamental reality, whereas for another it represents a network of compatibilities and exchanges between individuals. In one society it participates in the corporal staging of acts of language and in another ensures the circulation of declared values: this means perceiving that mistakes or innovations in spoken language are the signs of a practice that has come from elswewhere and the "signature" of different customs and other ways and practices. Only then can any attempt be made to develop a tactical diversity in one and the same language which might enrich it without erasing certain specific operational features.

Fundamental though it is, language is only a system of such practices. All the essential "factors" of a society such as law, marriage and the family, heritage, crime and punishment, medicine and cooking, personal hygiene, the use of day and night, and the organisation of space and time, are less specifically defined by the objects, instruments or concepts that surround them than by the ways in which this series of factors is appropriated, used and thought of. It is not certain that these ways are mutually consistent.

Their combination is already the result of a multitude of historical compromises which make adjustment and future selection possible. But it is certain that if we were to extract from this labyrinth of tactics the objects or statements that we consider are to the point, we would be left with the inert and moreover irrelevant parts of this different social body, even though we were able to base the most brilliant constructions on them. We must turn instead to those unassimilable practices which "animate" a special characteristic.

But here they appear spontaneously in our midst. Immigrant experience brings this tactical economy onto our own doorstep. Procedures that were yesterday regarded as exotic or replaced by our own practices have infiltrated the way we organise the space in which we live. So it is not surprising that, with a kind of lucidity about the true nature of ethnic confrontation, people display the most violent allergies to foreign "ways" of re-investing our space, and towards "errors" or "barbaric behaviour" which show, in contrast to our way of doing things, they are using our territory differently.

Fragments of history

This strong reaction actually clarifies the issue. The confrontation with these different ways of using our terrain triggers a change of ownership. It entails a loss for the "owners" which will seem still more menacing when the conflict leads to status or property being appropriated and when any advancement of the "foreigner" appears to oust a native. In any event, the encounter does not leave the majority unscathed. Clashes and reciprocal changes everywhere join the remnants of former monopolies to introduce the danger which is inseparable from a common renewal.

But for minority groups the cost is much higher and accompanied by greater risks. In particular, the immigrant is playing with high stakes: he loses proportionately more, but in order to win more. If one limits oneself to those aspects of the challenge which relate to "belonging", the loss first concerns the need to continue to live a history away from the territory, the language and the system of exchanges which were previously its support. Practices, as we have seen, develop on the basis of this loss. This distance becomes the measure of everything that is missed: tradition moves to imaginary regions of the memory; the implicit assumptions of personal experience become strangely lucid, often in many respects imitating the objective perspicacity of the ethnologist. Lost places are transformed into fictitious areas for mourning and meditating on the past.

But a much more notable, because more significant, phenomenon is that adaptation to a different social setting also makes the old references crumble away and some of the remnants that stay with the traveller begin to play a role which is both intense and silent. They consist of fragments of rites, forms of politeness, ways of dressing or eating habits, and gift-giving customs or standards of honour. They include smells, colour references, noises and tones of voice. These relics of a lost social body detached from its parent group then grow stronger, though not integrated in a whole, as though isolated, inert and grafted on to another body, like the "small bits of truth" that Freud found precisely in the "travels" of a tradition (34). They no longer have a language to symbolise or unite them. They no longer form an individual history born out of a disintegrating collective memory. They are there as though asleep. Yet this sleep is only apparent. You have only to nudge, and unpredictable violence breaks out.

These fragments refer to an increasingly widespread different "cultural" pattern. Enshrined in habits, latent and scattered about like the household statuettes that people used to put in every corner of their homes, silent spirits of place, but "spirits" which are only material details, they have this special feature that they no longer organise social, occupational, administrative or family life; they *punctuate* it with points of reference which are apparently insignificant but nonetheless important.

A notable example is provided by the survival of a religious tradition (Islamic, Protestant or Catholic) among migrants who no longer practise and even say that they have lost their faith. It nonetheless remains significant, but in the form of fragments of collapsed or abandoned systems. Indeed, certain gestures, certain objects, manners, anniversaries and fragrances punctuate the text of daily life and act like the essential punctuation of a written text. With signs that differ from the letters which organise meaning, they punctuate the lexical and syntactic order imposed by the dominant society. They are the (Barthism) "signifiers", but we no longer know for what. We call these material signs "superstitions", from a word designating something that exceeds (from the Latin *superstare*) and refuses assimilation. Their role is *metonymic* (expressing part for the concealed whole), *historical* (indicating a potential danger), *elliptical* (quotations whose meaning or reference has been forgotten) and *poetic* (inducing fantasy).

Because of them, ethnic otherness is maintained -- obstinate, fragmented, silent and illusive. This form of belonging, worn in social practice like worthless family jewels, is probably no less vital than conformity with socio-cultural orthodoxy was in the past since we have gradually discovered to what extent this conformity is cunning, tactical and speculative within the space provided for it by a system of beliefs. With these apparently trivial relics, less is at stake; they create obligations, albeit silently and sporadically; they bring into that area of what "everyone knows" irruptions of "but all the same". They represent what is most overlooked by the educational systems, which place a naïve trust in the content of knowledge and cannot even see the prosaic way in which a group manipulates this knowledge behind the teacher's back to preserve its present relationship with a scattered heritage.

CONCLUSION: SCHOOLING FOR DIVERSITY

These different groups, shaped either by the way we see them or by the depredations of exile from their home country, suggest possible approaches in the educational field. There is one precondition. The experience of the encounter is above all for us a schooling in diversity, an initiation into the social "economies" whose secrets we will never grasp (they are foreign to the paradigms that we have officially adopted) which nonetheless disclose aspects of our society ruled out of order by our own criteria. Our teaching methods might take advantage of this in several specific ways:

i) By unearthing from our acquired knowledge the real stages by which it is produced: in fact education often hides these by presenting the results. At the various levels of technical work and its past or present history, these practices belong to the general category of know-how, procedures and techniques which are also shared by the social practices of other ethnic or cultural groups. Clarifying them would tell us more about the selected operations which give access to our knowledge. It would also help the members of minority groups to recognise the different "styles" which distinguish the operations preferred by the host country from their own and, through a sort of pragmatic polyglotism, to develop various practices to match the environment and the objectives (35);

ii) At the same time, to show the relationship of knowledge to the social training which still responds to an <u>ethnic or family</u> type: education frequently presents a complex system of knowledge and imposes it on "foreigners" as a homogeneous whole. This educational theatre effectively indexes the existence of a coherent minimum number of rules for checking or falsifying knowledge. But it is nonetheless imaginary. It removes from view conflicts which are often savage, though muffled, between "families" (be they of genealogies, of clienteles or of "old boy" networks) since our official discourse, democratic and scientific, does not wish to "know" about the ethnic element involved. The aim is not to demystify the credibility of knowledge (which would be ridiculous, dangerous and wrong) but to bring it back into a discourse which masks the existence of collective competitive forces and thereby to provide instruments of analysis for minorities who live their own lives in terms of "belonging". Since ideology hides the "ethnic factor", thus preventing any discussion of the matter, and runs the danger of delivering it to unbridled racist passions, it would be better to elucidate the tacit laws, initiations, and rules of honour, allegiance and solidarity of these "families" in consultation with the members of groups who are in a better position than we are to control subtle or fierce reactions. They would thus no longer be given a deceptive picture of the society on whose fringes they live, and which finally ends up by giving them a deceptive picture of themselves (36);

iii) To promote the <u>management of conviviality</u> in the school. Often education wavers between an approach based on personal relationships and one based on the objective content of knowledge. Between the two there is supposed to be a knowledge of, and an apprenticeship to, conventions and social contract. In some institutions, such as US high schools, this social apprenticeship appears to be favoured at the expense of knowledge. These institutions are nevertheless the laboratories in which experiments are being conducted by trial and error of objective and regulated forms which can be built into competition. These ways of doing things are the motive force in society. They make it grow. It is no longer a question of expressing personal views, but of undertaking practical work in conviviality, the tensions and conflicts which disrupt relations between the races in particular urgently call for such exercises, which would be analogous in the social domain to what has already been done in linguistics -- and would be a real schooling in diversity.

NOTES AND REFERENCES

1. See the OECD/CERI report The Education of Minority Groups. An Enquiry into Problems and Practices of Fifteen Countries, Gower Publishing Co., Aldershot, U.K., 1983.

2. See ALLARDT E., "Implications of the Ethnic Revival in Modern Industrialised Society: A Comparative Study of the Linguistic Minorities in Western Europe", in Commentationes Scientiarum Socialium, 12, Helsinki, Societas Scientiarum Fennica, 1979, and for the United States, NOVAK M., The rise of the unmeltable ethnics, Macmillan, New York, 1972.

3. BENNETT J.W., The New Ethnicity: Perspectives from Ethnology, St. Paul, West Publishing, 1975. Particularly important contributions have been made on ethno- and socio-linguistics by FISHMAN J.A. (Advances in the sociology and languages of wider communication in developing nations, Stanford University Press, Stanford, 1972, etc.).

4. ISAJIW W., "Definitions of ethnicity", in Ethnicity, 1974, 1, pp. 111-124. See also the older journal Plural Societies, The Hague.

5. French research on this subject will be found in Pluriel, 1982/1983, No. 32-33, Minorités. Ethnicité. Mouvements nationalitaires (symposium held in Sèvres by the Association Française des ethnologues). In this article, SIMON J-P. notes French ethnological tradition's "distaste for inter-ethnic and minority issues" apart from a few "oases" (BASTIDE, BALANDIER) (op. cit., pp. 13-26). The absence of a specific field (still patent in the GODELIER Report, Les sciences de l'homme et de la société en France, Documentation française, 1982) is probably due both to a centralising tradition, the anti-republican past of minority group demands and the structuralist or Marxist leanings of research until very recently.

6. Notable socio-political work has been done in this connection by GLAZER N. (see Ethnic dilemmas, 1964-1982, Harvard University Press, 1983) and interesting comparative studies by Jerzy Smolicz on ethno-linguistic practices (see "Is the monolingual nation-State out of date?", in Comparative Education, Vol. 20, No.2, pp. 265-286; "Multiculturalism and an over-arching framework of values: some educational responses for ethnically plural societies", in European Journal of Education, Vol. 19, No. 1, 1984, pp. 11-25; etc.).

7. The concept of "identity" is currently the subject of debate. See L'identité, a seminar chaired by LEVI-STRAUSS C., Grasset, 1977;

ORIOL M., "Identité produite, identité instituée, identité exprimée ...", in Cahiers internationaux de sociologie, 6, No. 6, 1979, pp. 19-28; see CAMILLIERI C., "Identités et changements sociaux"? in Identités et changements sociaux", Privat, Toulouse, 1980, pp. 331-344; ABOU S., L'identité culturelle. Relations interethniques et problèmes d'acculturation, Anthropos, 1981; GRANDGUILLAUME G., "Langue, identité et culture nationale au Maghreb", in Peuples méditerranéens, No. 9, 1979, pp. 3-38; etc.

8. See ACUNA R., Occupied America. The Chicano's struggle towards liberation, Harper & Row, 1972. Another more recent example is provided by the large number of North American blacks who have been separated by advancement from a proletariat which is more deprived than ever and who are now persuaded that the racial problem in the United States is "out of date" or "archaeological"; in their view, economic competition is the real name of the game.

9. See, for example, ARONOWITZ S., False promises. The shaping of American working class consciousness, McGraw-Hill Book Co., 1974.

10. BIOT F. and VERBUNT G., Immigrés dans la crise, Ed. Ouvrières, 1981, pp. 171-181.

11. On the emergence and growth of Western individualism (a much debated problem), see MACPHERSON C.B., The political theory of possessive individualism, Oxford University Press, 7th edition, 1977; MACFARLANE A., The origins of English individualism, Cambridge University Press, 1979.

12. Thus, for KELSEN H., founder of the Austrian school (translated into French as Théorie pure du droit by Ch. Einsenman and published by Dalloz, 1962, p. 438), law is based on the "assumption of the sovereignty and liberty of the individual". Similarly, for RAWLS J. (A theory of justice, 1971, Harvard University Press, 7th edition, 1976), the "concept of the well-ordered society" is based on the category of "everyone" (pp. 453 et seq.) and the notion of the "unity of self", which defines society as consisting of individuals and their associations (pp. 560-567). Hence the two principles on which justice is based: 1) everyone must have an equal right to the widest freedom base compatible with a similar freedom for others; 2) social and economic equalities must be so organised as to be simultaneously: a) reasonably likely to benefit everyone; and b) attached to jobs and responsibilities accessible to all (op. cit., p. 60).

13. In his Leçons sur l'égalité (Fondation Nationale des Sciences Politiques, 1984), SFEZ L. submits the historical aspects of what he calls the "theology of equality" to a critical analysis.

14. On the concept of "house" and "house societies", see in particular LEVI-STRAUSS's lectures during the period 1976-1982 and Paroles données, Plon, 1984, pp. 189-241.

15. Such practices (reciprocal services, hospitality, exchange of gifts, etc.) obviously have an economic value and do not escape supercilious social observation, but they are not part of the law of the market,

which is based on a general equivalent represented by money. Hence their absence from financial and budget calculations.

16. More broadly, "cultures" are economies conquered or misunderstood by others, or are transversal and minor, or else lag behind the dominant economies and expand suddenly when circumstances permit (as in France during the Occupation). Neither more nor less symbolically than others, they represent different types of "commerce" which are perfectly compatible on the same territory but in a hierarchical order. In French society, for example, "events" which are assumed to be "cultural" (a carnival, the village festival and even the family reunion) are economies (provisionally?) repressed by history: even though these islets are being gradually taken over by a tourist technology, they still punctuate the country with places organised according to mixed economic principles (collective ownership, exchange of gifts, family allegiance, etc.).

17. The withdrawal of paternal authority (Act of 24th July 1889), followed by increasing intervention by the courts and the State to defend the individual rights of the child, also corresponds to "the separation of Church and State" (Act of 9th December 1905). Synchrony has its logic.

18. See the comments by HERITIER-AUGE F, "Famille", in Encyclopaedia Universalis, Supplément, Vol. 1 Le savoir, 1985, pp. 534-538; and LEFORD C, "L'individu", in Passé présent, No. 1, Ramsay, 1982.

19. "Hybrid monism": see SMOLICZ J., "Culture, ethnicity and education: multiculturalism in a plural society", in MEGARRY J., NISBET S. and HOYLE E. (eds.), World Year Book of Education 1981: Education of Minorities, Nichols Publishing Co., New York, p. 19.

20. See CITRON S., Enseigner l'histoire aujourd'hui. La mémoire perdue et retrouvée, Editions Ouvrières, 1984.

21. Concerning its present forms, see Franjo Tudjman, Nationalism in contemporary Europe, Columbia University Press, 1981. In France, it would be necessary to consider the analysis of the relationship between "Republic", "Patrie" (mother country) and "nation". See, for example, RENOUVIER C., Manuel républicain de l'homme et du citoyen, 1848, Garnier, 1981; or the history of "national ideology". See the following still essential books: GUIOMAR J-Y., L'idéologie nationale, Champ libre, 1974; WEILL G., L'Europe du XIXe siècle et l'idée de nationalité, Paris, 1938; etc. Identification of the State with the nation calls for a consideration of the distinction between them and of the political forms of national autonomies within one and the same State. See some examples and assumptions in Les autonomies en differents Etats. Expériences et perspectives, published by Abadia de Montserrat, 1979. The opposite argument is expounded by HECHTER M. in Internal colonialism: The Celtic fringe in British national development, 1536-1966, Routledge & Kegan Paul, London, 1975, which puts a higher value on nationalism.

22. Article 77 (subparagraphs 2 and 3) of the 1958 Constitution, which nonetheless lagged well behind the Constitution of 24th June 1793, whose Article 4 allowed certain foreigners at all levels to "exercise

the rights of French citizens", but has never been enforced. See COSTA-LASCOUX J. and DE WENDEN-DIDIER C. in Les droits politiques des immigrés, Cahiers de la Pastorale des Migrants, No. 10-11, 1982, pp. 47-58.

23. See the research on a "situational" concept of ethnicity, which stresses ethnic adaptability and its development or rigidities, etc., since BENNETT J. (ed.) The new ethnicity, Minnesota West Publishing, Saint Paul, 1975; DESPRESS L.A., Ethnicity and resource competition in plural societies, Mouton, The Hague, 1975; EPSTEIN A.L., Ethos and identity. Three studies in ethnicity, Tavistock, London, 1978.

24. LEVI-STRAUSS C., "Race et histoire", Anthropologie structurale deux, Plon, 1973, pp. 377-422.

25. See already, for example, the whole North American "interactionist" wave since the founding studies by BARTH F. (1969), etc.

26. See, for example, KATUSZEWSKI J. and OGIEN R., Réseaux d'immigrés, Ed. Ouvrières, 1981, on the successive "disconnection" and "reconnection" of a relational network and on trends in the traditional rules governing alliances.

27. In this connection, the experience of the teacher, who is well able to recognise the common formality of the problems of Gypsy, Portuguese and Breton pupils, already has exemplary value. Some too few and far between analyses of French experience may be found in Migrants formation, the journal of the CEFISEM. See also Cahiers de l'éducation nationale, No. 26, June 1984, especially concerning the intercultural educational action projects (PAE), as illustrated in the 11th arrondissement of Paris (research on the story) or the 15th arrondissement (twinning with African schools). For many teachers, as for those in Douai, this experience shows that "the difficulties encountered by immigrant children are not specifically educational problems" and that ghetto classes should therefore be avoided (ibid., p. 16).

28. SAYAD S., "Les trois âges de l'émigration algérienne", in Actes de la recherche en sciences sociales, No. 15, June 1977, pp. 59-79, and "From 'Immigrants' to 'Minorities'", Chapter 5 in this volume.

29. See GRANGER G.G., Essai d'une philosophie du style, A. Colin, 1968, whose discussion of a "stylistics" of scientific writings is more to my purpose than his search therein for a "principle of individuation".

30. HYMES D., "On communicative competence", in PRIDE J.B. and HOLMES J., Sociolinguistics, Penguin, Harmondsworth, 1972 ("communicative competence" consists in knowing when, how and with whom it is appropriate to adopt a particular form of linguistics and applies "rules for using the language"). Since GUMPERZ J. and HYMES D. (eds), Directions in sociolinguistics. The ethnography of communication, Holt, Rinehart & Winston, New York, 1972, and BAUMAN R. and SHERZER J., Explorations in the ethnography of speaking, Cambridge University Press, 1974, research has also been carried out by FERGUSON C.A., LABOV W., WATZLAVICK P., etc. See also WINDISH U., "Pensée sociale,

langage en usage et logiques autres", L'Age d'homme, 1982. Important research has also been carried out in this connection on pragmatism; see Langue française, No. 42, 1979, "La pragmatique"; Actes de la recherche en sciences sociales, No. 46, March 1983, "L'usage de la parole"; etc.

31. In this context, "mistakes" are signs of elocution in the normal system of expression. They indicate speakers' "ways of speaking". See already, in a similar connection relating to the "functions" of language, FREIN H., La grammaire des fautes (1929), Slatkine, Geneva, 1971.

32. See an example in SMITHERMAN G., Talkin' and testifyin'. The language of Black America, Houghton Mifflin, Boston, 1977.

33. The art of reusing and appropriating the products of another economy in one's own practice has been analysed many times. Concerning books, the telephone or radio, see the subtle observations made by N'DIAYE C. in Gens de sable, POL, 1984, etc., or the model worked out by AFFERGAN F., Anthropologie à la Martinique, Fondation des Sciences Politiques, 1983, and a general exposition in M. DE CERTEAU's, L'invention du quotidien, 1, Arts de faire, 10/18, 1980. Two revealing cases concern reading (M. de Certeau, op. cit., pp. 279-296), which Wolfgang Iser stressed as being very much determined by the reader's habits (The act of reading, Johns Hopkins Paperbacks, 1981, pp. 107-134, and television, whose most "colonising" programmes (e.g. Dallas, the target and leading example of a sociology of communication), which lend themselves to a thousand different "uses" or applications (see KATZ E. and LIEBES T., "Once upon a time, in Dallas", in Intermedia, May 1984, pp. 28-32; etc.).

34. FREUD S. "Moses and monotheism", in Gesammelte Werke, Vol. 16, pp. 190-191) analyses the "special power (Macht)" of "small fragments" scattered far and wide from an abandoned origin.

35. The conclusion of the results of a pilot project carried out at the Jules Guesde II school (Argenteuil, 1982) might be applied to this particular point: the aim was "to give the children the necessary tools for understanding the other person's culture and hence their own" (quoted in Cahiers de l'éducation nationale, June 1984, p. 12).

36. In particular, a history or institutional analysis would not only have to show the working class struggles and industrial movements that have triggered advances in law but also the role played in past or present struggles by the "belonging" (in almost "clannish" form or for adaptation) which the official argument conceals. In France, the always difficult relationship between the school itself and families is still bound up with this problem and might throw further light on social reality.

37. In a similar perspective relating to the education of young Gypsies, LIEGEOIS J-P. wants them to be given "negotiating tools" including both technical practices and hints for understanding the non-gypsy environment (the Gorio) and its institutions. See Formation des enseignants des enfants tziganes (Donaueschingen, 20th-25th June 1983), Council of Europe, Strasbourg, 1983, pp. 4-5.

Commentary by Egle BECCHI

Professor at the University of Pavia, Italy

I think there are a number of points which merit special attention. The first and most general is the approach whereby Michel de Certeau considers multiculturalism not merely from an educational and scholastic standpoint. He says his approach is "problematic" and also, more traditionally, epistemological and that it is an analysis of ways of thinking, social codifications, ideological and historical prejudices as regards the categories used in discussion and research on multiculturalism. This is an analysis of the tools we can use to think about this problem, which affects relationships in many systems -- both ours and those of "others" -- relationships which, it should be stressed, are dialectical and conflictual. The ensuing detailed examination employs one of the most dynamic, least sclerotic and least formal of these tools. It is a continual solicitation to "reflect" on our thinking about ourselves, when this is compared with the problems of "others" and at the same time an analytical and "critical" return to all those practices, rites, linguistic codes in the very widest sense (and not just "knowledge" in the strict sense) which are at one and the same time both an object of study and field for intervention as regards multiculturalism, and which, in addition, are also specific matrices from which reflections and interpretations of this phenomenon can begin.

This approach seems to me not only to open up a field of theoretical reflection which is more complex than usual, but also to inaugurate a proper pedagogical dimension to this reflection, a dimension which anticipates the final considerations of de Certeau's paper, relating to new educational methods in schools. We are given an invitation to de-intellectualise our conception of "other" (albeit on a high-powered level of reflection) and to do so in such a way as not to be hyper-respectful towards forms of otherness that are not always understood. We are faced with a pedagogy of the interminable because it leads us to analysing our own analyses, the instruments used, their past fortunes, their partial nature, their current risks. But we are also issued with a challenge as regards the over-weak theoretical bases of our assumptions about study, which precisely in the analysis of multiculturalism are all too easily turned into practice with excessive rapidity. These assumptions use dated and peculiar constructions. The challenge is to find "another" knowledge distinct from what has so far been adopted -- a knowledge for which the school itself, freed from compensatory designs, ought to be the springboard.

The robustness and speculative originality of this approach is demonstrated in the discussion of the cases that Michel de Certeau puts forward (from the Basques in France to the Jews in the United States to the Catholics in Northern Ireland) and in the "criticism" of the categories so far used by the various treatises (and treatments!) relating to multiculturalism. There the interpretative approach to the realities examined -- and the ways in which they have been examined -- is highly relevant: all the more so (and here I come to the second of my observations) if one insists, firstly, on the partiality of an approach in merely economic terms, secondly, on the non-exhaustive nature of any analysis of production structures and class relationships as the only decisive factors to multiculturalism, and, thirdly, on the consequent need to proceed by means of much wider and more complex concepts, where "cultural" is assigned a more significant, though not exclusive, role.

Nevertheless, in the "folds" of a dichotomy (recognised as basic and perhaps uneliminable) between the "historical" approach (which analyses the economic dimension) and the "ethnological" approach (concerned with the cultural dimension), the cultural pole would appear to be more interesting, richer, less schematic, and much more able to justify a series of relationships, not least the economic ones, such as the use and exchange of both material and symbolic goods. Turning to the examples given, this suspicion of a mainly cultural outlook is not weakened. The groups cited are "others" by virtue of their ethnic origin, religious creed, language but they are also graded differently within the structural web of society: the Chicanos in the subproletariat, the Jews in America in the middle class, while the Catholic Irish and French-speaking Canadians are found at various levels in the hierarchy of production and society.

But if we choose other examples, the balance changes and the relationships seem to change. The current "case" in Europe demonstrates this. There were the migrations in Europe between 1950 and 1970; there have been more recent ones from the Third World to many states on the old continent, those inside many European countries and the return of many emigrants to their place of origin, commuter migration, so significant, for example between Italy and Switzerland. These are all migrations that have led to confrontation with "others" as regards language, history, use of symbolic goods but with respect to which educational programmes have so far proved to be inept. None of these migrations are explainable in a complete way, when a merely "ethnological" key is used or when it is overstated. The priority should be with production dynamics, structural relationships of hegemony and inferiority, and class compensations.

The very forces, or rather agencies, at work (entrepreneurs and unions) prove this contention. Here the "other" is primarily the person in a certain position in the dynamics of production and his social role derives from this and, albeit only in part, his cultural destiny (we need merely think of the difficulties in educating the children of immigrants). If, therefore, we vary the examples, the proposed approach changes: the paths to be followed when trying to understand the knowledge and the savoir-faire of the "other" and to "impart" knowledge and savoir-faire to the "other" are no longer the same -- the existential and conceptual tools to analyse and to be used are different.

Certainly, the basic perspective, the "basic issues" are sufficiently flexible to withstand this diversification, whenever an epistomology of other knowledge of and about "others" is proposed. But it will still be necessary to reckon not only with ideologies and practices but with structures as well, with markets of symbolic and material goods in which these ideologies and practices are found with productions and reproductions of relationships. All these operations are feasible given the latitude and flexibility of the approach but need to be rooted in the social and economic circumstances in which they occur.

But -- and with this I would like to turn to my final consideration -- although the basic hermeneutic disposition does not change, nevertheless when we consider the realities I have indicated, there are certainly great changes to be made to the type of school that Michel de Certeau proposes. In them, we must ensure that it is possible in a meaningful and significant way to restore the most archaic, yet most fundamental, types of savoir-faire, to recognise the ethnic and family matrices of cognitive competence and to manage sociality. This very fine formative institution which de Certeau proposes cannot be planned sic e simpliciter.

In fact, in the reality of the great confrontations with "others" in the polyethnic migrations overseas in the first half of the century and the great European migratory movements of our days, it has only rarely been possible to reformulate a school in such a way that it is not a place of violence as regards integration, emargination, elitist knowledge. And when this has happened, it has happened outside the official educational systems, in small alternative experiences, which are hardly known and which are far from being widespread.

But if we wish to remain in a utopian design -- and the scholastic practices that de Certeau proposes certainly are -- and move in the environment of the possible, where other paths which would otherwise have been precluded can be explored, we must ask ourselves this: by ignoring and overlooking "structural" co-ordinates, are we not running the risk of going backwards in history and obtaining human advantages through operations which end up being archaic and reductive unless we change the cultural and productive circumstances and social relationships within which new exchanges, new practices and new knowledge take place.

Commentary by Marc GUILLAUME

Director of the Institut de Recherche d'Information Socio-Economique,
University of Paris IX-Dauphine

Michel de Certeau argues that schooling for diversity paves the way for an understanding of usages or an understanding of the operations and the operants; it leads to something more than merely the ability to control the results of these processes. What he is saying is, to my mind, something new and fundamental, and the logical outcome of his research on usages, the problems of languages and the assimilation of an environment. It seems to me that it is essential to emphasize that schooling for diversity is primarily a schooling in usages; a way of genuinely coming to terms with a new world, a world that is in the throes of change. It is a means of access to something that has been kept from us, by which I mean understanding: it involves thinking about the actual processes of thought, comprehending the processes of comprehension, understanding the processes of understanding.

A good analogy would be the new technologies. It could be said that in relation to these we are all in a position not unlike that of the immigrant, finding ourselves in a world that frightens us and from which we are excluded or, at least, in which we are only occasionally called upon to participate in some economic or practical capacity. Genuine assimilation of these new technologies requires just such a schooling in usages and the question is what conditions are necessary to ensure that these usages become more widespread.

This brings to mind a concept used by Kafka, who coined the phrase "minor literature" to describe a school of writers where there was no recognised "master" like, for example, the group of Jewish writers in Warsaw or Prague, who were in precisely the situation of a minority, using a language which was not their own, acutely aware of the political dimension -- even where seemingly personal matters were concerned -- and speaking with one voice. This literature, to which Kafka is referring, is literature of the common man. By and large, as Michel de Certeau says, minorities that have been plunged into a social code that is not their own are faced with the same situation, the same challenge.

Deleuze and Guattari had raised these questions a few years ago: how does one become the nomad, the immigrant, the Gypsy of one's own language? The answer might be to accord it minor usage in order to revive its immediate political and collective pertinence. It would seem to me that it is also on this level that Michel de Certeau is posing the question: what conditions are conducive to a minor usage, how does one organise minor usage of the new technologies of the environment, of learning? These are questions that should be directed to the architects and the educationists, not in terms of targets but in terms of criteria of change. How can a curriculum be changed so that it caters for these potential minor uses?

My second comment concerns what seems to me to be a central point: the question of the violence of the inter-ethnic relationship, the hostility that the alien can arouse. Having first of all underlined the violence of this relationship and the fact that it is fundamentally a matter of life or death, Michel de Certeau goes on to say that the cost of this violence is considerably higher for the members of a minority group. I wonder, however, whether it could not also be said that their gain too is higher. I would say that the member of a minority group, an immigrant within a society, is a person living under stress, who undoubtedly has more to lose but also more to gain. I base this premise on certain aspects to which passing reference is made: for example, the position of strength in which the weaker partner finds himself where the operant is obliged to obey a code that is not his own. This could well be the explanation for what is often the role played by the outsider, the immigrant, the member of a minority -- that of a forerunner, a pioneer -- a role moreover which is the outcome of the necessity for hybridisation, to which frequent reference is made, and which stems from the fact that the outsider has, as it were, a foot in both camps: the individualistic culture of the West on the one hand and his own culture on the other, which is a culture where the group takes precedence over the individual, what Louis Dumont describes as holistic cultures.

These holistic cultures, which have a hard time of it in the industrialised West, are transplanted into a society that is governed by the principles of individualism. As Michel de Certeau says, the immigrant or minority way of life brings a foreign economy into our own environment; procedures that had been excluded or exorcised suddenly reappear in our midst. It is, as it were, the re-emergence of something we had repressed, but not necessarily destroyed, whence the discomfort that can so easily become hostility. Hostility towards the foreigner, the foreigner from a holistic culture, is aroused by the fact that this foreigner has more room for manoeuvre than we do, in one way he has more freedom than we do and he brings with him a cultural element which we have not completely banished from our own. I agree completely with what Michel de Certeau says: he loses more (I shall not go into the reasons why) but he perhaps gains more and perhaps as a result of this he provokes, attracts hatred because of this kind of strength that is contained within his weakness. Were it not for this second component, it would be easy to understand the marginalisation, the subjugation and the losses suffered, but it would perhaps not be so easy to understand the extremely violent reactions triggered off by the presence of foreigners, although an explanation would always be the fact that this conflict is to some extent unavoidable.

I should also like to make some comments of a methodological character on the frame of reference that has been adopted, the formulation of the problem from which the foregoing premise is derived. First of all, a brief remark on the subject of "economy/culture". It is perfectly correct to say that we use the term "cultural" to describe what pertains to another economy. It is the usual, safe way of describing an economy that we do not accept, that does not conform to the principle of profitability. But it could also be said, and here I am merely looking at the reverse side of the coin, that what we call economy, our economy, with its strategic rules and its usages, is also a culture. If we swap the terms in this way, we can then appreciate that what we call an economic crisis is a cultural crisis, and we can then analyse it properly. The tricks of vocabulary which lead us to describe as a culture what is an economy and, conversely, to speak of an economy when what we are dealing with is a culture, creates serious confusion when it comes to analysing the situation. This distinction between economy and culture is a usage that has to be accepted, but it is a usage that introduces a separation between disciplines and one needs to be well aware of this since it tends to cloud the issue. Being an economist by training, I would tend to switch the words in order to incorporate cultural explanations in what are usually considered matters for the economist, in the same way as economic parameters can be introduced into what are regarded as cultural phenomena.

Another comment I have concerns the question of identity. I am fascinated by the correlation that Michel de Certeau establishes between identity and alienation. If this concept of identity is taken literally, it can be seen to contain the definition of alienation. From this concept of identity, which has legal, administrative, law enforcement and even ethical connotations (ethical because without identity there can be no responsibility), it becomes clear that identity operates within society both as a refuge and as a prison. The procedure of identification is a source of alienation, it converts an individual into an object.

In the light of this, I wonder whether the hyper-individualist character which our societies are assuming is not giving rise to new phenomena that are likely to undermine their legal, administrative, law enforcement and ethical bases and weaken the procedures of identification. What I mean by this is that hyper-individualism produces quite unusual forms of alienation, that moreover are accentuated by the new technologies, and results in an erosion of these identification procedures, in anonymity, for example. When we become anonymous, our behaviour within society becomes that of aliens (Georg Simmel's analyses of the positivity of the alien are very close to these ideas). The position of being an alien and that of being anonymous are sometimes identical. Once one accepts this idea of modern hyper-individualist society moving towards a spread of these procedures of anonymity, of under-identification, society can be said to be gradually becoming alien to every single person and that the individual's relationship to this society is like the relationship of a foreigner to a new world. We are all getting closer to the position of a foreigner, which is a position that is both under-identified and over-identified.

One last point: the question of the importance of the national ideology. In this connection I think that the worst is perhaps over, that we are perhaps reverting to a situation where society is to some extent rid of the delusion of the necessity for solid unity, a totalitarian form of social unity. I state this somewhat guardedly because there are forces working in the opposite direction, but it seems to me that progressively a certain division of society, that does not instantly conjure up the threat of a break-up, is becoming culturally possible, conceivable. In other words, the question of the social bond, established and safeguarded by the State, no longer appears so crucial as it was a few decades ago. It has perhaps lost some of its force with the (albeit relative) disappearance of the enemy; nowadays, it seems to me that this authoritarian, centralising policy has been toned down somewhat.

Gradually a new awareness is emerging that recognises an individual's right to live without having constantly to remember that he is a member of a highly functional and highly organised society. Which means that democracy no longer has need of this kind of general allegiance in order to function, that it has become more of a context than a social project dedicated to preserving a fragile social bond that is held to be under constant threat.

8. CULTURAL DIFFERENCES AND EQUALITY OF EDUCATIONAL ACHIEVEMENT

by
Nathan GLAZER
Graduate School of Education, Harvard

FROM CULTURAL DEMANDS TO ACHIEVEMENT DEMANDS

For an American to dip into the literature on the education of minorities in Europe, is to experience a sense of _déjà vu_: the discussion in some of the papers for this conference (Verne, Mullard, Churchill, Chombart de Lauwe) deals with issues that have lost salience in the United States during the past ten years. These issues can be summarised as: What is the impact of a national system of education on the culture of a minority group? Can that culture be maintained in a national system originally designed to impose a single national language and a single national culture? What is the ability of a national system of education to recognise these differences?

These issues of course continue to be discussed in the United States. But they are today confined to academic circles. The major period of their discussion in larger public arenas was the late 1960s and the early 1970s, concurrently with the period of great expansion of civil rights for minority groups represented by the major civil rights legislation of 1964, 1965, 1968 and 1972, and with the period of civil disturbances in American cities during the summers of the late 1960s. This was a period in which the theme of "black power" -- increasing the independent power of the black minority -- was prominent, and expressed heightened rhetoric: and this rhetoric inspired or was echoed by similar rhetoric from Chicano (Mexican American), Puerto Rican, American Indian, and Asian-American militants.

The chief repercussion of these demands were in the field of education. Ironically, the demand for minority power had few effects in changing the structure of politics and government, local, state, or national. The impact on institutions of higher education was particularly marked. Hundreds of programmes of black studies, Chicano studies, Puerto Rican studies, Native American (American Indian) studies, Asian studies were launched. The character of these programmes was, in the context of American higher education, exceptional: they were programmes that emphasized advocacy of group maintenance, of group values, of group power rather than analysis of group history, culture, and problems. Their faculties were drawn in large measure from persons without traditional scholarly or scientific education; their students often formed a separate enclave on campuses; the objectives of these programmes aimed at neither occupational nor professional qualification, nor were they well-linked with traditional fields of scholarship for which their students could be prepared as researchers or teachers. It was not therefore surprising that these fields, after the early 1970s, lost their appeal to students who were increasingly concerned with occupational futures.

They declined in number, and were in many places transformed into departments with a more traditional academic flavour.

Higher education thus bore the brunt of early demands for minority group recognition. A rather steadier presence was forged in the elementary and secondary schools, but there the social dynamics were very different. In the higher schools, the argument was that enclaves of power and recognition had to be created in the form of free-standing and independent departments and programmes. In the elementary and secondary schools, which are more oriented toward skills than content-laden studies, the argument was that the recognition of culture -- and, for those of foreign language background, language -- and the use of culture and language in teaching was essential for the academic progress of children of minority background.

Two reasons were set forth for this. The first was purely educational: children speaking foreign languages could not learn when taught in another language, and would fall behind until they learned the language of instruction. Thus, it was necessary to at least provide transitional education in the home language. The second reason was rather different and had a stronger connection with the politics of minority protest: it asserted that children of foreign language background and the black English-speaking minority would not learn unless they saw that their culture and language were respected by the school and the teacher. Otherwise they would feel denigrated, would withdraw, would feel resentment. Respect on the other hand would lead to heightened self-image, heightened self-image would lead to greater academic achievement and would close the gaps in academic achievement between minority and "majority" -- that is, white non-Hispanic -- children.

During the 1970s, a great deal was made of this argument about self-respect, in part because of the findings of the famous Coleman Report of 1966 and its reanalyses in the 1970s (Coleman, Mosteller and Moynihan). This research suggested the importance of positive self-image for achievement, though it was not at all clear whether self-image contributed to achievement, or achievement contributed to self-image, or whether any part of self-image was shaped by respect for a minority ethnic or racial heritage.

The argument that education required attention to culture and language was made for all groups that were considered minority: blacks, Mexican-Americans, Puerto Ricans, other Latin Americans, American Indians, Asians, despite the enormous differences among these groups, the great differences in their experiences, and, one would think, differences in their educational needs. But an argument was forged, and for a while had considerable force, that applied to all of them: to blacks, whose native language was English, and whose forbears had been resident in the United States for three centuries; to Mexican Americans, some of whom were descended from ancestors who had settled in the territory of the United States as long or longer ago than blacks, but most of whom were recent immigrants and their children, and who were identified by foreign language rather than different race; to American Indians, whose presence on the continent preceded the first two groups and the majority, and who, it could be argued, differed more from the dominant society in culture than any other group; to Asian Americans, themselves diverse, and who, in contrast to all other minority groups -- despite severe prejudice and discrimination to which they had been subjected from the time of their arrival to the 1950s or so -- showed education and economic achievement superior to that of the white majority.

It was always doubtful whether similar claims could be raised effectively for all these groups, and whether similar programmes would meet their demands and their needs. In particular, there were striking differences between the demands of black political leadership, and Hispanic political leadership. The first, owing to the long history of segregation, against which they had fought, demanded that black children be widely distributed through the schools and that they nowhere be allowed to form a majority, for that would indicate segregation. The Hispanics were not concerned about concentration, and indeed demanded programmes in the Spanish language that could only be effective if there was some substantial degree of concentration. Since desegregation was a major demand of the black community, leading to many extended constitutional cases and programmes designed to break up black concentrations, black and Hispanic leaders were often at odds. Blacks were willing to undertake the trouble that desegregation required: very often this meant long bus-rides for black children into distant areas. Since redistribution of one group required redistribution of others, these programmes also meant long bus-rides for Hispanic children, and Hispanic parents and leaders could not see the reason for that.

These differences, however, did not overwhelm all efforts to form a common alliance, educationally and politically. Politically, we have seen as recently as the Presidential primary campaign of 1984 Jesse Jackson's effort to forge what he called a "rainbow coalition" of all minorities -- successful among black, more doubtfully so among Hispanics, not at all among Asians. But educationally a common analysis was forged to explain the educational difficulties of minorities. To some extent, even a common programme was forged, leading to such an anomaly as the demand in at least one case for the recognition of "Black English" as a separate language (Glazer, 1981). In this case, black claimants made use of civil rights protections that had been designed primarily for Hispanics from non-English-speaking homes. More commonly, Mexican Americans and Puetro Ricans made use of the legal techniques forged by blacks, and the legal remedies originally designed for their protection, to press their own demands. As we have indicated, these tended not to be demands for desegregation, but for special programmes -- which some blacks also demanded.

Yet another element justified common demands, common programmes, for all minorities. All, it was argued, were treated differently by teachers. Teachers expected less from them, therefore provided less direct teaching for them. In effect, the racism so common in American society affected teachers and administrators, too, and this was the explanation of educational failure. But how does one deal with a widespread racism that changes the school experience for the minority child? Law had gone just about as far as it could. Anti-discrimination law, it was argued, could be supplemented by independent power for minorities. That independent power would consist of programmes run by members of a minority for members of a minority, using the culture and the language of that minority. Their culture would be maintained, their respect enhanced. With this kind of analysis, all minorities, despite differential legal status, educational achievement, and educational need, could forge a common programme. And to some extent they did.

The common elements of this programme were the use of language and culture of minority groups in teaching; respect for language and culture of minority groups; and power for members of minority groups. The three of course worked together: if there were more use of minority language and culture in teaching, there would be more teachers and administrators of minority groups. More such teachers and administrators would illustrate that respect was being shown; and one could point to other connections.

How was this to be done? For blacks, committed to desegregation, the key element was the power of federal courts, and the power of federal agencies that enforce civil rights of minorities on the basis of federal legislation and court orders. Desegregation orders generally required not only the shifting of black and white students (and teachers), but could also require increased numbers of black teachers and administrators. But the major force increasing the number of black teachers and administrators was the increasing political power of blacks, who, by their numbers in the central cities, elected mayors, and began to dominate school systems (which are locally run under elected or appointed boards in the United States). The black mayors of Chicago, Philadelphia, Atlanta, Washington and other cities demonstrated that one element in this complex of demands by minority groups -- power -- was being won by one group -- blacks.

For Hispanic Americans, the problem was more complicated. They dominate few cities politically (the Cubans, Miami; the Mexican Americans, San Antonio). Language plays a much more important role for them: respect means the right to use Spanish, to maintain Spanish, to have Spanish-speaking teachers and administrators, and to incorporate Spanish language and elements of Hispanic culture (Puerto Rican, Mexican, Cuban, depending on the area) into teaching. They, too, won political victories in achieving these aims in the 1960s and 1970s. In 1968, a bilingual education Act was passed by Congress. It was expanded in 1974 (Schneider). It provided Federal grants to local school systems for the teaching of children of foreign-language background (overwhelmingly Spanish in the United States). It also required that these Federal funds could only be used in programmes that made use of the home language in teaching (1).

The Federal government's role was enhanced by the key _Lau_ decision of the Supreme Court in 1974, which ruled that a local school district must make special provision for children with a foreign language background. On the basis of this decision, the Office of Civil Rights of the Federal Department of Health Education and Welfare monitored the largest districts with large numbers of children of Spanish-language background and required programmes of education that made use of their mother tongue. Other cases filed in other jurisdictions -- perhaps the most important was the _Aspira_ case in New York City -- also guaranteed that there would be extensive programmes of bilingual education. And these continue (Glazer, 1983, Chapter 7). And many states with large numbers of foreign-language minorities passed laws requiring local school districts to provide such programmes.

In contrast to present-day European (and Canadian) discussion, however, the demand for maintenance of culture and language has weakened and is no longer a dominant element influencing bilingual education, or, more broadly put, education for minorities. The hard economic times of the 1970s, and the increasing strength of conservative and nationalist political forces in the United States, as indicated by the successive victories of Ronald Reagan in 1980 and 1984, have changed the emphasis in discussion of the education of minority children. Educators are still concerned about children's self-image and minority culture. Ethnic and racial nationalists and militants are of course concerned with the maintenace of culture, and in particular with control of the political and social content of education for minorities to encourage identity and militancy, but they have lost power in these communities. Ethnic and racial minorities are concerned -- as they have always been -- with jobs for their people, and this is perhaps now the sturdiest support for special programmes using foreign language, because it gives jobs to members of the community. But the dominant emphasis in education now, among majorities and minorities, is for traditional achievement, on the assumption that this is crucial for raising the economic level of minority communities.

Most striking is what has happened to black demands as the blacks have gained political power in local communities. Black became dominant demographically in city after city in the 1970s. First their children became majorities in big-city school districts (Ravitch), and not long thereafter political dominance, which now extends to the public school systems, followed in many cities.

If the black community truly wanted a black component in education, it had the power to implement that increasingly, without recourse to Federal power or to judicial intervention, in the later 1970s and 1980s. But power has strange effects. It might have been expected that black-run school systems would have greater concern for black culture, and in a measure they do. They certainly take Martin Luther King Day more seriously. Their textbooks may reflect black concerns. But power means responsibility. It was easy to demand black culture when blacks were out of power. Once in power, the constituents of black educational and political leaders insisted on educational achievement, and could not care less, it seemed, about black English, black history, black mathematics, or black science. They wanted the kind of achievement that led to competence to take jobs and to enter higher education. Black demands, now addressed to school systems often run by blacks, no longer emphasize concern for a distinctive culture, but for achievement in the common culture. And interest in desegregation also declined: leading black civil rights organisations are still committed to it, but the black populace in general is now much more interested in achievement than desegregation.

The situation for the Hispanic Americans, who were the major force pressing for bilingual education in the 1960s and 1970s, is somewhat different. Their power is less; their commitment to bilingual education and the use of culture and language in education of their children has not declined. But there has been a change in the degree to which the non-Hispanic majority accepts these demands. Until the Reagan administration came to power in 1981, the proponents of bilingualism had the strong support of the Office of Civil Rights of the Department of Education in Washington, and the requirements of the bilingual education law which allowed only programmes making sure of the home language. But when the Reagan administration came to power in 1981 it signalled its disapproval of a single approach to the education of children of foreign language, one using their language and culture. In this respect, it supported the complaints of many school districts who asserted that Federal education and civil-rights authorities insisted on this approach when, they argued, they could demonstrate they could effectively educate children of foreign language background using an "immersion" approach (intensive and exclusive English teaching). The Reagan administration agreed with them. In a long battle to renew the Federal Bilingual Education Act in 1984, this approach and other alternatives to bilingual education were accepted as legitimate -- though only a small part of the funds can be used for them.

The cultural component in education for minorities has thus lost power: fewer among minorities demand it, and hardly anyone but professional educators among majorities accede to it or consider it important. The language component is considered important by the majority and legislators only if it provides a base for academic achievement so as to enhance future economic performance. In law and opinion, the objective of maintenance of competence in a foreign, native language, declines, the objective of transition to competence in English predominates. And if the objective is competence in English, the argument that some years of learning in one's native language is necessary, becomes subjected to pragmatic test -- and may fail (Rotberg).

One should not overestimate this shift: if one visits the schools of New York, Los Angeles, Miami, and many smaller communities such as Lawrence, Massachusetts, one will find a good deal of education in Spanish, and a good deal of education for Spanish-background children emphasizing some knowledge of Puerto Rican or Mexican history and culture, depending on the group from which the children come. One will find similar Portuguese-language programmes in Fall River, Massachusetts, and programmes in many other languages in other communities (recently, programmes using Vietnamese and Cambodian have increased, as a result of substantial immigration of these groups). The teachers in these programmes, coming from the groups they are teaching, will inevitably introduce specific cultural and historical materials relating to the group. But at the level of public policy, those who emphasize purely pragmatic objectives, the objective of "transition" to English, rather than "maintenance" of language and culture -- to use the two terms that differentiate the two approaches -- dominate.

The pragmatic test may still be argued about: a great deal of research is under way on various kinds of programmes for children of foreign language background. The political test is a different one. It may be affected by research, but is more decisively affected by power and opinion, and by that test bilingual education in its strongest form -- use of foreign language, for as long a period as possible, for maintenance as well as transition, for as many children as possible -- has already, it would appear, reached its high point and is in recession. On the last day of the Carter administration, the Secretary of Education announced new regulations on bilingual education. These gave the advocates of the strongest form not everything they wanted, but a great deal. Federal regulations, supplementing Federal law, are extremely powerful. They govern not only the distribution of Federal funds for bilingual education, but also embody the Federal government's position as to what is illegal discrimination in the treatment of such children, and have great weight in Federal court decisions as to what is the statutory requirement for the education of these children. One of the first actions of the new Reagan administration in 1981 was to withdraw these regulations. The announcement of these regulations, and their withdrawal, was the high tide of influence of the advocates of bilingual education in a strong form.

WHY THE UNITED STATES IS DIFFERENT

In arguing that the age of cultural protest and cultural defence for minorities has been replaced by one in which cultural themes lose salience as against the objective of straightforward educational achievement, I am not suggesting any iron law of development according to which one stage must be followed by another. Stacy Churchill has done an excellent job of developing sequences of policies that seem to have characterised many countries -- and the United States in some respects reflects this sequence too -- but it is the case that each nation is different on a number of important dimensions, and the shift from cultural concerns to achievement concerns that has occurred in the United States may not develop to the same extent in European countries. I would make a number of points which support such a conclusion:

i) European minorities, while varied, and including some aborigines in small numbers of Scandinavian countries, equivalent perhaps to American Indians, and some regional groups with different language or dialect who have no equivalent in the United States (except perhaps for some of the Mexican Americans of New Mexico), are dominantly communities created by migrant labourers or guestworkers who will maintain citizenship in their native countries. (The only exception on a major scale is the United Kingdom, and with its West Indians, Pakistanis and Indians who are British citizens). As such, the question of language and culture must be important for them. It would infringe on their rights if the nations in which they are perhaps temporarily resident were to undertake a forceful assimilatory policy, as was typical in the United States during the period of the great migration. Such policies still have much stronger support in the United States than equivalent policies have on the continent. The question of the language in which Turkish children in Germany or Algerian in France should be educated, and the society for which they should be educated, is a meaningful one, even if it turns out, as most believe, that they will remain permanently in France and Germany. This question of language of education is less meaningful in the United States. No one there would dream of educating the masses of new immigrant children stemming from Mexico, Nicaragua, Colombia, and other Latin American countries in Spanish, to prepare them for a return to those countries, or of educating the most equally large numbers of Asian immigrants in their native tongues. The reason is simple: the United States is a country of immigration, expects immigrants to become citizens, and makes it easy for them to do so. The fact may be -- it is -- that great numbers of immigrants to the United States do return to their home countries, and many villages in Italy and Greece have substantial populations of returned immigrants, but this return process plays no role in American policy-making. American immigration policy assumes permanent immigration, makes no allowance for temporary workers. It once did, in the "bracero" programme, and it is often proposed that we should again, to deal with the enormous problem of illegal immigrants, particularly from Mexico, but there is a great resistance to such a policy, and since the bracero programme was ended in 1964 it has not been resumed.

ii) At the same time, Europe is acquainted with regional differences of dialect or of language. These dialects and languages are not considered a matter of indifference by those who use them, but are often culturally valued and the population of the region that uses them does not want to give them up. There is thus a model in Europe, despite the history of centralisation and the creation of a single national dialect taught in all the schools, for allowing or acceding to the maintenance of distinctive language and culture in the schools. There is nothing like this in the United States. Southerners may speak with an accent that often makes it hard for Northerners to understand them but there has never been a claim set forward that Southern English should be enshrined in the schools, that the dialectal variation should lead to a different spelling of English words, that a separate cultural curriculum should be taught and encouraged. The curricula of southern schools, despite their pride in their heritage, and despite local control which permits local variation, is identical today to that of Northern and Western schools. The United States has not experienced the kind of regional difference which might be used to support the idea of maintaining immigrant and minority group culture in the schools.

iii) Finally, one must point to the fact that the scale of immigration to the United States, and the resultant size of American minorities is so huge in contrast to that of Europe that it is considered a threat to national unity to encourage the maintenance of linguistic and cultural difference. A former Senator from California, himself of Japanese origin, S.I. Hayakawa, is one of the strongest opponents of giving legal recognition to non-English languages, and has helped create an organisation, "U.S. English", which fights against bilingual education and which calls for a constitutional amendment declaring English the national language of the United States. (Despite the fact that the Constitution was written in English for an overwhelmingly English-speaking nation, there is no such provision in it, and never has been. A knowledge of English is required for naturalisation, but this is waived for old persons, and no knowledge of English is paradoxically required to vote. Indeed, those who speak, Spanish, Chinese or Japanese, or American Indian languages, must by Federal law get special assistance in voting: for example, ballots must carry translations in their languages of state referenda, proposed state constitutional amendments, etc).

These three factors: that the United States is and expects to be a country of permanent immigrants who become citizens, that its history is not one of growth through accretion of territories with a different culture and language [with the one exception of the Mexican American settlements in the Southwest territories annexed from Mexico in 1845 (2)], and that as a country of immigration it is committed to the forging of people of many linguistic backgrounds and races into a common American people with a common loyalty and a common language and culture, all serve to deprive demands for a culturally distinctive education that maintains home language of the authority it might otherwise possess.

WHAT TARGET GROUPS FOR PUBLIC POLICY?

The terms we have used somewhat interchangeably up to now -- "minorities", "immigrants", "children from non-English speaking homes," -- do not of course coincide. Indeed, the question of what target groups one defines for public policy is no simple matter in the United States. Once again one senses that the situation in Europe is simpler: there the decisive line is between natives and immigrants -- immigrants including the children of immigrants -- a line which tends to coincide closely with the line between citizen and non-citizen, the line between native-language speaker and non-native language speaker, and the line between those whose school career does not raise difficult problems of what kind of curriculum and approach to use and those who do. It is true of course that within the native-born, citizen, and native-language speaking majority there are substantial differences in educational achievement by class, and much concern over raising educational achievement in Europe has focused on this class gap. The problems raised by the new immigrants and their children are seen as both similar and different: similar in that the immigrants are themselves overwhelmingly lower-working-class socially, and different in that differences of language and culture (and not simply "working-class culture") complicate the educational question.

The difference in the situation in the United States is that it is not so easy to define the target groups, or even find words for them. The term "minority" is the most common: it is "minority" children for whom we are concerned. The differences among the different "minorities" are enormous. But the conception of "minority" is so muddled that there is considerable dispute over just who we mean.

There is no category of "official minorities" in the United States, if one considers official status to be one recorded in personal documents, of defined by law, and definable in courts of law. There are citizens and non-citizens, legally or illegally immigrant, and the only ethnic or racial category that has a definition in law beyond that is that of the American Indian, the original native inhabitants of the territory that became the United States. Nevertheless, public policy does define various categories as minorities deserving some special protection or attention. Four categories are so defined: American Indians, blacks, Hispanic Americans, and Asian Americans. In addition, there is, particularly for educational policy, a category known as "limited English proficient", and of "non-English language background", who both overlap with some of the four defined minority groups, and include many others not in any of these minority groups.

The number of categories that are actual and potential targets for educational policies directed toward some cultural and linguistic features of a student group are numerous indeed: immigrant children in general, immigrant children of non-English background, immigrant children o this background deficient in knowledge of English, the four somewhat official minority groups, and yet other groups. Thus, European ethnic groups originating in the mass immigration from Europe of the late 19th and early 20th centuries have occasionally raised claims for the recognition of their cultural and linguistic background in the teaching of their children. The situation is thus enormously complex. The complexity is reflected in many arguments over just who is eligible or should be eligible for programmes taking account of language and cultural background. To briefly account for the major target groups:

i) Native Americans or American Indians

If there is anything like an officially-defined minority in the United States, it is American Indians. They are the only group that is defined in law: blood descent defines an Indian as a member of a tribe. This definition does not serve to deprive the Indian of any rights. It serves rather to give him certain rights in the governing of Indian reservation territory, rights sometimes of substantial worth since there are valuable resources of timber and minerals on many reservations. In addition to the legal definition, there is also a self-definition, and by self-definition the number of Indians in the United States has been increasing at a phenomenal rate, from 800 000 in 1970 to 1.4 million in 1980. Undoubtedly this is owing to individuals redefining themselves as Indians in responding to the Census.

Indians were once educated almost entirely on reservations in schools maintained by the U.S. Federal Government -- a rarity in American life. Concerning these schools, there has been endless dispute as to what account should be taken of Indian languages and culture. In the past they tried to forcefully assimilate Indian children. In recent decades, as Indian political power has increased, in part because the majority accepts more than it did the legitimacy of minority interests, these schools have incorporated a greater degree of Indian culture and language. But these schools play a steadily declining role in educating American Indian children: two-thirds of American Indians now live outside of reservations (American Indian Areas and Alaska Native Villages). Four-fifths of their children attend local public schools. Indians have participated in the movement to increase the amount of specific cultural content in their education, but their current interest, along with that of other American minority groups, is to improve educational achievement defined in traditional terms and to increase the numbers of Indians who attend college and professional school.

Indians are of course neither an immigrant community nor (except for small numbers) a community defined by non-English-language background -- most Indians today are raised speaking English. They nevertheless exhibit problems of educational backwardness, even if not as severely as our largest (also non-immigrant, and English-language) minority, blacks.

ii) Blacks

Blacks have been counted as a separate group since the first American Census in 1970. At 12 per cent of the population, they are by far the largest American minority. On many measures they are the minority which in general exhibits the most severe educational problems. They are politically the most powerful and effective. Many programmes that now benefit other minorities (or at least are applied to them) were originally launched to aid blacks. Their progress or lack of it is still the chief touchstone used in the United States to test the success of efforts to provide equal opportunity.

Blacks were before 1954 in the Southern states confined to separate school systems, taught by black teachers, administered by black administrators. In the North and West they were part of integrated, unitary school systems, but systems in which in fact most blacks attended all-black or largely black schools, owing generally to the residential concentration of blacks in central cities, itself owing to discrimination and poverty. Since 1954, when separate school systems were declared unconstitutional by the Supreme Court, and more effectively since the late 1960s, when the Federal Government, under legislation of 1964, took vigorous action against them, these separate school systems for blacks have disappeared. In the South, integration has been fairly effective in mixing black students with white students, but in the North blacks still attend, in the large cities in which they are concentrated, mostly black schools. This is because of the extreme residential concentration of blacks, and because whites leave areas in which they will be required to attend schools with blacks, and because of the suburban movement of the white population. Integration, if measured by actual degree of mixing of whites and blacks, is only a mixed success, more effective in the South, where blacks live in many small communities as well as in large cities, than in the North and West, where they are concentrated in the central districts of large cities. Desegregation has meant the loss of positions as administrators and teachers in segregated black school districts; this is now balanced by a substantial increase in black teachers and administrators in Northern and Western school districts where there were once few.

Blacks, as I have said, are neither an immigrant nor a foreign-language background group, though in recent decades there has been substantial immigration of blacks (whose native language is English) from the British West Indies, and more recently a substantial immigration of Creole-French Haitians. Only 12 per cent of the population, blacks make up a much larger percentage of the population in central cities of the large metropolitan areas, an even larger percentage of the school-age population of these cities owing to a population distribution skewed toward younger age groups, an even larger proportion of the public-school population of these cities, owing to a lesser participation of black children in private Catholic and non-Catholic education. This leads to school systems with a majority of blacks in many large American cities (Detroit, Cleveland, Chicago, Baltimore, Washington, D.C., St. Louis, New Orleans, and many others). Thus the processes of concentration, not unfamiliar in Europe, lead to a relatively small national minority becoming, in many social settings, a majority, and indeed an overwhelming majority.

The major thrust of black political leadship for 30 years or more has been for desegregation; a lesser but substantial thrust has been for more recognition of black culture and history, and perhaps its greatest success has been the declaration of Martin Luther King Day as a national holiday (the only other individuals whose birthdays are marked as national holidays are George Washington and Abraham Lincoln). Both thrusts, it was hoped, would improve levels of educational achievement, but that was by no means the motive that led blacks to support desegregation and recognition of black culture and history. On the whole, the improvement in educational achievement among blacks in the past twenty years has been disappointing, which is perhaps the principal reason black efforts, particularly at the local level, are now concentrated on measures to improve educational achievement directly.

iii) Hispanic Americans

If one thinks of educational programmes addressing problems of educational and cultural pluralism, it is the Spanish-speaking groups in the United States that are inevitably the principal target group. Arguments over bilingual and bicultural programmes, even though they may involve (and do) more than a hundred different language groups, are overwhelmingly programmes for Spanish-speaking children: for Mexican-Americans in the Southwestern states, from California to Texas, for Puerto Ricans in New York and other Northeastern states, for Cubans in Florida, for Dominicans, Colombians, Nicaraguans, Salvadoreans and other Latin Americans in the chief immigrant-attracting parts of the country (California and New York, pre-eminently). Despite the great differences among and within these groups, in class and occupational background, in recency of migration, in legal status (citizenship, immigration status), they are lumped together as a minority deserving special protection in education, occupation, and voting rights. They also form almost one half of current American immigration (more, if one takes account of illegal immigration), are the most rapidly growing group in the American population, through immigration and rapid natural growth, and raise an exceptionally complicated question as to how American educational policy should respond to their needs.

The overall Hispanic population increased between the Census of 1970 and that of 1980 from 9.1 to14.6 million -- 6.4 per cent of the population -- and was estimated by 1983 to have increased to 15.9 million. In the decade of the 1970s, while the American population aside from those of Spanish origin showed an increase of 9 per cent, the Spanish origin population increased 61 per cent, and the Mexican origin population almost doubled. But these increases probably reflect not only real growth but also the fact that the 1980 Census made a more intense effort to count Hispanic Americans, and perhaps the fact that, as with American Indians, there was more incentive for individuals to declare Hispanic origin (The Condition of Hispanics in America Today).

It should be pointed out that there has been great uncertainty as to just how to name and count these groups, in particular Mexican-Americans. At one time the Census considered them a "race", later it made a special count of the "Spanish-surnamed" population of the five Southwestern states, and term "Spanish/Hispanic" was used in the 1980 Census, but the term "Hispanic American" for the varied groups has become general.

The foreign-language population of the United States, as I have pointed out, is today preeminently the Spanish-language population. This group has come to dominate all arguments as to the need or suitability of bilingual or bicultural education in the United States. In 1980, a question on the usual language spoken at home showed 11 million persons reporting Spanish, three-quarters of whom said they also spoke English well or very well. More people responded that they spoke other languages at home, but these were divided among many language groups, and the largest of them -- Italian, German, French and so on -- do not make a strong demand for an education responsive to language and culture (Condition of Hispanics in America Today).

iv) Asian Americans

This element of the population is growing as rapidly as Hispanic-Americans, but from a much smaller base. Asian-Americans include Chinese, Filipinos, Japanese, Asian Indians, Koreans, Vietnamese, Laotians, Cambodians, and others. This is a more varied mix than even the Hispanic-American. The overall population of Asian Americans was 3.5 million in 1980, and had doubled since 1970 (Asian and Pacific Islander Population by State). Next to Hispanic Americans, it is these groups who provide the largest numbers for bicultural and bilingual programmes, in particular the recent immigrants from Indochina -- Vietnamese, Cambodian, Laotian. Asians show on the whole greater educational achievement than Americans in general, and do not present a problem in general of educational deficiency, but as the class and occupational sources of immigration change, in particular from Indochina, this condition may not be maintained for all groups.

v) All the "others"

Finally, we must say something about "all the others", even if not considered minorities. They nevertheless consider themselves in some degree distinctive, and their cultural and linguistic demands sometimes impinge on the educational system. But who are "all the others"? The United States is a country of immigrants, but it is also a country which radically changes immigrants and their children: they lose their native tongue and begin to speak English, lose aspects of culture, change their religions in form if not in name, intermarry. Is it still necessary to make a count of these assimilated Europeans by ethnic background? In the past, the Census did not think so. It counted the foreign-born, and the children of the foreign-born. As the period of mass immigration faded, a count of foreign-born and their children did not give an adequate measure of the size of the various European immigrant groups. The demand then rose that a question on ethnicity be incorporated in the 1980 Census.

Leaders of ethnic and racial groups in the United States, on the whole, want to see larger numbers of their own group in official statistics. There are social psychological and political reasons for wanting to maximise one's numbers. The argument over numbers is also important because it is on the basis of numbers -- if they come out right -- that one can claim the group is discriminated against or does not get enough services.

In the 1980 Census, European ethnic groups, alarmed at the degree to which numbers were being used as a basis for policy in favour of the old minority groups and recent immigrant groups (blacks, Hispanic American, American Indian, Asian), fought for a question in the Census on "ancestry". It is perhaps not an accident that this question almost by design had the effect of maximising the number of persons of each ancestry, since the question also permitted, and many respondents gave, multiple ancestries. Thus 50 million gave English, 49 million German, 40 million Irish, 13 million French, 12 million Italian, 10 million Scottish, 8 million Polish, 6 million Dutch, 4 million Swedish, 3 1/2 million Norwegian, etc. Many gave multiple ancestries; only 17 per cent answered American or gave no ancestry (Ancestry of the Population by State: 1980, pp. 1,2). Hispanic Americans were beneficiary of two questions trying to get their numbers: one, already discussed, asked "is this person of Spanish/Hispanic origin or descent?". The second was the general ancestry question, to which 7.7 million responded Mexican, 2.7 million Spanish/Hispanic, 1.4 million Puerto Rican (on the American mainland), .6 million Cuban, and smaller numbers Dominicans, Colombians, and others.

vi) Children without English

But what is to be made of the ancestry question in terms of education? Not much. For educational purposes, most crucial is what language is spoken in the home, and to what degree children come with problems with English to school, and there have been substantial efforts to document how many of these there are.

"Language-Minority" children 5 to 14 years old ("members of households where the usual or second, often spoken household language is other than English") increased from 3.5 to 4.5 million between 1976 and 1982, or 27 per cent. As a per cent of total population they increased from 9.4 to 13.3 per cent. Within this group, "limited English proficient" children ("scoring below the 25th percentile on a special test of English proficiency") were estimated to have increased from 2 million in 1978 to 2.4 million in 1982. (All children 5 to 14 years old numbered 34 million in 1982). A somewhat different measure, children who speak a non-English language at home, in 1980 showed a national average of 9.6 per cent -- but this figure rose to 23 per cent in California, 25.6 per cent in Texas, 17.2 per cent in New York, and of course the percentages are much higher in given metropolitan areas and school districts -- in the Los Angeles school district, a majority of children are now of Spanish-language background (The Condition of Bilingual Education in the Nation, 1984, pp. 13, 14).

WHAT PROGRAMMES?

Having revised this area of diversity, it will become immeditely apparent that there is no such thing, nor should there be, as a uniform response to children of such varied backgrounds, abilities, and statuses. Basically, we have seen three responses to the problems posed by children of different racial, ethnic, cultural and linguistic background.

The first has been desegregation: mix the children. This policy becomes so significant because in so much of American history, and so large a part of the United States, the effort had been made to segregate the children: blacks in the South, Chinese and Japanese in the West, Mexican Americans in the Southwest. If this was the evil, the response was desegregation, or integration, and in the most concrete sense, mixing. This is not the place to tell the complex story of the effort to mix, which continues to go on by means of busing programmes to move children out of schools in which their race or group would be dominant into other areas in which they could form part of a representative mix. Under the Reagan administration, Federal efforts to expand mixing in the face of steady opposition by white majorities, opposition or indifference among minorities other than black, and split opinion among blacks themselves, ceased. Busing programmes already instituted have continued, and various court cases continue in an effort to institute more. I have indicated that improved achievement was one objective of this enterprise. Whether it followed has been much disputed. Recent research suggests that there is a modest improvement in black achievement as the result of desegregation (Cook). Nevertheless, because of political opposition to the measures necessary, we will not see any expansion of desegregation programmes.

The second response has been policy directed at compensatory education for all poor children. This would effectively reach the blacks, the Puerto Ricans, Mexican Americans, and would be proportionately less effective with groups that do not have large numbers of children in poverty. This is from a financial point of view by far the greatest effort mounted by the Federal government. It includes "Head Start", begun in the middle 1960s, which provides pre-school for poor children, reaches over 400 000 children a year, and spends almost one billion dollars a year, at a cost of $2 200 a child. These pre-school programmes are run by community groups, and may well be conducted in foreign languages and have a strong cultural component. Even larger is Compensatory Education for the Disadvantaged, begun in 1965, and continuing at a rate of $3.5 billion a year, reaching 5 million children a year. Compensatory education is conducted by school districts, concentrates on reading and arithmetic, and while programmes vary from district to district and school to school, pays on the whole no attention to culture and background. The effects of such programmes have been much disputed: recent studies suggest modest positive effects. This is indicated most convincingly by the National Assessment of Education Progress, which tests large national samples of 9, 13, and 17-year olds. Black 9- and 13-year-olds showed a better rate of improvement than whites on reading performance between 1971 and 1980. In mathematics, between 1973 and 1978, there was a decline for white 9-year-olds, and an improvement for black; a small improvement for black 13-year-olds, a small decline for white 13-year-olds. For 17-year-olds, there were declines for both groups, but less for blacks than whites (The Condition of Education, 1982, pp. 184-185).

The third kind of programme relevant to our discussion is those that directly take into account language and culture; "bilingual" programmes as they are called. As we have indicated above, these programmes have lost some political support but continue; in view of the enormous flow of immigrant children not speaking English, some kind of programme, whether or not bilingual, is essential.

The controversy over these programmes can only be understood in the light of American history. The United States had taken in tens of millions of immigrants of foreign language, their children had attended public schools, and whatever their early backwardness on the basis of language, by the 1970s it had been forgotten. Jews, Italians, Poles, Germans no longer recalled vividly that their parents or grandparents once had had problems in attending or sending their children into English-language public schools. What they now remembered was their success in adaptation to English and the United States. And what they feared was that by acknowledging in schools the need for education in a foreign language this process would be delayed. The fear was all the greater because the great majority of children speaking a foreign language entering the public schools were Mexican American and other Spanish-speaking, and they were concentrated in certain areas, and in the Southwest adjacent to their country of origin. The process of assimilation that from the perspective of the 1970s had been so successful with European immigrants was to many Americans now threatened by the new bilingual and bicultural policies, introduced as a result of political action by Mexican American and other Spanish origin groups, action which coincided with the dominance of liberal attitudes in education.

These programmes continue, despite the coolness of the Reagan administration. They are also sustained by many state laws which permit or require them. Federal programmes reached in 1983 about 200 000 children, state-funded services almost a million. (These figures may be compared with the estimates of target groups above). (The Condition of Bilingual Education, 1984, pp. 2-3).

The most severe controversy rages around the effectiveness in terms of educational achievement of bilingual education. While there seems to be a consensus as to a small moderate achievement effect for desegregation, and a small modest achievement effect for compensatory education, there seems to be no such consensus regarding bilingual education. It is understandable that the problem of finding effects for programmes whose major dimensions are set by political considerations, as well as educational ones, and whose actual concrete character differs greatly from school district to school district, school to school and even teacher to teacher, would be very difficult. Why should very diverse approaches unified only by the term "bilingual education" and the regulations, variously and imperfectly satisfied, that define it bureaucratically, have a uniform effect? Yet such a uniform effect has been detected for desegregation and compensatory education, which falls into the same category: not yet for bilingual education.

It is of course a serious question whether a positivistic research orientation should dominate political and social judgments in determining the kind of education minority children should receive. In fact, they do not. Researchers will be influenced by the best-designed research, others less so. Parents may simply make an experience-based judgment that they want their children to move rapidly into English, whatever the psychological costs, for future achievement; or, if less achievement oriented, will be indifferent to what kind of education the children receive; or, if proud of their heritage, will want more of the native language and culture. Political leaders and school personnel will make their own decisions, based on other considerations. There is no decisive answer in the research: the fact that there is no decisive answer is important, because it means that political and social judgments, which will in any case tend to prevail, should prevail.

The weight of these judgments, among minority and majority, in my view, now leads to an insistence on achievement as a basis for economic mobility and social and political integration into American society. This becomes the dominant consideration affecting judgment on education for minority-group children, and outweighs all other considerations: preservation of culture and language, independent power in the educational sector, psychological ease for the students, jobs for minority group members, superiority of native over American culture, or any other consideration that can be set forward. These other considerations did play a substantial role in the 1960s and the 1970s. They play much less of a role now.

ACHIEVEMENT AND MINORITIES

It is because the United States is a country of immigration that the issue of the economic integration of immigrants and minorities becomes so urgent. I do not wish to suggest that it is less than urgent in the major European countries. But there is still the reality in these countries that there are home countries, emigrating countries, to which many of the migrant labourers and their families may return, and to which indeed substantial numbers have returned. The degree to which children should be integrated into the immigration society becomes questionable because of the possibility of return.

In the United States, I would argue, nativist resistance is weaker than in Europe. This may be surprising to those who think of American society as racist in the highest degree. But the fact is that all American opinion, left and right, business and labour, conservative and liberal, knows that the American people is made up of many peoples of very different races and original languages, and *expects this process to continue*. Immigration to the United States -- legal -- runs to 600 000 a year, four-fifths of which is considered "minority" in American thinking (that is, not European). Illegal immigration runs at a substantial volume, most of it "minority".

The majority not only expects this process to continue: it expects these immigrants to become citizens. One of the most striking demonstrations of the common American view on ethnic and racial differences has been the debate over a proposed new immigration law, the Simpson-Mazzoli bill, which was conducted in the press and in Congress through most of 1983 and 1984. The law ultimately failed (Glazer, 1985, Chapters 1, 2). One primary objective of this law was to legalise the status of millions of illegal immigrants, and to permit them to become American citizens. There was no argument at all between opponents and proponents of this law over whether American immigration should differentiate among immigrants on the basis of language or race, or whether it should give preference to English-speakers, or whites. The bias in American immigration law that favoured such groups was abandoned in 1965. The argument that finally sunk the law was whether the efforts to control illegal immigration by making employers responsible for inquiring into the immigration status of employees would discriminate against Hispanic Americans.

A public opinion that expects mass immigration to continue, and immigrants to become citizens, must also be concerned with their economic adaptation to society, must be concerned to overcome the differences in income and occupation that separates "majorities" from "minorities", and that separate immigrants from natives. The situation here is complex. Not all "minorities" show an economic status inferior to that of the majority (this is particularly the case with Asian immigrants, among whom Chinese, Japanese, and Asian Indian do better than the "majority"). Nor is this uniformly the case with immigrants. Immigrants from Asia tend to be fairly highly educated, and it is therefore no surprise that they do well. But there is surprising evidence that immigrants in general do well, better than the "native majority", after a few years (Chiswick, 1982).

Of course inequality among groups, and between natives and immigrants, or majority and minority is not an exclusively American phenomenon. We find the same in Europe. I suggest that it is more urgent in the United States because of the expectation of the majority and minority that all will form part of a common society with common rights and duties. The maintenance of culture and language is a matter of lesser urgency to the majority and the minority for the same reason.

The attitudes of the American majority, owing to this history and expectation, differs from that of the European majority; and the attitude of the American minorities themselves, I would argue, also differs from that of European minorities themselves, I would argue, also differs from that of European minorities, since they expect to become permanent parts of American society and policy. This affects in their minds how much they <u>should</u> demand from educational institutions in acknowledgement of their special culture and language. Historically, they have asked very little, and have been content to maintain ethnicity and language, to the extent they have, through voluntary organisation, generally religious. In the late 1960s and 1970s, they demanded more, less because they truly wanted to or hoped to maintain ethnic culture and language in a full-bodied way in the United States, than because this was a means of insisting upon respect and equal treatment. The terms on which respect and equal achievement are now demanded have in the minds of ethnic leaders changed: they realise academic achievement and economic achievement are crucial in their own right, and that respect for culture will do little to get it. National holidays for ethnic leaders, respect for language, as such, does not grant achievement.

The key questions become the measures of achievement, on which there is enormous concentration -- and great dispute -- in the United States. These measures include achievement on standardized tests (as is well known there is no single nationally set standard in the United States, and there is considerable resistance to expanding the sampling measures of the National Assessment of Educational Progress); rates of graduation from high school, which is the American equivalent of the school-leaving certificate, and lack of which is considered a sign of a less than adequate education for almost any job that involves literacy; entry into community college, college, and university. New measures are being set as a result of the American educational reform movement, in particular tests for high school diplomas, tests for teachers, higher requirements for academic subjects that must be taken in high school, higher requirements for entry into public and private colleges (Glazer, 1984). There is no question that blacks, despite the improvements indicated above, do poorly. Hispanic Americans do poorly, but there is variation among the major groups of Hispanic Americans; Puerto Ricans do worst, Cubans do fairly well. Asian Americans on the average perform better than white Americans, who may be taken as the norm, though there are great differences among Asian Americans. To take one of these measures of achievement, "dropout rates" -- failure to complete high school, measured by the per cent of high school sophomores (students in second year of high school) who did not graduate two years later: the white non-Hispanic rate is 17.0 per cent, the black rate is 17 per cent, the Hispanic rate 18 per cent, the Asian rate, 3.0 per cent (The Condition of Education, 1984, Table 5.1). Other measures suggest this is representative. These figures understate overall dropout rates: on the whole only about three-quarters of American youth gain high school diplomas.

The statistics vary greatly by region: the South, despite improvement, still does worse than the other sections, in general and for the black minority. Or course, the measures correlate with class position. But it would be an error to simply see these variations as an expression of class. A differentiel ethnic factor plays an independent role in achievement. Sociologists emphasize class as the key determinant in educational achievement. It explains much, but it explains rather less in the United States. There we see that some groups of low socio-economic position, as measured by parental income, education, and occupation, have done qell in school. Nor does class alone explain the poorer achievement of blacks: class held constant, they still do on the average worse. These ethnic and racial differences stand out boldly in the American mind. They substitute in American thinking for the class differences that in Europe have often been a driving force for educational reform.

But even if ethnic and racial factors -- we can substitute for this term the somewhat vague notion of "culture", as anthropologists understand it -- explain a great deal in the differential educational achievement of racial and ethnic groups, they cannot be used in devising the programmes that may overcome these differences. I make this bald statement on the basis of historical experience, and on the basis of the past twenty years. Historical experience tells us that groups do well, have done well educationally, in the absence of any recognition of their culture or language. The case of the Japanese and the Jews is particularly noteworthy: not only was there a total absence in school curricula of their culture and language, they also were doing well at a time when they were subjected to severe discrimination, in the 1920s and 1930s (Dinerstein, Vernon). Recent experience on the other hand tells us that the effort we have made to introduce racial and ethnic curricular materials, particularly for black and Hispanic groups, into reading materials, social science, literature, and the like, seems to have been without any discernible effect in dealing with their educational problems. This is not to say this should not have been done: a curriculum is not only determined by effects on achievement measures, but also by political and social decisions as to what should be taught and learned. From that point of view, to learn that the United States is a multi-racial and multi-ethnic country is necessary.

Of course an argument can be made to justify even more such content. If, as some (but steadily fewer) ethnic militants argue, their life has been and is being shaped by exploitation, cultural and economic, then they will insist on a revolutionary style of education that incorporates more and more of the material demonstrating this exploitation and calling for the need for revolutionary change. But this rings increasingly hollow in a society in which groups that have been subject to severe discrimination as outsiders nevertheless find themselves today fully integrated into the society.

Thus one major conclusion seems to result from our distinctive experience: culture explains some part of differences in educational achievement. But progress to overcome them cannot easily make use of the cultural differences themselves to determine approach or content. In a society where all aspire to equal participation, all must undergo education in the same modes: the language in use in the society, literacy suitable for fulfilling jobs in that society, the methods of calculation that have universal validity, the science that is everywhere the same. This conclusion is not unchallenged in the United States. In the middle 1970s national policy favoured the use of native languages and of distinctive approaches making use of the distinctive culture of each group. But the results of our efforts to overcome differences in educational achievement using such approaches are not encouraging. Majority and minority alike, in part for different reasons, in part for the same reasons, now come together in agreement on traditional approaches to education as the most effective means of raising the educational achievement of minority groups and groups of different language and cultural background.

NOTES

1. For European readers, it should be pointed out that the primary authorities in American public schooling (elementary and secondary) are local school districts, some 15 000, which raise about half the money necessary for elementary and secondary education. Most of the rest is provided by the fifty states, which have full power, constitutionally, over local school districts, but exercise this power variously. The Federal government played almost no role in public schooling until the passage of the Civil Rights Act of 1964 and the Elementary and Secondary Education Act of 1965. Under the former, they could intervene in local school districts, directly or through the courts, to protect the civil rights of minorities; under the latter, they began to provide sums of money to local school districts (this never reached more than 10 per cent of expenditure), and require that districts receiving Federal funds accept Federal regulations relating to the treatment of racial and linguistic minorities.

2. American Indians might be considered another exception, but it would be hard to think of them as equivalent to the Welsh or Bretons or other peoples incorporated into European national states. They occupied land for the most part as hunter-gatherers rather than agriculturalists, did not have developed state organisations, and European settlers did not acknowledge their rights to occupy the land. They were thus akin to the Australian aborigines in their relation to European settlers rather than small nations absorbed by the expanding European states.

BIBLIOGRAPHY

American Indian Areas and Alaska Native Villages: 1980, U.S. Department of Commerce, Bureau of the Census, PC80-S1-13.

Ancestry of the Population by State: 1980, U.S. Department of Commerce, Bureau of the Census, Supplementary Report PC80-S1-10.

Asian and Pacific Islander Population by State: 1980, U.S. Department of Commerce, Bureau of the Census, PC80-S1-12.

CHISWICK B.R., "The Economic Progress of Immigrants: Some Apparently Universal Patterns", in Chiswick, ed., The Gateway: U.S. Immigration Issues and Policies, American Enterprise Institute, Washington, D.C., 1982.

COLEMAN J.S. and others, Equality of Educational Opportunity, U.S. Department of Health, Education and Welfare, 1966.

The Condition of Bilingual Education in the Nation, 1984. A report from the Secretary of Education to the President and the Congress, U.S. Department of Education.

The Condition of Education, National Centre for Education Statistics, 1982, 1984.

The Condition of Hispanics in America Today, U.S. Department of Commerce, Bureau of the Census, 1984.

COOK T. and others, School Desegregation and Black Achievement, U.S. Department of Education, Office of Educational Research and Improvement, National Institute of Education, Washington, D.C., 1984.

DINERSTEIN L., "Education and the Advancement of American Jews", in WEISS B.J. ed., American Education and the European Immigrant: 1840-1940, University of Illinois Press, 1982, pp. 44-60.

GLAZER N., "Black English and Reluctant Judges", in The Public Interest, No. 62, Winter 1981, pp. 40-54.

GLAZER N., Ethnic Dilemmas, 1964-1982, Harvard University Press, 1983.

GLAZER N., "Education and Training Programs and Poverty; Opening the Black Box", University of Wisconsin-Madison, Institute for Research on Poverty, manuscript, 1984.

GLAZER N., "Le débat sur l'enseignement aux Etats-Unis", in Pouvoirs, No. 30, 1984, pp. 29-37.

GLAZER N., ed., Clamor at the Gates, San Francisco, Institute for Contemporary Studies (forthcoming).

MOSTELLER F. and MOYNIHAN D.P., On Equality of Educational Opportunity, Random House, New York, 1972.

RAVITCH D., "The 'White Flight' Controversy", in The Public Interest, No. 51, Spring 1978, pp. 104-105.

ROTBERG I.C., "Federal Policy in Bilingual Education", in Harvard Educational Review, 52:2, May 1982.

SCHNEIDER S.G., Revolution, Reaction or Reform: The 1974 Bilingual Education Act, Las Americas, New York, 1976.

VELTMAN C., Language Shift in the United States, Mouton Publishers, Berlin, 1983.

VERNON P.E., The Abilities and Achievements of Orientals in North America, Academic Press, 1982.

Commentary by Edo POGLIA

Head of General Education Section,
Office pour l'Education et la Science de l'Administration fédérale suisse,
Berne

Nathan Glazer's main argument seems to me to be as follows:

Demands for the educational system to take into account the specific culture of minority groups increased sharply in the United States in the 1960s and reached its peak towards the middle of the 1970s. Since then, these demands have subsided, for three main reasons:

-- The labour market situation and the ideology currently predominant in the United States impels the members of minority groups to attach more importance to the educational success of their children in terms of certificates and diplomas of value on the labour market than to the cultural content of education;

-- The hope that if "minority cultures" were taken into account in school curricula this would have a positive effect on the educational success of children from the corresponding groups was largely disappointed;

-- Moreover, some of the demands of these minorities had been met (e.g. bilingual) or the possibility of deciding more or less independently on curricular content.

The European countries, on the other hand -- behind as usual with any innovation -- are only now launching themselves on the course already followed by the United States some years ago, i.e. that of "maintaining the cultural identity of minorities".

At the risk of seeming somewhat disrespectful, it appears to me that the conclusion which is to be read between the lines of Professor Glazer's paper is: "Dear European Friends, don't waste your time re-doing what has already proved to be fruitless and which is likely to run counter to present historical trends".

So the question which Glazer's contribution obliges us to ask is whether the so-called "intercultural" option now developing in several European countries and which is particularly encouraged by the Council of Europe, is opportune or feasible. In what follows, I shall endeavour to propose some elements in answer to this question.

The definition of "interculturalism" used in the European countries is far from unambiguous. For clarity's sake I shall quote the five main points of one of these definitions, as proposed by the Council of Europe (Project No. 7, "Education and cultural development of migrants"):

i) A sociological argument: "Most of our societies have become multicultural and will become more and more so";

ii) An ethical argument: "Each culture has its own specific characteristics which, as such, are worthy of respect";

iii) An ideological argument: "Multiculturalism is a potential source of enrichment for the whole of society";

iv) A strategical argument: "To enable this potential to become a reality, there must be interpenetration between all cultures concerned without effacing the specific identity of any. The multicultural situation must be stimulated to make it truly intercultural, with all the dynamism which this implies (in terms of communication and interaction especially);

v) A socio-political argument: "Interculturalism is not an end in itself. It is mainly a tool to be used in promoting equality of chances and an optimum integration into social and economic life".

If one wanted to demonstrate, on the basis of American experience, that interculturalism is not "viable" in Europe, one would need to show that:

a) The concept of interculturalism has the same meaning on both sides of the Atlantic;

b) That American intercultural experiments did in fact lead to a dead end;

c) That the current social, political and cultural situation in Europe is similar to that prevailing in the United States when those experiments were under way.

It is not possible to dwell on the first assertion, since polysemy and imprecision are so prevalent in this connection (as several speakers at the meeting pointed out). So I shall base what I have to say on the assumption (which can, of course, be challenged) that we do find ourselves in roughly the same semantic field.

I do not have enough knowledge of American experience to discuss the second assertion (b), still less to dispute Nathan Glazer's views on this specific point. So I shall confine myself to looking -- very briefly -- at assertion (c), which assumes that in the fields we are discussing here, there are similarities between the situation in the United States and in Europe.

Some arguments leading us to doubt that the positions in America and in Europe are the same are provided by Glazer himself.

Minorities in the United States generally consist of American citizens permanently residing in the country and who have few real -- or even imaginary -- prospects of returning to their "country of origin". There may be exceptions (e.g. the return of Mexicans), but generally speaking that is how these groups see themselves and their place in society as a whole.

In most European countries, on the other hand, the migrants are not yet "stabilised", at any rate psychologically speaking. So much so that, at least for first-generation migrants, hopes or dreams of returning home are still very much alive. Because of the proliferation of minority groups and/or migrants and the differing socio-political situations in the European countries, etc., it is difficult to make any valid comparison between the United States and Europe; but it may be supposed that the cultural specificities of these groups with regard to the European host countries (e.g. language) are -- at least for first-generation migrants -- more marked than those of certain minorities (e.g. blacks) in American society.

Furthermore, migrant groups in Europe can count on the relative proximity of their country of origin and its cultural influence to help them maintain their cultural specificity. Here, we can point to the importance of periodical returns home for holidays, the family links which persist, and the availability of national newspapers. Then there are the frequently considerable efforts made by some countries of origin (e.g. Italy, Spain and Yugoslavia) to maintain contact with their migrants, and which specifically focus on the educational aspect, through the organisation of "language and culture classes" for migrants' children.

In theory, this situation should result, in the European immigration countries, in strong pressure exerted by the immigrant communities on local authorities in order to preserve their language and culture of origin, the need for which can easily be demonstrated by pointing to the case of an eventual return home (voluntary returns or those due to the economic situation, while they are not as frequent as the migrants themselves like to believe -- viz. the return myth -- are nonetheless not rare). However, the reality is somewhat different, as can be seen in my own country, Switzerland. Where pressure does exist (e.g. for the provision of language and culture courses in school hours) it far more often comes from the countries of origin, which organise and finance these courses, than from the migrant communities themselves. In reality, it sometimes even happens that those responsible for the courses (backed up by various Swiss school authorities conscious of the need to maintain the language and culture of origin) have difficulty in convincing some of the foreign parents of the need for these lessons, since the latter attach more importance to educational success, which they consider to be essential to their children's future careers, and are afraid it may be compromised if time and energy are spent on activities that do not affect educational appraisal and streaming. Hence the claim (in reality pretty weak and without much hope) that the marks obtained in language and culture courses be taken into consideration in assessing school results, so as to motivate the pupils.

So on this side of the Atlantic, too, and even before the economic crisis, educational success, considered to be the key to social success, seems to take priority over the cultural concern and demands expressed by migrant groups. Moreover, if an effort is made to assess the direct consequences of the fact that, unlike the American minorities, migrants in Europe (of the first but also of the second generation) are not citizens of the countries where they live, three things become apparent:

i) To begin with, this means that our migrant groups are far less able to exert political pressure (pressure on the parties, whether from the inside or the outside, use of the mass media in political campaigns, etc);

ii) Then they are assured (to varying degrees) of the backing of their countries of origin, for which they constitute an interesting political clientèle (a clear sign of this is the fact that political parties and movements based in the countries of origin are implanted in immigrant communities and sometimes have quite a wide following). As a consequence of this situation, the cultural questions that are an inherent feature of migrant groups become one of the stakes in the periodical negotiations between the host country and the country of origin. Negotiations, of course, mean compromise, and therefore the acceptance by the host countries of some of the cultural claims made by the emigration countries. This is what happened with language and culture courses.

The real problem arises at another level. There is no guarantee that the cultural demands made by the countries of origin truly reflect those of the migrants, particularly if the latter belong to regions, social categories or political movements remote from the central government. This was the case with Spanish migrants at the time of the Franco regime, and with supporters of Yugoslav, Turkish and other opposition movements. But it is also sometimes the case with migrants from poor or rural areas, and this is a far more significant sociological factor.

iii) Now, looking at the attitude of the authorities in the host country, it may be supposed that some of them may recognise the right to cultural difference for migrants who are not likely to remain in the country more readily than they would grant the same rights to minority groups among their own nationals. Sometimes, indeed, the temptation may be strong, for some host countries, to encourage migrant populations to retain their own culture so as to keep them mobile -- in other words, with a view to being able more easily to persuade or sometimes oblige them to return home when the economic situation deteriorates. In this case, interculturalism is liable to serve as a cover-up for a policy in flagrant contradiction with its underlying principles.

The argument put forward by Glazer, theoretically in favour of the interculturalist thesis and according to which the Europeans are more inclined to set a positive value on local cultural differences (e.g. dialects) and therefore more willing to accept the differences of minority groups (e.g. migrants) does not seem to me to be warranted. Taking the case of Switzerland, for instance, with its four languages and marked political decentralisation, particularly in the educational field, it cannot be said that there is a greater openness to the culture of migrant groups than in single-culture countries. The reason is, perhaps, that the various cultures or sub-cultures in the country have a strictly defined geographical basis. The linguistic frontiers, for instance, are well established, and apart from a few exceptions, Swiss citizens are not entitled to receive schooling in a language other than that of the majority living in the part of the country concerned (the so-called "school language territoriality" principle).

Moreover, in places where there is a "declining" or "encircled" culture, the defence and the promotion of features specific to a local village or regional culture may mean that rather than openness towards other cultures there is, on the contrary, an isolationist tendency and a distrust of anything "foreign", whether from the other side of the world or from the next village...

One of the hopes raised by interculturalism is that it might improve the school achievement of migrants' children and those of other disadvantaged minorities, insofar as it would favour personal development while encouraging school authorities to take two things into account in streaming: "educational disadvantages" related to a minority cultural status, but at the same time the extra skills this implies (e.g. knowledge of another language as well as the school language, etc.), -- skills which should be allotted points in the educational selection process. How do things stand now in this respect?

One fact confirms Glazer's observation. Not all the cultural minorities record school performance rates below the national average. A good example here is the situation in Geneva, where there are two types of migrants, two quite distinct minorities. The children of Italian and Spanish migrants, who are generally unskilled workers, or at any rate from a relatively low socio-economic category, generally do markedly less well than Swiss children, whereas the children of foreign civil servants working for international organisations and those of foreign executives with multinational enterprises have good success rates.

There are probably a number of reasons for this, including not only differences in social class but also the fact of belonging to cultures more or less highly regarded in educational circles. (It is obvious that so far as schooling in Geneva is concerned a far higher premium is set on knowledge of English than on that of Spanish or Portuguese!).

It is always difficult to come to any firm conclusion with regard to the basic factors at work, particularly since existing studies are not very exhaustive. However, according to scientific literature on positions in Switzerland, it seems possible to say that it is the "social class" factor that is the main reason for the low achievements of migrants' children in our countries -- though this certainly does not mean that cultural factors are negligible.

The main reason for analysing these problems is, naturally, to be able to propose effective solutions. The importance of American experience for Europeans lies in the scale of the measures proposed and implemented in order to take cultural factors into account. Glazer's rather pessimistic assessment of the impact of these measures should therefore not be ignored. And the meagre effects of the compensatory schemes which focus more directly on the "social class" factor do nothing to reassure us.

On the other hand, European experiments in this field are both more recent and more specific. Even if we often consider them to be positive, and thus if the arguments aimed at "rehabilitating" interculturalism as an instrument for reducing inequalities in school performance have a certain weight, they lack the element that would finally tip the balance: having proved their worth in a sufficiently meaningful context.

It would, of course, be possible to hold an extremely interesting discussion on various questions of substance and method relating to the assessment of the various measurements used. (Remember the argument emphasizing that the instruments measuring performance used in school selection processes are generally imbued with the dominant culture and the fact that for the sake of comparison the same measuring instrument has to be used for all children, which almost automatically places those from cultural minorities at a disadvantage). It should also be borne in mind that in its advocates' view, the "intercultural option" covers a good deal more than bilingualism at school and does not even necessarily include it. Furthermore, interculturalism does not focus solely on the children of minorities, but on the contrary asserts that majority groups ought to be able to profit from the minority cultures present in the school and in society.

Over and above the more or less explicit criticisms expressed by Nathan Glazer, some questions have been raised as to interculturalism and European efforts to recognise the value of the contribution that can be made by the culture of migrant groups in the educational and social context. It seems to me useful to list some of these questions, quickly and succinctly:

-- Can it really be said that migrant groups in Europe have a "specific culture", when migrants of the second or third generation tend to predominate? If so, what are their ties with the cultures of their countries of origin? Furthermore, are the cultural differences between host countries and certain countries of origin (Germany, France, Belgium and Switzerland on the one hand and Spain, Italy, Greece and Yugoslavia on the other, for example) still as great as they were earlier?

-- When the cultural differences between the majority of a country's population and its minorities are strongly marked, or when they affect the very basis of a society, and even more so if those minorities regard their specific cultural traits as a "flag" to rally round and an instrument for use in political and social campaigning, is it conceivable that the majority will really allow the educational system to sustain such specific traits?

-- What are the real chances of interculturalism succeeding in Europe today, when the age-old bugbears of racialism and xenophobia are raising their heads again in politics and in everyday life?

-- Who can claim to have the ability and the right to decide which cultural traits are "different" but compatible with the dominant culture and would thus be "acceptable", and which ones are incompatible and therefore unacceptable at school?

-- Is the intercultural option in schools always "technically" workable? It would mean, for example:

that majority and minority children would have to go to school together (something which is sometimes difficult because minorities tend to be concentrated in particular areas or neighbourhoods);

that teaching staff must be able to instil the cultural traits of the minorities and give them their due value, something which requires preparation and teaching resources which for the moment are simply not available, as well as ability on the part of all teachers to keep an open mind and overcome any xenophobic instincts. It would also require curricular changes likely to run counter to the present tendency to return to the basic subjects (reading-writing-arithmetic...).

CONCLUSIONS

Comparison between the United States and Europe unfortunately seems to provide no support for the view that the intercultural option is likely to gain a stronger foothold in European educational systems. Moreover, a certain number of questions with regard to interculturalism have not yet been answered and several of the practical propositions it implies remain rather hazy.

It seems to me that because of this some participants in this meeting have made up their minds that "interculturalism is not a suitable and effective response to the cultural, educational and social problems considered." I do not agree, for a number of reasons:

-- Whether we like it or not, European societies are already multicultural and they are likely to become more so with time. It is thus essential for us to find a "modus vivendi" between the various social groups before the end of the century if our societies are to remain united and viable;

-- With all its drawbacks, interculturalism provides a positive alternative to a return to parish pump politics, chauvinism, xenophobia and racialism;

-- Even if (which I do not believe) interculturalism were merely a myth rallying good will, particularly among teachers and school authorities, children and disadvantaged groups can only benefit from it;

-- From the point of view of educational policy, once it has been acknowledged that structural reforms and compensatory programmes have not really met the objectives aimed at, there are no other more effective ideas to put forward to solve the problems of educational inequality.

So there is only one sensible attitude: recognising the potentialities of interculturalism in no way means that we have to close our eyes to its theoretical and practical drawbacks or its possible "perverse effects". On the contrary, it means that we must be keenly critical of the concepts and proposals so far put forward, seeking to clarify them and to achieve greater coherence and effectiveness.

It also means that we must go ahead with more socio-cultural and pedagogical experiments which will provide "living" examples from which our countries' policies (and particularly education policies) could draw inspiration.

9. THE SOCIAL DYNAMIC OF MIGRANT GROUPS: FROM PROGRESSIVE TO TRANSFORMATIVE POLICY IN EDUCATION

by
Chris MULLARD
Professor, Department of Sociology of Education, University of London,
Institute of Education, University of Amsterdam

All questions are posed within assumptive frameworks. Sometimes these frameworks are hinted at vaguely in the way the questions are formed; sometimes they are so completely hidden that only a truly historical appreciation of the context of the questions can lead to the necessary unearthing of the frameworks, and at other times they are so openly articulated that only the questioner remains blind. As in most controversial fields, the questions asked in the general area of race and ethnic relations in education are of a kind which spring from rather entrenched and definitive frameworks. They are always tinged with the heat of fervent beliefs, denying to all any access to their meaning until these beliefs are broken down, examined, and reassembled as guideposts to where the questioner stands, has stood in the past, and hopes to stand in the future.

In other words, the questions in this field are invariably asked and thus are only answerable in terms of localities, which always extend beyond the field into the nether regions of the questioner's perception of education and society and the definition held of the problem under discussion in both education and society.

Given this social truism it is now possible, firstly, to raise the question I have been asked to comment upon within a European or, more accurately, Europeanised context and, secondly, to suggest why it is necessary to go beneath the question itself in order to examine its assumptive framework (1).

Set in a descriptive and historical account of the relationship between multicultural education and minority groups, the question is to be found in the following statement in the CERI background paper for the Conference:

> "In the very early days of multicultural education minority groups anxious to safeguard their cultural individuality did not generally look to the public education service for help. Cultural programmes and initiatives developed as the result of each community's own cultural dynamism. It is only relatively recently that such communities have called upon the state for official assistance in support of their cultural life. It seems to us important that we should consider the implications of this transition from a system of cultural autonomy to one of cultural assistance and, more particularly, the feasibility nowadays of maintaining the cultural vitality of these communities without the help of the public system of education." (2).

Clearly in order to begin to answer the question(s) contained in this statement, at least three prior points need to be made. Firstly, did cultural programmes and initiatives develop as a result of the cultural dynamism of minority groups, as a result of, and in reaction to, the assimilationist, monocultural educational policies of Europeanised states and educational systems, or, for that matter, did they in any real sense develop at all? Secondly, is it correct to say that migrant groups have called upon the state for official assistance or has the state in recent years deliberately created the conditions and encouraged Black and other migrant groups to apply for funding? Lastly, can the actual question even be phrased in terms of a "transition from a system of cultural autonomy to one of cultural assistance" without some understanding of what is called in the text above "cultural dynamism"?

None of these questions can be answered here without undermining the obvious good intentions of the author of the question. But it is necessary, however, to raise them in order to extract and confirm a proposition hidden in the very first sentence of this paper. Namely: all questions are not only posed in assumptive frameworks but they also reflect, when turned around, their opposite question. If this is the case and if it can be accepted that all questions are located within and emanate from specific interests and relations of power, then it becomes a fairly straightforward thing to say that in order to understand and ultimately answer a question, it is imperative to broadly categorise and address these interests and relations of power. For, essentially, it is out of these things and not out of any liberal and non-connected feelings and thoughts about a problem that the assumptive frameworks of most questions are constructed.

Once this point is recognised, it is then possible to abstract the pith of the quotation and to re-interpret it educationally or otherwise as a phenomenon and process of social dynamism. As what is perhaps indisputable about the quotation is that such a dynamism has and does exist and is, further, an essential part not only of Black and migrant group cultural life but is also an integral feature of the relationship between two given and, as argued in this paper, competing frameworks or definitions of objectives, problems, questions, and answers. Indeed, it is virtually impossible to understand the contemporary patterning of race and ethnic relations in education without an understanding of the working of this dynamic as exhibited in alternative definitions of objectives and problems and in the educational struggles of Black and migrant groups themselves (3).

With this said, it might now seem to follow that whilst engaging with the kind of question(s) raised in the quotation on one level, the argument in this paper will have to be concerned, on another level, with how questions, problems, and possible solutions are formulated in respect to their opposites. More clearly the purposes of this paper besides the encouragement of constructive and equal talk are to set out the competing definitions or ways of looking at the question in the field and to show how these definitions give rise to different definitions of the "problem" and two kinds of policy -- <u>progressive</u> and <u>transformative</u> policy in education. In the concluding section which will return to some of the issues raised already, an indication of a possible way forward and through the morass of good intentions in the field will be suggested.

COMPETING DEFINITIONS: CHANGE OR CONTROL

At the centre of the debate in the field of race and ethnic relations in education exist two clear sets of contradictory interests. Whether the debate surfaces as a struggle between the relative merits of multicultural and anti-racist education, as it does in Britain, or, as in the Netherlands, the significance and meaning of intercultural education, these interests appear to underpin all European-oriented discourses in the field. They are to be found within the very institutional fabric of Europeanised societies, reflected in the practices of education as far apart, geographically, as America and Australia, Canada and France, and they all appear to be expressed in terms of two main socio-educational concerns.

Rather bluntly these two concerns can be viewed as the dual objectives of socio-educational control and socio-educational change. The former in the recent histories of education in Europeanised societies which, demographically, have undergone fundamental changes, is concerned with the essential maintenance of the institution of education, its production, allocative, and cultural reproduction and transmission tasks. The carrying out of these aims in relation to a rather conspicuously dominant objective, the control of racial, ethnic and other minority groups, constitutes in effect the substance of the discourse in the field. Starting from a qualitatively different and in many ways oppositional standpoint, the second objective is concerned with the essential change of the institution of education, its production, allocative, and cultural reproduction tasks. The carrying out of these aims in relation to what might be seen as a dominated objective in Europeanised societies, the effecting of a change in the conditions, positions, and relations of racial, ethnic, and other minority groups, constitutes in many respects the counter-substance of the discourse in the field.

Clearly these dual objectives of socio-educational control and change are not only in relations of contest and struggle: but, as oppositionally positioned objectives, they are also socially articulated in relations of power. They live in their own competing definitions of social reality in respect to race and ethnicity in education.

For instance, the objective organised around the principle of control or rather the definition of reality associated with this objective tends to exhibit a downward conception of the problem. Sanctioned by governments and educational authorities, this dominant definition views Black, ex-colonial, European, and other migrant workers as constituting the "problem". Within an implicitly pathological perspective, one which explains the "problem" in terms of the social, cultural, economic, linguistic, and religious characteristics of minority groups themselves, such a definition underemphasises, as in the UK and France, or appears to neglect altogether, as in the Netherlands, Belgium, Germany, and Scandinavia, the problem of institutionalised White racism. In other words the definition held of the "problem" in these European societies and indeed several other Europeanised societies precludes any blame or searching critique of dominant White institutions, the way and purposes for which they have evolved or the practices and ideologies which characterise them as institutions as such (4).

The dominated definition of social reality, on the other hand, begins not with an account of the so-called problems of minority groups. Insisting on an upward conception of the problem its constructing point is to be found instead on the level of the institutional basis of society. Furthermore it is built up on the premise that White racism is an institutionalised feature, forming part of the common-sense knowledge of all Europeanised societies dependent upon the labour of Black, ex-colonial, European, or other migrant workers (5). From this position this alternative and largely dominated definition reflects a view of the world in which Whites, not Blacks, the cultural majority as opposed to the cultural minority groups and the institutional structures and ideologies they fashion and control constitute the "problem".

It is, of course, a definition of reality which is inextricably tied up with a critique of the making and continuing of most racist Europeanised societies -- the coming into being of the nationalistic capitalisms and states of Europe as a directly related result of slavery, colonialism, imperialism (e.g. Great Britain, France, the Netherlands, Belgium, Portugal); the development of the new-world-type colonies into Europeanised capitalist economies out of conquest, the massive extermination of Black indigenous peoples, the large-scale "forced" migration (e.g. America, Canada, Australia, New Zealand, South Africa, etc.); and the continuing and reconstructing of the productive capacity and surpluses of all these societies, in especially the post-war period, through the encouragement of migration and the exploitative employment of largely Black, or descriptively speaking, non-White labour.

In sum, then, the dominant definition stresses cultural features, conditions, and ahistorical explanations of the problem. The relational context of culture is its site for exposition, organisation, and <u>control</u>. The dominated definition, in contrast, emphasizes structural features, conditions, and historical explanations of the problem. And the relational context of structure is its site for exposition, organisation, and <u>change</u>.

THE PROBLEM: RACISM OR ETHNICITY

Clearly any account of competing definitions of reality, as given above, which does not with some precision identify the nature of the problem subsumed within such definitions is insufficient. For what this achieves is only a description of objectives, change or control, in terms of a rather blunt indicator of the existence of competitive positions. It says very little about either the genesis of objectives or what relations might exist between, in the case here, educational objectives and broader social interests. In order to say more about the nature of the problem other than to assert that for most Whites it is Blacks, ethnicity, and for most Blacks, it is Whites, racism, it is necessary to probe beyond the content and study the context of the competing definitions.

If this is done something quite striking and highly significant emerges. In the first place when it is understood that the problem for White educational groups and institutions only emerged and is correlated with the presence of Black and other minority pupils in socially White schools, the problem cannot be solely identified and explained in terms of ethnicity or ethnic and cultural differences (6). The reason for this is simply because to identify and explain it in such a way is to presuppose or to have been socialised into believing that such differences are both significant and implicitly problematic. If this is so then the question becomes why are they viewed consciously or otherwise in this way.

The answer, again, is not to be found in the content but in the context of the competing definitions. As it is in this domain that the actual presence of Blacks connects with the hidden and acknowledged history of the educational systems and of the societies of which they form an integral part. The Black presence then raises a problem for particularly European societies with colonial and imperial histories, because it both unlocks (and locks up again) some of the more, in retrospect, disturbing, unethical, and criminal aspects of these histories.

In its unlocking the Black presence exposes more than a racist White past: it also brings to the surface in a challenging sense a whole range of definitions held by Europeanised societies of themselves, definitions of, for instance, Frenchness, Britishness, Dutchness, Germanness or Swedishness which owe more to deep senses of chauvinism, nationalism, ethnocentricism _und so weiter_ than to any system of rational thought or set of "ethical" and "democratic" propositions reflected in the written or unwritten constitutions of these societies (7). So what is being suggested here is that in the unlocking which has come about as a result of the presence of non-Europeans in Europe or Europeanised societies a somewhat different deeper and more horrific definition of the problem is released, which shakes many of the hitherto established historical, social, and educational foundations of Europeanised societies (8).

But as it unlocks the Black presence when articulated in an explicit political and education way, it also locks up the very thing it exposes, the racist educational and general institutional structure, policies and practices of Europeanised societies. This is in part to do with the fact that racism as a structural and ideational phenomenon accepts and negates itself through continuously asserting, counter-asserting, and juxtaposing notions of superiority and inferiority to the point where it is possible for any group or individual to declare: "_I know_ I am not racist." Such a mechanism, especially in the field of education where teachers and agencies largely define themselves as being progressive, concerned with the whole development of the pupil and untainted by the world outside of the school playground, is also reinforced by what might be called the established, essential, and, for these reasons, valued order of things. In other words, another part of the locking up of racism is to be seen in the defensiveness of teachers and educational bodies when confronted by Blacks and anti-racist Whites. What often occurs in these situations is not only a declaration of non-racism, but also an affirmation of self as a "good teacher", of the school as a "good and much needed place", of the educational system, despite its shortcomings, as a necessary and inherently benign institution, and, lastly of society as being highly valued for what it stands for in the present if not always in the past.

Thus from these kinds of assertions (non-racism) and affirmations (established beliefs, values, norms) the racism that is unlocked by the Black presence in Europeanised societies is in effect locked up again by, firstly, racism itself, and, secondly, by a set of long-standing and firmly held beliefs about the essential "goodness" and worth of the educational and other institutions of Western societies.

False though it might be, from this point onwards the logic becomes within a racist framework quite obvious. Associations are then made between the essential "goodness" and worth of institutions and the protection of both these institutions and kind of socio-educational order to which they give rise. Groups, who question in their actions, demands, charges and, in the case of Black, ex-colonial and other migrant groups such as the Turkish and Maroccan communities in Europe, even presence, become identified as groups to be controlled: as problems to be contained. The general definition of the problem then has to be framed in terms of "them", not "us", because to accept the inversion would be to raise a host of uncomfortable and contradictory questions about "us" and the fundamental nature, past and present, of society and all in which "we" believe and define "ourselves" as members of predominantly White, Europeanised society. So it is largely for these reasons, out of these interests, that the dominant definition and discourse has centred around a notion of ethnicity -- a notion which rarifies and ritualised a concept of difference to the total exclusion of inference (9).

From the opposite standpoint and dominated definition of the problem as one of racism, the discourse also conceals its underlying meaning, interests, and objectives. As already shown earlier, the definition focuses on the institutional nature of racism, evoking a whole analysis of the role of race and racism in the making of Western capitalism and Europeanised societies. But as well as doing this it does in the actions of particularly ex-slave and colonial Blacks in America, Britain, France, and, increasingly so, in the Netherlands transcend the issue of race and racism to question, as correctly feared by White institutions, the entire institutional and normative structure, including the material base and resource and income distribution, of the majority of Europeanised societies in the Western World. Even for other than Black migrant workers such as the Turks in Germany and the Moroccan and Algerian communities in France, this questioning in respect to educational, non-chances, and discriminations has already started and is beginning to be conveyed in their conceptions of struggle in and outside of education. For several White migrant groups, and the experience and educational struggles of the Finnish community in Sweden stand out as an example, the same deepening extension and account of the problem is present in, for instance, the struggles around the mother-tongue versus second language teaching debate (10).

Within this dominated definition, as is the case with the dominant definition, this extension of meaning is at times firmly, and at all times loosely, connected with a set of value-based interests which are hardly ever openly expressed. One of the differences between the two sets of interests, apart from their racial frameworks, is that the dominant set arises from within, whereas the dominated set tends to come from outside the societies under discussion. In some respects this can be seen in the nationalistic base of, for instance, Finnish, Algerian, and Mollucan educational struggles in Europe, but in all respects these interests spring from a sense of belonging to, coming from, returning to, or, for many Blacks born and bred in Europe, of identifying with the histories, concerns and aspirations of under-developed or Third World societies. As interests they tend to be collectivistic as opposed to individualistic, socialist as opposed to capitalist, with deep roots in the history of contact, struggle, and the eventual overthrow or physical banishment of the colonial European presence. In as much as they are then alternative interests in that they have been forged partly in opposition to those sanctioned institutionally in Europeanised society, these interests can and often do in the struggles for "cultural autonomy" in education bring into sharp relief, if not always open conflict, the relative ethnical assumptions and merits of the core value systems of developed and underdeveloped, capitalist and socialist, White and Black societies.

So, arising from and feeding back into the dominated definition of the problem, these interests together with the substantive concern of racism prescribe for Europeanised societies the most bitter pill of all -- the swallowing of the necessity for real socio-educational change if one of the main objects of human activity and that of education is to bring about the conditions for the liberation of all. Thus, finally, the dominated definition of the problem is neither concerned with the protection of established beliefs and values and the socio-educational orders they give rise to. Nor is it concerned with the problem of ethnicity, the symbolic discourse of the dominant. But, instead, it is concerned with liberation through a process of change of these beliefs, values, and socio-educational orders: it is concerned with the problem of racism, the actual discourse of the dominated.

PROGRESSIVE OR TRANSFORMATIVE POLICY

The two competing definitions of objectives, change and control, and the two competing definitions of the problem, racism and ethnicity, do not just exist as static presentations of positions and existences. They are as already shown connected dialectically and related to each other in a dominant-dominated relationship. In education this power relationship can be seen today in the way in which national educational authorities and their respective national states have either appropriated (e.g. Britain, France, America) or constructed independently (the Netherlands, Sweden, Australia) one variant or another of multicultural education (11). At all times and in all national situations it has been against a background and in direct opposition to the anti-racist struggles either threatened or actually waged within schools and colleges, by pupils, parents, teachers, and community-based organisations.

Even in those societies which proclaim the non-existence of anti-racist struggles in education and hence the progressive intentions of the state in its construction and endorsement of multicultural education, it does not take much intellectual imagination to make the connections between, for instance, the Mollucan rebellion in the 1970s and the Dutch state's support of intercultural education in the early 1980s. Or, to take another example, the Aboriginal campaign for landrights and the White Australian government's response with policies of "self-determination" and multi-ethnic education in the 1970s. Indeed all these indirect as well as the direct examples which can be assembled from the educational experiences and histories of Britain, America, and France point to one incontrovertible conclusion: namely, that the existence and support of a dominant definition of the objective and problem in and outside of education is invariably constructed in relation to an alternative, dominated definition of the objective and problem.

Precisely because this has been historically the case, it is important to remember that the educational policies and practices associated with dominant definitions, <u>progressive policy</u> stands in apparently oppositional relations to those espoused by the advocates of dominated definitions which, in contrast, can be seen as constituting statements of <u>transformative policy</u>.

Indeed, it is possible to go one step further than this and state unequivocably that all progressive policy not only stems from dominant definitions in education, which are in most respects racist, but it is also formulated either to mask and confuse or to seriously undermine and negate the statements and preferred practices of transformative policy.

Yesterday and today the substantial truth of this observation can be seen in the British case over the last two or more decades. "Immigrant education", for instance, in the late 1950s, was established not only as an educational vehicle for the teaching of English as a second language, but it was also encouraged to ensure, firstly, that "immigrants" would not disrupt the normal education of White children; secondly, to safeguard established school values, beliefs, and practices from any kind of contamination that might occur as a result of the Black presence in schools, and, thirdly, to prevent the appearance within "a National system of education" of the cultures, languages, and religions of Black peoples. All attempts by Black parents and pupils as well as those few White teachers and others to inject a multiracial dimension into the heavily monocultural and assimilative school environment and curriculum were thwarted.

It was not until Black groups in conjunction with others began to organise within and outside of education and to agitate vociferously for a change of educational policy and practice that the government and local educational authorities began slowly, under pressure with always the threat of disruption and violence lurking in the background, to reformulate their policies and consider a change in their practices. But the transformative policy of Black groups, which focused in the late 1960s, early 1970s, on the two issues of racism and monoculturalism was severely undermined by the state's absolute rejection of the issue of racism, which surfaced around a debate on the support or otherwise of Black Studies, and its appropriation and eventual redefinition in the mid-1970s of the cultural argument. What emerged in the late 1970s, early 1980s was a multicultural education, defined by Whites within their dominant definition of the problem -- a definition which precludes, as shown earlier, any real understanding or acceptance of the problem of racism (12).

Although this glimpse at what was in effect an extremely complex process illustrates the point being made here, it should not be understood as an example of the racist and negating effect of progressive policy that is idiosyncratically unique to Britain. Other examples as documented by researchers and educationalists in Sweden, Germany, France and the Netherlands as well as the illustrations given though not analytically commented upon by the author of a richly researched OECD/CERI document on "The Education of Linguistic and Cultural Minorities in OECD Countries", all question the problematic basis of what is termed here progressive policy (13).

Indeed what springs out of this literature and my own research and observation is that progressive policy, as developed in Europeanised societies, is progressive in a number of different though essentially interrelated ways. Firstly, and within a dominant definition of the problem it progresses within a racist framework, gradually over time covering up the overt racism of the assimilationist/integration era with the patchwork quilt of cultural heterogenity. Secondly, it progresses always in relation to what is actually seen or perceived to be the position and views of dominated migrant groups, appropriating all that does not disturb and as much else as can be realistically accommodated without a fundamental change in the conception and definition of the problem. Thirdly, it progresses often as a result of worldwide changes in the balances of power, economic relations, and arragements between developed and underdeveloped societies as well as changes that might occur between the West and East. Fourthly, it progresses in relation to the activities of the extreme right, neo-facist and racist groups as demonstrated recently in Germany with respect to the changes in policy and attitude towards particularly the Turkish Gästarbeiter (14). And, last but not least, it at all times progresses in relation to the street and classroom activities and rebellions of Black and other migrant groups, as was seen in the years of Black Power and "rioting" in the States during the 1960s and in the aftermath of Brixton and Liverpool in the Britain of the early 1980s.

Central to all these progressions is the factor of what might become a new and appreciably disturbing reality from the point of view of the dominant. In other words endemic in all progressive policy is the possibility of an existence of its own transformation. Not to progress in the way and as a result of the interactions just identified would be to accept in most cases the dominated definition of reality, objectives, and problems. But, of course, to continue to progress in the way that it does, all progressive policy will continue to be, however well camouflaged, racist.

Transformative policy, on the other hand, is both non-racist and anti-racist. It stands in direct opposition to progressive policy in the field of race and ethnic relations in education. Emerging in Britain, the Netherlands, and, perhaps to a lesser extent, in France is anti-racist education, which exists in relations of context and struggle with all the various forms of multicultural education, transformative policy and practice seeks not to progress within but to transform dominant definitions of reality, objectives, and problems, and the oppressive and exploitative relations they give rise to. Looking more towards emancipatory than to compensatory education, transformative policy and practice then possesses a root in the struggles of the victims of and activitists against racism (15). Because it does this, and because in the form of anti-racist education it is concerned with the problem of challenging and dismantling racism in all its manifestations and disguises, it, unlike progressive policy, continuously makes the connection between knowledge and consciousness, action and freedom, truth and untruth, right and wrong, and in so doing helps to generate a practice of structural challenge and change.

Without wishing here to repeat the case for anti-racist education, which has been published elsewhere, it should be noted that transformative policy can be seen to be developing in tangential though discretely different areas other than those to do openly with racism (16). For instance in Sweden at the moment the Finnish struggle already referred to and centred around the Stockholm area not only culminated, in part, in a school strike of pupils with Finnish parents removing their children from urban schools, but, more significantly, it gave rise to: firstly, the setting up of alternative school and teaching sites; secondly, the recruiting of Finnish teachers from Helsinki to Stockholm expressly interested in the teaching of the curriculum and the conveying of alternative cultural values in the Finnish language; thirdly, the discussion and development of a critical practice of transformational policy; and, lastly, it heralded in a new era of community educational politics and practice in which connections and relations are being forged with, particularly, Yugoslavian and Turkish educational concerns around and within a broadly construed anti-racist perspective in education. Whether or not this struggle "succeeds" in all its objectives in the short term is as irrelevant as whether or not the mating call is sung by a nightingale or a crow, for the point is that it has happened, is happening and, now, will continue to happen through one voice or another (17).

Of equal importance as its happening is the fact that it has occurred on and with respect to a specific terrain in anti-racist educational struggle -- the terrain of language in general and the fight for mother-tongue teaching and instruction in particular. The enveloping significance of this terrain is to be found in that it is precisely the terrain where cultural considerations (multicultural education, progressive policy) meet structural considerations (anti-racist education, transformative policy). This is the case, because evoked in this debate are not just matters to do with technical and communicative competences and their probable correlations with academic performance and achievement. But, on quite another level, this debate and its manifest educational politics also evokes a whole set of questions to do with the structural position, experiences, and conditions of Black and migrant groups in both the educational and social structure of Europeanised society. This is to say that it is through an ostensibly cultural debate and educational politics on language that dominant racist definitions of the problem are reflected to a degree where it is possible to see, in the reactions to Black and migrant group demands, the view held of the position of these groups in a society which clings onto a definition of itself as being White Swedish, White British, or White French.

To accept fully, as opposed to bend towards, the demands of the Finns in Sweden, the preferences for Asian and Afro-Caribbean schools in the U.K., or, for example, the Surinamese staffing of and non-Dutch teaching in schools in the Bijlgermeer, the Netherlands, would be, again, to reject most of that which informs all dominant definitions and progressive policy. But to articulate these demands, preferences, and objectives in the first place and to organise around them is as clear an example of transformative policy as is the whole struggle for Black alternative education in America and Aboriginal education in Australia.

So, unlike progressive policy, transformative policy is anchored into a qualitatively different conception of the world or individual society and its educational system as well as in a dominated definition of the problem. Firstly, in its challenging of the social inequalities (racism, classism, sexism) exhibited in Europeanised societies, it poses a need for a structural change in the relations of power, control, and legitimation. Secondly, it reflects an alternative definition of national identity, a new Europeanism, and one in which it is accepted that Black and other migrant groups in Europeanised societies are there for the most part to stay and fully contribute to the making and defining of the new definition of these societies. Thirdly, it conveys a notion of Pan-Worldism, one which forges breaks from the old and the construction of new relations with Third World and other societies represented in the migrations to Europeanised societies. Fourthly, as it is not concerned like its counterpart with the management of the appearance of change, it begins from and takes seriously the claims and demands of those with the experience of racial, ethnic or other forms of oppression, exploitation, and discrimination. Finally, all types of transformative policy is in any objective or other sense of the concept ethically based, involved with that kind of liberation necessary for the development of a consciousness of history and being that in its coming will lead to the equitable relations of power, resources, and education, that, in turn, can only but lead to a new concept and vision of humanity.

CONCLUSION: COMPROMISES OR CHOICES

To return to the principal point made in the introductory discussion to this paper no question can be understood or answered without some reference to the framework in which it is located. What I have therefore subsequently attempted to do in this paper is to identify the two umbrella frameworks or definitions of socio-educational objectives and problems in the fields, indicating that each has spawned its own special kind of policy orientation and focus. Although a good deal more could have been said about the competing definitions of objectives and problems as well as progressive and transformative policy itself, enough, however, has been conveyed to suggest two concluding points.

Firstly, it is almost inconceivable that dominant definitions together with progressive policy in the field of race and ethnic relations in education could have existed as such without the socially dynamic and relational presence of Black and other migrant groups in Europeanised societies. And conversely, dominated definitions and transformative policy could not have emerged if it had not been for the kind of contact that has occurred between Black and White, Third World and First World, Underdeveloped and Developed societies. But, above all else, there would have been no evolution of competing definitions, irrespective of presence or contact, if Black and migrant groups had chosen deliberately to remain (as was the case in the early years of migration), or have been kept in the margins of the making of everyday social and educational life.

The second and shorter point to be concluded answers in part the question raised in the quotation produced in the first pages of this paper. There has been no real transition "from a system of cultural autonomy to one of cultural assistance". Instead, what has occurred has been a shift in the perceptions of the state and the public system of education. Along a socio-educational avenue of control yet across a landscape of progressive policy, this shift has been one from cultural domination (monoculturalism) to now in most Europeanised societies a publicly supported and funded institutionalisation of this domination through the discourse, practices and policies of ethnicity solely conceived in respect to Black and migrant "ethnic" groups (multiculturalism) (18). Thus, what this point raises when taken with the other concluding points is in effect an ethical question, as phrased in the quotation, about "the feasibility nowadays of maintaining the cultural vitality of these communities without the help of the public system of education".

In short, what all these conclusions point to educationally, socially, and politically, is to an uncomfortable crossroads at which major decisions by all national states and educational systems in Europeanised societies have to be made. There are two frameworks or socio-educational definitions of objectives -- change or control? there are two definitions of the problem -- racism or ethnicity? There are two kinds of policy that can be pursued -- transformative or progressive policy? There are many compromises that can be botched together, but the fundamental choices should not belong to the history of the making of the past, but instead to the history of the making of the future of Europeanised societies and their educational systems.

For many Black and migrant peoples living in these societies, working in their factories, and attending their schools, these choices were made a long time ago.

NOTES AND REFERENCES

1. This paper was written for the OECD/CERI project in the area of the education of cultural and linguistic minorities in the OECD countries. The term "Europeanised" is used throughout the paper not only to describe geographically speaking European societies but also all those of migration and which themselves historically were founded by and at present are culturally (languages, Christianity, family systems, etc.) oriented to one or more (e.g. Canada) European society.

2. From the OECD/CERI background conference working paper and the subject area of my address.

3. Such a belief in more global terms was held by Oliver Cromwell Cox. See CROMWELL COX O. (1959), Caste, Class, and Race: A Study in Social Dynamics, Monthly Review Press, New York.

4. See MULLARD C. (1981), "The Social Context and Meaning of Multicultural Education", Educational Analysis, Vol. 3, No. 1, for an account of the downward model, and (1985), Race, Power, and Resistance, Routledge and Kegan Paul, London, for a more theoretical description of these models unfolded around the Mannheimian concepts of "ideology" and "utopia".

5. The notion of "common-sense racism" is fully elaborated on by LAWRENCE E., GILROY P., CARBY H. and others in the Centre for Contemporary Studies (1982), The Empire Strikes Back: Race and Racism in 70s Britain, Hutchinson, London.

6. The kind of correlation mentioned here has been fully documented in a number of the published working papers produced by the Race Relations Policy and Practice Research Unit/Sociological Research Unit at the University of London, Institute of Education. See, for instance: MULLARD C., BONNICK L., KING B., Working Paper I: Racial Policy and Practice in Education: A Letter Survey, 1983; Working Paper II: Local Education Authority Policy Documents: A Descriptive Analysis of Contents, 1983; Working Paper III: Process, Problem, and Prognosis: A Survey of Local Education Authorities' Multicultural Education Policies and Practices, Part One: The Multicultural Process, 1984; Working Paper IV: Process, Problem and Prognosis: A Survey of Local Education Authorities' Multicultural Education Policies and Practices, Part Three: The Prognosis, 1984.

7. Most of the societies that fall within the purview of the discussion here have either enshrined in their constitutions such as the Netherlands, passed several pieces of legislation, or issued several national policy statements and reports concerning their commitment to "racial equality".

8. For further detail on this and particularly the relationship between assimilation, integration, and cultural pluralism and the protection and maintenance of the social and educational order see MULLARD C. (1980), Racism in Society and Schools: History, Policy and Practice, Centre for Multicultural Education, University of London, Institute of Education, London, and (1982), "Multiracial Education in Britain: From Assimilation to Cultural Pluralism" in TIERNEY J. (ed.), Race, Migration and Schooling, Holt, Reinhart and Winston, London.

9. There are of course other reasons, but these would be more appropriately discussed in work on, for instance, the social management of racism in European societies. See, in respect to the U.K., note 6, above.

10. This example of the Finnish struggle in Sweden will be discussed in greater detail shortly, but in order to understand analytically, educationally, as well as politically the full dimensions of this struggle and other pertinent issues, it is necessary to consult the work of SKUTNABB-KANGAS T. See especially SKUTNABB-KANGAS T. (1983), God Bedre Dansk? Om invandrarbørns integration i Danmark, Forlaget Børn and Unge, København, and (1984), Bilingualism or Not: The Education of Minorities, Multilingual Matters Ltd., Avon.

11. The various names used in different societies include multicultural, multi-ethnic, poly-ethnic, intercultural. For a descriptive account of some of these usages see BULLIVANT B. (1981), The Pluralist Dilemma in Education: Six Case Studies, George Allen and Unwin, Sydney, and MULLARD C. (1984), Anti-Racist Education: The Three "O's", NAME Publications, London, especially Chapter One, "Anti-racist Education: A Theoretical Basis".

12. For a closer account of the actual and analytical history of this process from assimilation and immigrant education to cultural pluralism and multicultural education in the United Kingdom, see MULLARD C. (1982).

13. CHURCHILL S. (1983), in The Education of Minority Groups: An Enquiry into Problems and Practices of Fifteen Countries, OECD/CERI, Gower Publishing Company Ltd., Aldershot, United Kingdom, 1983.

14. An interesting and critical educational review of the German "experience" is to be found in TSIAKALOS G. (1983), Ausländer Feindlichkeit: Tatsachen und Erklärungsversucht, Verlag C.H. Beck, München.

15. Although owing an allegiance to the work of P. FREIRE the notion of emancipatory education suggested here is being developed at the Centre for Race and Ethnic Studies, Pedagogisch-didaktisch Instituut, Universiteit van Amsterdam. See, in particular, MIEDEMA W. (1983),

Kritische Evaluatie van Het Project "Moedertaalklassen" in Enschede, unpublished paper prepared for the European Community Project, and (1984), School success: Reproduction, Emancipation, and Transformation, unpublished paper prepared for the European Conference on Multicultural Education, Paris.

16. MULLARD C. (1982), op.cit.

17. The school strike referred to here started in February, 1984, and these remarks are based upon my own observation of it during a visit to Sweden at that time and the attending of and discussing with the parents at a strategy meeting of the campaign.

18. Canada provides a possible exception to this, as its multicultural policies came about and, historically, at least, are concerned with a political as well as an educational resolution to or management of the British-French conflicts in the construction of the Canadian state, which was possibly symbolically completed with the "repatriation of the Constitution" in 1983.

Commentary by Dominique SCHNAPPER (1)

Directeur d'études, Ecole des Hautes Etudes en Sciences Sociales, Paris

Between the late 1960s and the early 1980s a wide-ranging debate grew up in the United States concerning the education of children from "disadvantaged minorities". With varying degrees of success a number of States established forms of education variously described as bi-, inter-, multi- or cross-cultural schooling, separate from the education provided to the population as a whole and including variable doses of bilingual content. The presence in France of millions of immigrant workers and their families is setting off the same debate, some dozen years later, and bringing out the same arguments. As Nathan Glazer notes, the European discussion gives a sense of "déjà vu" (2).

That is because among the American and European experts we may discern the same inspiration, or the same temptation, to transpose arguments derived from the thesis of the education system's "symbolic violence" to the particular case of migrant children. That violence is held to be especially reprehensible here inasmuch as the migrants and their children are doubly or absolutely "dominated" and the culture of the parents' country of origin is caught up in a veritable ethnocide. Whence the dream of trans-cultural or inter-cultural or cross-cultural education which, so its advocates claim, would pass "their" culture on to migrant children and instill them with a legitimate pride in it.

The problem is not to be taken lightly, it is serious, and one that is not easy to settle inasmuch as primary education is not managing, in either France or Germany, to teach the basics even to "native" children. We may recall the sensation Mr. Chevènement caused in 1985 by stating that the primary school has a duty to teach every child the three Rs.

Arguments can no doubt be set out, with varying skill, about the contradictions between the requirements of the education system and the traditions of certain migrant families. This is particularly tempting inasmuch as the sociologists who look at the problems of culture contact or modernity are, professionally so to speak, alert to the specific cultural features of minority groups. Hence it is easy to stress the inevitable coercion that any form of socialisation -- at school or elsewhere -- presents for the behaviour of the people involved. French experts consistently demonstrate far greater ability to mine the vein of uprooting, exile and contradiction than people trained in the English-speaking system. But the rhetoric ultimately slides around the true question that any faithful reader of Raymond Aron is familiar with: what has to be done?

One might have thought that the experts assembled by the OECD in January 1985 (Michel de Certeau, Paul-Henri Chombard de Lauwe, Chris Mullard, François Raveau, for instance) would have felt bound to find some form of answer to that question. But the system of values peculiar to the intellectual world, and especially in France, which places value on theoretical or abstract development at the expense of policy analysis, leads the experts to write more for their peers than for decision-makers (perhaps they feel that they will, in any case, receive scant attention) and to present difficult theoretical papers on culture, language and the relation between culture and society. Well-intentioned decision-makers would be very largely at a loss if they sought to draw any practical conclusions.

It should be added that the experts assembled by the OECD were following the grand example of the prestigious professors at the Collège de France who, in their report to the President of the Republic, observed that "harmonious education needs to be capable of reconciling the universalism inherent in scientific thought and the relativism taught by the human sciences alive to the plurality of modes of life, wisdom and cultural sensibility". That is a formulation (and one they repeat a little later) that must draw unreserved approval, but yet again it holds back from the true question -- how?

How to educate?

It is an easy matter to criticise the policies being followed to educate migrant children, because solving the problem is by no means simple: how to educate migrant children, giving them the best opportunity of participating in the society in which they are living and where, in all probability, they will continue to live, without at the same time assaulting some of the norms and values transmitted by family socialisation?

Since the 19th century France, as a country of immigration, has educated immigrant children in the same way as French children, implicitly accepting that the possibility of participating in French society was the prime object (and an excellent one too) of schooling. That policy no doubt makes greater demands on children being brought up by immigrant parents but imperfect though it is (and what policy is perfect?) even today it seems to me to be the only one possible and in fact the one that is least bad, even though the new appreciation of different cultures may somewhat attenuate the way it is applied.

No going back

Political leaders in the country of origin, those in the country of immigration, and immigrants themselves in many cases nurture the dream of return, believing in it without really believing. The immense majority of their children raised in France, and often born in France, will remain there. All the surveys of young French people of foreign origin show that they do not feel at home in their parents' country of origin. Socialisation in France, in a society that is not just wealthier but more modern as well (with all the values attaching to that expression) in fact prohibits their going back to a country many of them have never known -- except possibly on holiday, and so outside the context of ordinary life.

The moral and social duty of the school hence lies in giving them, as best it can, the means to participate in the society in which they are to live. It is precisely because cultures are not globally and in themselves unequal but are unequally placed in historical and political terms that migrant children need to be given the means of participating in the majority culture, which is also the culture bound up with modernity and to which their parents' country of origin also aspires. In any case, it would be singularly slighting to regard the latest arrivals as being in principle less capable than migrants of earlier generations of participating in our society.

The dangers of separate education

It may be objected that more would return to their parents' country of origin if they had attended a bi-, trans-, inter- or cross-cultural school. The argument carries little conviction. In France, a school that endeavoured to give due place to a foreign language, literature or history could only add a special curriculum to the normal French one -- or else appear inferior. The example of the Jewish schools shows that this is not impossible. In practice, however, the difficulties seem enormous. The very great majority of migrant children come from the working classes. It seems singularly unrealistic to suppose that a twofold education system can be forced on them with any chance of success, or that they can be taught a twofold learned culture -- all the more since both learned cultures are likely to be foreign to the socialisation process in the families. Literary Italian, the Italian of Tuscany, is not the language that immigrants from Sicily or the Mezzogiorno speak. Literary Arab is not the family language of the immigrants from the Maghreb. I will not even mention the difficulties that would be involved in organising twofold schooling in a country as centralised as France, and the unfathomable decisions that the authorities would face -- bi-culturalism with Italian, Spanish, Portuguese, Serbo-Croat, Turkish, Arabic, Chinese, Vietnamese? Where would it stop? Problems without end, problems without solutions.

The "specialised" education found in other countries always consists of separating children who are considered to be badly placed because they speak a different language at home and of treating cases which are all different as though they were uniform. Nathan Glazer makes the point, not without humour, that educational achievement by young Americans of Asian origin is greater than for "majority" Americans. Segregating children, and imposing a fictitious uniformity, can only exacerbate inferiority, where it exists, or generate it where it does not. Subject to special conditions, excluded from the normal curriculum, the children come, by a process with which psychologists are familiar, to adopt the behaviour that is expected of them. As Sophie Mappa (3) notes, the effect of the Finnish bilingual schools in Sweden have been to turn young Finns into skilled workers for Swedish industry. Much the same has been found in Germany, in the United States, in Australia. Italy, which simply puts young foreign children into the ordinary system, and France, where the special system is small-scale (2.4 per cent of children at primary level), have achieved much better results in integrating migrant children.

What is more, parents and children, showing more wisdom than educationists, reject special education. What the "immigrants" and the "minorities" look first of all to the school to provide is that it should give their children the best means of participating in the economic and social activity of the society they are joining. In the United States, minorities are concerned with educational achievement by their members, success and status in American society. We may ask whether immigrants and their children have ever asked for anything else and whether in many cases the advocacy of cultural identity does not stem from difficulty in penetrating and succeeding in French society -- in short, whether they are not making a virtue of necessity. These immigrants do not want bi-cultural education (or inter-, trans- or cross-cultural education), they know it would be liable to jeopardise the chance of their (objectively disadvantaged) children succeeding in and through education. Doing people good whether they like it or not is a questionable principle of democracy. Are we to think, as Nathan Glazer and Sophie Mappa suggest, that the reason the inter-cultural education experiment is continuing lies in the vested interests of educationists in a time of unemployment?

If it is accepted that the school cannot inculcate a second learned culture, is it to be given the role of preserving culture in the sense that anthropologists use the term: ordinary ways of thinking and acting, a set of specific values and practices? This is not to deny the specific forms of family relationships, religious practices and sensibilities among certain immigrants. Yet it is in the family or in social life as a whole that these specific forms can and should continue to find expression. The school should simply strive not to offend them. It is not the function of education to transmit family modes of life; that is the family's business.

Recent narratives have revealed the harshness of French primary education in "the good old days", when the schoolmistress made distinctions between "real French" boys and Poles and Italians. It is reasonable to think that their beliefs and the spirit of the age have made today's schoolmistresses more aware of the diversity of cultures. Removing pork from the canteen menu in schools with large numbers of Jewish or Moslem children, knowing when Yom Kippur or Ramadan falls, allowing (but not compelling) children to study Arabic or Turkish as a foreign language, extending history and geography syllabuses beyond France, are all ways in which teachers can recognise the specific traits of some of their pupils -- provided they do not forget that their prime function is still to teach them how to use the French language and to do mathematics.

The transmission of learning is the true objective of education, and there is no reason to think a priori that the proportion of migrant children capable of acquiring such learning is smaller than the proportion of French children who are in the same social and economic circumstances. Migrant children are no doubt a little more disadvantaged than French children: the language spoken in the family is still further removed from the language at school, and material circumstances are often more insecure. Yet while the challenge is greater, it can still be taken up. History shows us minority groups who take the very circumstance of their minority as a reason to do better than others. Why should the children of Turkish or Algerian migrants do less well than the children of Jewish craftsmen or Polish and Italian miners between the two world wars?

The transmisssion of learning is especially necessary as it forms a condition for access to modernity. Should a migrant child eventually return to his parents' country of origin, will he not have a better chance of participating in social life as a skilled technician or engineer? Should he remain in France, he is most likely to "recuperate" his parents' culture of origin, in one form or another, once he has secured a place in French society. That is how we see the Bretons, now assured of a full part in national life, keeping a symbolic and sentimental connection with the language, history and area of their childhood or of the childhood of their parents and their grandparents; in the same way migrant children, once the school has given them the means to participate fully in the economic and social activity of their country of settlement, will have the opportunity of rediscovering and preserving ties, sentimental or learned, with the country from which their parents came. Not enough attention, possibly, has been paid to the origins of foreign language and civilisation teachers in France, at every level. That is simply one illustration, among many, of the intercessor role that migrant children may play, provided the school, rather than setting them apart in specialist education which does them no service, has first enabled them to take a part in the society to which they belong.

NOTES AND REFERENCES

1. Published under the title "Education des enfants de migrants" in Commentaire, No. 32, 1985-86.

2. GLAZER N., "Cultural Differences and Equality of Educational Achievement", Chapter 8 in this volume.

3. MAPPA S., "Education for Immigrants' Children in the OECD Member countries", Chapter 10 in this volume.

10. EDUCATION FOR IMMIGRANTS' CHILDREN IN THE OECD MEMBER COUNTRIES

by
Sophia MAPPA
Former Consultant to CERI/OECD

INTRODUCTION

It is no easy task to analyse educational policies for immigrants' children inasmuch as these policies are based on a variety of parameters which are often contradictory and difficult to define, reflecting as they do the explicit objectives and implicit options of the policymakers, ideological and administrative reflexes, social trends and pressure by special group interests, etc.

Since the subject is too vast to be dealt with adequately in a paper such as this, the study will be confined to a discussion of those host country objectives that, in our view, are the most controversial or the least aired. The policies of the so-called "sending" or emigration countries, though their role in setting up the schemes studied here is admittedly considerable, can only be touched on. For purposes of clarity we shall begin by describing briefly the educational reforms undertaken in the OECD countries and the explicit objectives they are designed to meet. We then move on to a critical analysis of governments' educational options, focusing on what is implicit and left unsaid in these policies as they are expressed in the educational structures and teaching content.

A SCHOOL FOR IMMIGRANT CHILDREN

The many educational initiatives "for migrants" that have blossomed over the last ten years or so in OECD countries have several features in common. The educational reforms brought in to meet the schooling needs of children of foreign origin are based, with very few exceptions, on the same principles, despite the apparent diversity of objectives and terminologies (special, bilingual, bicultural, multicultural or intercultural education), and irrespective of whether the countries concerned are European or non-European countries (United States, Canada, Australia), or whether they are "receiving" countries or countries with a historically high rate of emigration.

The economic and political context of these educational reforms, the 1970s, is the first common strand in these educational policies. This decade constituted a watershed, considering that almost two centuries have elapsed since the foundation of the modern nation state and the institution of state education whose main function has been the linguistic unification of those living within its national boundaries. It still maintains this function despite the extraordinary linguistic and cultural diversity, constantly renewed and enriched by successive migratory waves, that has characterised all OECD Member countries since the advent of modern society.

The turning point in Europe, as in the non-European countries, was the 1970s, for while a few educational measures had been taken earlier to assist immigrants -- or traditional ethnic minorities -- it was then that such provision was institutionalised on a wide scale: while the period saw almost all countries taking steps to curb immigration, it also saw the emergence of an array of educational initiatives. In the early 1970s a whole host of bilateral agreements and other official measures concerning the education of immigrant children were signed in Europe between the "sending" and "receiving" countries. In 1971 Prime Minister Trudeau laid down guidelines for a "multicultural" policy in Canada and in 1973 special schemes were launched in Quebec. In 1970 the first of a series of similar special programmes was launched in Australia by the Commonwealth Child Migrant Education Program (CMEP) and 1973 saw the first pilot schemes to provide bilingual education for the aborigines, extended later to immigrant children. In the United States, the 1968 Bilingual Education Act was amended in 1974 to extend the provision for Portoricans to all children deemed deficient in English language skills. In 1973-74 the French Ministry of Education carried out the first census of "foreign" children in French schools. Last, in 1977 the EEC Directive was issued, laying down the broad framework for Member States' educational policies in this area.

What is the significance of the economic background to this change in the attitude of the educational authorities to minority groups? More precisely is there a close correlation between the economic crisis and this change in policy? To our knowledge this is a question that is seldom posed and we shall attempt here to provide some measure of response.

The second common strand in the reforms undertaken during this period, and the most evident, was the establishment of special educational structures targeted at a special group -- young people of foreign origin -- and limited to specific geographical areas -- those with a high concentration of immigrants. The third is the rationale underlying these initiatives -- that the frequent school failure of immigrant children is the result of linguistic deficiencies -- and the objectives assigned to them -- namely to remedy these deficiencies so as to integrate these children into normal schooling at some later stage.

Thus, from closer at hand, the changes that occurred, far from altering official educational systems as a whole, led to an expansion in certain specific sectors. In Europe, for example, right up to the publication of the 1977 EEC Directive, the receiving countries simply built on to the existing educational system special arrangements reserved in principle for young people of foreign origin, irrespective of nationality, and based on the teaching of the official language of the host country. The sending countries had taken the same line, i.e. exporting their domestic educational model and setting up classes based, here again, on their own official language. This provision implicitly assumed that the children concerned would eventually return to their homeland though this was explicitly stated only by Yugoslavia which, even today, maintains that its nationals are residing abroad only on a "temporary" basis. In the various bilateral agreements and other official documents signed between the sending and receiving countries and relating to the education of young people of foreign origin, reference is frequently made to the need to maintain their nationals' linguistic and cultural ties with their country of origin.

These approaches hence appear to constitute a provisional response to what is perceived -- whatever is actually said -- as transitory. Now that the integration of young people of foreign origin has become stated policy, how have the educational policies of the European countries changed?

The 1977 EEC Directive, it may be remembered, appeared at a time when the European countries, while affirming their willingness to integrate immigrants, were in fact applying policies encouraging them to return. The objectives set in this Directive (1) would not seem to be breaking fresh ground, since in fact it encapsulates the policies that countries had been pursuing since the early 1970s: special classes teaching the official language of the host state and/or that of the country of origin.

However, it did embody a number of new features: first, the earlier measures took on, with this Directive, the nature of an educational model valid and mandatory for all Member States which were called upon "to comply with this Directive within four years of its notification". The second new feature was that the host country was required to promote "the teaching of the mother tongue and of the culture of the country of origin in co-operation with States of origin", and the ambiguity of such provision in that the Directive associated it with "their possible reintegration into the Member State of origin", whereas the countries of origin saw the end purpose as "maintaining their language and culture" abroad.

Of the European receiving countries, only Sweden has refused to base its policy in this regard on the assumption of a "return to the homeland" and stresses the development of active bilingualism among young people of foreign origin.

The same approaches and principles have prevailed in the non-European countries. Despite the apparent diversity stemming from the differing objectives of the different federal countries, they are very similar in their broad lines to those of the European countries: the special educational arrangements are designed to teach both the official language of the host country and that of the country of origin: these educational structures are intended for the less privileged social groups and for areas with large migrant communities or comprising traditional minorities whose linguistic skills are deemed deficient. In the United States the 1974 Bilingual Education Act defines the target groups and schools as follows: "An applicant school must enrol high concentrations of children from families whose income is below poverty levels, who receive benefits from the Aid to Families With Dependent Children Program" (2). These groups are defined as being "educationally deprived" and "culturally deprived" or qualified as "disadvantaged" (3). Canada and Australia have similar programmes.

The rationale that has prevailed in Europe again underlies the educational provision for immigrant children: poor social integration is seen as the outcome of poor school performance which in turn is ascribed to inadequate mastery of the official language and/or that of the country of origin.

The main difference relative to the EEC countries is that this special teaching, especially of the language of the country of origin, does not assume a "return to the homeland", but is aimed at improving skills in the official language, enhancing the child's self-confidence through a knowledge of his mother culture and promoting a multicultural society. These objectives are admittedly affirmed in Europe too. The wide variety of terms used to describe this provision -- "ancestral languages" in Canada, "native languages" in the United States, "community languages" in Australia -- reflect philosophies specific to each country, but the underlying assumption is that the groups concerned will ultimately settle in the host country.

Another fundamental difference working in the same direction and whose political implications are considerable, is that these programmes are the outcome of negotiations between the social groups concerned and the host country, without the country of origin intervening. The fact that the latter is not involved in the host country's school system removes some of the ambiguities surrounding the legal status of immigrants: outside Europe they are full citizens of the State in which they live; in Europe they remain citizens of their country of origin. Admittedly ambiguities persist -- this is another common strand in the policies of both groups of countries -- in regard to another and steadily growing segment of the school population since the early 1970s: namely, the children of irregular or temporary immigrants (4). For the time being, however, this problem has had little impact on how these programmes are set up and is hence not discussed here.

It is not the place here to describe in detail the arrangements that have been set up, since the initial objectives -- teaching both the official language and that of the country of origin -- have led to the introduction of a wide array of special measures. A typology can, however, be established. Since the EEC model best illustrates this burgeoning of educational initiatives and covers the whole range of measures adopted by OECD countries we will take it as our frame of reference.

Reception arrangements

Based on the assumption that difficulties with the official language are the reason for the school failure of the young people concerned, the EEC model takes three forms: the most common form of provision in all the European countries is that of the "preparatory" classes ("introductory", "reception" or "special temporary placement" classes). Coming outside the normal schooling from kindergarten to secondary level they are, at least in theory, a temporary arrangement. The time pupils spend studying in the classes varies from 6 months to 6 years; these classes cater for a wide range of nationalities, age groups and prior educational backgrounds. This model is applied not only in the European receiving countries, but also in the sending countries (Greece, Turkey, Spain, Portugal, though not Italy). The clientele in the latter case consists of the children of migrant workers returning to their home country and who find themselves once again in special classes, this time to learn their "mother" tongue. This model is applied only rarely in non-European countries, with the exception of Quebec where it has gained increasing popularity since 1972 (5).

Another variant, which is also quite common in the European countries and geared to young people attending normal schools, consists of "special" or "remedial" classes. Here the language teaching catering to as varied a group as above is integrated into the normal school curriculum and simply replaces another subject. This approach is apparently quite popular in Australia (6).

A third and quite distinct variant is offered by bilingual schools catering for groups of similar cultural background who receive tuition in the language of the country of origin in parallel to the official language of the country of residence which progressively becomes the language used in regular teaching. Theoretically, except in Sweden where these schools have been assigned a permanent role, participation in these bilingual classes is intended to be only temporary and they are seen as a means of integrating pupils into mainstream schooling. In practice, however, the arrangement tends to be continued throughout the children's compulsory schooling. In Europe, where they form a halfway house between the national educational systems of the country of origin and the country of residence, such classes tend to be few in number, confined to a handful of countries and catering to specific target groups, e.g. the Greeks (7) and Turks in Germany, and the Finns in Sweden (8). This third variant, however, predominates in the United States where such classes are primarily intended for young Hispanics with the range of nationalities this term implies. For the most part these arrangements are organised by the countries of residence, except for the bilingual schools in Europe which are set up in co-operation with the countries of origin.

Among the major problems encountered both in Europe and elsewhere may be cited: the lack of cohesion between this system and normal schooling (to a degree varying from one scheme to another), the absence of any real links between the two structures and hence the enforced separation of the group concerned from those attending normal schooling, the unsuitability of the teaching materials, and the poor qualification and status of the teachers involved. Teachers assigned to these classes, for example, are often less qualified, do not have permanent status, are frequently underpaid or paid at subsistence level (9). In the United States, for example, the Teachers Language Skills Survey (TLSS) showed that, in 1980-81, out of a total of 500 000 teachers whose pupils included young people with a limited command of English, only 56 000 used a language other than English and of these only 21 000 had the requisite academic qualifications.

In sum, the system is characterised by two increasingly contrasting trends: on the one hand a growing differentiation (educational structures, text books, teachers, etc.) between the groups concerned and the "national" school population in mainstream education; and on the other a lack of differentiation within these groups whose great cultural and linguistic diversity is reduced to the label of "immigrant", "migrant" or "foreign".

Of the receiving countries, the only one that would appear to have applied a policy of integrating the children of foreign origin rapidly into normal schooling without any special arrangements is Italy. As the EEC Commission reported (10), Italian would seem to be considered an easy language to learn; we shall be returning to this point later.

How many children are concerned by such arrangements? The available data, though incomplete, would suggest that numbers are growing at a rate varying from country to country; this is somewhat surprising given the entry restrictions on migrants and the fact that the vast majority of the children concerned were born in their country of residence and started school there and that the official language of the country of residence takes over from the language of the country of origin as soon these children enter school, which tends to be at an ever younger age. In France, for example, of the million or so children of foreign origin in French schools (11) there are only around 20 000 non-francophone foreign children who came to join their families at a later stage. In the European receiving countries as a group, 75 to 90 per cent of young people of foreign origin go to school for the first time in their host country and only rarely have lived in any other country (12).

Among the European countries, the proportion is relatively high in Belgium (13), the United Kingdom and Germany. In the United Kingdom according to the -- again incomplete -- information contained in the EEC Commission's report, one third of pupils receiving special provision did not have English as their mother tongue (7 per cent in the reception centres, 70 per cent in the reception classes). In Germany 47.8 per cent of pupils of foreign origin are in the Land of Bavaria, of whom Turks accounted for 78 per cent; 10.6 per cent are in Berlin. In Nord-Wurtemburg, 20 per cent are in reception classes and 20 per cent in remedial classes etc. Given the high proportion of the same target group in "special education" (14), one must conclude that a considerable proportion of young people of foreign origin in Germany are not integrated in mainstream schooling.

In other European countries such as France and Luxembourg the proportion of young people benefiting from special provision is low: in France 2.4 per cent in primary reception classes and 1.1 per cent at secondary level, and 5 per cent in remedial classes in 1981-82; in Luxembourg the figures are 0.53 per cent for Italians, 0.57 per cent for Spanish and 5.89 per cent for Portuguese. Here again, attention should be drawn to the relatively high representation of these young people in special education (15).

In Quebec and in the United States the trend is also upward. In Quebec the number of such pupils rose from 382 in 1971-72 to 2 559 in 1981-82 (16). In the United States there were 76 bilingual programmes catering for 26 521 pupils in 1969-70 against 565 programmes for 350 000 in 1979-80, and notwithstanding some subsequent reservations by the authorities, and despite a slight reduction in appropriations, there has been no change in policy; the number of languages used for instruction in these programmes rose from 79 in 1980 (14 in 1969-70) to 106 in 1982-83 (17).

Teaching the language and culture of origin

Two models are predominant in Europe as well as in the non-European countries: classes integrated into the state school system of the country of residence and out-of-school classes.

In Europe integration is generally held to mean the incorporation of such provision into the reception arrangements described above which in this case provide teaching of both languages. When integrated into the normal curriculum, this teaching takes the place of other subjects and is intended -- except for a few pilot schemes in Sweden, where classes are composed of both Swedes and foreigners -- exclusively for young people of foreign origin. This formula is also the norm in the non-European countries offering such provision except in the United States where the legislation defines teaching in the "native" language solely as a transitional means of learning English;

there is however a clear and growing shift towards teaching such languages as an end in itself; we shall return to this point later.

Such provision is offered in kindergartens and primary schools. When it is integrated into secondary education, the language of origin is taught as a second language and often, as in the case of Turkish in Germany, in the place of English, the first foreign language and one that plays a decisive role in the children's school career. In Europe it is organised by the countries of residence in collaboration with the countries of origin, though the former are becoming increasingly involved in setting up the arrangements, producing teaching materials, and in recruiting and paying teachers. As in the case of the programmes mentioned earlier, the main problems encountered are the absence of links with the normal curriculum, the under-qualification and the low and precarious status of the teachers who, in principle, are trained in the sending countries and often do not speak the language of the country they have come to, as well as the unsuitability of the teaching materials, that are mostly devised for use in the sending countries' schools and exported as they stand.

Here too it will be observed that young people of foreign origin are catered for in an <u>undifferentiated</u> fashion in structures that <u>differ</u> from those of the normal system: while on the one hand there are special structures, teachers, methods, equipment and teaching tools catering for a population group concentrated in geographical areas with a high proportion of immigrants, on the other hand the wide differences within the same group are ignored; children of Turkish origin in Germany and Australia are, for example, all subsumed under the sole characteristic of being children of Turkish immigrants. This is borne out by the fact that special teaching material, produced in the framework of a German pilot project, in co-operation with the EEC, for young people of Turkish origin in Berlin and which, in the words of its initiators was intended to be "relevant to real life, and especially the pupils' environment" (18) was used in a number of other EEC countries and even further afield in Australia. The rationale for this transfer, decided by the German and EEC authorities, even before the teaching material had been finalised (19) was that since the living conditions of Turkish pupils were the same throughout the EEC (...), <u>their problems derived primarily from moving without transition from the essentially agricultural society of Turkey</u> to a highly developed technological society" (20). Yet the vast majority of these young people were born in their country of residence.

It would appear, however, that despite the expansion in such provision in certain cases (e.g. 600 courses in Bavaria in 1979-80, 798 in 1980-81) and the various means adopted by some countries (Belgium, Sweden, Germany) to promote such education, pupils and parents did not on the whole view them favourably.

In the Netherlands for instance, in 1982 8 per cent of the relevant groups benefited from such provision at primary level and 1 per cent at secondary (21). In Germany the number of young people of Turkish origin who opted for such courses was much lower than expected (22). In Baden-Wurtemburg, out of the 50 000 children concerned, only 700 attended such classes (23). As the report of the EEC Commission noted (24) the trend is not very marked, while officials from the Baden-Wurtemburg education authorities noted that the scheme had not been nearly as successful as hoped (25). In Rhineland-Westphalia, too, the provision is not being fully taken up. In

1982-83 more than 250 courses were on offer to young people of different cultures, but the education authorities noted that participation, especially at secondary level, was not encouraging (26). In the same Land 45 per cent of young people of Greek origin attending German schools receive no teaching in their native language and the integrated classes receive only a very small proportion of those who do (27). The same resistance is found in Sweden; in the bilateral commission reports, the countries of origin emphasise the lack of interest among the children and call for additional incentive measures.

In Europe the term "out-of-school classes" is used to denote the provision of education by the countries of origin in the countries of residence outside the official school system, leaving aside the wealth of private initiatives in this area. In the non-European countries, on the other hand, this term is used to denote only classes organised on the initiative of the immigrant communities themselves; the countries of origin are only marginally involved in setting up such schemes. The Greek communities provide a good illustration of this difference. In 1979 the education of Greeks in Germany absorbed 50.66 per cent of total Greek government subsidies to schools abroad, while in Australia such subsidies covered only 3.3 per cent of the budget for Greek schools in this country; similarly, in 1981-82 89.3 per cent of Greek primary school teachers in Germany and 100 per cent in Belgium were recruited by the Greek government against 2.95 per cent in Canada, 1.12 per cent in Australia, and 4.3 per cent in the United States (28).

These classes, which antedated integrated provision, are still, both inside and outside Europe, the commonest means of teaching the language of the country of origin; there is a growing trend, however, to integrating them into the schools of the country of residence: in Europe, the countries of origin hope that they will help to raise the low rate of pupil attendance since they feel the problem is due to the extra workload demanded of pupils and to the financial burden this may impose on immigrant communities; the cost of hiring school premises is often quite high (29). The same trend may be observed within communities in the non-European countries, which have begun to put pressure on governments in recent years. There is a dearth of quantitative data in this area but what there are show the relative importance of the different models.

In France, for example, numbers attending out-of-school classes in 1981-82 were frequently greater than those in integrated schooling (30). This could be due to the lack of infrastructures and teachers of certain nationalities in France referred to earlier, but the same applies in Germany for certain nationalities. In the Land of Baden-Wurtemburg and Berlin, for example, 58.3 and 49.3 per cent respectively of the target groups concerned receive out-of-school provision. The proportions by nationality are 45.8 per cent for Greeks, 95.5 per cent for Spaniards, but only 7.7 per cent for Turks and 13.3 per cent for Italians. This last group would appear to be reluctant to participate in any form of State provision, tending to prefer voluntary arrangements organised by associations, trade unions etc.

Last, we should note the out-of-school provision offered by wholly foreign schools. In Europe it is usually the country of origin or the Churches that are behind such ventures, while private initiative is predominant in the non-European countries where these schools -- like the out-of-school classes -- are subsidised by the host country government. The children enrolled in these establishments must naturally comply with the educational requirements of the host country. Such schools would seem to be fairly few in number, but few data are available. There are, for example, Italian schools in Switzerland and Greek schools in Belgium, the United Kingdom and especially in Germany, as well as Finnish schools in Sweden.

In Europe their raison d'être is to facilitate ultimate return to the country of origin. Other considerations, however, are also involved, in particular the poor attainment of the young people concerned in the schools of the country of residence and, in consequence, the desire of parents to provide a more appropriate type of education. In the non-European countries, on the other hand, these schools, of which there would seem to be few, would appear to have a predominantly religious vocation (31).

THE EXPLICIT OBJECTIVES: WHAT IS SAID AND WHAT IS LEFT UNSAID

The question that in our view needs to be elucidated is whether the objectives explicitly assigned to the educational provision for immigrant children -- whether in the form of programmes teaching the official language of the host country or those teaching the languages of the countries of origin -- are in accord with the economic, social and cultural policies pursued in regard to immigrants. Given the limited space available, we shall confine consideration here to three of the objectives underlying these programmes: integration, multiculturalism and "return to the homeland".

i) Integration: theory and practice

The special measures for teaching the official language of the countries of residence are aimed at combating underachievement by young people of foreign origin, facilitating their integration into the school system and hence into the community, and ensuring equality of opportunity with the country's nationals. These aims were recently reaffirmed by the Council of Europe: at the Conference of Ministers of Education held in Dublin in 1983 the Resolution adopted recommended educational measures "appropriate to migrants so that they are able to participate fully in the social life of the host country and enjoy the same opportunities for their personal and professional development as nationals" (OECD translation).

If one looks, however, at economic and social policies relative to immigrants since the 1970s and the various measures taken in OECD countries, the emphasis would seem to be more on controlling flows (in terms of volume and composition) and sometimes on repatriation of at least some immigrants than on integration. Such policies reflect changing economic or demographic demand and must be seen in the historical perspective of migration policies and attitudes towards immigrants over the years. While, in the post-war period immigration policies were determined by the growth requirements of the industrialised countries, they are today dominated by the needs arising from the economic upheavals which these same countries are now experiencing.

In Australia, for example, the volume and composition of permitted immigrant flows are determined by short-term market needs and calculations of the requisite long-term demographic growth: a major factor in this country's policy towards immigration is the memory of the shock of Japan's military advance in World War II. The criteria on which the composition of the flows is based -- which are common to all receiving countries -- are: youth, good health (the fittest being selected) and skills for a particular labour market need on the job market.

In the United States the successive reforms introduced since the early 1970s to control immigrant flows -- especially illegal immigration -- have not affected the Texas Proviso under which the hire of irregular workers is allowed on the grounds that they play an important role in agriculture and the services. Consideration is also being given to reintroducing the "guest worker programs" which, from World War II until 1964, provided job oppportunities for temporary or seasonal migrants, jobs that were later to be filled by illegal immigrants (32).

The same holds true for Europe where the immediate response to firms' economic problems was a clampdown on labour and residence permits as from 1980.

A considerable number of administrative and statutory measures have been adopted by central governments to this end: government controls on workers' entry; tighter conditions for family reunification and political refugee status; a refusal to regularise (above all in Europe) or selective regularisation (non-European countries) of illegal workers whose numbers are rising in OECD countries; entry visas for certain nationalities, with admission quotas by firm and region.

These policies for curbing immigrant flows, which are based on economic and administrative rather than social considerations, are often cited by the authorities as proof of their concern to ensure more effective integration for those immigrants already resident. It would nonetheless appear that the policies applied in this area have failed to respond to the complexity of the problem posed by immigration.

The measures that stand in the way of family reunification fall outside the scope of this report. It should simply be noted that family reunification, a sine qua non for integration, is blocked in both groups of countries by stringent entry requirements (age restrictions on members of the family wishing to join immigrant workers, proper housing, stable employment, etc.) and by rules precluding members of the family already resident from taking a job.

In Europe the refusal of labour and residence permits to first-time applicants or those with no stable employment, the possibility of opposing applications on labour market grounds, the subordination of right of residence to stable employment, age restrictions and health controls (33), quotas, financial incentives to return home, and the right of countries to expel immigrant workers etc., are all measures that are inimical to integration. In the non-European countries, the successive amnesties granted to illegal immigrants have so far failed to tackle the problem of the precarious status of illegal immigrant workers, while the institutionalisation of the temporary status of some of them (34) testifies to the similarity of these countries' policies to those applied in Europe.

Clearly -- and we would stress this point which explains, inter alia, the similarities of the educational policies mentioned earlier -- historical facts and present-day experience do not bear out the idea that the non-European countries' policies are designed to promote permanent immigration while those of the European countries, and these countries alone, are designed with a view to temporary immigration determined by labour market needs. In fact, in both cases, immigration has been employment oriented and the mobility of immigrant workers has been reflected in their status. In both cases, too, there has been the same trend to settle in the countries where they came to work, irrespective of host country policy.

In Europe, for example, notwithstanding policies of rotation, immigration, which was intended to be temporary, has in reality become permanent; conversely, the non-European countries have always, whatever their stated policies, resorted to temporary labour-market oriented immigration, sometimes on a massive scale; the Guest Worker Programs and clandestine employment in the United States bear out this assertion. Furthermore, while permanent immigration -- settlement -- was a feature of both groups of countries during periods of economic growth, the precarious position of immigrant workers became all too evident in times of political and economic crisis in the European and non-European countries alike. The establishment of "tolerated" nationality quotas and even the withdrawal of citizenship rights from nationals of foreign origin in the 1920s (35), and the expulsion of immigrants in the 1930s are part of a historical process common to both and one which was not confined to the inter-war crisis years but continued throughout the 1950s and 1960s. In the 1950s for example, under "Operation Wetback" immigrants were expelled from the United States while in the 1960s some 300 000 immigrant workers were sent home from Germany.

The non-European and European countries reacted similarly to the economic crisis of the early 1970s with labour-market oriented immigration gaining ground, not infrequently to the detriment of the social integration of workers of foreign origin.

Similarly, the de jure denial of political rights, such as the right to vote, in Europe (36) and the de facto absence of such rights in the non-European countries for illegal and temporary workers, as well as the social segregation suffered by immigrant workers -- felt more keenly in the second group of countries -- are a further obstacle to integration and one that adversely affects the schooling of immigrant children and their social integration.

ii) Multiculturalism

Similar questions are raised by a study of the objectives assigned to the teaching of the languages and cultures of origin.

The point on which all are agreed -- sending and receiving countries alike both inside and outside Europe -- , is that such teaching can help to transform present-day societies, promote a multicultural society, combat racism, democratise the school and enhance children's self-confidence through knowledge of their country of origin. In Canada, for example, the Minister of State for Multiculturalism, Jim Fleming, explained that "multiculturalism within a bilingual framework" was a means to combat racism: "...To my regret, a regret which is shared deeply by my colleagues in cabinet, this assault on the integrity and pride of fellow Canadians appears to be on the rise again as can be witnessed from the resurgence of extremist, and particularly racist groups in our country (...) I see heritage language education as an important strategy to combat racist attitudes and behaviour. Attitude formation is shaped to a large degree by the educational system. (...) Tolerance is taught (...)" (37). Similarly, the French Minister for Education, Alain Savary, defined his vision of a multicultural society as follows: "There is a narrow path to be trod between standardisation that crushes the cultural and social identity of each and every one of us and fragmentation resulting from a host of specific measures. Sometimes the school lights upon this path to the benefit of all" (38). On similar lines the Swedish authorities assign the school the task of educating pupils so that they acquire a sense of solidarity with other countries, peoples and cultures and understand and develop a sense of community with the minorities in their own country (39); the promotion of active bilingualism is a further objective in this country.

A considerable body of literature has grown up around this theme among intellectuals and militants who consider that the integration of the languages and cultures of ethnic minorities into the state system will pave the way to its becoming "more democratic and truly of the people" (...) and call into question its underlying objective" (40) (i.e. assimilation). Even in the United States where the teaching of "native" languages is seen by the authorities as a transitional step towards learning the official language, the shift in the campaign against segregation towards "the presence of the ethnic culture of the patio" (41) and "the strengthening of the child's pride" is manifest among intellectuals of Hispanic or other minority origin.

But apart from the fact that the concept of multiculturalism is somewhat vague and ill-defined, one may also wonder whether this objective assigned to the school is not part of a change in the perceived reality and symbolic representation of the nation, and of a transformation in the intellectual categories commonly used to denote the idea of "belonging" or not to a nation. Today's societies are still hierarchically organised and the struggles of the different groups to gain access to power or a share in it are expressed in or disguised as cultural and linguistic conflicts.

The official language, a binding force, both historically and mythically, of the Nation, defines above all -- in non-European and European countries alike -- the group holding the reins of power in the territory over which the group has sovereignty. There is no possible sharing of this power or territory with linguistically different groups; countries founded on the federal principle are no exception to the rule; indeed they illustrate more cogently what is at issue. Here, as elsewhere, any deviation from the official code is seen as a reprehensible departure from the norm often leading to the marginalisation of the social group in question. The very term "minority", used to designate any non-official language does not indicate a quantitative difference -- often it is the official language that is the minority tongue in terms of numbers speaking it -- but defines the "majority" in terms of exclusion: those who have the power to define the "other" and determine his status in society. The terminology used to designate the language of biligual or multicultural programmes -- "original" languages in Europe, "native" languages in the United Kingdom, "community" languages in Australia, "ancestral" or "heritage" languages in Canada -- reflects the ideological premises of those who so label them and underlines the "foreignness" of the groups concerned vis-à-vis the nation (e.g. the "original languages") and/or the lower status of their language relative to the official language through their association either with a particular and limited territory within the national territory (the "native languages") or with a legal status lower than that of the nation ("community languages") or again with a mythical past external to the nation ("ancestral languages").

The conflicts between the different national languages in the conquest of other territories, the internationalisation of English and the decline of other languages, even within their own territory, express the same aspirations for power and the same social and political hierarchies at international level.

But language, aside from this social function which is bound up with the very life of the modern nation state, plays just as crucial a role as guarantor of national unity, a role reinforced by the economic crisis and the resurgence of nationalism which is itself a recurrent symptom of any society in a time of crisis.

In the national framework, the immigrant, the "foreigner", the "other" has a dual function: first, through his "otherness" he imparts a reality to the notion of national unity, a concept that is difficult to define in relation to itself because of the diversity of the nation and its internal conflicts, and one that is more clearly expressed in terms of what it excludes, what it is not; second, he sparks off the cultural violence inherent in every society and especially among the less privileged social groups who normally come into closest contact with immigrants.

What precisely is the meaning of multiculturalism, assigned as an objective for schools in societies founded on the principle of monolingualism and cultural unification? The question becomes more pressing when it is realised that the recent move to open up the school system is addressed not to the school population and the community at large but to those on the fringes of society, those at the bottom of the social pyramid, those who are farthest from power and the most oppressed, whose languages and cultures have no market or symbolic value in the society in which they live and where, on the contrary, they are rejected.

iii) Returning home

Another ambiguity and even contradiction in the objectives assigned to the school provision for immigrants merits closer scrutiny. The EEC associates such tuition with the "possible integration (of young people) into the Member States of origin". This policy shift and its implications has been little discussed in the countries of origin or by the upholders of the system. "Return to the homeland" is now enshrined in EEC legislation and it is for this reason that the receiving countries have taken on the task of integrating the teaching of the "languages and cultures of origin" into their schools and shouldering the costs.

The sending countries which see in the integration of their languages into the school system of the receiving countries a solution to the problems of the out-of-school classes for which they are responsible, have been generally content and little thought seems to have been given as to the implications of giving schools the task of preparing for a possible "return" at a juncture when the countries of residence were pursuing policies encouraging immigrant workers to return. The question is nonetheless an important one: what in fact is the meaning for young people born or brought up in the countries of residence, of these policies, which have had little impact on first-generation workers? And why should these policies enter the schoolroom? Is this not a way of legitimising a perception of young people of foreign origin as "foreign", whose right to residence is fraught with the same uncertainty as that of their parents?

Is "return" indeed the aim of all EEC Member States? And is this aim shared by the sending countries? It is true that, with the exception of the Portuguese President, who recently urged Portuguese immigrants in France to integrate into their country of residence, the notion of "return" often figures large in official government declarations. What is said, however, seems more destined for home consumption than a reflection of actual objectives. Since unemployment and underemployment, which are the main cause of migratory movements, are aggravated by the crisis, return could only be at the price of considerable economic and social upheaval. Furthermore, the real concerns -- the need for new emigration outlets, the inadequacy of resettlement measures for returning workers -- reveal that immigrants have in fact no option but to remain in the country where they work and fulfil the same role as before: guaranteeing, through their departure, social order in their country of origin, and contributing through their remittances, to its economic development as interpreted by the authorities. The protests by the Turkish authorities in 1983 at the German policy of incentives to return and their recommendation that workers refuse voluntary repatriation (42) illustrate a situation which appears to be general.

The bilateral education agreements, signed in the 1970s, lend support to this view. Apart from Yugoslavia, which considers its citzens abroad as "temporary" residents, the other countries stress "maintaining the language and customs of origin" and even the "national identity" of second-generation immigrants. This is another controversial point and many questions remain unanswered on the meaning of national identity, culture and language outside national frontiers, and on the cui bono. Space limitations preclude a further discussion of this issue here. The crucial problem in our view is that raised by "return to the homeland" which does not appear to be an objective genuinely shared by all the countries that publicly subscribe to it.

A MISSED OPPORTUNITY FOR REFORM

First, creating of special structures for immigrant children instead of introducing comprehensive reforms would seem to be a matter of deliberate choice reflecting, in the same way as migration policies, the long-term thrust of education policies. For want of a major overhaul which would take due account of the special social and cultural needs of immigrants, schools will simply maintain their traditional functions which, as is frequently pointed out, serve to perpetuate social inequalities and promote a single culture, that of the urban élites of the industrialised societies.

Schools are hence not really fitted to the task of integrating young people of foreign origin. The languages and cultures of the non-industrialised countries may have penetrated school buildings but they have had little impact on the content of education and hence on the school population as a whole. Furthermore, the determining role of social conditions in underachievement at school has been recognised but little has been done to remedy the situation.

The education provision for immigrant children has a number of drawbacks and some fundamental questions have yet to receive a satisfactory answer. The measures taken would appear to reflect ingrained administrative and ideological responses and/or the outcome of political considerations rather than being based on an honest analysis that would identify the real educational needs of young people of foreign origin. The political and economic crisis which formed the backdrop to the implementation and extension of these educational developments, reinforces this view and again illustrates that this provision is based on a broader rationale in which national interests, the conflict of social groups and corporate concerns tend to outweigh purely educational considerations. There is no space here to go into all the questions raised by a study of all these systems. We are of necessity forced to focus on some of the more important among them.

The fundamental problem is the failure to mesh in this special provision with the normal school system with the result that it is difficult to establish a bridge between the two, and young people -- especially in the preparatory classes and in bilingual schools -- find the transition to normal schooling somewhat fraught and uncertain.

The educational considerations underlying this approach are not easy to appraise. Whether the classes are explicitly designed to teach the official language of the country of residence or that of the country of origin, the separation they tend to maintain often appears as an end in itself, as a means of safeguarding the educational standards of young nationals. The concentration of immigrants in poor areas and schools, itself a source of racial tensions and racist behaviour, has fostered the idea that the presence of "foreigners" brings down educational standards for "nationals".

Thus, the separation of this portion of the school population from that attending normal classes for purposes of learning the host country's language does not necessarily facilitate the process. Research findings lend no support to the idea that the language of the host country should be taught as a foreign language, without integrating the children concerned into mainstream schooling. Experience in Italy is a useful pointer in this regard; despite what is often said, it is probably not the fact that "Italian is an easy language" that facilitates its acquisition but that tuition is given within the normal school system.

Similarly, the criteria used to identify pupils deficient in the official language are seriously contested by the specialists. In the case of Hispanics in the United States, it has been pointed out that "Tests and other instruments have not been developed to measure the cognitive and English speaking abilities of linguistic minority children" (43). Quite simply, as C. Paulston notes, we do not know what the tests measure (44).

Assessing these programmes is another problem that has yet to find a satisfactory solution. By and large, there is no agreement among specialists as to what criteria should be used to produce reliable assessments. This question has long been keenly debated, especially in the United States. But despite the controversy surrounding the issue and frequent negative evaluations, these programmes are being extended. In the United States, for example, the GAO and the American Institute of Research published a highly negative evaluation of bilingual education in 1979. But despite mounting scepticism in academic and political circles since the early 1980s, no reforms have yet been put in hand. In Montreal a survey of young people attending special classes between 1979 and 1983 showed that in one school as many as 45 per cent were behind in their studies -- the national average for children of immigrants is 17 per cent. Despite the manifest failures, note the authors, these special classes are not being called into question; the demand is rather for their expansion (45). In Europe, the educational performance of the young people in question has not improved since these classes were set up; research by CERI in this field has shown that many young people of foreign origin have been relegated by the school system. Nevertheless, in a number of European countries both reception classes and bilingual schools are being expanded on the same bases as before.

Parental opposition to such schemes, particularly outside Europe, is a further indication that all is not well. Haitians in Quebec, for example, do not understand why their children should be placed in special compulsory classes when French in Haiti, as in Quebec, is their official language. The authorities contend that young Haitians are deficient in international French (46). Others, in the United States, have asked that the teaching of Creole be abolished and that courses be given directly in English or French (47).

A final problem merits attention. Not only is this segment of the school population treated differently from the school population as a whole, it is also viewed en bloc by the authorities despite its innate cultural and other diversities (age group, previous schooling etc.). Recent years have seen an increasing specialisation of this system: special arrangements have given way to special teaching of the official language, now taught as a "foreign language" and special teaching techniques "adapted to foreign children" and special instructors etc. What is the significance of this development? How are we to interpret the teaching of German or French as a "foreign language" to a school population living within national frontiers? If the objective is to make the undifferentiated teaching of a language more accessible to a multicultural public, the solution proposed is as undifferentiated as before; is French, for example, a foreign language in the same way for young people of Portuguese or Asiatic origin? And why the term "foreign" rather than "second" language? Does this not betray a symbolic shift in emphasis that designates as "foreign" not the language but the population for whom it is destined?

Similar considerations apply to the sending countries, which play a major role in setting up systems for teaching the "languages and cultures of origin", systems that are perceived as a means for maintaining their economic and cultural ties with their nationals abroad. These ties are crucial for these countries' economies and are threatened by the (possible) assimilation of their citizens in the host country. As the Italian senator, Valitutti, wrote recently (48): we have unconsciously accepted a nationalist prejudice in considering that the most important thing was maintaining ties with the mother country; for Italian emigrants the aim was not purely and simply one of conserving their identity at the price of their isolation which would ultimately scar them just as much as the loss of their identity, but a more active and more fertile presence of Italian culture in the countries in which they lived. (The underlining is ours.)

The approach we have taken throughout this report to education for immigrant children is somewhat different from that normally adopted. This was in our view necessary to highlight the fact that so far genuinely educational objectives have played a smaller role in the creation and development of such provision than might be thought and that non-educational considerations have often prevailed over reasoned debate and serious reflection on educational issues. It is hence urgent to embark on the painstaking process of reconsidering the school system as a whole, its theoretical bases and its future development.

NOTES AND REFERENCES

1. Provision of suitable tuition including teaching of the language of the host State; measures necessary for the training and further training of the teachers who are to provide this tuition; promotion of the teaching of the mother tongue and of the culture of the country of origin, Council of the European Communities Directive, 77/486/EEC, 25th July 1977.

2. 39 Fed. Reg. 19966 (1974).

3. FOSTER W.P., "Bilingual Education: An Educational and Legal Survey", Journal of Law-Education, Vol. 5, No. 2, April 1976, p. 150.

4. See FLORES E.T., "Research on Undocumented Immigrants and Public Policy: A Study of the Texas School Case" in International Migration Review: Irregular Migration: An International Perspective, Vol. 18, Fall 1984, pp. 505-519.

5. CRESPO M. and PELLETIER G., "Performance scolaire, intégration sociale et 'classes d'accueil' francophones pour jeunes immigrants. Analyse diachronique d'une expérience montréalaise (1974-1983)", paper for the First Conference of the European Society for Comparative Education, Würzburg, Fed. Rep. of Germany, pp.3-4. See also CRESPO M. and HACHE J.B.: Gestion et décroissance, le cas d'une commission scolaire québecoise, Montreal University Press, Montreal 1983.

6. See Schools Commission for the Triennium 1979-1981 cited in MILLS J., "Bilingual Education in Australian Schools". In Australian Education Review, No. 18, 1982, p. 39.

7. MAPPA S.: "Education et Pluralisme Culturel et Linguistique, Examen par pays: Grèce", CERI/OECD, not published.

8. Commission on Migrants' Languages and Culture in School and Adult Education in Sweden: English Summary from the Main Report on "Different Origins -- Partnership in Sweden", SOU: 1983, 57, pp. 12 and 18.

9. EEC, report by the Commission to the Council on the implementation of the Directive 77/486/CEE, p. B.3; US Department of Education, 1984, pp. 17-20.

10. EEC, op.cit., I.2.

11. BOULOT S., BOYSON-FRADET D., "Echecs scolaires des enfants d'immigrés" in Les Temps Modernes: L'Immigration maghrébine en France, March-April-May 1984, p. 1912.

12. LEBON A., Migrants' Children and Employment. The European Experience, OECD, Paris, 1983, p.7.

13. In 46 Flemish-speaking schools, 48.1 per cent of foreign children were attending special classes in 1981-82, made up as follows: 13 per cent French, 27 per cent British, but 47 per cent Yugoslav, 48 per cent Spanish, 50 per cent Greek, 51 per cent Portuguese, 52 per cent Italian, 62.2 per cent Turk and North-African (EEC Commission Report B.4).

14. In Belgium (French-speaking) foreign children accounted in 1981-82 for 30.7 per cent of kindergarten classes for children with learning disabilities, against 23.8 per cent of the total (normal and special); 24.6 per cent in primary schooling against 23.1 per cent of the total; in Germany, in 1981-82, 9.5 per cent overall, though the rates are particularly high in some Länder: in Berlin (1980-81) 13.7 per cent; in Hamburg 10 per cent; in Hesse 9.4 per cent. In Switzerland, too, in 1982 young foreigners accounted for 26.4 per cent in special education, against 18 per cent overall (Immigrants' Children at School, OECD/CERI, Paris, 1987).

15. In France (1980-81), 15.15 per cent in special elementary education (9.3 per cent of the total) and 15.2 per cent (1982-83) in special secondary education (6.4 per cent of the total). In Luxembourg, 40.9 per cent of special primary education in 1981-82 against 35.8 per cent of the total (Immigrants' Children ..., ibid.).

16. CRESPO M. and PELLETIER G., op. cit, pp. 3-4.

17. M.B. ARIAS, R. NAVARRA, "Title VII, Bilingual Education: Developing Issues of Diversity and Equity". In IFG 1981.

18. Pilot-project: "Turkish instead of the first and second modern language". In Bildung und Wissenschaft, BW 1983, No.11/12, pp. 194-197.

19. Ibid.

20. Ibid.

21. EEC Commission Report, Netherlands.

22. "Should foreign children learn their mother tongue?" in Der Spiegel, (Hamburg), No. 51, December 1983.

23. Ibid.

24. EEC: DE (BW) 8

25. Immigrants' Children at School, op. cit.

26. Ibid.

27. Programme for producing audio-visual teaching materials for teaching Greek to children of Greek migrants in Germany (in Greek), Ministry of National Education, Athens, 1982-83, p.4.

28. MAPPA S., art.cit., pp. 15-16.

29. See STENOPU A., "Report on the situation of migrants' children in Belgium" (in Greek). In Logos kai Praxi, V.4, Athens, 1983, p. 56.

30. EEC: FR. 5.

31. See MILLS J., op.cit. in note 6, p.52.

32. SIMPSON A.K., "The Politics of Immigration Reform" in International Migration Review, Vol. 18, autumn 1984, pp.487-494.

33. In the Netherlands, for instance, unskilled immigrant workers may only be employed between the ages of 18 and 35 and skilled workers between the ages of 18 and 45; medical examinations are required by all receiving countries.

34. Hence, for instance, in the United States, the regularisation of the situation of certain illegal immigrants who have been in the country for more than eight years. In 1977 new measures were introduced to regularise the situation of illegal immigrants provided that they had resided clandestinely for five years without interruption The 1977 regularisation measures in the United States, for example, granted temporary right of abode for a period of five years to those entering before 1977, but did not state what would happen after that time (SIMPSON A.K., art. cit.).

35. The provisions adopted in the United States and Europe during World War I under which naturalisation could be rescinded were applied on a massive scale in the inter-war years; these were supplemented by the measures rescinding nationality rights from citizens by birth and the introduction of laws rescinding such rights by decree, as was done by Belgium and some other Western democracies in the 1930s.

36. Only Sweden, the Netherlands and Belgium have granted the right to vote at municipal elections.

37. TRUDEAU T. (James Fleming, Keynote speech in) "Heritage Language Education: Issues and Directives". In Proceedings of a Conference Organized by the Multiculturalism Directorate of the Department of the Secretary of State, Ed. J. Cummins, p.12, Saskatoon, Canada, June 1981.

38. SAVARY A., "L'intégration scolaire des enfants d'immigrés". In Cahiers de l'Education Nationale No.26, Paris, June 1984, p. 3.

39. Commission on Migrants' Languages and... (English Summary), op.cit. in note 8, pp. 31 and 62.

40. ALLOUCHE Ab. "La problématique de l'enseignement des langues et des cultures d'origine aux enfants d'immigrés maghrébins: l'exemple de la banlieue parisienne" in Les sciences sociales de l'éducation, Revue internationale francophone, 1/2 January-June 1984, pp. 45-46.

41. See COHEN G. "The Politics of Bilingual Education". In Oxford Review of Education, Vol. 10, No. 2 1984, p.230.

42. SERTEL Y. "La crise économique et l'immigration turque en Europe" in Les temps modernes, No.456-457, July-August 1984, p. 308/

43. IFG (Institute for Research on Educational Finance and Governance), Bilingual Education for Hispanics, Vol. 2, No. 4, Autumn 1981, p.1.

44. BRATT PAULSTON C.: Swedish research and debate about bilingualism. National Swedish Board of Education, 1982, p. 50.

45. CRESPO M. and PELLETIER G., "Performance scolaire ...", op.cit. in note 5, pp. 9 and 14.

46. Ibid., p. 12.

47. FOSTER C.R., "Instruction of Haitian Bilingual Children in the United States". In Seattle Center for Research on International Language Problems, 1980 (ED 1976 19).

48. Ministero Affari Esteri: "Atti del convegno sulla riforma della normativa italiana in materia di scolarizzazione dei figli degli emigranti", Instituto Poligrafico e Zecca dello Stato, Roma e Urbino, March 1983, pp. 14-15.

IV. FOCUS ON THE LANGUAGES

11. LINGUISTIC CONSEQUENCES OF ETHNICITY AND NATIONALISM IN MULTILINGUAL SETTINGS

by
Christina BRATT PAULSTON
Chairman, Department of General Linguistics
University of Pittsburgh

INTRODUCTION

This paper presents an analytical framework for explaining and predicting the language behaviour of social groups as such behaviour relates to educational policies for minority groups. It argues a number of points:

i) If language planning is to be successful, it must consider the social context of language problems and especially the forces which contribute to language maintenance or shift;

ii) The linguistic consequences for social groups in contact will vary depending on the focus of social mobilisation, i.e. ethnicity or nationalism;

iii) A major problem in the accurate prediction of such linguistic consequences lies in identifying the salient factors which contribute to language maintenance or shift, i.e. answering the question "under what conditions". Rational policy-making requires that all these factors be considered in the establishment and understanding of educational policies for minority groups.

The theoretical model is grounded on a wide variety of data: my own fieldwork data and school visits on five continents; impressions and observations from my own work with training teachers from ethnic groups and directing doctoral dissertations on language shift and spread; and examination of some thirty case studies of social and political groups in multilingual situations.

The paper seeks to present basic linguistic facts before presenting the arguments for the analysis, which are based on those facts. After some initial comments about language planning and language problems, a major section of the paper discusses the possible linguistic consequences of ethnic groups in contact, namely language maintenance, bilingualism or shift. A shorter section on language (and religion) as social resources in competition for social advantage follows. The paper concludes with a discussion of ethnicity, ethnic movements, ethnic nationalism and geographic nationalism and how they result in differential outcomes of language maintenance and shift. A concluding section makes a few general comments for policy-makers on the setting of education policies for minority groups.

LANGUAGE PLANNING AND LANGUAGE PROBLEMS

Most scholars limit the term language planning to "the organised pursuit of solutions to language problems, typically at the national level" (Fishman, 1973:23-24). The degree of "organised" varies; a language planning process which shares Jernudd's specification of the orderly and systematic -- i) establishment of goals, ii) selection of means, and iii) prediction of outcomes (Jernudd, 1973:11-23) -- is an exception rather than the rule. Heath makes clear in her study of language policy in Mexico (1972) that language decisions are primarily made on political and economic grounds and reflect the value of those in political power. Linguistic issues *per se* are of minor concern. Since the matters discussed are overtly those of language, there is frequently confusion about the salient issues discussed in language planning, whether they are, in fact, matters of political, economic, religious, socio-cultural or linguistic concerns, or even moral concerns. The OECD's interest in the educational policies for minority social groups serves to emphasize the legitimate and important economic implications such language policies have; one can even argue that the most important factor influencing language choice of ethnic groups is economic, specifically one of access to jobs (Brudner, 1972).

Language choice is one of the major language problems, whether it be choice of national language (as in Finland and Israel), choice of national alphabet (as in Somalia) or choice of medium of instruction (as in Norway). In Israel, social conditions and religious attitudes towards Hebrew and the Promised Land made possible the rebirth of Hebrew and its implementation as a national language. "As to the success of the Hebrew revival, it was probably due largely to the prevalence of the required conditions" (Nahir, 1984:302); that is Israel serves as an example of social forces facilitating national language planning. In contrast, Peru during the Velasco government officialised Quechua as a national language (Mannheim, 1984) with resounding failure of implementation. In Peru, as in much of Latin America, race is defined primarily by cultural attributes: wear a long braid, and many faldas, wide Indian type skirts, and speak Quechua and you are Indian; cut your hair, wear European style clothing and speak Spanish, and you become if not white, at least Mestizo (Patch, 1967). To embrace Quechua would be to declare oneself Indian with all the accompanying socio-economic stigmatisation, and such planning held no hope of successful implementation. Peru serves as an example of language planning which goes counter to existing socio-cultural forces.

The problem is of course to be able to identify relevant social forces and predict the outcomes they will have. For example, contrary to expectation, choice of medium of instruction in the schools, especially for minority groups (1), has very little predictive power in the final language choice of the ethnic group. The difficulty is that we have a very poor grasp of what the relevant social forces are and what the corresponding educational, social, and cultural outcomes will be. Three points need to be made here. The major point to understand about language as group behavior (2) is that language is almost never the causal factor, never the factor that gives rise to, brings about, causes things to happen, but rather language mirrors social conditions, mirrors man's relationship to man. It is quite true that denying Blacks access to schooling as was common in the U.S. South in the last century made them unfit for anything but menial jobs, but Black illiteracy was not the cause of Black/White relations and exploitation, it was the result of it.

The corollary to this simple, yet hard to grasp point is that bilingual education (mother tongue education, home language education, i.e. education in the national language plus the ethnic group's own language) is in itself not a causal factor. One reason why there is no conclusive answer in the research on BE to the seemingly simple questions whether a child learns to read more rapidly in a second language if first taught to read in his primary (Engle, 1973:1) is that medium of instruction in school programs is an intervening variable rather than the independent variable it is always treated as. One cannot hope to achieve any consensus in research findings by examining intervening variables without identifying the independent variables (Paulston, 1975). Schools and schooling can facilitate existing social trends, but they cannot be a successful counter to social and economic forces. English-medium schools were the major language learning facility for the children of the European immigrants to the United States, but the same schools have not been successful in teaching English to Navajo children on the reservations and they have had their fair share of failure in Chicano education "Under what social conditions does medium of instruction make a difference for school children in achieving success" remains one key question.

The third point relates to the possible linguistic outcomes of the prolonged contact of ethnic groups within one nation -- the typical background situation which necessitates special educational policies for minority groups. There are not many possibilities: the three main ones are language maintenance, bilingualism, or language shift. Another possibility is the creation of pidgins and creoles but they entail bilingualism or shift and will not be further considered in this paper. For an overview of the range of language problems and their intended treatments, see Nahir's "Language Planning Goals: A Classification" (1984).

LANGUAGE MAINTENANCE AND LANGUAGE SHIFT

To the study of language maintenance and shift, we need to add two other related topics, language spread (Cooper, 1982) and language death (Dressler and Wodak-Leodolter, 1977). Cooper defines language spread as "an increase, over time, in the proportion of a communication network that adopts a given language or language variety for a given communicative function" (1982:6). Most language spread probably takes place as lingua francas, as LWC's (languages of wider communication), and English is a good example (Fishman, Cooper and Conrad, 1977). On the whole, such spread is neutral in attitudes.

But languages also spread for purposes of within-nation communication, and when they do so, not as an additional language like English in Nigeria, but as a new mother tongue, then language spread becomes a case of language shift. When such language spread through shift takes place within groups who do not possess another territorial base, we have a case of language death. Languages do become extinct, and the many dead Amerindian languages are now a mute witness to the spread of English (Bauman, 1980). Language shift, especially if it involves language death, tends to be an emotional topic; and economists and other social scientists who are not basically interested in language and culture *per se* will simply have to accept that it is often fairly futile to insist on a reasoned view in matters of language shift where it concerns the opinions and attitudes of the speakers of the shifting groups. Linguists and anthropologists frequently belong in this category as well.

In addition, the data base is very small. For example, in Gal's fine dissertation (1979) the ten page bibliography only contains six entries which mention shift or maintenance in the title. I know of no major study on language maintenance, presumably because it is not considered problematic.

Still there are some generalisations we can make about language shift and maintenance which seem to hold in all cases. One of the primary factors in accounting for subsequent course of mother tongue diversity, to use Lieberson's phrase, lies in the origin of the contact situation (Lieberson, Dalto, and Johnston, 1975; Schermerhorn, 1970). Voluntary migration, especially of individuals and families, results in the most rapid shift while annexation and colonialisation where entire groups are brought into a nation with their social institutions of marriage and kinship, religious and other belief and value systems still in situ, still more or less intact, tend to result in much slower language shift if at all.

The mechanism of language shift is bilingualism, often but not necessarily with exogamy, where parent(s) speak(s) the original language with the grandparents and the new language with the children. The case of bilingualism holds in all cases of group shifts, although the rate of shift may vary with several bilingual generations rather than just one.

A thoroughly documented fact is that language shift frequently begins with women, as manifest in choice of code (Schlieben-Lange, 1977); in choice of marriage partner (Gal, 1979; Brudner, 1972); and eventually in the language in which they choose to bring up their children (Eckert, 1983). The most common explanation is that women who are in a subordinate position in society, are sensitive to issues of power, including the language of power, but there really exists no generally accepted explanation.

Maintained group bilingualism (3) is unusual. The norm for groups in prolongued contact within one nation is for the subordinate group to shift to the language of the dominant group, either over several hundred years as with Gaelic in Great Britain or over the span of three generations as has been the case of the European immigrants to Australia and the United States in an extraordinary rapid shift. It was exactly the language shift and attempts to stop it which have caused much of the trouble in Quebec, from French to English (Gendron, 1972), and in Belgium, from Flemish to French (Verdoodt, 1978).

Language shift is often treated by laymen and social scientists alike as an unarguable indicator of cultural assimilation, and it is often the painful thought of forsaking the culture and values of the forefathers that is at the root of the strife over language shift. Assimilation is a much more complex issue than language shift, but a few points need to be considered. First, we need carefully to make the distinction, in Schermerhorn's terms (1970), between social and cultural institutions. Economic incorporation of an ethnic group with access to the goods and services of a nation, the common goal of minority groups and the most common reason for migration in Europe (some also claim religious freedom or refugee status), is different from cultural assimilation and the giving up of values and beliefs. It is primarily to the perception of forced assimilation that the issue of the medium of instruction in the national language becomes tied, and so many Chicanos bemoan the loss of Chicano culture with the loss of Spanish. But there is not necessarily an isomorphic relationship between language and culture; Spanish is the carrier of many other cultures besides Chicano, and less commonly accepted, language maintenance is not necessary for culture and ethnicity maintenance, as indeed Lopez (1976) documents for the Chicanos in Los Angeles. In other words, it is possible for groups to maintain their own ethnic culture even after language shift, as we see in groups like the English Gypsies and many Amerindian tribes.

Although most ethnic minority groups within a nation do shift language, they will vary in their degree of ethnic maintenance and in their rate of shift. Some causal factors can be identified. For example, in Pittsburgh the Greeks shift over a four generation span compared with the three generation shift of the Italians. Some factors which contribute to the slower Greek shift are i) knowledge and access to a standardised, written language with cultural prestige and tradition, which is taught by the Greek churches in Pittsburgh, and ii) arranged marriage partners directly from Greece (who then are monolingual in Greek). The Italians in contrast speak/spoke a non-standard, non-written dialect with no prestige, and they shared their Roman Catholic churches with the English-speaking Irish, typically with Irish priests and sisters, so they found no language maintenance support in the churches. Nor was there any pressure for endogamy as long as the marriage was within the Roman Catholic Church.

Ethnic groups also vary in, quite vaguely, ethnic pride or ethnic stubborness in culture maintenance -- even after they have shifted language and become socially incorporated into a nation. Alba (1975) says in the preface to his book about Catalunya: "Catalonia is not especially notable for anything except its persistence -- its stubborness in existing despite the most adverse conditions". The survivial of Catalan may best be explained as a result of nationalism but it does exemplify the notion of stubborness, as Alba calls it, in group maintenance.

Groups also vary in group adhesion and there is wide intra-group variation in members' attitude toward language maintenance and cultural assimilation. A case in point is Robert Rodriguez' beautiful, autobiographical but controversial Hunger of Memory (1982) in which he argues for assimilation -- and against bilingual education. Carrillo's comments (1984) on this work are worth citing:

> "Mexican-American children were a minority in the schools. There was a strong pressure to assimilate; the overwhelming presence of the dominant anglo society was enough to cause this pressure. Add to this the impression of a sensitive child that the rewards of the society were limited to those who were members of the dominant culture, and you can begin to understand Rodriguez' conflicting feelings about learning English, maintaining his Spanish, assimilating to anglo society, and maintaining his ties to Mexican-American culture.
> Today, growing up Mexican-American in California is very different. As the minority group has grown, it has influenced the dominant culture significantly. ... Today, a Mexican-American child in California has many options on the scale from complete assimilation to strong pride in Mexican-American culture." (1984:9, 30).

Carillo does not write as a social scientist but as a participant Chicano and ESL (English as a Second Language) professional, and he documents his perception of social change, in the host culture as well as the minority group, in his defence of the much criticised Rodriguez (4). Carillo's point about many options available stresses the need for flexible educational policies.

Where shift does not take place, it is for three major reasons:

i) Self-imposed boundary maintenance (Barth, 1969), always for reasons other than language, most frequently religion, e.g. the Amish and the orthodox Jewish Hassidim. The Hassidim are perfectly aware of the role of English but their choice is for group cohesion for religious purposes:

> Many (Lubovitch) families elect to send their children to the Yiddish speaking school (no English curriculum). In so doing, they increase the possibility of upward mobility within the ethnic group and decrease the probability that these children will gain the secular and technical skills necessary for employment in the economy of the larger society. All Lubovitchers are aware of the potential usefulness of secular skills and an English curriculum, but few... families elect the bilingual school for their children.

Such extreme measures of language maintenance are very unusual and never undertaken over time only for the sake of language itself.

ii) Externally imposed boundaries, usually in the form of denied access to goods and services, especially jobs. The Black community of the past in the U.S. is an example. Geographic isolation (which is theoretically uninteresting but nevertheless effective) is also a form of external boundary which contributes to language maintenance, as Gaelic in the Hebrides or Quechua in the Andes.

iii) A diglottic-like situation where the two languages exist in a situation of functional distribution where each language has its specified purpose and domain and the one language is inappropriate in the other situation, as with Guarani and Spanish in Paraguay (Rubin, 1968) or with Modern Standard Arabic and the mother tongues in the Maghreb (Grandguillaume, 1983).

We see then that the major linguistic consequence of ethnic groups in prolongued contact within one nation is language shift of the subordinate groups to the language of the dominant group. The major dependent variable is the rate of shift. But this shift only takes place if there are opportunity and incentive for the group to learn the national language. There are probably many kinds of incentives (the data base here is very inadequate) but the two major ones are i) economic advantage, primarily in the form of source of income, and ii) social prestige. In Brudner's terms (1972), jobs select language learning strategies, which is to say wherever there are jobs available that demand knowledge of a certain language, people will learn it. Without rewards, language learning is not salient. Sometimes language shift is held to be problematic (Quebec), sometimes it is encouraged as national policy (France), sometimes it is resisted by the ethnic groups (Catalan) and sometimes encouraged (European immigrants to Australia and the United States), but it is invariably to the social conditions one must look to understand the attitudes and values which accompany language shift.

Another less common result of languages in contact is language maintenance, frequently with bilingualism, and it is always for reasons other than appreciation of the language per se. The third consequence is prolonged group bilingualism. This paper is not the place for a thorough discussion on the nature of bilingualism (Albert and Obler, 1978; Grosjean, 1982; Hornby, 1977; Lambert, 1972; Mackey, 1976; Miracle, Jr., 1983), but it should be mentioned that full-fledged, balanced bilingualism is the exception rather than the rule. Bilingualism spans a range from passive, imperfect knowledge of dead sacred languages (Sanskrit, classic Arabic, classical Hebrew, Suryoyo, etc.) to the linguistic competence necessary for simultaneous interpretation (but even so U.N. interpreters only translate into one language, not back and forth). Degree of proficiency has little to do with language attitudes, and the sacred languages particularly assert a vast influence on attempts to orderly language planning (e.g. choice of alphabet in Somalia). When we talk about bilingualism and bilingual education as an educational policy, we should therefore be careful to consider the degree and functional possibilities of the linguistic competence of the group discusses. I have observed "mother tongue" education for Assyrian children in Sweden who could not even count to ten in their mother tongue but were fluent in the national language (5). In the same country, I have seen classes for Turkish primary students who knew very little Swedish. The highly varied nature of bilingualism forces us to face the problem whether equity in education will allow the same educational policies for all ethnic groups. Indeed, the United States Supreme Court has suggested that equal treatment does not constitute equal opportunity in the matter of education of ethnic minority children compared to mainstream children. One can easily take that argument a step further and consider that the various ethnic groups may merit differential treatment.

LANGUAGE AND RELIGION AS SOCIAL RESOURCES

Language can be seen as a resource which is available to ethnic groups in their competition for access to the goods and services of a nation. All groups do not avail themselves of language as a symbol in their fight for independence or economic shares or for whatever goal they see as in their best interest. When they do, language can be a very effective power base, to which the nationalistic movements in Europe in the last century bear witness. Language loyalty was so often romanticised during these movements, that one does well to remember that there is nothing inherently "natural" about group language loyalty, but rather that it is a deliberately chosen strategy for survival.

Mohammed Kabir documents these points in an important dissertation on "Nationalistic Movements in Bangladesh" (1985, MS). His claim is that the economy is the crucial factor in bringing about change in a nation, and as change occurs, so do members' loyalties and their bases therefor. Members choose political identity and mobilise particular strategies depending on their particular demands. So language, ethnicity, and religion are available resources and are chosen as identity bases variously over time as strategies to achieve specific demands.

Bengal, Kabir's case study, was populated by the same ethno-linguistic group, roughly half of whom were Muslim and the other half Hindu. Eventually the Hindu group came to dominate education and agriculture. In 1905 Bengal was split into East and West Bengal against the opposition of the Hindus, and in 1912 Bengal was reunited this time against the will of the Muslims. The 1940 Lahore resolution granted Pakistan sovereign status so Muslims could have a separate homeland; consequently the East Bengali claimed Muslim status to join Pakistan and become free of Hindu competition. But power became concentrated in West Pakistan, and the Bengali had little or no share in education and other social-economic spheres. In spite of the Bengali constituting 54 per cent of the population, Urdu was the only national language of Pakistan, and this time the language controversy was the beginning of the separatist movement. Muslims in East Bengal joined with Hindus in separatist demands based on Bengali linguistic identity, and Bangladesh achieved independence in 1971 as a linguistic unity. To date, no one has raised the point of a united Bengal, because, Kabir points out, neither group (Hindu and Muslim) perceives reunification to be in their best interest (6).

We see then an example of a group, East Bengal Muslims who, when they perceived such action best suited to their purposes and demands, claimed religious status and identity and Pakistani nationalism, later linguistic-ethnic nationalism and separatism and, at present, status for Bangladesh founded on religio-linguistic identity. Throughout the course of the last hundred years, language and religion have been available resources, variously utilised in the battle for survival in a harsh world.

Immigrant groups are not very different from the Bengalis. When they see learning the national language well and fluently in the best interest of their children (and there are social institutions available like the schools and the church, which can help them do so), there are very few problems associated with the educational policies for minority groups. Within the single city-state of Singapore with her four official languages and three major religions, there is no sign of ethnic strife or educational problems (Crewe, 1977). In fact, the ex-colonial English is favoured as medium of instruction by many (McDougall & Foon, 1976). I must admit that I looked very carefully for competition along ethnic lines but saw none. The simple explanation is to be found in Singapore's very strong and expanding economy. There is enough of the good of this life to go around for everybody, and competition takes place on the basis of individual qualities, not along ethnic lines.

But when these same immigrant groups instead of socio-economic opportunity see stigmatisation, economic exploitation and systematic unemployment, they are perfectly likely to use the original mother tongue as a strategy for mobilisation. Language boundary maintenance reinforced with religion is an even stronger tool. The Turks in Europe have frequently followed this latter process (Sachs, 1983). It is not that mainstream members and those from assimilated former ethnic groups like the Poles and the Slovaks in Pittsburgh don't face difficulties in a declining economy; it is rather that they don't feel a we-they injustice and antagonism and also that they have (through language shift) lost language as a resource for mobilisation strategy. As I write this, the City Council has decide to merge the Police Force and the Fire Fighter units in Pittsburgh. Both groups perceive this as being against their best interests and are violently opposing the new policy. As both groups share the same ethnic mix, language and ethnicity were not available resources and instead both groups mobilised along the lines of their labor unions. Had ethnicity been an available resource, they very likely would have mobilised along ethnic lines to judge from Elazar and Friedman's

(1976) case study of teachers in Philadelphis who didjust that and who were able to successfully defend their jobs in that fashion.

Almost twenty years ago, Glazer asked: "Just why America produced without laws that which other countries, desiring a culturally unified population, were not able to produce with laws -- is not an easy question" (1966:360). There is a fable by Aesop which holds the answer to that question and which best illustrates the points I have been trying to make. The sun and the wind see a man with a cloak (read language) walking along the road. They decide to enter a contest to see who can first cause him to shed his coat. The wind tears at him for hours but the man only wraps himself more tighly in his cloak. The sun takes over and spreads her benevolence over the man who after a short time divests himself of his cloak. Moral: In hard times, man will cling to his language and ethnic group; in times of plenty, man pays little attention to resources like ethnic languages.

ETHNICITY AND NATIONALISM

Introduction

The past discussion has dealt exclusively with the course of language and the linguistic consequences of ethnic minority groups in prolongued contact within one nation. But groups can find another focus of social mobilisation than ethnicity, and in the rest of this paper I shall argue that there are four distinct types of social mobilisation, which under certain specified social conditions result in different linguistic consequences: ethnicity, ethnic movements, ethnic nationalism and geographic nationalism. I am attempting a theoretical framework which will allow us to explain and to predict the language behaviour of groups who have access to or are exposed to more than one language. I have argued earlier that such an understanding is vital to helpful educational policies and successful language planning in general.

This paper represents the first attempt to organise these thoughts in writing, and as always some revision will be in order. I have long thought about the social mobilisation of religious groups within this framework and eventually opted for considering religion as a social resource similar to language. Linguistic groups may choose a religious identity as the main base in strategies of competition, but they do so as pre-existing ethnic or national groups. For purposes of explaining language behaviour of groups, I doubt that religion needs to be considered a primary force of group cohesion. More data will help support, modify or disprove this point. Religious groups are also theoretically problematic because of the preponderance of "irrational" behaviour where it is difficult to predict behaviour on the notion of acting in their own best interest.

A definite weakness of the framework is the present inability to incorporate the social organisation of tribes and clans when those tribes exist within a single ethno-linguistic group spread over several nations, such as Kurdistan. Somalia has a tribal social organisation but with one language within one nation, and so adherents for the various alphabets simply take on aspects of special interest groups which is not theoretically problematic. Nigeria's tribes are isomorphic with ethnic groups and can be so understood. It may be that Kurdish behaviour is more explainable with a better understanding of faciliting or constraining social conditions. More data and more reflection are needed on the linguistic consequences of this fairly unusual social organisation.

Another weakness is the lack of consideration given to the role of pan-movements in language maintenance. The role of English and French in pan-Africanism, the role of classical and literary standard Arabic in pan-Arabism, and the role of the Chinese character writing system all share certain features one of which is maintenance beyond what might reasonably have been expected. Future development of the topic of this paper will have to consider both tribes and pan-movements within the same framework.

Earlier Explanations

The focus of social science research and its scholarly writing as it relates to the language behaviour of social groups has very much reflected actual events in the real world. The one-nation-one-language national movements of 19th-century Europe provided the beginning of this field of literature, where nationality often was used synonymously with ethnic group (Deutsch, 1953).

Fishman has argued for a distinction between nationalism and nationism in his "Nationality-Nationalism and Nation-Nationism" (1968) where he attempts to sort out some of the terminological confusion accompanying nationalism. He suggests that "the transformation... of tradition-bound ethnicity to unifying and ideologised nationality... be called nationalism" (1968:41) and that "wherever politico-geographic momentum and consolidation are in advance of socio-cultural momentum and consolidation (be called) nationism" (1968:42). He goes on to discuss the different kinds of language problems such recent nation-states face. Van den Berghe in the same volume (1968) also addresses the terminological confusion. He suggests

> "that tribe (7) and its derivatives be scrapped altogether. To refer to a political movement based on ethnicity, I shall use the term 'nationalism' (e.g. Yoruba nationalism,...). To refer to political movements that use the multinational state as their defining unit, I shall speak of 'territorialism' (e.g. Nigerian territorialism,...)" (1968:215).

Fishman's and van den Berghe's linking of ethnicity with nationalism is typical of the thinking reflected in this set of scholarship.

The concern for nationalism was followed by an interest in ethnicity. Glazer and Moynihan point out in the "Introduction" to their Ethnicity: Theory and Experience that the word ethnicity made its appearance in the Oxford English Dictionary first in the 1972 Supplement where the first recorded usage is of David Riesman in 1953. They suggest "that a new word reflects a new reality and a new usage reflects a change in that reality." They continue:

> "The new word is "ethnicity" and the new usage is the steady expansion of the term 'ethnic group' from minority and marginal subgroups at the edges of society -- groups expected to assimilate, to disappear, to

continue as survivals, exotic or troublesome -- to major elements of a society." (1975:5).

This concern and focus of research on ethnicity and ethnic minority groups is not only an English language world phenomenon although the term ethnicity may not be used. To mention just a few representative publications, Recherches sociologiques of Louvain-la-Neuve published in 1977 a special issue on "Langue et identité nationale" which deals with language maintenance of ethnic minority groups in Europe. So did the Second International Conference on Minority Languages in Abo/Turko, Finland in 1983 (Molde & Sharp, 1984). Lenguas y Educacion en el Ambito del Estado Espanol (Siguan, 1983) deals with the emergent concern for the educational problems of linguistic minority groups in post-Franco Spain. UNESCO has just published a special issue of Prospects on "Mother Tongue and Educational Attainment" (14:1, 1984).

This resurgence of ethnic awareness brings into question the goal of complete assimilation for these groups. Elazar and Friedman discuss this new development of ethnic affirmation (in groups who have all shifted to English) in their Moving Up: Ethnic Succession in America (1976). They point out that ethnic identity has often been seen as a problem that must somehow be overcome. Social scientists have often considered religious and ethnic groups as "vestiges of a primitive past that are destined to disappear" (1976:4) but recent "writers on the 'new pluralism' have argued that racial, religion and ethnic groups are a basic component of our social structure" (p. 5) who affect our institutions and are at times more powerful than economic forces in their influence.

What Elazar and Friedman are discussing in their study of ethnic groups reflects not only a "change in reality", in Glazer and Moynihan's term, but also a paradigm shift (Kuhn, 1971) from equilibrium theory to a conflict perspective. This shift in focus on ethnicity is provocatively explored in John Bennett's The New Ethnicity: Perspectives from Ethnology (1975) whose shift in basic theoretical outlook also reflects the change in the phenomenon of ethnicity. The old notion of ethnicity looked on ethnicity as a group-cultural phenomenon where ethnicity was taken to refer to shared norms, artifacts, values, and beliefs within a "culture-population-group frame of reference" (Bennett, 1975:4), groups mobilising around cultural symbols (R.G. Paulston, 1977:181), of which language when it was available formed one of the most obvious. The major function of the new ethnicity can be seen as "a set of strategies for acquiring the resources one needs to survive and to consume at the desired level" (Bennett, 1975:4); above all, it differs from the old ethnncity in that it is "a cognitive ethnicity, a self-chosen ethnicity" (Bennett, 1975:9).

And that is roughly where we stand today with the scholarship on the background situation to language problems and educational policies of linguistic subordinate minority groups (8).

A New Theoretical Framework

I suggest now that there is merit in reconsidering the literature and that instead of entwining the concepts of ethnicity and nationalism, we would be better served in our endeavours to understand the nature of educational language policies, if we were to differentiate the two. I suggest four types of social mobilisation, which come close to forming a continuum rather than four distinct types: i) Ethnicity which very much corresponds to the notion of old ethnicity; ii) Ethnic movement which is based on the concept of the new ethnicity; iii) Ethnic nationalism; and iv) geographic nationalism which correspond to Kohn's closed and open nationalism (1968) as well as to Fishman's nationalism and nationism (1968) (see Chart 1).

It is perfectly possible for social groups to embrace a different type of mobilisation at different stages of their history and to move back and forth on the continuum of types; the Flemish have at various times occupied all four niches. No sense of evolution or development is implied in the notion of stage, only time in the historical sense, nor is any ameliorative value implied by any type; ethnicity and nationalism are simply descriptive labels for sets or syndromes of behaviour, attitudes and perceptions of groups of peoples. Given certain social conditions, they will behave in certain predictable fashions in regard to language, which behaviour it is my purpose to explore.

It is, however, an unavoidable fact that nationalism as a social phenomenon is a stigmatised behaviour in present day Europe for reasons of historical events during the last century. It is understandable that a region that has experienced the excesses of National Socialism and found economic recovery in a united Europe hesitates to again encourage nationalism. To use nationalism as a concept analytically for organising sets of behaviours is, however, very different from advocating nationalism as a political and economic system, but it should be recognised that the concept of nationalism may be difficult to use in the present day European climate. I do not intend these comments as a criticism of the analytical power of nationalism, only as a recognition of possible tactical drawbacks when explaining education policies.

Ethnicity

> "An 'ethnic group' is a reference group invoked by people who share a common historical style (which may be only assumed), based on overt features and values, and who, through the process of interaction with others, identify themselves as sharing that style. 'Ethnic identity' is the sum total of feelings on the part of group members about those values, symbols, and common histories that identify them as a distinct group. 'Ethnicity' is simply ethnic-based action." (Royce, 1982:18)

Ethnicity tends to stress roots and a shared biological past and the common ancestors (factual or fictional). The basis of personal identity is cultural (including religion), and ethnicity is a matter of self-ascription. The cultural values and beliefs, which are held in common, are unconsciously learned behaviour, and ethnicity is just taken for granted. The members tend to feel comfortable with past and future, and there is no opposition and no violence involved.

There is in fact little power struggle and not much purpose with ethnicity, and so the common course is assimilation and concomitant language shift, like the Walloons, who were brought to Sweden in the 1600s to develop the iron industry, have completely assimilated into Swedish culture (Douhan, 1982). Ethnicity will not maintain a language in a multilingual setting if

Chart 1

LINGUISTIC CONSEQUENCES OF SOCIAL MOBILIZATION IN MULTILINGUAL SETTINGS

<table>
<tr><th></th><th>ETHNICITY</th><th>ETHNIC MOVEMENT</th><th>ETHNIC NATIONALISM</th><th>GEOGRAPHIC NATIONALISM</th></tr>
<tr><td>1. Definig Characteristics</td><td>As identity

Unconscious learned behavior

Shared ancestors, roots

Taken for granted, not goal oriented, no violence

Common values and beliefs

Survives language shift</td><td>As strategy in competition for scarce resources

Goal: socio-economic advantage

Cognitive
self-chosen
militant
violent
charismatic leader

Language as rallying point

Boundary maintenance

Glorious

Etc…</td><td colspan="2">Territory

Closed n (Kohn) | Open n

Exclusive

Intellectual leaders
Middle class
Loyalty (important)

Common ennemy
Taught behaviors

Goal: independence
Political self-determination

past

External distinction
Internal cohesion (Haugen)

Cultural self-determination
Etc… as identity</td></tr>
<tr><td></td><td colspan="4">Less ◄—— Legislation Involved ——► More</td></tr>
<tr><td>2. Facilitating or constraining factors</td><td colspan="4">UNDER WHAT SOCIAL CONDITIONS ?
e.g : particpation in social institutions, schooling, exogamy, military service, religious institutions, mass-media, roads and transportation, travel, trade, commerce, war, evangelism, occupations, in-migration, back-migration, urbanization, etc……</td></tr>
<tr><td>3. Linguistic consequences (also: language spread language death language reformation)</td><td>Language shift</td><td>Language shift but slower rate</td><td>Maintenance national language as powerful symbol
Language planning
academies
Strong language attitudes</td><td>Maintenance national language</td></tr>
<tr><td></td><td></td><td></td><td colspan="2">Standardization
Modernization
Literacy-teacher training
Language problems: choice of a national language</td></tr>
</table>

the dominant group allows assimilation, and incentive and opportunity of access to the second language (L2) are present. Some general factors of social conditions which influence access to the L2 are:

i) Participation in social institutions, primarily universal schooling, exogamy, and required military service, and often religious institutions.

ii) Access to mass-media, especially TV;

iii) Access to roads and transportation versus physical isolation, like islands and mountains;

iv) Travel, including trade, commerce, war, and evangelism;

v) Some occupations;

vi) Demographic factors, like size of groups, vast in-migration, continued migration, back-migration, urbanisation.

The major social institution facilitating L2 learning in a situation which favours language shift is without a doubt public schooling. With children from socially marginal groups like the Navajo Indians (Rosier & Holm, 1980; Spolsky, 1977), bilingual education tends to be the moreefficient form of public education, but with children from socially favoured groups, education in the national language is a viable alternative, as the vast literature on the Canadian immersion programs for middle class children attests to (Cohen & Swain, 1976; Lambert & Tucker, 1972; Swain & Lapkin, 1982). There is a vast literature on the pros and cons of bilingual education, and the issues are too complicated to discuss in this paper (see, e.g. Center for Applied Linguistics, 1977; Cummins, 1976; Hartford et al., 1982; N. Epstein, 1977; Paulston, 1980; Spolsky, 1972).

A social institution for adults which can contribute markedly to L2 learning is the Armed Forces. In Peru, military service paired with the necessary travel to the coast district has been the major means of learning Spanish for many Quechua young men, former school drop-outs. In Zaire, during the colonial times of the Belgian Congo, Flemish officers did not insist on French, and the Armed Forces became a major force in the spread of Lingala, a local pidgin which became the language of the army.

Exogamy, marrying outside the ethnic group or other social unit, obviously necessitates language shift for one partner, at least within the family. This shift typically is in the direction of the language of the socio-economically favored group. This is exactly what happened in French Canada, but the French-speaking Canadians held political power and through legislation have been able to protect the position of French. Language maintenance and shift in regions where political and socio-economic power is divided between the ethnic groups is difficult and probably impossible to predict. Exogamy, showing definite trends of direction, is the most positive indicator of incipient shift. Once it is clear whom the children of migrant workers in Europe will marry, the setting of educational policy will be much facilitated. If they commonly marry nationals of the host culture, there will be no need of special or different educational policies for their children. If, however, they marry exclusively within their own ethnic group, learn the national language poorly and show other trends of strong culture maintenance (arranged marriages with partners from the home country, vacations in the home country, etc.), then a strong case can be argued for the case of bilingual education (9).

Demographic data are troublesome. Apart from concerns about reliability and validity of the data base (de Vries, 1977; Thompson, 1974) and methods of analysis (see Section II, "Demography", in Mackey and Ornstein, 1979), we do not really know what constitutes a critical mass in language maintenance of an ethnic group. We recognise that maintenance is easier for a large group, but we do not know how large is large. Clearly other factors like elitist status and prestige are at work here as well.

Most of the other factors are self-explanatory although I should point out that there exists no hard quantificational data base, and this list has been collected from a reading of case studies where these conditions are often treated observationally and anecdotally. No doubt there are additions to be made.

Ethnic Movement

The major difference between ethnicity and ethnic movement is when ethnicity as an unconscious source of identity turns into a conscious strategy, usually in competition for scarce resources. An ethnic movement is ethnicity turned militant, consisting of ethnic discontents who perceive the world as against them, an adversity drawn along ethnic boundaries. While ethnicithy stresses the content of the culture, ethnic movements will be concerned with boundary maintenance, in Barth's terms, with "us" against "them". It is very much a conscious, cognitive ethnicity in a power-struggle with the dominant group for social and economic advantage, a struggle which frequently leads to violence and social upheaval. Many ethnic movements have charismatic leaders (probably always born a member of the ethnic group) like Stephen Biko in South Africa and Martin Luther King, but they need not have an intellectual elite or a significant middle class.

Movements need rallying points, and language is a good obvious symbol if it is available. (It may not be. The IRA, the Irish Republican Army, uses English). So is religion. Original mother tongues and sacred languages are powerful symbols and may serve to support men in their struggle for what they perceive as a better life (10). But note that language as a symbol need not be the ethnic group's original mother tongue. Both Stephen Biko and Martin Luther King used English and partially for the same reason -- the diversity of African languages. The symbol in Biko's case was the choice of language, English rather than Afrikaans; in King's case, the symbol lay with the characteristic style of Black English rhetoric, many of which features originated with the West African languages.

When an ethnic movement draws on religion as a resource for identity base as strategy in social competition, when cognitive ethnicity is joined with religious fervor, the likely consequence is one of language maintenance, probably of a sacred language (only). Sacred languages tend with great diligence to be kept unchanged (11). The result is that sacred languages often are not spoken and only exist in written form. Groups maintaining a sacred language like the Syrians will typically shift their everyday language to that of the surrounding community so that we find Syrians all maintaining Suryoyo (a form of Aramaic) but speaking Arabic, Turkish, Swedish or American English. Maintaining two extra languages seems too cumbersome a task.

There are exceptions. Pre-Israeli Jews maintained both Hebrew and Yiddish (or Hebrew and Ladino) but as a result of externally imposed boundary maintenance, of the environing community's refusal to let them assimilate. (Ladino was after all the result of an earlier assimilation into Spanish culture). When allowed to assimilate, Yiddish disappeared and that explains why Yiddish was maintained in Slavic East Europe but not in Germany, i.e. as a factor of degree of social enclosure (Schermerhorn, 1970). The drop out rate is likely to be high for such religious groups if the host community allows assimilation, as it is for the Amish and as Bennett cites for the New York Hassidim.

Ethnic movements by themselves probably cannot maintain a language but will affect the rate of shift so that the shift is much slower and spans many more generations. Such a long state of bilingualism affects the structure of the languages involved (Thomason & Kaufman, Ms.), as Spanish expressions in Peru like <u>no mas</u> and diminutives like <u>chicititito</u>, which are calqued on Quechua (Albo, 1970; see also Pfaff, 1981). What is less understood and really not studied at all is the degree to which such groups keep their communicative competence rules (12) and apply their own rules of appropriate language use to the new language. An Arab who speaks fluent Swedish but stands as close, touches as much, interrupts as often, etc. as it is appropriate to do in a conversation in Arabic will have a confusing and probably irritating effect on a Swede who has very different rules for using language. We know virtually nothing about this aspect of language shift, but it is easy to speculate that cognitive ethnicity is more likely to guard cultural ways of using language and we know that different standards for using language (like appropriate loudness of voice) easily becomes a source of friction between groups. This topic merits study because the different communicative competence rules show up clearly in the classroom (Philips, 1970), and the children suffer as a consequence, since the teacher's rules are always held to be the "right" ones. Certainly educational policies should be taken to include teacher training. We know with dismal certitude teachers' misinterpretation of the social meaning of the language used by children with different group norms for speech. All teachers of ethnic minority children, whether they are members of the ethnic group or not, need a working understanding of communicative competence and its implications for the classroom.

Nationalism

When ethnic discontents turn separatist, we get ethnic nationalism. For nationalism, there seems to be as many definitions as there are scholars of nationalism, basically because, in Shafer's words (1972), nationalism has many faces. The following definitions will give a sense of the range of phenomena scholars have attempted to identify:

> [Nationalism is] a consciousness, on the part of individuals or groups, of membership in a nation, or of a desire to forward the strength, liberty, of prosperity of a nation (Royal Institute of International Affairs, 1939).

Arab nationalism emphasized other facets:

> The nationalism is a wider conception than the state, greater than the people, and more meaningful than the fatherland. It is not necessary for a nation to have one state or one fatherland [this is peculiarly Muslim], or to be composed of one people, but it must have its own language [some do not], its own history, its own ideals, its own shared aspirations, its own shared memories, and its own natural links which bind its members in two respects, the moral and the economic (Abd al-Latif Sharara, 1962:228).

African nationalism yet again differs:

> African nationalism is a feeling among the African people. It is not only a feeling against something, but also for something. It is a feeling against European rule ... This is the fundamental feeling of African nationalism -- the African feeling against Eurocracy, in favor of Afrocracy ... African nationalism is therefore essentially a political feeling (Sithole, 1960).

Shafer, who has brought together these definitions (1976), concludes elsewhere that it is impossible to fit nationalism into a short definition (1972:5). Kohn points out that while all instances of nationalism will vary according to past history and culture, present social structure and geographical location, all forms of nationalism still share certain traits (1968:64). Cottam's insistence that nationalism should not be dealt with as a thing reified but rather interpreted as a manifestation of nationalistic behaviour is very useful here as he identifies some of the shared traits in his definition of nationalist "as an individual who sees himself as a member of a political community, a nation, that is entitled to independent statehood, and is willing to grant that community a primary and terminal loyalty" (Cottam, 1964:3; lecture notes, January 15, 1984). Group cohesion to the end, a goal-orientation of self-determination, a perceived threat of opposing forces, and above all access to or hope of territory are characteristics of all national movements. What is important to remember and what both Royce's and Cottam's definitions stress is that ethnicity and nationalism both are sets or syndromes of behaviour, perceptions, and attitudes of a group of people. Given certain social conditions, they will behave in certain predictable fashions, including language behaviour which is our present interest.

Ethnic and geographic nationalism share all these features. The goal is independence, their own political status and social institutions on their own territory. The most common ideal is the nation-state but there are others. Catalunya Quebec, and Flemish Belgium are content to remain part of a larger state as long as they can safeguard their own social and cultural institutions of which language (and language maintenance) becomes a very prominent symbol. When use of their own language is denied, other cultural acts acquire a national symbolism way beyond their actual significance. To illustrate, during Franco anti-Catalan days, to cheer for Club Barcelona when the soccer team played Real Madrid became a political statement as was dancing the _sardana_ after Sunday mass.

The improvement of one's own lot in life or at least of one's children's is probably a common goal of all national movements; the motivation, like in ethnic movements, is one of perceived self-interest, a self-chosen state. Very often nationalism takes place as a protest against oppression, against a common enemy, whether it be against a (dominant) group within the same state or against another state. Euskadi, the Basque nation within Spain, is an example of the first type and it introduces another problem of interpretation, the unanimity of degree of intensity of a national movement. The Basques range from terrorists and separatists to assimilists with language shift more common than admitted. There is typically a great emphasis on loyalty and group cohesion, which are consciously taught behaviours, taught through social institutions like school, church, and army, with typical symbols the flag (13), the national anthem, and above all the language. To admit to language shift is to be disloyal, and this very deep-seated feeling of disloyalty is an additional problem in eliciting valid survey data in this type of research (Thompson, 1974).

Goals in national movements, besides general independence, tend to be quite definite and specific. These goals are often legitimatised by or based on historical past events or conditions. During the Finnish school strike in Stockholm during February of 1984, when Finnish parents kept their children out of school in support of their demand for Finnish medium schooling in kindergarten through university level courses, the reason given was that Finland is bilingual in Swedish-Finnish and that Sweden should reciprocate. It is a demand legitimised on the national law of the ethnic immigrant group and its past history and is much more characteristic of nationalism rather than of ethnic movements which tend to base their claims on a rationale of equity with others within the nation-state.

Whether a defining characteristic or a necessary social condition, a national movement must have a well developed middle class in which condition it differs from ethnic movements. Alba's (1975) anecdote of the Catalan workers who considered issues of language immaterial is representative. "We don't care if we are exploited in Castilian or Catalan," was their rejoinder, and they aligned themselves with the workers' unions and the socialist party rather than mobilise themselves along national lines. Without a stake in property, nationalism is not perceived to further one's self-interest.

Royce considers the similar situation of the Basques. The ETA, the Basque national organisation, is led by members of the middle class. The lower class perceived no advantage in a Basque movement and the concerns and economic interests of the elite are primarily state/national and international. The regional economic interests are in the control of the middle class who feel that they carry an unfair share of Spain's economic burden with no adequate compensation. "The important point in this case is that the impetus for ethnic nationalism came from the sector whose privileges and power depended on the economic well-being of the Basque provinces. Basque nationalism was the obvious way to maintain their position" (Royce, 1982:104).

The crucial difference between ethnic movement and ethnic nationalism is access to territory; without land one cannot talk about Basque nationalism. It is also access to territory that gives viability to a separatist movement. We can talk about Chicano nationalism but without territory such a movement, were it genuine, is doomed to failure. Mostly such phraseology masks conceptual confusion and what is intended is a label for what in fact is an ethnic movement fighting for equal access to goods and services (Oriol, 1979).

Ethnic nationalism and geographic nationalism share a great many features as is obvious from the previous discussion. The difference between them is probably the same as Hans Kohn outlines for "open" and "closed" nationalism (1968:66). In ethnic or closed nationalism the ethnic group is isomorphic with the nation-state. The emphasis is on the nation's autochtonous character, on the common origin and ancestral roots. In ethnic nationalism language can come to carry an importance way beyond any proportion of its communicative functions. The typical claim is that the deep thoughts and the soul of the nation can only be adequately expressed in the common mother tongue. Hitler's Germany was the most extreme form of ethnic nationalism with its emphasis on racial exclusivism and rootedness in the ancestral soil. (It is an interesting observation that the leaders of national movements need not be original members of that nation; Hitler and Stalin did not have their original roots in the state of which they became national leaders).

Kohn calls "open" nationalism a more modern form; it is territorially based (hence geographic nationalism) and features a political society, constituting a nation of fellow citizens regardless of ethnic descent. The so-called great immigration countries of Canada, Australia and the United States are good examples. As Kohn comments, they rejected the notion of a nation based on a common past, a common religion or a common culture. Instead "[Americans] owe their nationhood to the affirmation of the modern trends of emancipation, assimilation, mobility, and individualism." (1968:66)

In ethnic nationalism, language is a prime symbol of the nation but that is not necessarily so with geographic nationalism. Actually the United States does not even legally have a national language. Canada has two national languages but English and French are not thought of as national symbols of Canada. Rather, the maintenance of a common language was primarily undertaken for pragmatic LWC purposes. At the same time, although one cannot change one's genes but uses language to define its membership, as does Catalunya, learning the new language obviously held both practical and symbolic significance: knowing the national language became the hallmark of membership and in-group status. The combination of voluntary migration, the social incentives of in-group membership, and easy access to the new language has tended to result in very rapid bilingualism, often with consequent shift.

SOME CONSIDERATIONS FOR POLICY-MAKERS

M. Pompidou is said to have commented that a politician can ruin himself in three ways, with women, by taking bribes, and by planning. Women, he said, is the most pleasant way, gambling the quickest, and planning the surest. What this anecdote illustrates is the uncertainty inherent in planning at the national level, a fact recognised by any experienced politician who has at the same time to face its necessity.

I have argued in this paper that the uncertainty of language planning in education will be reduced if the planners consider the social context of language problems and especially the social, cultural and economic forces which contribute to language maintenance and shift. The most elegant educational policies for minority groups are doomed to failure if they go counter to prevailing social forces, especially the economic situation. This is as true for maintenance efforts in an economically incorporating group as it is for shift efforts to the national language for a socially marginal group. In OECD countries, the language planning efforts most likely to be successful are those which are supported by economic advantage (or similar social incentives) for the minority groups.

At the same time, planners need to acknowledge and respect the fact that there are other points of view on language maintenance and shift than the strictly pragmatic aspects argued in this paper. Religious groups take language maintenance seriously without any immediately obvious incentives, and so do a few ethnic groups. Nations vary in their actual tolerance of religious disparity, but the principle of religious freedom is well recognised in the OECD countries. Simply, it is one of respect for the self-determination of a group to hold the values and beliefs as it chooses. Similarly we should hold the truth self-evident that an ethnic group has a right to its own language if it so chooses. The point made in this paper that ethnic groups very rarely opt for continued language maintenance if the social conditions favor a shift to the national language is no counter-argument to the ethical principle of a right for minority groups to cultural self-determination. However, planners need to realise that the social costs of such continued language and culture maintenance tend to be high to the minority group members, and consequently parents and children may be at variance on this point, a situation which enormously complicates the setting of educational policy.

While moral decency dictates the language rights of minority groups, it does not necessarily follow that the state is under any obligation to support such rights economically nor does it follow that minority groups have a right to impose their language on the nation. The context of the situation and its historical development will hold the key to such problems, which are invariably political in nature rather then linguistic. Honest planning does not confuse the two.

While the social factors may at times seem of such overwhelming importance in influencing the outcomes of language planning that one is tempted to dismiss any efforts of setting educational language policies for minority group children as quite futile, this perception is far from accurate. National efforts or indifference in teacher training, textbook development and other implementational stages of national policies do make a difference. The implementation of educational policies for minority groups is the area where the difference between the various planning efforts actually shows up and where planning will have tangible effects on the lives of individual children. The implementation of educational language planning is a topic clearly outside the scope of this conference, but my point is that policy makers, political as well as educational, should be cognizant of what is feasible inside as well as outside the classroom. We know surprisingly little about how the features of implementation fit into any typology of language planning and bilingual education, which can help us predict and understand educational success or failure. Clearly, it is a possible next step for CERI/OECD to explore this aspect of "Educational Policies and the Minority Social Groups".

NOTES

1. I am following the terminology of the conference in using the term minority but want to point out that in dealing with language outcomes, subordinate status is frequently more important than mere numbers.

2. Most studies on bilingual education are done from a psychological perspective with the individual as the unit of research. In this paper I am solely interested in the language behaviour of groups.

3. By group bilingualism I mean a group where all or most of the individual members are bilingual. This is not necessarily true of countries who legally recognise more than one national language. For example, German speaking Swiss do not typically speak French and Italian as well.

4. I should make clear that Rodriguez is criticised for ideological reasons by proponents for bilingual education, not for the quality of his writing.

5. Segregation in the name of bilingual education is a serious concern.

6. Indeed, almost all group language behaviour can be explained on the assumption that people act in their own best and vested interest. This assumption does not always apply to religious groups, at least not in any obvious way. The Hassidim and the Amish both reject mainstream definition of "best interest" as socioeconomic advantage and limit access to education in English (although in different ways) as one means of instead focusing on "best interest" as inner salvation.

7. In the preceding paragraph he talks about the "invidious connotations of tribalism". Whatever those connotations are, social scientists have "scrapped" the term tribe altogether, which for my purposes I regret since there is no more accurate way to discuss language problems and social organisation in e.g. Somalia and Kurdistan.

8. Although it would be misleading to claim that structural-functional theory has given way to neo-marxism. The leading research paradigm on bilingual education remains a structural-functional perspective (albeit with notable exceptions [see Paulston 1980, 1982]) which at times leads to infelicitous claims because the very nature of ethnic groups in contact frequently tends towards conflict, and so group conflict theory may hold greater insight. On the other hand in situations marked by calm and basic good will, neo-marxist theory can lead to misleading interpretations and mischief-making claims.

9. I am here only talking from a viewpoint of educational efficiency. There are many other strong arguments for mother tongue teaching of an

affective nature (Gaarder, 1977; Pascual, 1976; Pialorsi, 1974; Sevilla-Casas et al., 1973). There is also the argument that languages are national resources which are being wasted without support in the educational systems (Fishman, 1972).

10. That life may be after death, as in Jihad, Holy War.

11. All linguists know that we owe the original impetus for our discipline to Panini who more than two thousand years ago devised a way of describing the sound system of Sanskrit to keep people from changing the pronunciation.

12. Dell Hymes (1972) has coined the term communicative competence to include not only the linguistic forms ofa language but also a knowledge of when, how and to whom it is appropriate to use these forms. Communicative competence includes the social meaning of the linguistic forms, and Hymes points out that were a man to stand on a street corner and utter all and only the grammatical sentences of English (Chomsky's definition of linguistic competence), he likely would be institutionalised.

13. The significance of symbols can change. During the Vietnamese war, to fly the flag in the United States meant that you supported the war, and flag-burning was common. During this time, the U.S. flag lost a great deal of its national symbolism, but this significance has been restored as was obvious during the last Olympics in Los Angeles.

BIBLIOGRAPHY

AKZIN B., 1964: State and Nation. Hutchinson, London.

ALATIS J.E. (ed.), 1978: International Dimensions of Bilingual Education. Georgetown University Press, Washington, D.C.

ALBA V., 1975: Catalonia: A Profile, Praeger, New York.

ALBERT M. and OBLER L., 1978: The Bilingual Brain, Academic Press, New York.

ALBO X., 1970: "Social Constraints on Cochabamba Quechua", in Latin American Studies Program. Dissertation Series, Cornell University, Ithaca, NY.

ASMAH HAJI O., 1979: Language Planning for Unity and Efficiency, Penerbit University, Kuala Lumpur, Malaysia.

BARTH F., 1969: Ethnic Groups and Boundaries, Little, Brown & Co., Boston, MA.

BARTON A.H. and LAZARSFELD P.F., 1961: "Some functions of qualitative analysis in social research". In LIPSET S.M. and SMELSER N.J. (Eds.). Sociology: The progress of a decade. Prentice Hall, Englewood Cliffs, N.J.

BAUMAN J.J., 1980: A Guide to Issues in Indian Language Retention, Center for Applied Linguistics, Washington, D.C.

BELL W. and FREEMAN W.E. (eds.), 1974: Ethnicity and Nation Building: Comparative, International and Historical Perspectives, Sage, Beverly Hills.

BENNETT J.W., 1975: The New Ethnicity: Perspectives from Ethnology, West Publishing Co., St. Paul, MN.

BENNETT J.W., 1975: "A Guide to the collection". In BENNETT J.W. (ed.), The New Ethnicity: Perspectives from ethnology, West Publishing Co., St. Paul, MN.

BOYD S., 1984: "Minoritets spraken ar borta om 25 ar?", in Invandrare och Minoriteter, 5-6, pp. 43-45.

BRATT PAULSTON C., 1982: Swedish Research and Debate about Bilingualism, National Swedish Board of Education, Stockholm.

BRATT PAULSTON C., 1980: Bilingual Education: Theories and Issues, Newbury House, Rowley, MA.

BRATT PAULSTON C., 1977: "Language and Ethnic Boundaries", in Papers from the first Nordic Conference on Bilingualism SKUTNABB-KANGAS T. (ed.), Helsingfors Universitet, Helsinki.

BRATT PAULSTON C., 1977: "Language and ethnicity in bilingual education: Some further comments", in Conference Proceedings: Bilingual Education: Ethnic Perspectives, National Service Center and the Community College of Philadelphia, Philadelphia, PA.

BRATT PAULSTON C., 1975: "Ethnic Relations and Bilingual Education: Accounting for Contradictory Data", in Proceedings of the first inter-American conference on Bilingual Education, TROIKE R. and MODIANO N. (eds.), Center for Applied Linguistics, Arlington, VA.

BRATT PAULSTON C., 1974: Implications of language learning theory for language planning: Concerns in Bilingual Education, Center for Applied Linguistics, Arlington, VA.

BRATT PAULSTON C., 1974: "Linguistic and Communicative Competence", in TESOL Quarterly, 8:4.

BRESNAHAN M.I., 1979: "English in the Philippines", in Journal of Communication, 29,2: 64-71.

BRUDNER L., 1972: "The Maintenance of Bilingualism in Southern Austria", in Ethnology, 11:1, 39-45.

CARILLO L., 1984: "Reflections on Rodriguez' Hunger of Memory", In TESOL, Newsletter, 18:5, 9-30.

CASINO E.S., 1980: "Ethnicity, Language Demands and National Development", In Ethnicity, April 1: 65-72.

CENTER FOR APPLIED LINGUISTICS, 1977: Bilingual Education: Current Perspectives, Vol. 1, Social Science, Arlington, VA;
Vol. 2, Linguistics;
Vol. 3, Law;
Vol. 4, Education;
Vol. 5, Synthesis.

CHEUNG Yuet-wah, 1981: "Effects of Parents on Ethnic Language Retention by Children: The Case of Chinese in Urban Canada", in Sociological Focus 14,1: 33-48.

CHURCHILL S., 1976: "Recherches récentes sur le bilinguisme et l'éducation des francophones minoritaires au Canada : l'exemple ontarien", in Bilingualism in Canadian education, Yearbook. Edited by M. Swain. Canadian Society for the Study of Education.

COHEN A. and SWAIN M., 1976: "Bilingual Education: The 'Immersion Model' in the North American Context", in TESOL Quarterly, 10.1.45-53.

COOPER R.L. (ed.), 1982: "A Framework for the Study of Language Spread", in Language Spread: Studies in Diffusion and Social Change, Center for Applied Linguistics, and Bloomington, IN. Indiana University Press.

COTTAM R.W., 1964: Nationalism in Iran, University of Pittsburgh Press, Pittsburgh, PA.

COUNCIL OF EUROPE, 1976: Factors which influence the integration of migrants' children into pre-school education in France, Council for Cultural Cooperation, Strasbourg.

CREWE W. (ed.), 1977: The English Language in Singapore, Eastern Universities Press, Singapore.

CUMMINS J., 1976: "The Influence of Bilingualism on Cognitive Growth: A Synthesis of Research Findings and Explanatory Hypothesis", in Working Papers on Bilingualism, No.9, 1-43.

DAS GUPTA J., 1974: "Ethnicity, Language Demands and National Development", in Ethnicity, April 1: 65-72.

DAS GUPTA J., 1970: Language Conflict and National Development: Group Politics and National Language Policy in India, University of California Press, Berkeley, CA.

DEUTSCH K.W., 1968: "The Trend of European Nationalism - The Language Aspect" in FISHMAN J.A. (ed.), Readings in the Sociology of Language, Mouton, The Hague.

DEUTSCH K.W., 1966: Nationalism and Social Communication, 2nd ed., MIT Press, Cambridge, MA.

DEUTSCH K.W., 1953: Nationalism and Social Communication: An Inquiry into the Foundations of Nationality, MIT Press, Cambridge, MA.

DEUTSCH K.W. and FOLTZ W.J. (eds.), 1963: Nation-building, Atherton Press, New York.

DEVOS G. and ROMANUCCI-ROSS L., 1975: "Ethnicity: Vessel of Meaning and Emblem of Contrast", in Ethnic Identity: Cultural Continuities and Change, Mayfield, Palo Alto, CA.

DE VRIES J., 1977: "Explorations in the Demography of Language: Estimation of Net Language Shift in Finland 1961-1970", in Acta Sociologica, 20-2, 145-153.

DIL A.S. (ed.), 1972: Language in Sociolinguistic Change: Essays by J.A. Fishman, Stanford University Press, Stanford, CA.

DOUHAN B., 1982: "The Walloons in Sweden", in American-Swedish Genealogical Review, 2:1-17.

DRESSLER W. and WODAK-LEODOLTER R. (eds.), 1977: "Language Death", Special Issue, in International Journal of the Sociology of Language, N° 12.

DREYER J.T., 1978: "Language Planning for China's Ethnic Minorities", in Pacific Affairs 5,1: 369-383.

EASTMAN C.W. and REECE T.C., 1981: "Associated Language: How Language and Ethnic Identify are Related", in General Linguistics 21, 2: 109-116.

ECKERT P., 1983: "The Paradox of National Language Movements", in Journal of Multilingual and Multicultural Development, 4:4, 289-300.

ELAZAR D. and FRIEDMAN M., 1976: Moving Up: Ethnic succession in America. Institute on Pluralism and Group Identity of the American Jewish Committee, New York.

EMERSON R., 1960: From Empire to Nation: The Rise to Self-Assertion of Asian and African Peoples, Harvard University Press, Cambridge, MA.

ENGLE P.L., 1975: The Use of Vernacular Languages in Education, Papers in Applied Linguistics, Bilingual Education Series N° 3, Center for Applied Linguistics, Arlington, VA.

ENLOE C., 1970: Multi-Ethnic Politics: The Case of Malaysia, University of California, Center for South and Southeast Asia Studies, Berkeley, CA.

EPSTEIN N., 1977: Language, Ethnicity and the Schools: Policy Alternatives for Bilingual-Bicultural Education, The George Washington University, Institute for Educational Leadership, Washington, DC.

ERWIN-TRIP S., 1973: Language Acquisition and Communicative Choice, University Press, Stanford, CA.

ESCOBAR A., 1972: Lenguaje y discriminacion social en America Latina, Milla Batres, Lima, Peru.

ESCOBAR A. (ed.), 1972: El reto del multilinguismo en el Peru, Peru-Problema No.9, Instituto de Estudios Peruanos, Lima, Peru.

FEINSTEIN O. (ed.), 1971: Ethnic Groups in the City, Heath Lexington Books, Lexington, Mass.

FERGUSON C.A., 1962: "The language factor in national development", in RICE (ed.), pp. 8-14.

FERGUSON C.A., 1959: "Diglossia", in Word, Vol. 15:325-40, reprinted in GIGLIOLI (ed.), 1972, pp. 232-51.

FISHMAN J.A., 1980: "Minority Language Maintenance and the Ethnic Mother Tongue School", in Modern Language Journal 64,2: 167-172.

FISHMAN J.A., 1978: Advances in the Study of Societal Multilingualism, Mouton, The Hague.

FISHMAN J.A., 1977: "Language, Ethnicity and Race". In SAVILLE-TROIKE (ed.), Proceedings of the Georgetown University Roundtable on Language and Linguistics: Linguistics and Anthropology, Georgetown University Press, Washington, DC.

FISHMAN J.A., 1977: "Language Maintenance", in Harvard Encyclopedia of American Ethnic Groups, Harvard University Press, Cambridge, MA.

FISHMAN J.A., 1974: Advances in Language Planning, Mouton, The Hague.

FISHMAN J.A., 1973: "Language modernization and planning in comparison with other types of national modernization and planning", in Language in Society, Vol. 2, n° 1, pp. 23-42.

FISHMAN J.A., 1972a: Advances in the Sociology of Language, Vols. 1 and 2. Mouton, The Hague.

FISHMAN J.A., 1972b: Language and Nationalism: Two Integrative Essays, Newbury House, Rowley, MA.

FISHMAN J.A., 1972c: Language in Sociocultural Change, Stanford University Press, Stanford, CA.

FISHMAN J.A., 1971: "National languages and languages of wider communication in the developing nations". In WHITELEY (ed.), pp. 27-56.

FISHMAN J.A., 1968: "Nationality-nationalism and nation-nationism". In FISHMAN J.A., FERGUSON C.A. and DAS GUPTA J. (eds.), Language Problems in Developing Nations, Wiley, New York.

FISHMAN J.A., 1966a: Language Loyalty in the United States, Mouton, The Hague.

FISHMAN J.A., 1966b: "Language Maintenance and Language Shift: The American Immigrant Case", in Sociologus, NS16:19-39.

FISHMAN J.A., COOPER R. and CONRAD A. (eds.), 1977: The Spread of English Newbury House, Rowley, MA.

FISHMAN J.A., FERGUSON C. and DAS GUPTA J. (eds.), 1968: Language Problems of Developing Nations, Wiley, New York.

GAARDER B., 1977: Bilingual Schooling and the Survival of Spanish in the United States, Newbury House, Rowley, MA.

GAL S., 1979: Language Shift: Social Determinants of Linguistic Change in Bilingual Austria, Academic Press, New York.

GALLAGHER C.F., 1963: "Language, Culture and Ideology: The Arab World" in Expectant Peoples: Nationalism and Development, SILVERT K.H. (ed.), Random House, 19-231, New York.

GANS H.J., 1979: "Symbolic Ethnicity: The future of ethnic groups and cultures in America", in Ethnic and Racial Studies, January, 2:1, 1-20.

GENDRON J.D., 1972: The position of the French language in Quebec, L'éditeur officiel de Quebec, Quebec.

GIGLIOLI P.P., 1972: Language and Social Context, Penguin Books, Harmondsworth, England.

GLAZER N., 1983: Ethnic Dilemmas, Harvard University Press, Cambridge, MA.

GLAZER N., 1966: "The process and problems of language maintenance: An integrative review" in Language Loyalty in the United States, FISHMAN J. (ed.), Mouton, The Hague.

GLAZER N. and MOYNIHAN D.P., 1975: "Introduction", in Ethnicity: Theory and Experience, Harvard University Press, Cambridge, MA.

GRANDGUILLAUME G., 1983: Arabisation et politique linguistique au Maghreb, Maisonneuve and Larose, Paris.

GREELY A., 1974: Ethnicity in the United States, Wiley, New York.

GROSJEAN F., 1982: Life with two languages: An Introduction to Bilingualism, Harvard University Press, Cambridge, MA.

GUMPERZ J., 1971: Language in Social Groups, Stanford University Press, Stanford, CA.

HARTFORD B., VALDMAN A. and FOSTER C.R., 1982: Issues in International Bilingual Education, Plenum Press, New York.

HAUGEN E., 1972: The Ecology of Language, Stanford University Press, Stanford, CA.

HAUGEN E., 1966: Language conflict and language planning: The case of modern Norwegian, Harvard University Press, Cambridge, MA.

HAUGEN E., 1966: "Dialect, Language, Nation", in American Anthropologist, 68:4, 922-935.

HEATH S.B., 1972: Telling Tongues: Language Policy in Mexico -- Colony to Nation, Teachers College Press, New York.

HORNBY P., 1977: Bilingualism: Psychological, Social and Educational Implications, Academic Press, New York.

HYMES D., 1972: "On Communicative Competence" in Sociolinguistics, PRIDE J.B. and HOLMES J. (eds.), Penguin, Harmondsworth, England.

INHASLY B., 1977: "Language and Religion in Conflict Between Ethnic Groups", in Internationales Asienforum 8, 3-4: 337-355.

ISAJIW W., 1974, "Definitions of ethnicity", in Ethnicity, 1, 111-124.

JAKOBSON R., 1968: "The Beginning of National Self-Determination in Europe". In FISHMAN J.A. (ed.), Readings in the Sociology of Language, Mouton, The Hague.

JARET C., 1979: "The Greek, Italian, and Jewish American Ethnic Press: A Comparative Analysis", in Journal of Ethnic Studies, 7,2: 47-70.

JERNUDD B. and DAS GUPTA J., 1971: "Towards a theory of language planning". In RUBIN J. and JERNUDD B. (eds.), pp. 195-215.

JESPERSEN O., 1946: Mankind, Nation and Individual from a Linguistic Point of View, G. Allen and Unwin, Ltd., London.

JONZ J.G., 1978: "Language and La Academia, If English works, por que se emplea Espagnol?", in Journal of Ethnic Studies, 5, 4: 65-79.

KABIR M., 1985: "Nationalistic Movements in Bangladesh", Unpublished doctoral dissertation, University of Pittsburgh.

KENNEDY C., 1984: Language planning and language education, Allen & Unwin, London.

KHLEIF B.B., 1979: "Language as Identity: Toward an Ethnography of Welsh Nationalism", in Ethnicity 6, 4: 346-357.

KHUBCHANDANI L.M., 1979: "Language planning processes for pluralistic societies", in Language Problems and Language Planning, Vol. 2, N° 3, pp. 141-59.

KIRSCH P., 1977: "Review of B. Schliben-Lange, Okzitanisch und Katalanish. Ein Beitrag zur Soziolinguistik zweier romanischen Sprachen", in International Journal of the Sociology of Language, Language Death, Vol. 12, 113-114.

KLOSS H. and McCONNELL G.D., 1985: Linguistic Composition of the Nations of the World: Europe and the USSR, University of Laval Press, Quebec.

KOENIG E.L., 1980: "Ethnicity: Key variable in a case study of language maintenance and language shift", in Ethnicity 7, 1: 1-14.

KOHN H., Nationalism, 1968 International Encyclopedia of the Social Sciences, 11, 63-70.

KOHN H., 1944: The Idea of Nationalism: A Study of its Origins and Background, Macmillan, New York.

KUHN T.S., 1970: The Structure of Scientific Revolutions, University of Chicago Press, Chicago.

LAMBERT W.E., 1972: Language, Psychology and Culture, Stanford University Press, Stanford, CA.

LAMBERT W.E. and TUCKER R., 1972: Bilingual Education of Children: The St. Lambert Experiment, Newbury House, Rowley, MA.

"Langue et Identité Nationale", 1977, in Recherches Sociologiques, VIII:1.

LEPAGE R.S., 1964: The National Language Question: Linguistic Problems of Newly Independent States, Oxford University Press, London.

LEWIS G., issue editor, 1977: International Journal of the Sociology of Language. Bilingual Education, Vol. 14.

LIEBERSON S., 1981: Language Diversity and Language Contact, Stanford University Press, Stanford, CA.

LIEBERSON S. and CURRY T.J., 1971: "Language Shift in the United States: Some Demographic Clues", in International Migration Review, 5:125-137.

LIEBERSON S., DALTO G., and JOHNSTON M.E., 1975: "The Course of Mother Tongue Diversity in Nations", in American Journal of Sociology, 81:1, 34-61.

LOPEZ D.E., 1976: "The Social Consequences of Chicano Home/School Bilingualism", in Social Problems, 24:2, 234-246.

LOPEZ-ARANGUREN E., 1981: "Linguistic Consciousness in a Multilingual Society: The Case of Spain", in Language Problems and Language Planning, 5:3, 264-278.

MACDOUGALL J.A. and FOON C.S., 1976: "English Language Competence and Occupational Mobility in Singapore", in Pacific Affairs, 49:2, 294-312.

MACKEY W.F., 1979: "Language and Policy and Language Planning", in Journal of Communication 29, 2: 48-53.

MACKEY W.F., 1976: Bilinguisme et contact des langues, Editions Klincksieck, Paris.

MACKEY W.F. and ORNSTEIN H. (eds.), 1979: Sociolinguistic Studies in Language Contact, Mouton, The Hague.

MACKINNON K.M., 1977: "Language Shift and Education: Conversation of Ethnolinguistic Culture amongst Schoolchildren of a Gaelic Community", in Linguistics 198: 31-55.

MARJAMA P., 1979: "Bilingual, Multicultural Education: An Anglo-American Point of View", in Hispania 62, 1: 115-117.

MANNHEIM B., 1984: "Una nacion acorrolada: Southern Peruvian Quechua language planning and politics in historical perspective", in Language in Society, 13, 291-309.

MCKINNEY J.C., 1957: "The polar view variables of type construction", in Social Forces, 35, 300-306.

MCKINNEY J.C., 1954: "Constructive typology: explication of a procedure". In DOBY J.T. (ed.), Introduction to Social Research, Stackpole, Harrisburg, PA.

MIRACLE A., ed. 1983: Bilingualism, University of Georgia Press, Athens, GA.

MOLDE B. and SHARP D., 1984: "Second International Conference on Minority Languages (special issue)", in Journal of Multilingual and Multicultural Development, 5:3-4.

MORRIS H.S., 1968: "Ethnic Groups", in International Encyclopedia of the Social Sciences.

MYRDAL G., 1974: "The Case against Romantic Ethnicity", in Center Magazine, 26-30.

NAHIR M., 1984: "Language Planning Goals: A Classification", in Language Problems and Language Planning, 8:3, pp. 294-327.

NELDE P.H., 1980: SprachKontakt und SprachKonflikt (Languages in Contact and Conflict), Franz Steiner Verlag, Wiesbaden.

NGUYEN L.T. and HENKIN A.B., 1982: "Vietnamese Refugees in the United States: Adaptation and Transitional Status", in Journal of Ethnic Studies 9, 4: 101-116.

OHANNESSIAN S., FERGUSON G. and POLOME E. (eds.), 1975: Language Surveys in Developing Nations, Center for Applied Linguistics, Arlington, VA.

OKSAAR E., 1972: "Bilingualism", in Current Trends in Linguistics, SEBECK T.A. (ed.), Mouton, The Hague.

ORIOL M., 1979: "Identité produite, identité instituée, identité exprimée: confusion des théories de l'identité nationale et culturelle", in Cahiers internationaux de sociologie, 6:6, 19-28.

OSSENBERG R.J., 1978: "Colonialism, Language and False Consciousness: the Mythology of Nationalism in Quebec", in Canadian Review of Sociology and Anthropology 15, 2: 145-147.

PAINTER M., 1983: "Aymara and Spanish in Southern Peru: The Relationship of Language to Economic Class and Social Identity". In MIRACLE A. (ed.), Bilingualism, University of Georgia Press, Athens, GA.

PANNU R.S. and YOUNG J.R., 1980: "Ethnic schools in three Canadian cities: A Study in Multiculturalism", in Alberta Journal of Educational Research 26, 4: 247-261.

PASCUAL H.W., 1976: "La educacion bilingue: retorica y realidad", in Defensa 4 and 5:4-7.

PATCH R.W., 1967: "La Parada, Lima's Market. Serrano and Criollo, the confusion of race with class", in AVFSR, West Coast South America Series, XIV:2, February, pp. 3-9.

PAULSTON R.G., 1977: "Separate Education as an Ethnic Survival Strategy: The Findlandssvenska Case", in Anthropology and Education Quarterly, VIII:3.

PAULSTON R.G., 1970: "Estratificacion social, poder y organizacion educacional: el caso peruano", in Aportes, vol. 16, pp. 92-111; also in English version "Sociocultural constraints on Peruvian educational development", in Journal of Developing Areas, vol. 5, No.3 (1971), pp. 401-15.

PFAFF C.W., 1981: "Sociolinguistic problems of immigrants: foreign workers and their children in Germany (a review article)" in Language in Society, 10:155-188.

PHILIPS S., 1970: "Acquisition of Rules for Appropriate Speech Usage". In ALATIS J. (ed.), Bilingualism and Language Contact, 21st Annual Roundtable, Georgetown University.

PIALORSI F., 1974: Teaching the Bilingual, University of Arizona Press, Tucson.

POOL J., 1972: "National development and language diversity". In FISHMAN (ed.), Vol. 2, pp. 213-30.

RA'ANAN U. and ROCHE J.P. (eds.), 1980: Ethnic Resurgence in Modern Democratic States, Pergamon Press, New York.

RAMOS M. et al.: The Determination and Implementation of Language Policy, Quezon City: Alemar-Phoenix.

RICE F.A. (ed.), 1962: Study of the Role of Second Languages in Asia, Africa and Latin America, Center for Applied Linguistics, Washington, D.C.

RICHMOND A.H., 1974: "Language, ethnicity and the problem of identity in a Canadian metropolis", in Ethnicity, 1, 175-206.

RODRIGUEZ R., 1982: Hunger of Memory, Grodine, Boston, MA.

ROSIER P. and HOLM W., 1980: The Rock Point Experience: A Longitudinal Study of a Navajo School Program, Center for Applied Linguistics, Washington, D.C.

ROYCE A.P., 1982: Ethnic Identity: Strategies of Diversity, in Indiana University Press, Bloomington, IN.

RUBIN J., 1968: National Bilingualism in Paraguay, Mouton, The Hague.

RUBIN J. and JERNUDD B., 1972: Can Language be Planned?, University of Hawaii Press, Honolulu, HI.

RUBIN J., JERNUDD B., DAS GUPTA J., FISHMAN J.A. and FERGUSON C. (eds.), 1977: Language Planning Processes, Mouton, The Hague.

SACHS L., 1983: Onda Ogat eller bakterier, Liber, Stockholm.

SANDBERG N.C., 1974: Ethnic Identity and Assimilation, Praeger, New York.

SAVARD J.G. and VIGNEAULT R., 1975: Les Etats multilingues: problèmes et solutions, Université Laval, Québec.

SCHERMERHORN R.A., 1974: "Ethnicity in the Perspective of the Sociology of Knowledge", in Ethnicity, April 1: 1-14.

SCHERMERHORN R.A., 1970: Comparative Ethnic Relations, Random House, New York.

SCHLIEBEN-LANGE B., 1977: "The Language Situation in Southern France", in International Journal of the Sociology of Language, 12:101-108.

SCOTTON C.M., 1972: Choosing a Lingua Franca in an African Capital. Linguistic Research Associates, Canada and Champaign, IL.

SEVILLA-CASAS et al., 1973: "Addenda of Chicanos and Boricuas" to Declaration of Chicago, IX International Congress of Anthropological and Ethnological Sciences, Sept. 7.

SHABAD G. and GUNTHER R., 1982: "Language, Nationalism and Political Conflict in Spain", in Comparative Politics 14, 4: 443-477.

SHAFER, BOYD C., 1976: Nationalism: Its Nature and Interpreters, American Historical Association, Washington, DC.

SHAFER, BOYD C., 1972: Faces of Nationalism, Harcourt, Brace, Jovanovich, New York.

SHILS E.A., 1975: Center and Periphery: Essays in Macrosociology, University of Chicago Press, Chicago.

SIGUAN M., ed., 1983: Lenguas y Educacion en el Ambito del Estado Espagnol, Ediciones de la Universidad de Barcelona, Barcelona.

SITHOLE, Ndabaningi, 1970: Obed Mutezo, the Midzimu Christian nationalist. Nairobi.

SMITH A.D., 1979: Nationalism in the Twentieth Century, New York University Press, New York.

SMITH A.D., 1971: Theories of Nationalism, Harper and Row, London.

SMITH R.P. and DENTON J.J., 1980: "The Effects of Dialect, Ethnicity and an Orientation to Sociolinguistics on the Perceptions of Teaching Candidates", in Educational Research Quarterly 5, 1: 70-79.

SNYDER L.L., 1976: Varieties of Nationalism: A Comparative Study, Dryden Press, Hinsdale, Ill.

SNYDER L.L., 1968: The New Nationalism, Cornell University Press, Ithaca.

SNYDER L.L., 1964: The Dynamics of Nationalism, Van Nostrand, Princeton, N.J.

SNYDER L.L., 1954: The Meaning of Nationalism, Rutgers University Press, New Brunswick, N.J.

SORENSEN A.P., Jr., 1972: "Multilingualism in the Northwest Amazon". In PRIDE J.B. and HOLMES J. (eds.), Sociolinguistics, Penguin Books, Harmondsworth, England.

SOTOMAYOR M., 1977: "Language, Culture and Ethnicity in Developing Self-Concept", in Social Casework 58, 4: 195-203.

SPOLSKY B. (ed.), 1977: "American Indian Bilingual Education", in International Journal of the Sociology of Language, Vol. 14.

SPOLSKY B. (ed.), 1972: The Language Education of Minority Children, Newbury House, Rowley, MA.

SPOLSKY B. and COOPER R. (eds.), 1978: Case Studies in Bilingual Education, Newbury House, Rowley, MA.

SPOLSKY B. and COOPER R. (eds.), 1977: Frontiers in Bilingual Education, Newbury House, Rowley, MA.

STEIN W., 1972: Mestizo Cultural Patterns: Culture and Social Structure in the Peruvian Andes, New York State University Press, Buffalo, NY.

STEINBERG S., 1977: "Ethnicity in the United States: A Sociological Perspective", in International Journal of Group Tensions, 7:3, 5, 130-144.

STRUBBS M., 1980: Language and Literacy, Routledge and Kegan Paul, London.

SWAIN M. (ed.), 1976: Bilingualism in Canadian Education: Issues and Research. Yearbook, Canadian Society for the Study of Education.

SWAIN M. and LAPKIN S., 1982: Evaluating Bilingual Education: A Canadian Case Study, Multilingual Matters, Ltd., Clevedon.

SWING E.S., 1982: "Education for Separatism: The Belgian Experience", in Issues in International Education, PLENUM, HARTFORD et al. (eds.), New York.

THOMASON S. and KAUFMAN T.: Language Contact, Creolization, and Genetic Linguistics (manuscript).

THOMPSON R.M., 1974: "Mexican American Language Loyalty and the Validity of the 1970 Census", in International Journal of the Sociology of Language, 2, 6-18.

TIRYAKIAN E.A., 1968: "Typologies", in International Encyclopedia of the Social Sciences, 16, 177-186.

TIVEY L. (ed.), 1981: The Nation-State, St. Martin's, New York.

TOSI A., 1984: Immigration and Bilingual Education: A case study of movement of population, language change and education within the EEC, Pergamon Press, Oxford.

UNESCO, 1984: "Mother tongue and educational attainment", in Prospects XIV:1.

VAN DEN BERGHE P.L., 1970: Race and Ethnicity: Essays in Comparative Sociology, Basic Books, New York.

VAN DEN BERGHE P.L., 1968: "Language and 'Nationalism' in South Africa". In FISHMAN J.A., FERGUSON C.A.and DAS GUPTA J. (eds.), Language Problems in Developing Nations, Wiley, New York.

VELTMAN C., 1983: Language Shift in the United States, Mouton, The Hague.

VERDOODT A., ed., 1978: "Belgium", in International Journal of the Sociology of Language, Vol. 15.

VERDOODT A., 1972: "The Differential Impact of Immigrant French Speakers on Indigenous German Speakers: A Case Study in the Light of two Theories". In FISHMAN J.A. (ed.), Advances in the sociology of language, Part II, Mouton, The Hague.

WALLACE A., 1966: "Revitalization movements", in American Anthropologist 59.

WEINREICH U., 1968: Languages in Contact, Mouton, The Hague.

WEINSTEIN B., 1983: The Civic Tongue: Political Consequences of Language Choices, Longmans, New York.

WHITELEY W.H.W., 1971: Language Use and Social Change, Oxford University Press, London.

WHITELEY W.H.W., 1969: Swahili -- The Rise of a National Language, Methuen, London.

YOUNG C., 1976: Politics of Cultural Pluralism, University of Wisconsin Press, Madison, WI.

Commentary by M. Gilbert Grandguillaume

Maître Assistant to the Ecole des Hautes Etudes en Sciences Sociales, Paris

I should first like to say how interested I was in Professor Paulston's paper. Her mastery and experience of the subject of bilingualism are amply demonstrated by her previous publications (1). Her paper brought out very well some of the central points of our discussion, namely:

-- The connection between language planning and social context, due to two factors involved in language shift: economic advantage and the social prestige attached to language acquisition;

-- The distinctive roles of ethnicity and nationalism as regards the social rallying around a language considered as a symbol;

-- The conditions determining language maintenance, spread or shift to the dominant language, with bilingualism, which is rarely balanced, favouring absorption of the mother tongue in the dominant language. Professor Paulston laid stress on the causes of contact and de facto bilingualism: voluntary migration or an imposed presence, as with colonisation. The latter, because of the opposition of the colonised community, acts as a check on the disappearance of the mother tongue. In a bilingual situation, the maintenance of specific social and cultural structures is another factor in resistance by the mother tongue.

All of these topics, and many others that I do not mention, can provide food for a highly interesting discussion. Professor Paulston restricts herself to linguistics and educational planning, and one of her footnotes (No.9) indicates that what is "affective" has been left aside. I do not fault her for this but, in the context of our meeting, the realities of the problems raised warrant our overstepping the boundaries of our specialities. It is in this sense that I should like to develop her observations on two points: the case of Arabic, and the question of mother tongue and native culture.

The Arabic-speaking countries

As Professor Paulston emphasized, the fundamental factors (economic advantage and social standing) play an indeniably important role, but they do not suffice to explain the full range of linguistic developments. Stress should be given to the cultural reality, grounded in a historical tradition that is responsible for all the "Islamic awakenings" that abound in the columns of the press (and which at least serve to prove that Islam is not asleep).

The cultural reality includes a double source of identity:

-- A universal, Islamic identity, so diffuse however that it cannot be perceived as a distinct reference;

-- Personal, family, regional and national roots, expressive of a local culture.

It happens that each of these sources is sustained by a language: classical Arabic, corresponding basically to the Islamic identity; and a mother tongue (Arab dialect or, in some parts of North Africa, Berber) which, in the past, had an exclusively local connotation but now, as the communities have expanded, has spread its "settings". This persistent state of bilingualism demonstrates how multiple sources of identity can have a parallel in language.

In modern times, the linguistic frame has stretched to take in a third, foreign, language (French or English) linked to colonisation or development. In a way, this other language has taken over the universalist function previously exercised by Arabic. Associated with modernity and legitimised by development, this modern language introduces an extra source of identity, to the point where the national government attempt to incorporate it into a modernised Arabic supposed to be the official language (2).

These multiple linguistic connotations may also be approached from the standpoint of the social groups who speak the languages. To the extent that they are current and employed in a situation where functions and contexts are not cut off from one another, each language works upon each other one, and their connotations become more and more interwoven. Because of this, the social groups dispose of "linguistic instruments", ever more supple and better adapted to the social purposes to which they are put. As Michel de Certeau remarks (3), these instruments, insofar as they incessantly recreate it, represent the groups' authentic identity.

All of this presupposes, however, that the underlying mechanisms of such creativeness have not been jammed by a prohibition against the native language and culture.

Mother tongue and native culture

Mother tongue is to be understood as the very earliest language, unlike any other, in that it is the vehicle for an individual's first subjection to cultural dictates and his first experience of social behaviour. Compared with later language (other languages will necessarily follow, even though they may fall within the same linguistic register), the mother tongue certainly fulfils the same bridging function of reflexiveness and extraversion that D.W. Winnicott assigns to the face of the mother in child development (4).

The problem with the mother tongue, therefore, is not to cling to it but to transcend it by accepting other languages beyond those of the family -- the languages of the various external situations in which the individual must make himself recognised or, if one prefers, the various fields of knowledge which he must penetrate.

The obstacles in this connection are due possibly to over- or under-fixation with respect to the mother tongue. Over-fixation occurs when an enveloping family environment shuts out the call of the outside world or, in the case of a community, when chauvinistic glorification of the mother tongue appears to proscribe use of the other language. Conversely, an insecure fixation on or relation to the mother tongue invests it with a sense of loss (see M. de Certeau), a fantasy of a lost paradise that leads to an obsession with the past, as Jacques Hassoun has written (5). In its individual variant, this occurs when the parental language -- either its vocabulary or its cultural substructure -- is not transmitted. It happens on the social plane when the mother tongue is unappreciated, despised, or treated as thought it did not exist (as in the education systems of the North African countries, or possibly for immigrants in France). The process has something in common with the frequent and widely studied cases where an official language is forced on a population by the devaluation of its vernacular tongues (6).

At this point, I should like to come back to a fundamental question raised by Professor Paulston in her paper: to what extent does knowledge of the mother tongue enable a person to learn other languages? There are a number of ways of interpreting this question. At the "technical" level, it could be taken as asking how far knowledge of the mother tongue can help in learning the "useful" language, the one which will allow a foreigner to assimilate economically and socially, a child to succeed at school. The problem posed -- and this I took to be Professor Paulston's meaning -- is whether it is of use or not to teach the mother tongue in the classroom.

The question can, however, be read at a more challenging level: how much does the relationship with the mother tongue act as an obstacle to a relationship with other languages? This can be stated in cultural terms: does fidelity to one's native culture act as a help or a hindrance to one's accession to other cultures? Seen from this angle, the problem clearly predates schooling, although the school may be confronted with it in the following form: how may the conditions for transcendence be achieved when a situation of inhibition exists?

On the subject of inhibition, I should like to digress for a moment to express my agreement with those, like Chris Mullard here present, who refuse to lay every problem concerning migrants at the door of cultural factors. For several years now, the work of Jim Cummins has stressed the importance of the social factor in the various manifestations of bilingualism. In France, the surveys conducted by the CREDIF have shown that the curves for failure at school follow socio-professional patterns more than ethnic origins. Again, in Françoise Henry-Lorcerie's evaluation report (7) on a pilot experiment in the Bouches-du-Rhône department, the command of French revealed by the children of migrants is comparable to that of children from similar social backgrounds. Such constant reminders of reality should put an end to the false claims made for the impact of cultural or ethnic factors.

After this comment, I repeat that the inhibition connected with origins is something that precedes school education but which the school is liable to encounter. I am less concerned, however, with providing recipes for action than with trying to understand a situation that can have a deleterious effect on schooling.

The inhibition, which typically expresses itself through failure at school may be considered from two different angles:

- -- It may be psychological in character, in which case it may be traced to particular family circumstances rather than to cultural and linguistic differences (and may be treated on an individual basis);

- -- Another case may implicate society itself. This occurs when the mother tongue was handicapped in regard to the normal integration process I mentioned above. In the North African example, I am thinking particularly of the colonial situation followed by independence, in which the authorities have tended to deny recognition to the mother tongue and to banish it from the educational system, thus running the risk of extinguishing the creativeness inherent in the mother tongue, as a recent study on Algeria by El Hadi Saada makes clear (8).

When this happens, some means of recognition must obviously be imagined for restoring the mother tongue to a status where it can be transcended. This is a necessary condition both for satisfactory school performance and for integration into a world beyond the immediate family circle, as every human society requires. It hardly needs to be said that such recognition does not obligatorily entail teaching the mother tongue and culture.

Recognition should not be regarded as a therapy reserved for migrants. It should, instead, be applied to the whole educational community which then becomes an area where all difference is recognised and valued by what is said more than by what is done. The details of this recognition have been referred to on several occasions during our meeting, notably in the contribution by Michel de Certeau. Beliefs in the cohesiveness of cultural systems and the purity of origins should be superseded by the recognition of diversity.

Difference in other people is recognisable only if one recognises it in oneself, without fear. The problem lies in getting our society and school system to admit their diversity, to stop denying their true plural nature and to recognise its riches, in the individual self and in others. Mikhail Bakhtine's idea of "dialoguism" might be mentioned here -- Tzvetan Todorov (9) uses it to characterise the duality of languages and discourse, which he relates both to "the coexistence of cultural models within a single society" and "the internal multiplicity of personality".

Such a recognition of diversity as a reality and an asset could promote a climate of open-mindedness in the schools and society. This, in turn, would enable both migrants and nationals to surmount the obstacle to self-fulfilment represented by rejection of their native specificity.

NOTES AND REFERENCES

1. BRATT PAULSTON C., Bilingual Education, Theories and Issues, Newbury House Publishers Inc., Massachusetts, 1980.

2. As discussed in my book, Arabisation et politique linguistique au Maghreb, Maisonneuve et Larose, Paris, 1983.

3. DE CERTEAU M., "Schooling for Diversity", chapter 7 in this volume.

4. WINNICOTT D.W., Playing and Reality, Ass. Book Publishers Ltd., London, 1975.

5. HASSOUN J., "Eloge de la dysharmonie", in Du bilinguisme, Denoël, Paris, 1985.

6. We may quote, for example, DE CERTEAU M., JULIA D., REVEL J., Une politique de la langue, Gallimard, Paris, 1975.

7. HENRY-LORCERIE F., Scolarisation des enfants d'immigrés et enseignement interculturel, rapport d'évaluation, typescript, 1985 (on the pilot experiment in the Bouches-du-Rhône, 1979-1982, CCE, French Ministry of Education).

8. EL HADI S., Les langues et l'école, bilinguisme inégal dans l'école algérienne, Peter Lang, Berne, 1983.

9. TODOROV T., "Bilinguisme, dialogisme et schizophrénie", in Du bilinguisme, op.cit

12. THEORY AND POLICY IN BILINGUAL EDUCATION

by
Jim CUMMINS
Director, National Heritage Language Resource Unit,
The Ontario Institute for Studies in Education

INTRODUCTION

Goals of the Paper

This paper addresses the issue of what policy-makers need to know in order to institute educational programmes that promote high levels of academic achievement and a secure cultural identity for students in multi-ethnic societies. Specifically, what cognitive, academic and personal consequences can be expected from various forms of bilingual education instituted in different sociopolitical contexts? These contexts vary enormously and thus the language planning issues are highly complex. As pointed out in an article prepared for the National Seminar on Multicultural Education organised jointly by the CERI and the Institute for Ethnic Studies of Ljubljana, in Ljubljana from 15th to 17th October 1985:

> "There is no consensus among scientists, educators, government officials and politicians, or in the eyes of public opinion concerning the new directions to be adopted. These divergencies are hardly surprising. The social, historical, cultural and institutional contexts vary so greatly that differences of opinion are inevitable".

In his paper (Chapter 8), Glazer makes a similar point with respect to the debate in the United States regarding the effectiveness of bilingual education in promoting academic achievement for linguistic minority groups. He notes that there is no consensus among policy makers, educators, or the general public regarding the educational validity of bilingual programmes. Because there is no decisive answer in the research, he argues, "political and social judgements, which will in any case tend to prevail, should prevail". The final conclusion of Glazer's paper is worth quoting because it is diametrically opposed to the conclusion in the present paper:

> "In the middle 1970s national policy (in the United States) favored the use of native languages and of distinctive approaches making use of the distinctive culture of each group. But the results of our efforts to overcome differences in educational achievement using such approaches are not encouraging. Majority and minority alike, in part for different reasons, in part for the same reasons, now come together in agreement on traditional approaches to education as the most effective means of raising the educational achievement of minority groups and groups of different language and cultural background".

In other words, because both minority and majority groups now agree that improved academic achievement should be the primary educational goal for minority groups, traditional instructional approaches using the majority language (English) are favoured over those that make use of the minority group's language and culture.

A major goal of this paper is to argue, contrary to public opinion in many countries and to Glazer's analysis, that there is an empirical and theoretical basis for educational policy-decisions in this area. In other words, a psycho-educational knowledge base exists whereby policy-makers can predict, with considerable accuracy, at least some of the outcomes of different types of bilingual education programs in a wide variety of contexts. The present paper will make this psycho-educational knowledge base explicit and will also examine the sociological conditions under which different outcomes can be predicted.

Organization of the Paper

It is first necessary to clarify the role of theory in the policy-making process. In the United States, for example, the widespread confusion about the effects of bilingual education programs for minority students is largely due to an almost total absence of concern for theory in the formation of educational policy. Political and social judgements prevail not, as Glazer suggests, because there is little consistent research evidence, but because the relationship between research, theory and policy has been ignored.

This is followed by a brief outline of a logical sequence that might be followed in the planning and implementation of bilingual programs. The importance of both theory and research in addition to political considerations is emphasized.

Three psycho-educational principles, for which there is considerable evidence, are then reviewed and their implications for bilingual education policy discussed. These principles appear applicable to virtually all forms of bilingual education including programs aimed at reversing educational failure among minority students (e.g. home language programs for Finns in Sweden) as well as programs that are intended to enrich students whose educational development is not in jeopardy [e.g. middle-class students in second language (L2) immersion programs].

However, in order to understand the causes of school failure for many minority students, much more than just linguistic factors must be taken into account. The sociological context of dominant-dominated group relationships must be examined in relation to the educational program (Mullard, Chapter 9 in this volume). It will be argued that in order to promote academic and personal development for minority students, the patterns of interaction between educators and students in the school must reverse the established pattern of dominant -- dominated group relations in the society at large. Active incorporation of the language and culture of the minority within the school program is just one of a number of interventions that are required to empower rather than to disable minority students within the school context.

RESEARCH, THEORY, AND POLICY IN BILINGUAL EDUCATION

The Relation between Theory and Policy

A major reason why many policy-makers and educators regard the research basis for bilingual education as minimal or even non-existent is that they have failed to realise that data or "facts" from bilingual programmes become interpretable for policy purposes only within the context of a coherent theory. It is the theory rather than the individual research findings that permits the generation of predictions about programme outcomes under different conditions. Research findings themselves cannot be directly applied across contexts. For example, the fact that kindergarten and grade 1 Punjabi-background students in a bilingual programme in Bradford, England, learned English just as successfully as a control group in a traditional English-only programme (Rees, 1981) tells us very little about what might happen in the case of Greek background students in Bradford or Hispanic students in the United States. Similarly, the findings of French immersion programmes for majority students in Canada cannot be directly applied to policy decisions regarding programmes for minority students in the United States. Yet clearly the accumulation of research findings does have relevance for policy. This relevance is achieved by means of the integration of the findings within a coherent theory from which predictions regarding programme outcomes under different conditions can be generated.

In short, although research findings cannot be applied directly across contexts, theories are almost by definition applicable across contexts in that the validity of any theoretical principle is assessed precisely by how well it can account for the research findings in a variety of contexts. If a theory cannot account for a particular set of research findings, then it is an inadequate or incomplete theory.

Theory and the U.S. Bilingual Education Policy Debate

Two opposing theoretical assumptions have dominated the U.S. policy debate regarding the effectiveness of bilingual education in promoting minority students' academic achievement. These assumptions are essentially hypotheses regarding the causes of minority students' academic failure and each is associated with a particular form of educational intervention designed to reverse this failure. In support of transitional bilingual education where some initial instruction is given in students' first language (L1), it is argued that students cannot learn in a language they do not understand, thus, a home-school language switch will almost inevitably result in academic retardation unless initial content is taught through L1 while students are acquiring English. In other words, minority students' academic difficulties are attributed to a "linguistic mismatch" between home and school.

The opposing argument is that if minority students are deficient in English, then they need as much exposure to English as possible. Students' academic difficulties are attributed to insufficient exposure to English in the home and environment. Thus, bilingual programmes which reduce this exposure to English even further appear illogical and counterproductive in that they seem to imply that less exposure to English will lead to more

The following passage from a New York Times editorial (October 10, 1981) is typical:

> "The Department of Education is analysing new evidence that expensive bilingual education programmes don't work... Teaching non-English speaking children in their native language during much of their school day constructs a roadblock on their journey into English. A language is best learned through immersion in it, particularly by children... Neither society nor its children will be well served if bilingualism continues to be used to keep thousands of children from quickly learning the one language needed to succeed in America."

Viewed as theoretical principles from which predictions regarding programme outcomes can be derived, the "linguistic mismatch" and "insufficient exposure" hypotheses are each patently inadequate. The former is refuted by the French immersion data which clearly demonstrate that for English background students in Canada a home-school language switch results in no academic retardation. The success of a considerable number of minority students under home-school language switch conditions similarly refutes the linguistic mismatch hypothesis.

The "insufficient exposure" hypothesis fares no better. Virtually every bilingual programme that has ever been evaluated (including French immersion programmes) show that students instructed through a minority language for all or part of the school day perform, over time, at least as well in the majority language (e.g. English in North America) as students instructed exclusively through the majority language. The fact that two such patently inadequate theoretical assumptions have dominated the bilingual education policy debate in the United States illustrates the power of politics over logic. It also shows the necessity of integrating theory explicitly into the decision-making process. One possible decision-making sequence or "flow-chart" with respect to bilingual education policy in different contexts is presented in the next section.

A Framework for Theoretically-Based Decision-Making in Bilingual Education

Any language planning process will first identify a particular problem (e.g. underachievement of certain groups of minority students) and then focus upon solutions to this problem. These solutions will involve either explicit or implicit hypotheses about the causes of the problem (e.g. "linguistic mismatch" or "insufficient exposure" to the school language) followed by the identification of alternative goals and means to resolve the problem. An idealised (and undoubtedly over-simplified) sequence for this type of decision-making is presented in Figure 1.

The decision-making process can be illustrated by comparing the highly successful implementation of French immersion programmes in Canada during the late 1960s and 1970s with the generally much less successful implementation of bilingual programmes for linguistic minority students in the United States during the same period (1). In both situations the general perceived problem was similar, namely, lack of student proficiency in a socially-valued language (French in Canada and English in the United States). A major difference,

Figure 1

SEQUENCE FOR ANALYSING LANGUAGE PROBLEMS IN EDUCATION

1. EXAMINE PERCEIVED PROBLEMS
2. GENERATE HYPOTHESES ABOUT CAUSES IN LIGHT OF THEORY AND RESEARCH
3. PLAN SOLUTIONS TO PROBLEMS: IDENTIFY GOALS AND MEANS
4. IMPLEMENT INTERVENTIONS TO RESOLVE PROBLEM
5. MONITOR (OR INITIATE) RESEARCH RELEVANT TO THEORY ABOUT CAUSES OF PROBLEM
6. EVALUATE SUCCESS OR FAILURE OF INTERVENTION
7. COMMUNICATE INTERVENTION RESULTS TO POLICY-MAKERS, EDUCATORS AND PUBLIC

however, was that in the United States situation, poor academic achievement in English was the major identified problem.

With respect to causes of the problem, sociopolitical considerations have been largely ignored in the policy debates. However, as Paulston (see Chapter 11 in this volume) has frequently pointed out, the major causes of most language planning problems are sociopolitical in nature with psychoeducational and linguistic factors acting as intervening variables. By the same token, the effects of educational interventions aimed at resolving such problems can usually be understood only in terms of their interaction with sociopolitical factors. In other words, interventions based on linguistic or psychoeducational hypotheses in isolation from the context of inter-ethnic group relations will frequently fail to produce the predicted outcomes. This issue is considered in a later section. Here we are primarily concerned with policy-making process as it has evolved in the Canadian and United States situations.

In the Canadian situation, the writings of the Montreal neurosurgeon Wilbur Penfield were influential. Penfield (1965) had speculated (partly on the basis of neuropsychological evidence) that there is an optimal prepubertal period for acquiring an L2 and our language learning capacity declines after this period; he also suggested that second languages should be taught by what he called "the mother's method" by which he meant used as a medium of communication in the classroom to permit children to acquire their L2 in much the same way as they acquired their L1. It is not difficult to see how these hypotheses gave rise to early French immersion programmes.

In the United States situation, as discussed previously, linguistic hypotheses ("linguistic mismatch" and "insufficient exposure") have tended to dominate the debate regarding causes of linguistic minority students' underachievement. The linguistic mismatch hypothesis tends to give rise to "quick-exit" transitional bilingual programmes, whereas the insufficient exposure hypothesis justifies English-only programmes, often with some English-as-a-second-language (ESL) instruction. It is at this point that the planning process begins to break down in the United States context since neither of these hypotheses is consistent with the research data. Thus, it is not surprising that programmes implemented on the basis of these hypotheses have not been particularly successful.

In Canada, at the third stage, the goals and means of immersion programmes were clearly defined and problematic. This, however, was not the case with bilingual education in the United States. All parties agreed with the goal of improved English academic skills but many minority advocates also desired bilingual programmes to further the development of a pluralistic society through an emphasis on native culture and language maintenance. This goal was vehemently resisted by many "mainstream" educators and policy-makers. During the late 1970s, the suspicion grew that bilingual programmes were in reality intended only to promote Hispanic political and economic goals (even Hispanic separatism à la Québec) under the guise of developing students' English language skills. Thus, lack of consensus on goals and means compounded difficulties created by questionable psychoeducational assumptions used to justify bilingual education.

Problems of implementation followed naturally from the confused psychoeducational rationale and disputed goals of bilingual education in the

United States. An enormous variety of programmes resulted, ranging from considerable use of L1 in the early grades to virtually no use of L1. Some programmes appeared to work extremely well, others much less so. By contrast, immersion programmes started off on a very small scale with the St. Lambert programme in the Montreal area (Lambert and Tucker, 1972) and a team of researchers monitored the progress of students through the grades. No further implementation was carried out until the initial results of this evaluation were available.

In both the United States and Canadian contexts, a considerable amount of evaluative research was carried out to assess the effects of the bilingual programmes. In the case of the immersion programmes, the initial St. Lambert programme was thoroughly evaluated over a period of seven years and students were also followed through high school and beyond. As the immersion programme spread to other areas, large-scale evaluations were also carried out to assess the consistency of findings with those of the St. Lambert programme (e.g. Swain and Lapkin, 1982). One of the reasons for this was continued doubts among educators and parents that children could spend so much instructional time through French with no negative consequences for their English academic skills. Although some problematic issues have emerged (Cummins, 1984), the weight of research evidence has overwhelmingly confirmed the initial St. Lambert findings. Over time, theoretical principles emerged which could account for the absence of negative effects on English academic skills (Cummins, 1984 and below). It is interesting to note that, with respect to the initial theoretical assumptions underlying immersion, the research has refuted Penfield's hypothesis of an optimal age for language learning in that students in late immersion programmes (usually beginning at grade 7, age 12-13) also succeed very well.

The story has been very different in the evaluations of bilingual programmes in the United States. Much of the research carried out was poorly designed (Baker and de Kanter, 1981), in part because of the much more complicated sociopolitical and educational context. For example,students were frequently exited from bilingual programmes at very early stages (e.g. after one year) with the result that if students continued to perform poorly in English academic skills it was unclear whether this was due to premature exit to an all-English programme or to the lack of effectiveness of bilingual education. Evaluations also tended to be atheoretical in that theory-based predictions regarding outcomes were seldom generated and tested. Thus, evaluators attempted to assess the "effectiveness" of bilingual education without any well-articulated hypotheses regarding how long it would take minority students to acquire age-appropriate levels of English academic skills and under what sociopolitical and instructional conditions (e.g. length and intensity of L1 instruction)(2).

In Canada, the overall conclusion of immersion programme evaluations is that the programmes have been a resounding success and this has been effectively communicated to policy-makers, parents and educators. The result has been a huge increase in parental demand for French immersion programmes which now have an enrolment of more than 120 000 students and are offered in every Canadian province. Sociopolitical and administrative problems have emerged as a result of the increased demand for immersion programmes (e.g. concerns by minority francophones of increased competition for bilingual jobs, layoff of teachers who do not speak French, etc). However, these problems have not slowed the momentum of immersion.

By contrast, as Glazer (Chapter 8) indicates, bilingual programmes in the United States are perceived much more equivocably by policy-makers and educators. This perception was reinforced by the research review conducted by Baker and de Kanter (1981) which concluded that transitional bilingual programmes overall were not much more successful than English-only programmes in promoting minority students' achievement. This review reflects the major problems of transitional bilingual education in that it is almost completely atheoretical and consequently ignores the consistent patterns that do emerge in the research data (see below).

In summary, a framework has been presented for policy-making in the area of bilingual education (and other areas of educational language planning). The importance of generating and evaluating predictions from a coherent theory has been emphasized as a central, but frequently neglected, aspect of rational policy-making. Particularly in the case of academic difficulties involving minority groups, sociopolitical rather than psychoeducational causes are likely to be more fundamental. Thus, theory that ignores these sociopolitical influences is unlikely to result in effective educational policy or intervention.

With respect to the effects of bilingual education on students' cognitive and academic development, some consistent theoretical principles do emerge from the research and these are considered in the next section.

PRINCIPLES OF BILINGUAL ACADEMIC DEVELOPMENT

The Additive Bilingualism Enrichment Principle

In the past many students from minority backgrounds have experienced difficulties in school and have performed worse than monolingual children on verbal I.Q. tests and on measures of literacy development. These findings led researchers in the period between 1920 and 1960 to speculate that bilingualism caused language handicaps and cognitive confusion among children. Some research studies also reported that bilingual children suffered emotional conflicts more frequently than monolingual children. Thus, in the early part of this century bilingualism acquired a doubtful reputation among educators, and many schools redoubled their efforts to eradicate minority children's first language on the grounds that this language was the source of children's academic difficulties.

However, virtually all of the early research involved minority students who were in the process of replacing their L1 with the majority language, usually with strong encouragement from the school. Many minority students in North America were physically punished for speaking their L1 in school. Thus, these students usually failed to develop adequate literacy skills in this language and many also experienced academic and emotional difficulty in school. This, however, was not because of bilingualism but rather because of the treatment they received in schools which essentially amounted to an assault on their personal identities.

More recent studies suggest that far from being a negative force in children's personal and academic development, bilingualism can positively affect both intellectual and linguistic progress. A large number of studies have reported that bilingual children exhibit a greater sensivity to linguistic meanings and may be more flexible in their thinking than are monolingual children (Cummins, 1984a).

Most of these studies have investigated aspects of children's metalinguistic development; in other words, children's explicit knowledge about the structure and functions of language itself. A problem in interpreting these studies is that the notion of "metalinguistic development" is not yet clearly defined in the literature. Bialystok and Ryan (1985) have recently attempted to clarify this notion in terms of two underlying dimensions: namely, children's analysed knowledge of language and their control over language. They predicted that bilingualism would enhance children's control over and ability to manipulate language but not their analysed knowledge of language. These predictions regarding the likely consequences of bilingualism for metalinguistic development have generally been borne out in a number of studies (Bialystok, 1984).

In general, it is not surprising that bilingual children should be more adept at certain aspects of linguistic processing. In gaining control over two language systems, the bilingual child has had to decipher much more language input than the monolingual child who has been exposed to only one language system. Thus, the bilingual child has had considerably more practice in analysing meanings than the monolingual child.

The evidence is not conclusive as to whether this linguistic advantage transfers to more general cognitive skills. McLaughlin's review of the literature, for example, concludes that:

> "It seems clear that the child who has mastered two languages has a linguistic advantage over the monolingual child. Bilingual children become aware that there are two ways of saying the same thing. But does this sensitivity to the lexical and formal aspects of language generalize to cognitive functioning? There is no conclusive answer to this question -- mainly because it has proven so difficult to apply the necessary controls in research" (1984, p. 44).

Hakuta and Diaz (1985) and Diaz (in press) have recently reported evidence that bilingualism may positively affect general cognitive abilities in addition to metalinguistic skills. Rather than examining bilingual monolingual differences, Hakuta and Diaz employed a longitudinal within-group design in which Hispanic primary school children's developing L2 (English) skills were related to cognitive abilities with the effect of L1 abilities controlled. The sample was relatively homogenous both with respect to socio-economic status (SES) and educational experience (all were in bilingual programmes). L2 skills were found to be significantly related to cognitive and metalinguistic abilities. The positive relationship was particularly strong for Raven's Progressive Matrices -- a non-verbal intelligence test; further analyses suggested that if bilingualism and intelligence are causally related, bilingualism is most likely the causal factor.

An important characteristic of the bilingual children in the more recent studies (conducted since the early 1960s) is that, for the most part, they were developing what has been termed an <u>additive</u> form of bilingualism (Lambert, 1975); in other words, they were adding a second language to their repertory of skills at no cost to the development of their first language.

Consequently, these children were in the process of attaining a relatively high level of both fluency and literacy in their two languages. The children in these studies tended to come either from majority language groups whose first language was strongly reinforced in the society (e.g. English-speakers in French immersion programmes) or from minority groups whose first languages were reinforced by bilingual programmes in the school. Minority children who lack this educational support for literacy development in L1 frequently develop a subtractive form of bilingualism in which L1 skills are replaced by L2. Under certain sociopolitical conditions (see below) these children fail to develop adequate levels of literacy in either language.

This pattern of findings suggested that the level of proficiency attained by bilingual students in their two languages may be an important influence on their academic and intellectual development (Cummins, 1979). Specifically, there may be a threshold level of proficiency in both languages which students must attain in order to avoid any negative academic consequences and a second, higher, threshold necessary to reap the linguistic and intellectual benefits of bilingualism and biliteracy.

Diaz (in press) has questioned the threshold hypothesis on the grounds that the effects of bilingualism on cognitive abilities in his data were stronger for children of relatively low L2 proficiency (non-balanced bilinguals). This suggests that the positive effects are related to the initial struggles and experiences of the beginning second-language learner. This interpretation does not appear to be incompatible with the threshold hypothesis since the major point of this hypothesis is that for positive effects to manifest themselves, children must be in the process of developing high levels of bilingual skills. If beginning L2 learners do not continue to develop both their languages, any initial positive effects are likely to be counteracted by the negative consequences of subtractive bilingualism.

In summary, the conclusion that emerges from the research on the academic, linguistic and intellectual effects of bilingualism can be stated thus:

> "The development of additive bilingual and biliteracy skills entails no negative consequences for children's academic, linguistic, or intellectual development. On the contrary, although not conclusive, the evidence points in the direction of subtle metalinguistic, academic and intellectual benefits for bilingual children".

The Linguistic Interdependence Principle

The fact that there is little relationship between amount of instructional time through the majority language and academic achievement in that language strongly suggests that first and second language academic skills are interdependent, i.e. manifestations of a common underlying proficiency. The interdependence principle has been stated formally as follows (Cummins, 1984a, p. 143):

> "To the extent that instruction in Lx is effective in promoting proficiency in Lx, transfer of this proficiency to Ly will occur provided there is adequate exposure to Ly (either in school or environment) and adequate motivation to learn Ly".

In concrete terms, what this principle means is that in, for example, a Gaelic-English bilingual programme in Ireland, Gaelic intruction which develops Gaelic and writing skills (for either Gaelic L1 or L2 speakers) is not just developing <u>Gaelic</u> skills, it is also developing a deeper conceptual and linguistic proficiency which is strongly related to the development of literacy in the majority language (English). In other words, although the surface aspects (e.g. pronounciation, fluency, etc.) of different languages are clearly separate, there is an underlying cognitive/academic proficiency which is common across languages. This "common underlying proficiency" makes possible the transfer of cognitive/academic or literacy-related skills across languages. Transfer is much more likely to occur from minority to majority language because of the greater exposure to literacy in the majority language outside of school and the strong social pressure to learn it. The interdependence principle is depicted in Figure 2.

Figure 2

THE LINGUISTIC INTERDEPENDENCE MODEL

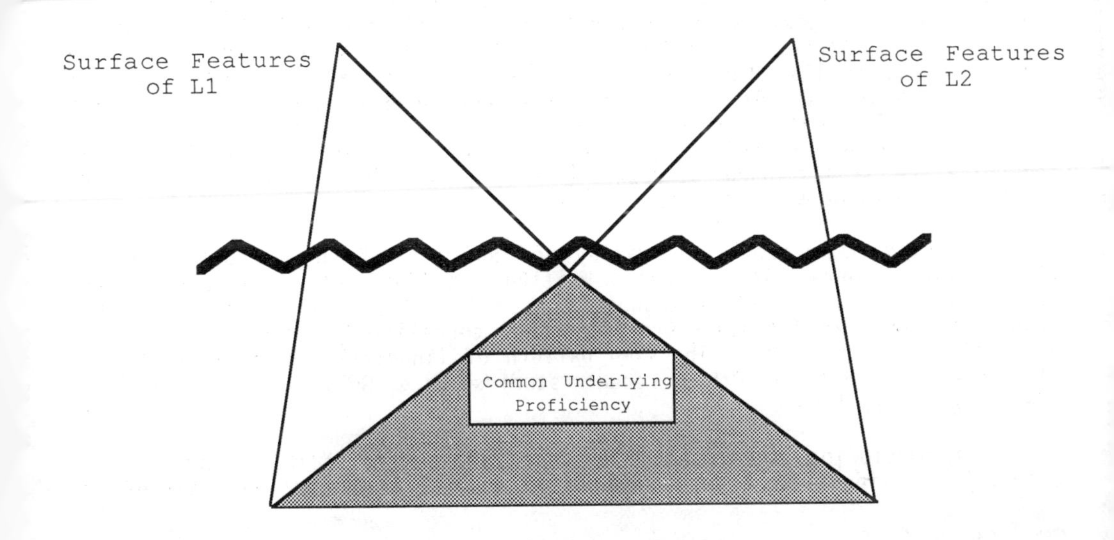

A considerable amount of evidence supporting the interdependence principle has been reviewed by Cummins (1983, 1984a) and Cummins and Swain (in press). The results of virtually all evaluations of bilingual programmes for both majority and minority students are consistent with predictions derived from the interdependence principle (see Cummins, 1983). The interdependence principle is also capable of accounting for data on immigrant students' L2 acquisition (e.g. Cummins, 1981) as well as from studies of bilingual language use in the home (e.g. Bhatnagar, 1980; Dolson, 1985). Correlational studies also consistently reveal a strong degree of cognitive/academic interdependence across languages.

Recent studies continue to support the interdependence principle. Kemp (1984), for example, reported that Hebrew (L1) cognitive/academic abilities accounted for 48 per cent of the variance in English (L2) academic skills among 196 seventh grade Israeli students. Treger and Wong (1984) reported significant positive relationships between L1 and English reading abilities (measured by cloze tests) among both Hispanic and Chinese background elementary school students in Boston. In other words, students above grade level in their first language reading also tended to be above grade level for English reading.

Two longitudinal studies also provide strong support for the notion of linguistic interdependence. Ramirez (1985) followed 75 Hispanic elementary school students in Newark, New Jersey, enrolled in bilingual programmes for three years. It was found that Spanish and English academic language scores loaded on one single factor over the three years of data collection. Hakuta and Diaz (1985) with a similar sample of Hispanic students found an increasing correlation between English and Spanish academic skills over time. Between Kindergarten and third grade the correlation between English and Spanish went from 0 to .68. The low cross-lingual relationship at the Kindergarten level is likely due to the varied length of residence of the students and their parents in the United States which would result in varying levels of English proficiency at the start of school.

An on-going study of five schools attempting to implement the Theoretical Framework developed by the California State Department of Education (1981) showed consistently higher correlations between English and Spanish reading skills (range $r = .60 - .74$) than between English reading and oral language skills (range $r = .36 - .59$) (California State Department of Education, 1985). In these analyses scores were broken down by months in the programme (1-12 months through 73-84 months). It was also found that the relation between L1 and L2 reading became stronger as English oral communicative skills grew stronger ($r = .71$, $N = 190$ for students in the highest category of English oral skills).

Finally, Cummins, Allen, Harley and Swain (1985) have reported highly significant correlations for written grammatical, discourse and sociolinguistic skills in Portuguese (L1) and English (L2) among Portuguese grade 7 students in Toronto. Cross-language correlations for oral skills were generally not significant. The same pattern of linguistic interdependence has also been reported in other recent studies (e.g. Goldman, 1985; Guerra, 1984; Katsaiti, 1983).

In conclusion, the research evidence shows consistent support for the principle of linguistic interdependence in studies investigating a variety of issues (e.g. bilingual education, memory functioning of bilinguals, age and second language learning, bilingual reading skills, etc.) and using different methodologies. The research has also been carried out in a wide variety of sociopolitical contexts. The consistency and strength of support indicates that higly reliable policy predictions can be made on the basis of this principle.

The Sufficient Communicative Interaction Principle

Most second language theorists (e.g. Krashen, 1981; Long, 1983; Schachter, 1983; Wong Fillmore, 1983) currently endorse some form of the "input" hypothesis which essentially states that acquisition of a second language depends not just on exposure to the language but on access to second language input which is modified in various ways to make it comprehensible. Underlying the notion of comprehensible input is the obvious fact that a central function of language use is meaningful communication; when this central function of language is ignored in classroom instruction, learning is likely to be by rote and supported only by extrinsic motivation. Wong Fillmore (1983) has clearly expressed this point:

> "Wherever it is felt that points of language need to be imparted for their own sake, teachers are likely to make use of drills and exercises where these linguistic points are emphasized and repeated. And when this happens the language on which students have to base their learning of English is separated from its potential functions, namely those that allow language learners to make the appropriate connections between form and communicative functions. Without such connections language is simply not learnable" (p. 170).

A limitation to the term "comprehensible input" is that it focuses only on the receptive or "input" aspects of interaction whereas both receptive and expressive aspects appear to be important (Swain, 1984). Swain and Wong Fillmore (1984) have expressed the importance of meaningful interaction for second language learning by synthesizing the views of leading researchers in the field in the form of an "interactionist" theory whose major proposition is that "interaction between learner and target language users is the major causal variable in second language acquisition" (p. 18). It is important to emphasize that meaningful interaction with text in the target language and production of text for real audiences is also included within this interactionist framework (see Cummins, 1984a).

The principle of sufficient communicative interaction also characterizes first language acquisition. Young children rarely focus on language itself in the process of acquisition, instead, they focus on the meaning that is being communicated and use language for a variety of functions, such as finding out about things, maintaining contact with others, etc. According to Wells (1982), children are active "negotiators of meaning" and they acquire language almost as a by-product of this meaningful interaction with adults.

One important link between the principle of sufficient communicative interaction and the common underlying proficiency principle is that knowledge (e.g. subject matter content, literacy skills etc.) acquired through linguistic interaction in one language plays a major role in making input in the other language comprehensible (Cummins, 1984a; Krashen, 1981). For example, an immigrant student who already has the concept of "justice" in his or her first language will require considerably less input in the second language containing the term to acquire its meaning than will a student who does not already know the concept. In the same way the first language conceptual knowledge developed in bilingual programmes for minority students greatly facilitates the acquisition of L2 literacy and subject matter content.

Conclusion

This review of psychoeducational data regarding bilingual academic development shows that, contrary to the opinions of some researchers, a theoretical basis for at least some policy decisions does exist. In other words, policy-makers can predict with considerable reliability the probable effects of bilingual programmes implemented in very different sociopolitical contexts.

First, they can be confident that if the programme is effective in continuing to develop students' academic skills in both languages, no cognitive confusion or handicap will result; in fact, students may benefit in subtle ways from access to two linguistic systems.

Second, they can be confident that spending instructional time through the minority language will not result in lower levels of academic performance in the majority language provided, of course, that the instructional programme is effective in developing academic skills in the minority language. This is because at deeper levels of conceptual and academic functioning, there is considerable overlap or interdependence across languages. Conceptual knowledge in one language helps to make input in the other language comprehensible.

Both these principles involve conditions with respect to the effectiveness of the instruction in developing language skills. The third psychoeducational principle addresses this issue. Specifically, policy-makers need to realise that conceptual and linguistic growth are dependent upon opportunities for meaningful interaction in both the target language and the student's L1. Exposure to the target language by itself is insufficient to ensure either language acquisition or conceptual growth. The input students receive must be modified to make it comprehensible and students must have ample opportunities to use language actively to express and negotiate meaning in both oral and written modes. The development of L1 conceptual skills provides the underlying basis for students' ability to negotiate meaning in the L2.

These psychoeducational principles open up significant possibilities for the planning of bilingual programmes by showing that, when programmes are well implemented, students will not suffer academically either as a result of bilingualism *per se* or as a result of spending less instructional time through one of their two or (more) languages. In sociopolitical situations which are not characterized by persistent school failure by certain minority groups, these principles by themselves provide a reliable basis for the prediction of programme outcomes (e.g. immersion programmes for majority students). However, these principles do not attempt to account for the variability in academic performance among minority groups exposed to similar educational programmes (see for example Ogbu, 1978) and thus, do not constitute a fully adequate basis for policy and planning in the case of minority students experiencing persistent academic difficulties.

In order to generate accurate predictions regarding the probable outcomes of school programmes for such students, the psychoeducational principles must be placed in the context of a broader theoretical framework that incorporates interactions between sociopolitical and psychoeducational factors. This framework is outlined in the next section.

EMPOWERING MINORITY STUDENTS: A THEORETICAL FRAMEWORK

A major issue for theory and policy is to explain the variability in the pattern of school success and failure among minority students. As outlined earlier, the two conventional wisdoms (the linguistic mismatch and insufficient exposure hypotheses) that currently dominate the policy debate in the United States are each patently inadequate to account for the research data. It is hardly surprising that this should be so since each of these conventional wisdoms involves only a unidimensional linguistic explanation. Consideration of the variability of minority students' academic performance under different social and educational conditions (see Ogbu, 1978; Wong Fillmore, 1983) indicates that multidimensional and interactive causal factors are at work. In particular, sociological and anthropological research (for example, Fishman, 1976; Obgu, 1978; Paulston, 1980) suggests that factors related to status and power relations between groups must be invoked as part of any comprehensive account of minority students' school failure. However, a variety of factors related to educational quality and cultural mismatch also appear to be important in mediating minority students' academic progress (see for example, Cummins, 1984a; Wong Fillmore, 1983). The framework outlined below attempts to integrate these hypothesized explanatory factors in such a way that the changes required to reverse minority student failure are clearly indicated.

The proposed theoretical framework incorporates sets of constructs that operate at three levels: i) the societal context of inter-group power relations; ii) the context of the school as an institution reflecting the values and priorities of the dominant societal group in its interactions with minority communities, and iii) the context of classroom interactions between teachers and minority students which represent the immediate determinants of students' success or failure.

As outlined in Figure 3, the central tenet of the framework is that students from what Mullard (see Chapter 9) has termed "dominated" societal groups are "empowered" or alternately, "disabled" as a direct result of their interactions with educators in the school context. Students who are empowered by their schooling experiences develop the ability, confidence and motivation to succeed academically. They participate competently in instruction (Cummins, 1984b; Tikunoff, 1983) as a result of having developed a confident cultural identity as well as appropriate school-based knowledge and interactional structures. Students who are disempowered or "disabled" by their school experiences do not develop this type of cognitive/academic and social/emotional foundation. Thus, student empowerment is regarded as both a mediating construct influencing academic performance and also as an outcome variable itself.

Figure 3

EMPOWERMENT OF MINORITY STUDENTS : A THEORETICAL FRAMEWORK

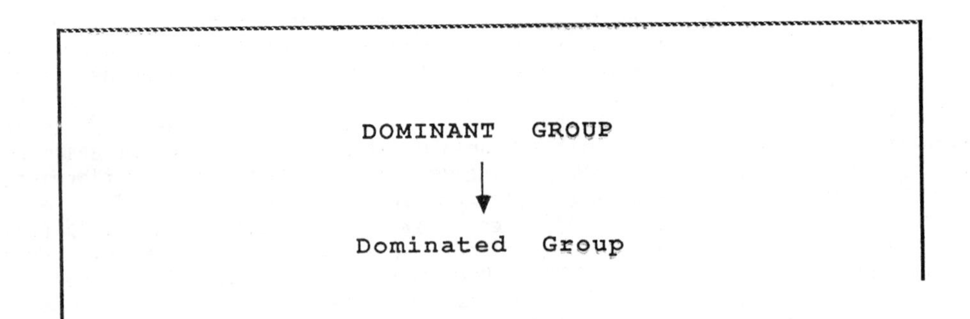

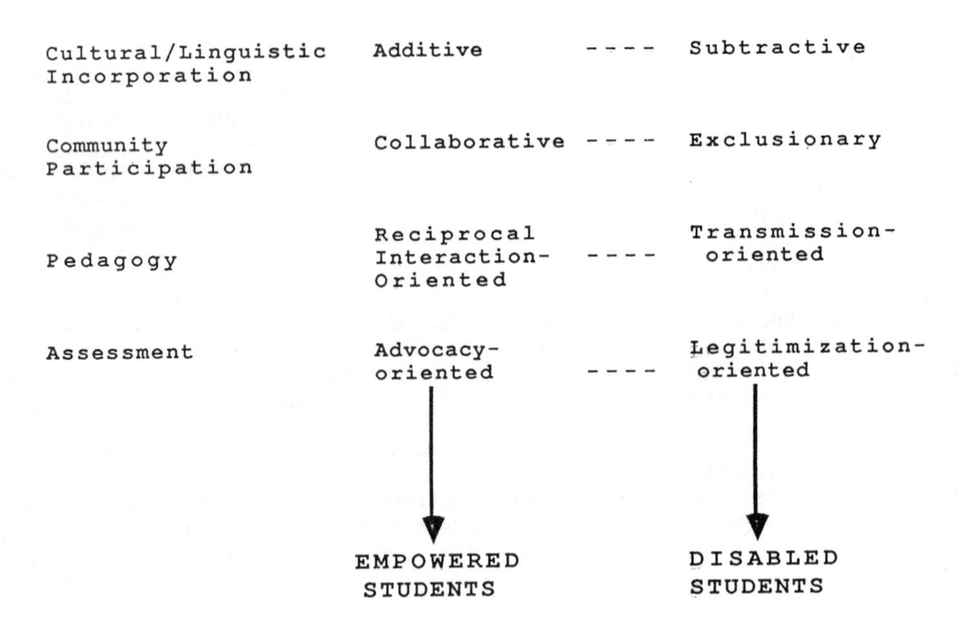

These student-educator interactions are mediated by the implicit (or explicit) role definitions that educators assume in relation to four institutional characteristics of schools. These characteristics reflect:

- -- The extent to which minority students' language and culture are incorporated within the school programme;
- -- The extent to which minority community participation is encouraged as an integral component of children's education;
- -- The extent to which the pedagogy promotes intrinsic motivation on the part of students to use language actively in order to generate their own knowledge;
- -- And finally, the extent to which professionals involved in assessment become advocates for minority students as opposed to legitimizing the location of the "problem" within the student.

For each of these dimensions of school organisation, the role definitions of educators can be described in terms of a continuum with one end of the continuum promoting the empowerment of students while the other contributes to the disabling of students.

The three levels analysed in the present framework (i.e. majority-minority societal group relations, school-minority community relations, educator-minority student relations) are clearly not the only ones that could be discussed. The choice of these levels, however, is dictated by hypotheses regarding the relative ineffectiveness of previous educational reforms, and directions required to reverse minority students' school failure. The relative ineffectiveness of previous attempts at reform (e.g. "compensatory education" and "bilingual education" in the United States) is attributed largely to the fact that the individual role definitions of educators and the institutional role definitions of schools have remained largely unchanged despite "new and improved" programmes and policies. The framework outlined in Figure 3 sketches the individual and institutional redefinitions required to reverse that pattern.

Inter-Group Power Relations

When the patterns of minority student school failure are examined within an international perspective, it becomes evident that power and status relations between minority and majority groups exert a major influence. Examples frequently given are the failure of Finnish students in Sweden (where they are a low status group) compared to their academic success in Australia where Finns are regarded as high status (see Troike, 1978); similarly, Ogbu (1978) reports that low status Buraku outcasts perform poorly in Japan but as well as any other Japanese students in the United States.

In accounting for the empirical data, theorists have employed several related constructs to describe characteristics of minority groups that tend to experience school failure. Cummins (1984a), for example, discusses the "bicultural ambivalence" (or lack of cultural identification) of students in relation to both the home and school cultures; similarly, Ogbu (1978) discusses the "caste" status of minorities that fail academically and attributes their failure to economic and social discrimination combined with the internalisation of the inferior status attributed to them by the dominant group. Feuerstein (1979) attributes academic failure to the disruption of intergenerational transmission processes caused by the alienation of a group from its own culture. In all three conceptions, minority groups that are positively oriented towards their own and the dominant culture (Cummins), have not internalised the dominant group attribution of inferiority (Ogbu) and are not alienated from their own cultural values (Feuerstein) tend to achieve academic success despite a home-school language switch.

Extensive analyses of inter-group power relations and their consequences for minority students' educational development have been carried out (e.g. Mullard in Chapter 9 of this volume; Ogbu & Matute-Bianchi in press; Paulston, 1980 and Chapter 11 of this volume; Skutnabb-Kangas, 1984, 1985). These analyses go beyond the scope of this paper. It is sufficient to note that there is general agreement with respect to the importance of status and power relations in determining minority students' success in school. However, few analyses have examined closely the interactions between sociopolitical and psychoeducational factors. The four structural elements in the organisation of schooling that contribute to the extent to which minority students are empowered or disabled are described below.

Cultural/Linguistic Incorporation

Considerable research data suggested that for dominated minorities the extent to which students' language and culture is incorporated into the school program constitutes a significant predictor of academic success (for example, Campos & Keatinge, 1984; Cummins, 1983; Rosier & Holm, 1980). Students' school success appears to reflect both the more solid cognitive/academic foundation developed through intensive L1 instruction and also the reinforcement of their cultural identity (Cummins, 1984a).

Included under incorporation of minority group cultural features is the adjustment of instructional patterns to take account of culturally-conditioned learning styles. The Kamehameha Early Education Program in Hawaii provides strong evidence of the importance of this type of cultural incorporation (see e.g. Au & Jordan, 1981).

With respect to the incorporation of minority students' languages and culture, educators' role definitions can be characterised along an "additive-subtractive" dimension. Educators who see their role as adding a second language and cultural affiliation to students' repertoire are likely to empower students more than those who see their role as replacing or subtracting students' primary language and culture in the process of assimilating them to the dominant culture.

It should be noted that an additive orientation is not dependent upon actual teaching of the minority language. In many cases this may not be possible for a variety of reasons (e.g. low concentration of particular groups of minority students). However, educators communicate to students and parents in a variety of ways the extent to which students' language and culture is valued within the context of the school. Even within a monolingual school context, powerful messages can be communicated to students regarding the validity and advantages of first language development.

Community Participation

Students from dominated communities will be empowered in the school context to the extent that the communities themselves are empowered through their interactions with the school. When educators involve minority parents as partners in their children's education, parents appear to develop a sense of efficacy that communicates itself to children with positive academic consequences (see for example the "Haringey Project" in Britain; Tizard, Schoefield and Hewison, 1982).

The teacher role definitions associated with community participation can be characterized along a collaborative-exclusionary dimension. Teachers operating at the collaborative end of the continuum actively encourage minority parents to participate in promoting their children's academic progress both in the home and through involvement in classroom activities. A collaborative orientation may require a willingness on the part of the teacher to work closely with the mother tongue teachers or aides in order to communicate effectively and in a non-condescending way with minority parents. Teachers with an exclusionary orientation, on the other hand, tend to regard teaching as their job and are likely to view collaboration with minority parents as either irrelevant or actually detrimental to children's progress.

Clearly, initiatives for collaboration or for a shared decision-making process can come from the community as well as from the school. Under these conditions, maintenance of and exclusionary orientation by the school can lead communities to directly challenge the institutional power structure. This was the case with the school strike organised by Finnish parents and their children at Bredby school in Rinkeby, Sweden. In response to a plan by the headmistress to reduce the amount of Finnish instruction, the Finnish community withdrew their children from the school. Eventually (after eight weeks) most of their demands were met. According to Skutnabb-Kansas (1985), the strike had the effect of generating a new sense of efficacy among the community and making them more aware of the role of dominant-group controlled (i.e. exclusionary) education in reproducing the powerless status of minority groups. A hypothesis that the present framework generates is that this renewed sense of efficacy would lead to higher levels of academic achievement among the minority students in this type of situation.

Pedagogy

Several investigators have suggested that the learning difficulties of minority students are often pedagogically-induced in that children designated "at risk" frequently receive intensive instruction that confines them to a passive role and induces a form of "learned helplessness" (e.g. Beers & Beers, 1980; Coles, 1978; Cummins, 1984a). Instruction that empowers students, on the other hand, will aim to liberate students from dependence on instruction in the sense of encouraging them to become active generators of their own knowledge.

Two major orientations can be distinguished with respect to pedagogy. These differ in the extent to which the teacher retains exclusive control over classroom interaction as opposed to sharing some of this control with students. The dominant instructional model in most western industrial societies has been termed a "transmission" model (Barnes, 1976; Wells, 1982); this will be contrasted with a "reciprocal interaction" model of pedagogy.

The basic premise of the transmission model is that the teacher's task is to impart knowledge or skills that s/he possesses to students who do not yet have these skills. This implies that the teacher initiates and controls the interaction, constantly orienting it towards the achievement of instructional objectives. The instructional content in this type of program derives primarily from the internal structure of the language or subject matter; consequently, it frequently involves a predominant focus on surface features of language or literacy (e.g. handwriting, spelling, decoding, etc.) and emphasizes correct recall of content taught. Content is usually transmitted by means of highly structured drills and workbook exercises, although in many cases the drills are disguised in order to make them more attractive and motivating to students.

It has been argued that a transmission model of teaching contravenes central principles of language and literacy acquisition and that a model allowing for reciprocal interaction between teachers and students represents a more appropriate alternative (Cummins, 1984a; Wells, 1982). This "reciprocal interaction" model incorporates proposals about the relation between language and learning made by a variety of investigators, most notably in the Bullock Report (1975), and by Barnes (1976), Lindfors (1980) and Wells (1982). Its applications with respect to the promotion of literacy conform closely to psycholinguistic approaches to reading (e.g. Goodman & Goodman, 1977; Holdaway, 1979; Smith, 1978) and to the recent emphasis on encouraging expressive writing from the earliest grades (e.g. Chomsky, 1981; Giacobbe, 1982; Graves, 1893; Temple, Nathan & Burris, 1982).

A central tenet of the reciprocal interaction model is that "talking and writing are means to learning" (Bullock Report, 1975, p.50). Its major characteristics in comparison to a transmission model are as follows:

- -- Genuine dialogue between student and teacher in both oral and written modalities;
- -- Guidance and facilitation rather than control of student learning by the teacher;
- -- Encouragement of student-student talk in a collaborative learning context;
- -- Encouragement of meaningful language use by students rather than correctness of surface forms;
- -- Conscious integration of language use and development with all curricular content rather than teaching language and other content as isolated subjects;
- -- Focus on developing higher level cognitive skills rather than factual recall;
- -- Task presentation that generates intrinsic rather than extrinsic motivation.

In short, pedagogical approaches that empower students encourage them to assume greater control over setting their own learning goals and to collaborate actively with each other in achieving these goals. The development of a sense of efficacy and inner-direction in the classroom is especially important for students from dominated groups whose experiences so often orient them in the opposite direction. In support of this, Wong Fillmore (1983) has reported that Hispanic students learned considerably more English in classrooms that provided opportunities for reciprocal interaction with teachers and peers.

Assessment

Historically, assessment has played the role of legitimizing the previous disabling of minority students. In some cases, assessment itself may play the primary role but usually its role has been to locate the "problem" within the minority student thereby screening from critical scrutiny the subtractive nature of the school program, the exclusionary orientation of teachers towards minority communities, and transmission models of teaching that inhibit students from active participation in learning.

This process is virtually inevitable when the conceptual base for the assessment process is purely psycho-educational. If the psychologist's task (or role definition) is to discover the causes of a minority student's academic difficulties and the only tools at her disposal are psychological tests (in either L1 or L2), then it is hardly surprising that the child's difficulties will be attributed to psychological dysfunctions. The myth of bilingual handicaps that still influences educational policy was generated in exactly this way during the 1920s and 1930s.

Recent studies suggest that despite the appearances of change with respect to nondiscriminatory assessment, the underlying structure has remained essentially intact. Mehan, Hertweck and Meihls (in press), for example, report that psychologists continued to test children until they "found" the disability that could be invoked to "explain" the student's apparent academic difficulties. A similar conclusion emerged from the analysis of more than 400 psychological assessments of minority students conducted by Cummins (1984a). Although no diagnostic conclusions were logically possible in the majority of assessments, psychologists were most reluctant to admit this fact to teachers and parents. In short, the data suggest that the structure within which psychological assessment takes place orients the psychologist to locate the cause of the academic problem within the minority student herself.

The alternative role definition that is required to reverse the traditional "legitimizing" function of assessment can be termed an "advocacy" or "delegitimization" role (see Mullard's Chapter 9 for discussion of delegitimization strategies in anti-racist education). The psychologist's or special educator's task must be to "delegitimize" the traditional function of psychological assessment in the educational disabling of minority students; in other words, they must be prepared to become advocates for the child (Cazden 1985) in critically scrutinizing the societal and educational context within which the child has developed. This involves locating the pathology within the societal power relations between dominant and dominated groups, in the reflection of these power relations between school and communities, and in the mental and cultural disabling of minority students that takes place in classrooms. These conditions are the cause of the 300% overrepresentation of Texas Hispanic students in the "learning disabled" category (Ortiz & Yates, 1983) rather than any intrinsic processing deficit unique to Hispanic children.

Clearly, and for obvious reasons, the training of psychologists and special educators does not prepare them for this advocacy or delegitimization role. However, from the present perspective, it must be emphasized that discriminatory assessment is carried out by (well-intentioned) individuals. Rather than challenging a socio-educational system that tends to disable minority students, these individuals have accepted a role of definition and an educational structure that makes discriminatory assessment virtually inevitable.

CONCLUSION

I have suggested that in most western industrialized countries the planning of educational interventions to promote academic success for minority students has not been characterized by a particularly rational process. Two major reasons can be suggested for this. First, sociopolitical considerations have often been rationalized in psychoeducational terms, and second, the crucial role of theory in the policy-making process has been ignored. Consequently, there is considerable confusion among policy-makers about appropriate educational options for minority students under different sociopolitical conditions. A recent example is the characterization of bilingual education in the United States as "a failed path" by the U.S. Secretary of Education, William Bennett (see Time, October 7, 1985). As has been suggested, the failure in the United States context is not the path of bilingual education which has scarcely been tried, but rather the path of a policy-making process that has failed to take account of the theoretical basis that does exist for predicting minority student outcomes under different educational and social conditions.

In this regard, certain psychoeducational principles appear to have considerable predictive power with respect to student outcomes. We can be confident, for example, that bilingualism in itself will not impede students' academic development and may, in fact, enhance academic and linguistic growth when both languages continue to develop throughout schooling. It is also clear that academic skills and knowledge are interdependent in that effective instruction through a minority language will not result in any educational deficits in the majority language, given adequate motivation and exposure to the majority language. A major reason for this is that the development of conceptual skills in one language helps to make input in the other language comprehensible. Sufficient communicative interaction in both languages appears to be necessary for adequate academic development; however, it is important to note that interaction involves comprehensible input rather than just exposure and students' L1 abilities are a major factor in helping students assimilate academic input in the L2.

Thus, there *is* a psychoeducational basis for policy in the areas of bilingual education. However, these psychoeducational factors do not address all the questions of policy-makers concerned with the educational difficulties of some minority groups. For example, they do not account for the variability in academic performance among different groups, nor do they adequately explain why certain forms of bilingual education appear particularly effective in reversing these difficulties (see e.g. Campos & Keatinge, 1984).

In order to address these issues, a theoretical framework was proposed for analysing minority students' academic failure and for predicting the effects of educational interventions. Educational failure among minority students was analysed as a function of the extent to which schools reflect, or alternatively, counteract the power relations that exist within the broader society. Specifically, language minority students' educational progress will be strongly influenced by the extent to which individual educators become advocates for the promotion of students' linguistic talents, actively encourage community participation in developing students' academic and cultural resources, and implement pedagogical approaches that succeed in liberating students from instructional dependence.

The educator-student interactions characteristic of the disabling end of the proposed continua reflect the typical patterns of interaction that dominated societal groups have experienced in relation to dominant groups. Students' language and cultural values are denied, their communities are excluded from participation in educational decisions and activities and they are confined to passive roles within the classroom. The failure of minority students under these conditions is frequently attributed on the basis of "objective" test scores to deficient cognitive or linguistic abilities.

In order to reverse the pattern of minority group educational failure, educators and policy-makers are faced with both a personal and a political challenge. Personally, they must redefine their roles within the classroom, the community and the broader society so that these role definitions result in interactions that empower rather than disable students. Politically, they must attempt to persuade colleagues and decision-makers (e.g. school boards and the public that elects them) that the school should redefine its own institutional foundations so that rather than reflecting society by disabling minority students it begins to transform society by empowering them.

NOTES

1. Recent implementation of bilingual programmes in California represents an exception to the general picture of the US bilingual programmes described here in that it conforms to the sequence outlined in Figure 1.

2. One consistent finding of the research is worth noting, namely that, on average, students' L1 tended to be used for considerably less time (approximately 5 per cent to 25 per cent) than most media and political commentators believed (Tikunoff, 1983).

BIBLIOGRAPHY

AU K.H. and JORDAN C., 1981, "Teaching reading to Hawaiian children: Finding a culturally appropriate solution". In TRUEBA H., GUTHRIE G.P. and AU K.H. (Eds.) Culture and the Bilingual Classroom: Studies in Classroom Ethnography. Rowley, Mass.: Newbury House.

BAKER K.A. and de KANTER A.A., 1981, Effectiveness of Bilingual Education: A Review of the Literature. Washington, D.C.: Office of Planning and Budget, U.S. Department of Education.

BARNES D., 1976, From Communication to Curriculum. Harmondsworth: Penguin.

BEERS C.S. and BEERS J.W. 1980, "Early identification of learning disabilities: Facts and fallacies. The Elementary School Journal, 81, 67-76

BHATNAGER J., 1980, "Linguistic behaviour and adjustment of immigrant children in French and English schools in Montreal". International Review of Applied Psychology, 29, 141-149.

BIALYSTOK E., 1984, "Influences of bilingualism on metalinguistic development". Paper presented at the symposium "Language awareness/reading development: Cause? Effect? Concomitance?" at the National Reading Conference Meeting, St. Petersburg, Florida.

BIALYSTOK E. and RYAN E.B., 1985, "Metacognitive framework for the development of first and second language skills". In FORREST-PRESSLEY D.L., MacKINNON G.E. and WALLER T.G. (Eds.), Meta-cognition, cognition, and human performance. New York: Academic Press.

BRATT PAULSTON C.B., 1980, Bilingual education: Theories and issues. Rowley, Mass.: Newbury House.

BULLOCK Report, 1975, A Language for life: Report of the Committee of inquiry appointed by the Secretary of State for Education and Science under the Chairmanship of Sir Alan Bullock. London: HMSO.

California State Department of Education, 1985, Case studies in bilingual education: First Year Report. Federal Grant G008303723.

CAMPOS J. and KEATINGE B., 1984, The Carpinteria Pre-School Program: Title VII Second Year Evaluation Report. Report submitted to the Department of Health, Education and Welfare, Office of Education, Washington, D.C.

CAZDEN C.B., 1985, "The ESL teacher as advocate". Plenary presentation to the TESOL Conference, New York.

CHOMSKY C., 1981, "Write now, read later". In CAZDEN C. (Ed.), Language in Early Childhood Education 2nd Edition. Washington, D.C.: National Association for the Education of Young Children.

COLES G.S., 1978, "The learning disabilities test battery: Empirical and social issues". Harvard Educational Review, 48, 313- 340.

CUMMINS J., 1979, "Linguistic interdependence and the educational development of bilingual children". Review of Educational Research, 49, 222-251.

CUMMINS J., 1981, "Age on arrival and immigrant second language learning in Canada: A reassessment". Applied Linguistics, 2, 132-149.

CUMMINS J., 1983, Heritage language education: A literature review. Toronto: Ministry of Education, Ontario.

CUMMINS J., 1984a, Bilingualism and special education: Issues in assessment and pedagogy. Clevedon, England: Multilingual Matters. Co-published in the United States by College-Hill Press, San Diego.

CUMMINS J., 1984b, "Functional language proficiency in context: Classroom participation as an interactive process". In TIKUNOFF W. (ed.), Significant instructional features in bilingual education: Proceedings of symposium at NABE 1983. San Francisco: Far West Laboratory, 1984.

CUMMINS J. and SWAIN M. (in press), Bilingualism in education: Aspects of theory, research and practice London: Longman.

CUMMINS J., ALLEN P.A., HARLEY B. and SWAIN M., 1985, "The development of bilingual proficiency among Portugese-speaking students in Toronto". Unpublished report, The Ontario Institute for Studies in Education.

DIAZ R.M. (in press), "Bilingual cognitive development: Addressing three gaps in current research". Child Development.

DOLSON D., 1985, The effects of Spanish home language use on the scholastic performance of Hispanic pupils. Journal of Multilingual and Multicultural Development, 6, 135-156.

FEUERSTEIN R., 1979, The Dynamic Assessment of Retarded Performers: The Learning Potential Assessment Device, Theory, Instruments, and Techniques. Baltimore: University Park Press.

FISHMAN J., 1976, Bilingual education: An international sociological perspective Rowley, Mass.: Newbury House.

GIACOBBE M.E., 1982, "Who says children can't write the first week?" In WALSHE R.D. (Ed), Donald Graves in Australia: "Children Want to Write" Exeter, New Hampshire: Heinemann Educational Books Inc..

GOLDMAN S.R., 1985, Utilization of knowledge acquired through the first language in comprehending a second language: Narrative composition by Spanish-English speakers Report submitted to the US Department of Education.

GOODMAN K.S. and GOODMAN Y.M., 1977, "Learning about psycholinguistic processes by analysing oral reading". Harvard Educational Review, 47, 317-333.

GRAVES D., 1983, Writing: Children and teachers at work. Exeter, NH: Heinemann.

GUERRA V., 1984, Predictors of second language learners' error judgements in written English. Doctoral dissertation, University of Houston.

HAKUTA K. and DIAZ R.M., 1985, "The relationship between degree of bilingualism and cognitive ability: A critical discussion and some new longitudinal data". In NELSON K.E. (Ed.), Children's Language, vol. 5 Hillsdale, New Jersey: Erlbaum.

HOLDAWAY, 1979, Foundations of literacy. New York: Ashton Scholastic.

HOOVER W., MATLUCK B., and DOMINGUEZ D., 1982, Language and literacy learning in bilingual instruction: Cantonese site analytic study. Final report submitted to the NIE.

KATSAITI L.T., 1983, Interlingual transfer of a cognitive skill in bilinguals. M.A. Thesis, Ontario Institute for Studies in Education.

KEMP J., 1984, Native Language Knowledge as a Predictor of Success in Learning a foreign Language with Special reference to a Disadvantaged Population. Thesis submitted for the M.A. Degree, Tel-Aviv University.

KRASHEN S.D., 1981, "Bilingual education and second language acquisition theory". In California State Department of Education, Schooling and language minority students: A theoretical framework. Los Angeles: Evaluation, Dissemination and Assessment Center.

LAMBERT W.E., 1975, "Culture and language as factors in learning and education". In WOLFGANG A. (Ed.), Education of immigrant students. Toronto: Ontario Institute for Studies in Education.

LAMBERT W.E. and TUCKER G.R., 1972, Bilingual education of children: The St. Lambert Experiment. Rowley, Mass.: Newbury House.

LINDFORS J.W., 1980, Children's Language and Learning. Englewood Cliffs, New Jersey: Prentice Hall.

LONG M.H., 1983, "Native speaker/non- native speaker conversation in the second language classroom". In CLARKE M.A. and HANDSCOMBE J. (Eds.), On TESOL '82: Pacific perspectives on language learning and teaching. Washington D.C.: TESOL.

McLAUGHLIN B., 1984, "Early bilingualism: Methodical and theoretical issues". In PARADIS M. and LEBRUN Y. (Eds.). Early bilingualism and child development. Lisse: Swets & Zeitlinger B.V.

MEHAN H., HERTWECK A. and MEIHLS J.L. (in press), Handicapping the handicapped: Decision making in students' educational careers. Palo Alto: Stanford University Press.

OGBU J.U., 1978, Minority education and caste. New York: Academic Press.

OGBU J.U. and MATUTE-BIANCHI M.E. (in press), "Understanding sociocultural factors: Knowledge, identity and school adjustment". In California State Department of Education (Ed.), Sociocultural factors and minority student achievement. Sacramento: California State Department of Education.

ORTIZ A.A. and YATES J.R., 1983, "Incidence of exceptionality among Hispanics: Implications for manpower planning". NABE Journal, 7, 41-54.

PENFIELD W., 1965, "Conditioning the uncommitted cortex for language learning". Brain, 88, 787-798.

RAMIREZ C.M., 1985, Bilingual education and language interdependence: Cummins and beyond. Doctoral dissertation, Yeshiva University.

REES O., 1981, "Mother tongue and English Project". In Commission for Racial Equality (Ed.), Mother Tongue Teaching Conference Report. Bradford: UK.: Bradford College.

ROSIER P. and HOLM W., 1980, The Rock Point Experience: A Longitudinal Study of a Navajo School. Washington, D.C.: Center for Applied Linguistics.

SCHACHTER J., 1983, "Nutritional needs of language learners". In CLARKE M.A. and HANDSCOMBE J. (Eds.), On TESOL '82: Pacific perspective on language learning and teaching. Washington D.C.: TESOL.

SKUTNABB-KANGAS T., 1984, Bilingualism or not: The educating of minorities. Clevedon, England: Multilingual Matters.

SKUTNABB-KANGAS T., 1985, "Resource power and autonomy through discourse in conflict: A Finnish migrant school strike in Sweden". Unpublished manuscript, Roskilde University.

SMITH F., 1978, Understanding reading. 2nd edition. New York: Holt, Rinehart and Winston.

SWAIN M. (in press), "Communicative competence: Some roles of comprehensible input and comprehensible output in its development". In CUMMINS J. and SWAIN M., Bilingualism in education: Aspects of theory, research and practice. London: Longman.

SWAIN M. and LAPKIN S., 1982, Evaluating bilingual education. Clevedon, England: Multilingual Matters.

SWAIN M. and WONG FILLMORE L.W., 1984, "Child second language development: Views" from the field on theory and research". Paper presented at the 18th Annual TESOL Conference, Houston Texas, March.

TEMPLE C.A., NATHAN R.G. and BURRIS N.A., 1982, The Beginnings of Writing. Boston: Allyn & Bacon.

TIKUNOFF W.J., 1983, "Five significant bilingual instructional features: A summary of findings from Part 1 of the SBIF descriptive study". In FISHER C. et al. The significant bilingual instructional features study. Final report submitted to The National Institute of Education.

TIZARD J., SCHOFIELD W.N. and HEWISON J., 1982, "Collaboration between teachers and parents in assisting children's reading". British Journal of Educational Psychology, 52, 1-15.

TREGER B. and WONG B.K., 1984, "The relationship between native and second language reading comprehension and second language oral ability". In RIVERA C. (Ed.), Placement procedures in bilingual education: Education and policy issues. Clevedon, England: Multilingual Matters.

TROIKE R., 1978, "Research evidence for the effectiveness of bilingual education". NABE Journal, 3, 13-24.

WELLS G., 1982, "Language, learning and the curriculum". In WELLS G., Language, learning and education. Bristol: Centre for the Study of Language and Communication, University of Bristol.

WONG FILLMORE L., 1983, "The language learner as an individual: Implications of research on individual differences for the ESL teacher". In CLARKE M.A. and HANDSCOMBE J. (Eds.), On TESOL '82: Pacific perspective on language learning and teaching. Washington, D.C.: TESOL

V. A RETROSPECT

13. CULTURAL ISSUES IN EDUCATIONAL POLICIES: A RETROSPECT

by
Walo HUTMACHER
Director of Sociological Research Service,
Public Education Department, Canton of Geneva

The comments that follow were written subsequent to the Experts' meeting at which the papers here reproduced were presented, and were prompted by these and by the ensuing discussions. They are offered, not so much as a summary, but as an attempt to put into perspective the current discussion (of which the meeting formed part) concerning the development of new relationships, particularly within schools, between different cultures in contact with one another.

An observation that was by no means original started off a train of thought: in most OECD Member countries, the presence of what are described as minority groups poses a problem as regards educational policy and teaching practice; in these countries the tendency is to consider this problem as being of a cultural nature. Now, these two facts that no one nowadays would seriously think of questioning were by no means self-evident even thirty years ago. In short, the problem of the education of immigrants and other minorities has only come to the fore in recent decades, as has the perception of it as a cultural matter. Yet neither the way a social problem is perceived nor the form it assumes at a given point in time are self-evident. So it would seem useful here to examine what links there are between the emergence of this problem and the economic, social and cultural changes taking place in the industrialised societies -- particularly the changes in their education systems.

THE CONSTRUCTION OF SOCIETAL PROBLEMS BY SOCIETY

The fact that, at the request of several Member countries, an international organisation like the OECD should invest resources in the study of Education and Cultural and Linguistic Pluralism must surely reflect the conviction that a problem exists in this area, that it resides at government level and that it is therefore a societal problem. A societal problem exists once there is a fairly widespread perception of a social reality being not what it should be -- litter because it is unfair, inconsistent, outdated, scandalous, disturbing, dangerous, intolerable, contrary to the social order or the interests of the community, or all of these things. As Fuller and Myers (1941) maintain, "Social problems are what people think they are".

There are obviously countless perceptions of this kind. For there to be a societal problem in the sense that I am using the term here, it is not sufficient that an individual or a small group should consider a social reality (their own, for example) as problematic. What I shall be describing herein as a "societal problem" supposes that the reality that is perceived as problematic is related to one or more social aims (e.g. the prevention of delinquency, birth control, the democratisation of education, full employment, the reduction of environmental pollution), and resources are allocated to tackling them by decisions at societal level, i.e. involving action on the part of the State and/or other major social institutions such as business, professional or trade union organisations, religious institutions, etc. There has also to be strong evidence for believing that a number of people share (or probably share or are supposed to share) the same aims and consequently the same vision of the problem and of ways of solving it.

However, the definition of a societal problem, in the sense we are using the term here, excludes the type of perceptions of problematic social realities that call into question the social order itself (blueprints for society, utopias, revolutionary programmes for changing the social order). This implies that the aims and the means are defined within the framework of the existing social and political system and rely on this system's own mechanisms of regulation. As a corollary, in many cases this means that "the actors tailor societal problems to match the aims that appear achievable within the context of the 'normal' operation of managing conflicts and claims" (Perrenoud, 1976).

This concept of a social or societal problem is a basic category in the political practice and culture of modern capitalist societies where political parties, social movements and pressure groups are constantly at work to get societal problems recognised or solved, and where one of the permanent features of the debate and the conflicts is precisely the question of the reality, importance and urgency of the problems and the validity, relevance and pertinence of the definitions that they are given and the solutions that are applied. This process of selective formulation and definition of legitimate social problems, that is to say problems that are considered as deserving attention and requiring regulatory or remedial action on the part of the State and/or other major organisations, manifest the capacity of these (Promethean) societies to produce themselves, to put the way they operate at distance and to invest resources and energies in their own transformation (Touraine, 1973).

The construction of a societal problem is in itself a social process. The form that a problem assumes at a particular point in time cannot be understood without reference to the historical process of collective fashioning, definition, recognition and symbolic acceptance which has given it form and meaning. A process of problematisation brings into confrontation, sometimes over a very long period, a series of groups, organisations, agencies and bodies involved in the production and discussion of ideas as well as in the conflict itself. The actors involved in the construction and definition of a societal problem, who may find themselves sometimes on the same side and sometimes on opposing sides, invariably differ in terms of:

-- Their interests and plans as regards firstly the social reality that is becoming a problem, and secondly the consequences that the defining of the problem will have on their status, their social position, their independence, their resources, etc.;

-- The disproportionate resources they have at their disposal, not only material but also social resources (an acknowledged legitimacy and competence, influence, etc.), to enable them to designate a social reality as a problem and get their definition of the problem accepted;

-- The information and experience they already have in dealing with this type of situation;

-- Their position in respect of the overall balance of power within the society and, in particular, the forces involved in the process of problematisation.

It is the interaction between these actors that will give its specific form and legitimacy to the recognition of the reality of the problem, the definition of its nature, and its degree of seriousness and urgency. In the last analysis, the outcome of the process of construing a social problem depends on the balance of power between the various protagonists involved. The influence that can be exerted by the groups or categories whose presence, situation or actions are beginning to be considered as a problem depends on their weight in relation to the other forces involved in the process of problematisation.

Education and cultural pluralism as it exists today

In our present context, the groups defined as presenting or representing a problem as regards education are the cultural minorities or immigrants. Etienne Verne very rightly reminded us during the meeting that the presence of such groups in the countries concerned is nothing new; it is a long-established fact, created and maintained by a long tradition of settlement, migration (for religious, economic or political motives) and international trade.

However, the definition of these minority groups or immigrants as the source of a particular problem in terms of educational achievement or adjustment, and the focusing on them as subjects for debate and special educational policy measures are relatively recent phenomena which seem to me indicative of a change in the social issues involved, not only in educational achievement but also in legitimate perceptions to do with the nature and origin of educational difficulties and problems. What is the reason for this change? How does one explain the emergence in many countries of policies that reflect a feeling that there is a special problem of educational achievement and adjustment in the case of immigrants or what are considered to be cultural minority groups? Furthermore, why is it that the problem should be defined as being of a cultural nature? These are the questions to which I shall be trying to provide some tentative answers against the background of the theoretical considerations briefly outlined above.

There is a tendency, in Europe at least, to consider that the great increase in migration over the past thirty years is in itself enough to explain the development of educational policies specifically directed to immigrants. It is true that this vast influx of foreigners has helped to create large groups speaking a language other than that of the local inhabitants, holding beliefs and values different from theirs and moreover observing different practices as regards many aspects of everyday life such as social relationships, religion, marriage, education, dress and diet.

Furthermore, in some large urban areas, the size and pace of immigration from certain countries has led to the creation of groups (or even mini-communities or social networks) within which the immigrants are able to control the strain between preserving their original identity and adjusting to the culture of the host country. In situations like these, cultural differences become socially more visible and this generates attitudes of non-acceptance, xenophobia or racism amongst the indigenous population, particularly amongst those sections who are in daily contact with the immigrants and/or have the impression that their interests are threatened, for example with regard to working conditions or housing. These widespread sources of tension and potential threat to law and order are naturally of concern to the State authorities.

There can be no disputing the fact that the vast migratory flows of recent years have increased social tensions. However, the urbanisation and industrialisation of western countries in the last century was marked by transfers of population which, relatively speaking, were at least as massive as those in recent years. To this it may be replied that these more recent movements differ from the earlier ones in terms of the distance involved as well as the cultural, and especially the language, gap that separates the immigrants from the indigenous population of modern urban societies. Perhaps. But in many cases these earlier movements were also cross-national in character (for example, Poles into France and Italians into Northern Europe) and even when the migration was from largely rural areas, this was at a time when the cultural differences between town and country were far more pronounced than they are nowadays.

In these cases, the school system remained for many years relatively aloof from these cultural differences and any tension. In fact, wherever educational policy had to deal with the issue of cultural heterogeneity, it was usually to urge schools to ignore it for the sake of national or linguistic unity, secularism, rationalism or progress. Even in the United States, a country with a very long tradition of immigration, there is no evidence to suggest that the culture of immigrant groups was considered to pose a particular problem as regards education. And although the "melting pot theory" does indeed acknowledge the existence of differences, it implies also and above all a confidence in the ability of a dominant "American model" to assimilate these differences without undergoing major changes.

In other words, the United States and European societies have for many years been able to adjust to the presence of culturally different groups or regions, their educational policy however being aimed at reducing these differences, either by ignoring them or by combating them. Moreover, as Jacques Revel in his contribution claims, indifference to schoolchildren's different origins was a characteristic feature of education systems well before the industrial revolution.

What, then, are the reasons for the apparent break with this tradition of engendering homogeneity, evidenced over the past fifteen or twenty years by the educational policies of most industrialised countries moving towards recognition and respect for cultural differences and even towards a positively "multicultural" system of instruction? I am interested first of all in the reasons for this quite remarkable change. Considering education systems to be one of the mechanisms by and within which modern societies both produce and reproduce themselves and applying the theory of societal problems outlined in my introductory section, I should like to examine the merits of a hypothesis that can be formulated in three parts:

i) In spite of appearances, national education systems still retain undiminished their inherent vocation of cultural homogenisation;

ii) On the other hand, national education policies are increasingly focusing on aims bound up with the international system of competition that encourage them to increase the resources devoted to education, whilst at the same time;

iii) Placing the emphasis on a new, ostensibly universal dominant cultural referent which is the aim of the homogenisation work.

THE RAISING OF THE GENERAL STANDARD OF EDUCATION: AN ASPECT OF THE COMPETITION BETWEEN COUNTRIES

Since the late 1950s the education policies of the industrialised countries, in one form or another and with growing force, have been aimed at expanding available educational resources and raising the general standard of education of the younger generations. The debate concerning these policies in some instances refers to the concept of democratisation education (and even equal educational opportunities) and in others to the concept of investment in "human capital" or "human resources", to use the term that came into fashion later. These two approaches reflect two major social currents which combined in different ways in each country to give force to a new objective assigned to the education system, that of raising the general standard of education. Let me begin by briefly describing these two movements.

On the one hand, there is the increasing aspiration among the population for more education and for equal opportunities as regards educational achievement and choice, regardless of sex, race or social origins, coupled with a belief in the emancipatory virtues of a good formal education and the hope by this means of improving one's social and career prospects. As the result of, among other things, economic growth and changes in the social structure of the various countries, this movement has consistently gained momentum over the past forty years, mainly because:

-- The middle classes are expanding, at least among the indigenous population in each country (i.e. the electors) and it is a well-known fact that their social status is particularly dependent on the value of the academic qualifications they have obtained;

-- With the improvement in living standards the middle-class system of values and beliefs has spread to a section of the working classes;

-- For different reasons, the policy statements (from the left as well as the right) supporting educational reforms and measures to promote formal training urge every boy and girl to raise their educational ambitions; and lastly,

-- The higher qualifications required by employers provides proof to those concerned that these higher ambitions make social and economic sense.

On the other hand, and coupled with this first set of social forces, is the growing influence of a number of prominent, political and economic groups which, as economic growth adds to the resources of the nation, are intent on channelling an ever larger proportion of these resources into the training of a labour force of a high professional, technical and therefore intellectual level. The attitudes of these groups indicate that they are anxious to preserve or strengthen their chances in the face of international economic competition and eager to be able for this purpose to recruit a higher standard of scientific, technical and management know-how and skills in order to be able to develop new products and introduce new production methods.

The thinking behind the policies of educational expansion pursued over the past thirty years in the industrialised countries have, on the whole, been rooted in social factors considered as specific to each country. In this, too little importance was attached to the fact -- glaringly obvious though it was -- that the process of educational expansion was taking place simultaneously in all of the countries with which we are concerned. To explain away this coincidence, the usual theory was that the same (internal) causes were producing similar effects in the different national contexts. To my mind, however, this overlooks the genuinely inter-national dimension of the process and the vital part played by the dynamics of relations between countries in the definition of national policies. The fact is that all of these countries are involved in an economic competition where the chances of winning depend increasingly on the capacity to innovate in scientific and technological fields and consequently on the availability of the corresponding skills among the labour force (the "human resources" in fact). With the result that these countries drag each other into a sort of upward spiral from which it is difficult for them to escape without undermining their future, this movement encourages them constantly to expand the facilities for training invested in this area while the demands made on education resources and the requirements for output and quality of training are on the increase.

The embroiling of national education policies in the rivalry of the system of competitive interdependence between countries is evidenced first of all by the frequent reference to international competition in the statements of national aims in support of new educational policies. It is also evident in the part played by international organisations in this respect as fora for debate and confrontation between countries and as promoters of the game of international comparisons where each country has the education policies of other countries held up as an example. It is particularly significant in this respect that the OECD, an organisation for economic co-operation, has played a major role in inspiring, defining and legitimating the expansionist educational policies of its Member countries.

It is this concern with the way international relations are evolving that explains why in most countries the raising of the standard of education (and in particular vocational, scientific and technical education) has remained a high priority despite the economic recession and the budgetary restrictions and restructuring of recent years. Although, from a domestic standpoint, this educational policy coincides with the constant desires of parents and at the same time helps to regulate entries into the labour market, it is also, and perhaps mainly, the result of the attention paid to the international situation by countries and their leaderships. An outcome of the fact that the economic crisis is viewed as a crisis involving the structural adjustment of national economies and their productive forces as part of a major realignment of the international division of labour has been that international competition has become an even more powerful stimulus to expansionist education policies.

Mutatis mutandis, the present situation is somewhat reminiscent of that in Western Europe during the second half of the 19th century. At that time, following a phase of consolidation of the new political regime, the modern states were embarking upon the vast social and economic restructuration associated with the process of industrialisation which, in turn, involved a radical reorganisation of the division of labour both within these countries and between them. During this same period, virtually every western country reorganised, each in its own way, its system of education in line with a new set of objectives. It was at this time that the utilitarian orientation of education towards economic activity finally gained legitimacy and took its place, alongside the values of morality, rationality and nationality, in education policies emancipated from the religious referent. It was during this period, too, that governments undertook the reorganisation of the hitherto separated educational networks into co-ordinated systems, integrating a set of schools differing in terms of recruitment and opportunities, but nevertheless much more specifically oriented towards preparing the young for an economic activity. Showing a strong capacity to preserve their unity while adapting their internal differentiation and their expansion in response to external constraints and demands, these systems are still in operation nowadays, at least with regard to their fundamental principles.

Now, at least the studies carried out in Geneva would suggest it, the leaders supporting the modernization of the school, in those times, were already very aware of international competition. Although there was as yet no international organisation capable of developing and systematizing comparisons between countries, in the discussions on educational policy it is by no means unusual to find references to what was being done elsewhere and better, as well as a concern about the possible decline of the competitiveness of the national economy through a lack of effort in the education field.

Once the utilitarian orientation of the school is legitimated, international competition in educational matters becomes part of the very existence of nation-states within an international economic environment. Awareness of this competition appears to be more marked at certain key periods of major change, as would seem to be the case at present insofar as the so-called highly industrialised countries are shifting over to what, for want of a better term, is called a "post-industrial" structure. Alain Touraine (1973) considers the main feature of post-industrial society to be its emphasis on the accumulation of creative abilities (science, technology, organisation), whereas Peter Heintz (1973) sees it also as a strong concentration on economic activities of a service nature geared towards the steering, organisation and management of production processes in other parts of the world, coupled with the abandonment to some degree of the more traditional industrial activities and the specialisation of the residual secondary sector in high technology production.

All western countries are involved in this change which, as far as economic occupations are concerned, increases the demand for constantly renewed scientific and technical knowledge and, in addition to rational thought, tends to emphasize the ability to formalize and abstract, independence of judgment, flexibility of mind, the capacity to learn as well as technical and organisational efficiency. All of these skills, the education systems are expected to develop to a high level in an increasing number of young people.

Therefore, although it is still a matter of catering for all children, it is no longer sufficient that education systems should provide them with formally equal chances of success whilst at the same time ensuring the relative scarcity of elites. In the policy debate about reforms in education and in teaching practice, the provision of the highest possible level of education for all is increasingly emerging if not as a reality at least as a legitimate aim and even as a priority. It would scarcely be an exaggeration to say that the task now being assigned to education systems is to ensure maximum achievement for every child, at least at the primary level if not throughout compulsory education, and that this task is regarded as an aspect of both domestic and international policy.

From a domestic standpoint, over the past few decades developed societies have been frequently troubled by more or less vigorous protests against discrimination of all kinds organised by groups defined or defining themselves in terms of their cultural or racial or even sexual identity. The virtually worldwide feminist protest movements are good examples of this. Equally well-known are the protests of the Blacks, Indians and other groups traditionally regarded as "minorities" in the United States. In Europe too, traditional minorities and immigrant groups (encouraged and occasionally supported by their countries of origin) have demonstrated in various ways an increasing ability to mobilize protest and demonstrate their strength.

It is a sign of the times that these demonstrations against political discrimination and economic and social inequalities in general have frequently also been based upon educational problems. They certainly contributed to change the position of these groups in the overall balance of power, if only by altering the perception that State leaders had of their relative strength and the potential threat to law and order deriving from their discontent. At the same time, the change in educational aims briefly described above, made it easier for prominent groups to meet the demands related to schooling. In this process, the representation of educational problems specific to so-called cultural minorities took roots.

In many cases these attacks against discrimination of all kinds are evidence of cultural changes occurring within the groups concerned. The very fact of their mobilisation, and in particular on educational issues, is a sign of a broader appreciation of the values of modernity, its representations and its beliefs, and consequently of those transmitted by the school (individualism, rational thought and action, compliance with the standards of a formal organisation, the work ethic, and so on). This change denotes on the part of these groups a form of participation in social issues and struggles based on a perception of society and their own place within it that is less one of subservience and acceptance and less dictated by a destiny outside of their control.

ANOTHER DOMINANT CULTURAL REFERENT?

If it is true, as just suggested, that the more recent activities of minority groups indicate their reconciliation with the dominant modern cultural model (individualism, rationalism, career, etc.), then part of the work of assimilation and cultural homogenisation entrusted to schools a century ago is reaching completion and, if this assumption is correct, minority groups will henceforth be culturally more integrated and more anxious to integrate than ever. This is borne out by, among other things, the fact that disadvantaged minority and immigrant groups increasingly expect that schools provide the same opportunities and the same type of education for their children as for the children of the majority or indigenous groups and without devoting too much time to their own native language and culture.

However, in the case of certain groups, this trend does not prevent the residual differences (language or linguistic usage, religious traditions and more or less folk and private customs) from acquiring an enhanced symbolic value in this process by virtue of the fact that, as Michel de Certeau says in his paper, they are in some ways transformed into "relics", fetishes or mementoes of another cultural universe and in some cases invested as symbols of the difference.

But to a certain extent, in the cultural environment of the late 20th century, which has seen a tremendous increase in the ability to produce and disseminate information, knowledge, skills and expertise, such localised and partially privatised conservatisms are characteristic of every social group and every particularism in every country, including those that are nationalist.

Nor can one ignore the effects of the tremendous scientific breakthroughs of the past thirty or forty years on "traditional" symbolic systems. Too frequently alas it is only the technological and economic consequences of scientific discoveries that are considered and not their profound impact on the central core of all cultures, which is their concept of the world and of man himself, whereas it is these fundamental concepts that are being called into question throughout the world as a result of the pressure from the increasingly rapid pace of scientific discovery. On the one hand, physics is proclaiming a new concept of matter and astronomy forcing us to revise traditional cosmologies, while biology is changing accepted beliefs as to the nature of life and the human sciences (from paleontology to sociology) are helping to create a new concept of human nature and a new anthropology. In this seemingly inexorable process whole sets of former beliefs and convictions are crumbling, although this is not without friction, regrets, tension, conflicts and wars.

Science, which considers itself as supra- and trans-cultural, is forcing upon the most widely diverse national, ethnic, racial and religious allegiances a claim to universality and relative compatibility, that derives most of its force from the product of its research and, more particularly, its technological spinoffs in the worldwide political and economic arena. Confronted with the development of science as a valid cultural referent and a universally accepted source of knowledge and valid perceptions, local allegiances and susceptibilities all tend to become relatively minor particularisms. The accelerated obsolescence not only of skills, techniques and practices, but also of beliefs, values and moral and ethical standards affects every social group, majority or minority, in every country.

It would seem, therefore, that a new universal culture has become the principal objective towards which the drive for homogenisation is being directed. All the cultural media are helping directly or indirectly to consolidate the legitimacy of rational thought and scientific research and to disseminate their content. The systems of education are no exception to this. In every country and particularly in those that are economically more advanced, the legitimate and important subject matters taught in schools have been revised in order to give more emphasis to the development of logical-mathematical thought right from primary level and, also at this level, to the spread of scientific knowledge and skills. Admittedly, the pace differs depending on the traditions in each country, but what is important is that the trend is universal. The increasing stress placed on science in legitimate educational culture is leading to a situation where education in the various countries is becoming increasingly similar. In this respect, even the wide ideological/military gap between the two blocks is narrowing.

It is important to realise that this process is also playing a part in the relativisation of national cultures in a context where, in addition, the international, political and economic system of interdependence is in turn helping to reduce the range of possibilities available to each nationalism to enhance its own image by denigrating the others. For example, as Stacy Churchill points out in his paper, practically all the countries he studied have at least eliminated from their school textbooks and their official educational culture discriminatory or derogatory references to social, ethnic, racial or national groups that were formerly belittled.

Nationalism still exists of course, but national identities are less and less nourished on self-admiration and veneration of a supposedly glorious past, of which merely the memory would constitute a source of pride. National feelings are increasingly being directed to the various fields of international competition where pre-eminence is measured by transnational criteria of excellence. In this respect, what is happening in the field of sport is a good illustration. It is significant, too, that technological and scientific achievement remains one of the fields of transnational rivalry which provide matter for nationalist sentiments although, paradoxically, the cultural spinoff from scientific research tends in the long run to reduce these to residual particularisms within a worldwide culture.

Inside the individual countries, however, reactions to this relativisation as it relates to national, religious or ethnic particularisms seem to be marked by a social division. Large sections of the upper, intellectual and middle classes, who by virtue of their education or their activities form part of the new universal, are much in favour of cultural pluralism or ecumenism whether this be with respect to diet, language or music and even aesthetic or metaphysical matters. They have a taste for "things exotic" and they advocate tolerance of otherness, the right to be different and inter-cultural dialogue and exchange for the sake of mutual enrichment and as a way of reducing tension between groups within a country and between countries themselves.

Other and for the most part less privileged classes and groups, having neither the same cultural references nor the same social horizons and not expecting the same benefits from these radical changes, react to what they consider the erosion of values and established beliefs by adopting attitudes of resistance, opposition and/or nostalgic attachment to traditions. Some of the recent resurgences of religion and some xenophobic attitudes no doubt have their roots in the sentiment of losing touch with "one's own world".

Thus, the promotion via the schools of cultural pluralism, and even multicultural education, may be viewed in very different ways. Some will see this as a means of reducing tension and promoting peaceful coexistence between groups, peoples or nations by relativising or endowing with an aesthetic charm cultural differences otherwise considered as secondary or merely picturesque. Others will see this as the loss of a sense of "recognised" values and the order of things, and an unacceptable risk. To some parents (and probably also to some teachers) it seems astonishing, not to say inadmissible, that the school should be willing to give children an education designed to promote a positive (or less negative) perception of ethnic, racial or national groups that they themselves had been taught, partly through the same schools, to regard as inferior and even contemptible. It is not my intention here to pass judgment on these reactions or to seek to justify them, but merely to note their existence and relate them to the rationalities of these groups and to their material and symbolic objectives in the process that is taking place.

From the symbolic standpoint in fact, the promotion of multi- or intercultural education implies striking a balance between the perceptions that the groups involved have of one another which modifies the social identity and status of their members. The supporters of this doctrine would certainly refuse to consider this as a zero-sum game with one person's gain being necessarily someone else's loss. The question is whether the potential gains will appear credible and desirable to those who, being less able to cope with the difficulties of intercultural exchange, are afraid of losing in the process their own convictions and sense of superiority.

This risk of hostility and opposition is heightened by the fact that the issue is concerned not only with the legitimacy of the differences and inequalities but, at another level, with their nature, that is to say, the appropriate and legitimate definition of the nature of the differences and inequalities between groups within society as a whole and with regard to educational achievement in particular.

DEFINING THE PROBLEM AS BEING OF A CULTURAL NATURE

Defining these differences as being (essentially) of a cultural nature implies altering the cultural model (Touraine, 1973), the perception of the nature of human nature which is still widely accepted and is at issue in the revision of anthropology.

I submit that the school is one of the more important places where the gestation of this change in the cultural model can be observed, and specifically by the way it interprets underachievement. To say that the educational achievement or adjustment of children from certain social groups is related to their cultural origin is tantamount to ascribing this to the way in which relationships at school, the behaviour, skills and educational performance of these children are shaped and dictated by the systems of predispositions to perceive, think, believe, evaluate, feel and act that have been acquired through the experience gained within the groups to which they belong. Adopting such a view as regards the etiology of success and failure at school is not simply an intellectual operation, socially neutral and gratuitous. It ascribes a specific meaning to educational inequalities which reflects a particular anthropological interpretation. This view, a determinant of both the conceivable and the inconceivable, conflicts with other explanatory postulates.

The history of education is strewn with examples of the failure in respect of a number of school children of a system's plans for teaching and standardization -- examples that are always specific and situational perceptions of the nature and causes of this failure. Broadly speaking, these perceptions fall into two main categories. In the first case, blame for this failure is laid primarily on the school itself, whether it be its educational structure, its bureaucratic organisation, its norms, its rhythms, its methods, or its isolation from its environment. In the second, the underachievement of a section of the school population is blamed on certain characteristics specific to them. According to the first of these explanations, the education would work if the school were different, changed, reformed or even, as certain recent theories advocate, abolished. According to the second explanation, however, the school is not to blame: it would be able to perform its educational task successfully if the pupils (or some of them) were different.

The choice between these two viewpoints, which involves adopting a clearly delineated pattern of thought and action as well as unevenly desirable consequences for the various groups of people concerned, is never a matter of indifference to these groups and depends to some extent on the balance of power between them. By and large, the views and actions of the schools themselves tend to support the second type of perception. Since the latter blame educational inequalities on the characteristics of the pupils or their family or social environment, they do not call into question either the existence of the school or the way it operates. On the contrary, they allow it in many cases to demand and obtain extra material or symbolic resources to enable it to cope in its way with the problems of particular groups of children, whether the undisciplined, lazy, slow, incapable or unintelligent, or those disadvantaged by their ethnic, racial or national origins.

The cultural paradigm (the perception of inequalities in educational achievement and adjustment as related to cultural differences that result from being of a particular ethnic, racial or national origin) clearly falls into our second category of perceptions, where it finds itself in competition with others, including:

-- The biological paradigm, which attributes the differences to biological heredity, the biogenetic makeup or to other morphological or even physiological characteristics of individuals or groups; it frequently refers to race and supposedly innate talents and aptitudes;

-- The economic paradigm, which attributes educational inequalities to the characteristic differences between social groups in terms of material resources (incomes and material living conditions) which can have either a direct effect (e.g. diet, access to cultural goods) or an indirect effect (e.g. greater or less opportunity for study depending on the degree of prosperity or deprivation);

-- The social paradigm, which attributes inequalities to the patterns of discrimination, segregation, marginalisation, exclusion or domination between social groups which result in, for example, social rejection, the lowering of social status, differences as regards the aspirations and life goals that are subjectively and objectively possible or probable depending on social position.

Although not exhaustive, this list is sufficient to give some indication of the different types of explanation for educational underachievement in current usage in the professional literature and in the discussions on social affairs. We know, of course, that the way a problem is defined will determine the type of solution proposed and indeed we teach our children in school that a problem well stated is a problem already half solved.

This fundamental truth seems more especially relevant at a time when our industrialised societies are tending gradually to adopt the cultural paradigm as the basic explanation for the differences between groups, classes and nations, and in particular for educational inequalities. Even as recently as the early 1960s the biological paradigm was very prevalent in political and educational thinking. Yet, at all events while man is unable directly to manipulate the genetic code or other possibly relevant characteristics, this biological paradigm is at odds with the aims inherent in the growing movement towards making education available to all and raising the general standard of education. As long as educational achievement is regarded as dependent on a child's biogenetic or physiological heredity, there is nothing that either teachers or education policymakers can do.

By contrast, the cultural paradigm brings the underachievement problem of at least some schoolchildren into the realm of the treatable and tractable. Unlike the biological paradigm therefore, it sees the problem as one that is soluble. If it is adopted, then a policy of raising the general standard of education becomes feasible, provided a) the underlying causes and mechanisms of underachievement are correctly identified, and b) the necessary steps are taken to offset or remedy their effects.

It is worth noting that, in their way, the economic and social paradigms also see the problem as soluble. Indeed both have given rise to educational demands and policies over the past thirty years (e.g. free education, grant systems, legal measures to desegregate access to schools). But, in the last analysis, both would require a lessening or even the disappearance of certain of the fundamental inequalities in modern societies connected with the technological and social division of labour and resulting in inequalities of social status, which in turn are increasingly bound up with differences in the levels of formal education acquired and certificated.

To define the problem of educational achievement as a problem of a cultural nature means to some extent defining it as not being one of an economic or social nature, or at least only indirectly so. This approach therefore implies that, with respect to education systems, the success of the cultural paradigm is due to the very conditions that have rendered the biological paradigm socially and politically obsolete, given that the social and economic paradigms are only partially compatible with the functions of the school in today's social, economic and political system.

The cultural paradigm has assumed several forms during the past thirty years. One of its original versions involved what in Western societies is a traditional definition of culture as being the highest expression of abilities, intellectual and artistic activities as well as taste which, among other things, the education system was expected to inculcate. The early stages of the debate about the democratisation of education saw the emergence in the 1950s of interpretations of social inequalities in relation to education which, while rejecting the biological paradigm (aptitudes being considered innate), did not however attribute these directly to inequalities in the social and material conditions of life of different social classes, but to cultural differences associated with these inequalities such as parents' standard of education (Clerc, 1964) or more generally with the family's cultural "level" (i.e. in relation to the standard represented by the culture of the education system).

These interpretations continued to endorse the theory of an uneven distribution of innate (and more especially intellectual) aptitudes amongst individuals, but refused to accept that this uneven distribution from birth was related to social class. Rather it was thought that the disparities between the conditions of life of different classes provided greater or less opportunities for these aptitudes to emerge and develop at school. Whence the concept, subsequently considered to be too quantitativist, of a cultural or socio-cultural "lag" that needed to be "offset" by remedial action on the part of the school in order to facilitate the acquisition of a formal education that otherwise remained unchanged as far its cultural components, its practices and criteria of excellence were concerned. This remedial action should or could be essentially quantitative in character (extra resources in the schools, aid and assistance to backward pupils, etc.) and/or structural (e.g. postponement of the first streaming stage).

However, with the sudden emergence on the social and educational scene in the aftermath of May 1968 of new psychological, sociological and anthropological theories (Piaget, Bourdieu, Levi-Strauss, Morin, Foucault, etc.) the very possibility of separating nature and nurture, innate and acquired abilities was called into question. In some educational as well as social circles it led to development and learning being considered as a self-organising and accumulative process of construction bound up with the interactions of the human being with a given material, social and symbolic environment.

With the concept of cultural or socio-cultural "handicaps", educational thinking moved a step closer to this more qualitative interpretation of cultural differences. A handicap always has a specific form within an overall structure while still being a shortcoming in relation to what is considered to be a normal state. More or less explicitly acknowledging this concept, virtually all of the education systems in the industrialised world, when faced with the need to raise the level of achievement of more of their pupils, introduced remedial measures to help children considered to have a handicap or a learning problem. Amongst these are first and foremost those cases where the difference is perceived straight away by those concerned as being cultural, i.e. children whose language, ethnic, national or racial origin immediately marks them out as being from another culture.

It seems to me that the doctrine of multicultural education differs from this concept in that it proclaims the principle of equal value and status for the cultures associated with different nationalities, ethnic groups or other racial minorities. It has its roots therefore in a definition of culture of a descriptive and analytical type, such as that put forward by cultural anthropology, ethnology or sociology.

The egalitarian recognition by schools of the cultural differences associated with children's national, ethnic or racial origins now seems likely, the avowed desire responding to local circumstances:

-- To do away with the downgrading that comes from considering the different cultures to be of unequal value or status;

-- To enrich the children's experience by allowing them opportunities to relate positively to cultures other than their own;

-- To help reduce the tensions and conflicts between groups during their time at school and thereafter;

-- To enhance the educational achievement and adjustment of children from cultural "minority" groups by adopting a constructive attitude to their differences and taking these into account in the form of a differentiated teaching approach.

The aims of the doctrine of cultural pluralism would thus seem to be consistent with the overall process, described earlier, of relativising national, regional, ethnic, racial and, to some extent, religious particularisms. What is more, our approach enables these to be positioned more accurately within the social relationships which, in our emerging "post-industrial" society, are forming around the new dominant cultural referent and around the cultural model.

A point that should be made here is that, in schools at least, cultural pluralism is still overshadowed by the priority accorded to the culture they uphold and its criteria of excellence, the yardstick for measuring the educational achievement they are also expected to promote. There is little evidence to suggest that the vast investment in modernising and updating the subject matter taught by schools in every country is specifically aimed at ensuring equal chances of achievement for children from different social classes or cultural groups. The priority given to the development of mathematics/logic skills, and scientific, technical and organisational knowledge and abilities, is more directly related to the objectives set for national education systems in the new context of international competition. In the swim of the current move towards cultural homogenisation, this is primarily a response to demands from a section of the ruling classes and the leaders of society who, over a period of about twenty years, have abandoned classical scholarship as the criterion of social as well as educational excellence in favour of scientific education.

Moreover, a similar trend towards scientific observation and apprehension is emerging in the area of teaching practice and pupil guidance, which is an essential element in scholastic culture in the anthropological sense of the term. One example of this is the individualisation of instruction and pupil-centric methods based on knowledge of the individual's development provided by psychology and other observational sciences. It is debatable whether these changes too are not more in line with the sentiments and wishes of the upper and middle classes rather than with those of the working classes, who often do not see either the logic or the advantages of this (Perrenoud, 1985). In the case of some parents, these new methods do not only bewilder but make them feel even more lost in a world that is already strange to them. This inevitably makes it more difficult for them to help their children with their school work.

In any case, it is now a firmly established fact, and one that again applies to all countries, that the likelihood of educational achievement -- right from the primary stage onward -- is directly related to the social position of the family to which a child belongs. The educational policies pursued over the past thirty years as part of the move to make education available to all and provide "equality of opportunity" have undoubtedly helped to raise the general standard of formal education acquired by the generations about to embark upon working life, but at the same time it has maintained the gaps between children from different social classes. In other words, the policy of ensuring educational achievement for everyone is still confronted by the obstacle of class inequality.

As the result of migratory movements over the past thirty years the proportion of generally low-skilled immigrant workers in the labour forces of European countries has been increasing. In the United States too, what are traditionally termed the minority groups (Blacks, Hispanics, Indians) are mostly in positions at the lower end of the social scale. Educationists tend to ascribe the underachievement of children from these groups to their lack of familiarity with the language of instruction or to other characteristics attributed to their nationality or their ethnic origin. This focusing of attention on the more visible differences is understandable given the currently accepted explanatory paradigm. However, this is not supported by the available statistical evidence which shows that, in the case of children from the same social class, the success rates for children of nationals or the "majority group" and children of immigrants or "minority groups" are virtually identical (Swann, 1985; Hutmacher, 1987). Conversely, within supposedly homogeneous national or ethnic groups the chances of educational achievement vary very considerably for children from different social strata.

Thus the raising of the general standard of education can thus be compatible with the preservation of social and educational hierarchies. But there is reason to believe that there is no (or no longer any?) specifically ethnic or national inequality as regards educational achievement, or at least that this inequality is slight compared with that associated with the family's position in the social hierarchy of modern society. There is a growing awareness of the extent to which this position is related moreover to the level of education and thus to the duration and intensity of exposure to school work and the degree of success achieved. It is this position therefore rather than a child's ethnic or national origin, that seems the factor at present determining how far he or she lags behind the standards of excellence of the school which, we all know, always represents something more and something other than merely what it teaches (Perrenoud, 1984).

Due to the lack of data going back even to the 1960s it is impossible to know whether in the past differences in the level of educational achievement of ethnic groups were greater than they are today for children with a similar social background, and thus to assess whether and to what extent the struggles described earlier may have helped to reduce these differences at least within the social classes. Notwithstanding this however, one thing that is certain is that women have achieved greater equality.

On the other hand, it is remarkable that over the past thirty years the struggle for equal chances of educational achievement has never really been a high priority for action or organised protest on the part of the working classes's own organisations (trade unions or genuine workers' parties). This is not due to a lack of information however: the facts about social inequality as regards education started to become available through surveys and published statistics back in the 1950s and ever since have frequently been referred to and commented on in public discussions. This lack of organised protest on the part of the social category that suffers most from educational discrimination, in a situation which has otherwise been marked by action on the part of ethnic, racial or feminist groups, is somewhat surprising. I shall not attempt to go into the reasons for this here, but it is possible that one of them was that these differences and inequalities were seen as a cultural problem. May it not be the case that sexual, racial and ethnic differences have become all the more powerful as divisive factors because the acceptance of the culturalist interpretation as valid has helped to direct energies and action away from what are inherently social inequalities and hence shared social causes as well?

CONCLUSION

The argument that I have been developing here began with a question raised by Etienne Verne concerning the ability of schools to adopt a multicultural approach after so long a tradition of cultural and linguistic homogenisation. In dealing with this question, it seemed to me essential to go beyond the purely nationalist framework within which educational questions are usually posed. Having therefore positioned countries and their education policies within the international context in which in fact they operate, I described the mechanism of the upward spiral in which each of them is caught up and which would seem to explain the high priority that they all still assign to increasing the output and "productivity" of their education systems. The task of education systems too is now governed by international considerations; which explains why virtually everywhere there is a shift of emphasis as regards the goal of education and its criteria of excellence towards the development of scientific skills and knowledge, which in addition are a guarantee of future economic competitiveness.

This approach helps to put the cultural reorientation of education policies into perspective by placing it within the dialectic between the de facto relativisation of national and ethnic cultures and the growing importance of the scientific and technical referent. Linked to this is the new homogenising task of education systems whose frame of reference is now that of society worldwide.

This reorientation of the cultural task of education systems does not however mean the abandonment of their tasks of selecting and ranking individuals, since essentially it does not involve changing the criteria of excellence.

BIBLIOGRAPHY

BOURDIEU P. (1964), "La transmission de l'héritage culturel", in DARRAS, Le partage des bénéfices, Paris, 1964.

BOURDIEU P. (1966), "L'école conservatrice", Revue française de sociologie.

BOURDIEU P. (1972), Esquisse d'une théorie de la pratique, Droz, Genève.

BERTAUX D. (1977), Destins personnels et structure de classe, PUF, Paris.

BERTHELOT J.M. (1983), Le piège scolaire, PUF, Paris.

CHURCHILL S. (1987), "Policy developments for education in multicultural societies: Trends and processes in the OECD countries", Chapter 3 in this volume.

CLERC P. (1964), La famille et l'orientation scolaire au niveau de la 6ème. Survey carried out in June 1983 in the Paris area, Population et enseignement.

FULLER R.C. and MYERS R.R. (1941), "The natural history of a social problem", in American Sociological Review.

HEINTZ P. (1973), The future of development, Hans Huber, Berne.

HUTMACHER W.(1981), Migrations, production et reproduction de la société, in GRETLER A., PERRET A.N. and POGLIA E. (ed.): Etre migrant, Lang, Berne.

HUTMACHER W. (1987): "Passport or social position?", Immigrants' Children at School, OECD/CERI, Paris, 1987.

MAGNIN, Ch. (1985), Les enjeux de la loi sur l'instruction publique du 5 juin 1886, Working Paper, Service de la recherche sociologique, Genève.

PERRENOUD Ph. (1976), "Déviance: objet sociologique ou problème de société ?", in Revue européenne des sciences sociales, n°36.

PERRENOUD Ph. (1984), La fabrication de l'excellence scolaire, Droz, Genève.

PERRENOUD Ph. (1985), Les pédagogies nouvelles sont-elles élitaires ? Réflexions sur les contradictions de l'école active, due to be published in the proceedings of the symposium on "Classes populaires et pédagogies", Université de Haute-Normandie, Rouen.

SWANN Lord (1985), Education for All, Department of Education and Science, London.

TOURAINE A. (1973), Production de la société, Le Seuil, Paris 1973.

OECD SALES AGENTS
DÉPOSITAIRES DES PUBLICATIONS DE L'OCDE

ARGENTINA - ARGENTINE
Carlos Hirsch S.R.L.,
Florida 165, 4° Piso,
(Galeria Guemes) 1333 Buenos Aires
Tel. 33.1787.2391 y 30.7122

AUSTRALIA-AUSTRALIE
D.A. Book (Aust.) Pty. Ltd.
11-13 Station Street (P.O. Box 163)
Mitcham, Vic. 3132 Tel. (03) 873 4411

AUSTRIA - AUTRICHE
OECD Publications and Information Centre,
4 Simrockstrasse,
5300 Bonn (Germany) Tel. (0228) 21.60.45
Local Agent:
Gerold & Co., Graben 31, Wien 1 Tel. 52.22.35

BELGIUM - BELGIQUE
Jean de Lannoy, Service Publications OCDE,
avenue du Roi 202
B-1060 Bruxelles Tel. (02) 538.51.69

CANADA
Renouf Publishing Company Ltd/
Éditions Renouf Ltée,
1294 Algoma Road, Ottawa, Ont. K1B 3W8
Tel: (613) 741-4333
Toll Free/Sans Frais:
Ontario, Quebec, Maritimes:
1-800-267-1805
Western Canada, Newfoundland:
1-800-267-1826
Stores/Magasins:
61 rue Sparks St., Ottawa, Ont. K1P 5A6
Tel: (613) 238-8985
211 rue Yonge St., Toronto, Ont. M5B 1M4
Tel: (416) 363-3171
Sales Office/Bureau des Ventes:
7575 Trans Canada Hwy, Suite 305,
St. Laurent, Quebec H4T 1V6
Tel: (514) 335-9274

DENMARK - DANEMARK
Munksgaard Export and Subscription Service
35, Nørre Søgade, DK-1370 København K
Tel. +45.1.12.85.70

FINLAND - FINLANDE
Akateeminen Kirjakauppa,
Keskuskatu 1, 00100 Helsinki 10 Tel. 0.12141

FRANCE
OCDE/OECD
Mail Orders/Commandes par correspondance :
2, rue André-Pascal,
75775 Paris Cedex 16
Tel. (1) 45.24.82.00
Bookshop/Librairie : 33, rue Octave-Feuillet
75016 Paris
Tel. (1) 45.24.81.67 or/ou (1) 45.24.81.81
Principal correspondant :
Librairie de l'Université,
12a, rue Nazareth,
13602 Aix-en-Provence Tel. 42.26.18.08

GERMANY - ALLEMAGNE
OECD Publications and Information Centre,
4 Simrockstrasse,
5300 Bonn Tel. (0228) 21.60.45

GREECE - GRÈCE
Librairie Kauffmann,
28, rue du Stade, 105 64 Athens Tel. 322.21.60

HONG KONG
Government Information Services,
Publications (Sales) Office,
Beaconsfield House, 4/F.,
Queen's Road Central

ICELAND - ISLANDE
Snæbjörn Jónsson & Co., h.f.,
Hafnarstræti 4 & 9,
P.O.B. 1131 – Reykjavik
Tel. 13133/14281/11936

INDIA - INDE
Oxford Book and Stationery Co.,
Scindia House, New Delhi I Tel. 331.5896/5308
17 Park St., Calcutta 700016 Tel. 240832

INDONESIA - INDONÉSIE
Pdii-Lipi, P.O. Box 3065/JKT.Jakarta
Tel. 583467

IRELAND - IRLANDE
TDC Publishers - Library Suppliers,
12 North Frederick Street, Dublin 1.
Tel. 744835-749677

ITALY - ITALIE
Libreria Commissionaria Sansoni,
Via Lamarmora 45, 50121 Firenze
Tel. 579751/584468
Via Bartolini 29, 20155 Milano Tel. 365083
Sub-depositari :
Editrice e Libreria Herder,
Piazza Montecitorio 120, 00186 Roma
Tel. 6794628
Libreria Hœpli,
Via Hœpli 5, 20121 Milano Tel. 865446
Libreria Scientifica
Dott. Lucio de Biasio "Aeiou"
Via Meravigli 16, 20123 Milano Tel. 807679
Libreria Lattes,
Via Garibaldi 3, 10122 Torino Tel. 519274
La diffusione delle edizioni OCSE è inoltre assicurata dalle migliori librerie nelle città più importanti.

JAPAN - JAPON
OECD Publications and Information Centre,
Landic Akasaka Bldg., 2-3-4 Akasaka,
Minato-ku, Tokyo 107 Tel. 586.2016

KOREA - CORÉE
Kyobo Book Centre Co. Ltd.
P.O.Box: Kwang Hwa Moon 1658,
Seoul Tel. (REP) 730.78.91

LEBANON - LIBAN
Documenta Scientifica/Redico,
Edison Building, Bliss St.,
P.O.B. 5641, Beirut Tel. 354429-344425

MALAYSIA - MALAISIE
University of Malaya Co-operative Bookshop Ltd.,
P.O.Box 1127, Jalan Pantai Baru,
Kuala Lumpur Tel. 577701/577072

NETHERLANDS - PAYS-BAS
Staatsuitgeverij
Chr. Plantijnstraat, 2 Postbus 20014
2500 EA S-Gravenhage Tel. 070-789911
Voor bestellingen: Tel. 070-789880

NEW ZEALAND - NOUVELLE-ZÉLANDE
Government Printing Office Bookshops:
Auckland: Retail Bookshop, 25 Rutland Street,
Mail Orders, 85 Beach Road
Private Bag C.P.O.
Hamilton: Retail: Ward Street,
Mail Orders, P.O. Box 857
Wellington: Retail, Mulgrave Street, (Head Office)
Cubacade World Trade Centre,
Mail Orders, Private Bag
Christchurch: Retail, 159 Hereford Street,
Mail Orders, Private Bag
Dunedin: Retail, Princes Street,
Mail Orders, P.O. Box 1104

NORWAY - NORVÈGE
Tanum-Karl Johan
Karl Johans gate 43, Oslo 1
PB 1177 Sentrum, 0107 Oslo 1Tel. (02) 42.93.10

PAKISTAN
Mirza Book Agency
65 Shahrah Quaid-E-Azam, Lahore 3 Tel. 66839

PORTUGAL
Livraria Portugal,
Rua do Carmo 70-74, 1117 Lisboa Codex.
Tel. 360582/3

SINGAPORE - SINGAPOUR
Information Publications Pte Ltd
Pei-Fu Industrial Building,
24 New Industrial Road No. 02-06
Singapore 1953 Tel. 2831786, 2831798

SPAIN - ESPAGNE
Mundi-Prensa Libros, S.A.,
Castelló 37, Apartado 1223, Madrid-28001
Tel. 431.33.99
Libreria Bosch, Ronda Universidad 11,
Barcelona 7 Tel. 317.53.08/317.53.58

SWEDEN - SUÈDE
AB CE Fritzes Kungl. Hovbokhandel,
Box 16356, S 103 27 STH,
Regeringsgatan 12,
DS Stockholm Tel. (08) 23.89.00
Subscription Agency/Abonnements:
Wennergren-Williams AB,
Box 30004, S104 25 Stockholm.
Tel. (08)54.12.00

SWITZERLAND - SUISSE
OECD Publications and Information Centre,
4 Simrockstrasse,
5300 Bonn (Germany) Tel. (0228) 21.60.45
Local Agent:
Librairie Payot,
6 rue Grenus, 1211 Genève 11
Tel. (022) 31.89.50

TAIWAN - FORMOSE
Good Faith Worldwide Int'l Co., Ltd.
9th floor, No. 118, Sec.2
Chung Hsiao E. Road
Taipei Tel. 391.7396/391.7397

THAILAND - THAILANDE
Suksit Siam Co., Ltd.,
1715 Rama IV Rd.,
Samyam Bangkok 5 Tel. 2511630

TURKEY - TURQUIE
Kültur Yayinlari Is-Türk Ltd. Sti.
Atatürk Bulvari No: 191/Kat. 21
Kavaklidere/Ankara Tel. 25.07.60
Dolmabahce Cad. No: 29
Besiktas/Istanbul Tel. 160.71.88

UNITED KINGDOM - ROYAUME-UNI
H.M. Stationery Office,
Postal orders only: (01)211-5656
P.O.B. 276, London SW8 5DT
Telephone orders: (01) 622.3316, or
Personal callers:
49 High Holborn, London WC1V 6HB
Branches at: Belfast, Birmingham,
Bristol, Edinburgh, Manchester

UNITED STATES - ÉTATS-UNIS
OECD Publications and Information Centre,
2001 L Street, N.W., Suite 700,
Washington, D.C. 20036 - 4095
Tel. (202) 785.6323

VENEZUELA
Libreria del Este,
Avda F. Miranda 52, Aptdo. 60337,
Edificio Galipan, Caracas 106
Tel. 32.23.01/33.26.04/31.58.38

YUGOSLAVIA - YOUGOSLAVIE
Jugoslovenska Knjiga, Knez Mihajlova 2,
P.O.B. 36, Beograd Tel. 621.992

Orders and inquiries from countries where Sales Agents have not yet been appointed should be sent to:
OECD, Publications Service, Sales and Distribution Division, 2, rue André-Pascal, 75775 PARIS CEDEX 16.

Les commandes provenant de pays où l'OCDE n'a pas encore désigné de dépositaire peuvent être adressées à :
OCDE, Service des Publications. Division des Ventes et Distribution. 2. rue André-Pascal. 75775 PARIS CEDEX 16.

70712-04-1987

OECD PUBLICATIONS, 2, rue André-Pascal, 75775 PARIS CEDEX 16 - No. 43983 1987
PRINTED IN FRANCE
(96 87 03 1) ISBN 92-64-12989-8